IPv6 Fundamentals: A Straightforward Approach to Understanding IPv6

Rick Graziani

Cisco Press

800 East 96th Street

Indianapolis, IN 46240

IPv6 Fundamentals: A Straightforward Approach to Understanding IPv6

Rick Graziani

Published by:
Cisco Press
800 East 96th Street
Indianapolis, IN 46240 USA

Printed in the United States of America 1 2 3 4 5 6 7 8 9 0

Second Printing: July 2014

The Library of Congress Cataloging-in-Publication Data is on file.

ISBN-13: 978-1-58714-313-7

ISBN-10: 1-58714-313-5

Warning and Disclaimer

This book is designed to provide information about IPv6 (Internet Protocol version 6). Every effort has been made to make this book as complete and as accurate as possible, but no warranty or fitness is implied.

The information is provided on an "as is" basis. The author, Cisco Press, and Cisco Systems, Inc. shall have neither liability nor responsibility to any person or entity with respect to any loss or damages arising from the information contained in this book or from the use of the discs or programs that may accompany it.

The opinions expressed in this book belong to the author and are not necessarily those of Cisco Systems, Inc.

Feedback Information

At Cisco Press, our goal is to create in-depth technical books of the highest quality and value. Each book is crafted with care and precision, undergoing rigorous development that involves the unique expertise of members from the professional technical community.

Readers' feedback is a natural continuation of this process. If you have any comments regarding how we could improve the quality of this book, or otherwise alter it to better suit your needs, you can contact us through email at feedback@ciscopress.com. Please make sure to include the book title and ISBN in your message.

We greatly appreciate your assistance.

Trademark Acknowledgments

All terms mentioned in this book that are known to be trademarks or service marks have been appropriately capitalized. Cisco Press or Cisco Systems, Inc. cannot attest to the accuracy of this information. Use of a term in this book should not be regarded as affecting the validity of any trademark or service mark.

Publisher: Paul Boger

Associate Publisher: Dave Dusthimer

Executive Editor: Mary Beth Ray

Managing Editor: Sandra Schroeder

Development Editor: Marianne Bartow

Editorial Assistant: Vanessa Evans

Cover Designer: Sandra Schroeder

Indexer: Tim Wright

Business Operation Manager, Cisco Press: Anand Sundaram

Cisco Press Program Manager: Sonia Torres Chavez

Technical Editors: Jim Bailey, Yenu Gobena

Copy Editor: John Edwards

Project Editor: Mandie Frank

Book Designer: Louisa Adair

Composition: Mark Shirar

Proofreader: Debbie Williams

About the Author

Rick Graziani teaches computer science and computer networking courses at Cabrillo College in Aptos, California. Prior to teaching, he worked in the information technology field for Santa Cruz Operation, Tandem Computers, and Lockheed Missiles and Space Corporation. He holds an M.A. in computer science and systems theory from California State University Monterey Bay. Rick also does consulting work for Cisco Systems. When he is not working, he is most likely surfing at one of his favorite Santa Cruz surf breaks.

Rick Graziani, the early years.

About the Technical Reviewers

Jim Bailey, CCIE #5275 (Routing & Switching; Service Provider) and CCDE #20090008, is a Services Technical Leader at Cisco Systems with more than 20 years of experience in networking. As part of the Central Engineering Network Architecture and Design Advanced Services team, he focuses on the architecture, design, and implementation of networks for Enterprise, Service Provider, and Government customers. He has focused on IPv6 integration into those networks over the last seven years.

Yenu Gobena is a Distinguished Service Engineer in a strategic role in the Borderless Network Architecture and Design Space. He is also a key player in evangelizing, consulting, and enabling multiple Cisco architectures such as BYOD, VDI/VXI, IPv6, converged Core infrastructures, and Data Centers. Yenu also focuses on consulting and providing design services to some of the leading IPv6 adopters globally. **Yenu** has been leading IPv6 customer delivery engagements and workshops for several years, and he has earned a trusted advisory role for dozens of accounts around the globe. He is a sought-after industry speaker and represents Cisco at key IPv6 initiatives around the world. Based in Research Triangle Park (Raleigh, N.C.), he has experience in a broad range of technologies, including Routing and Switching, MPLS, SP Mobility, IPv6 Architecture and Design, Enterprise, and SP NGN Architectures. Yenu holds a B.S. in telecommunications from the State University of New York. He has two children, Amara and Elena, with his wife, Molly. Yenu is CCIE certified, has published multiple white papers, and is an IPv6 Forum Certified Gold Trainer.

Dedication

This book is dedicated to my parents. Thank you for the many years of love and support.

Acknowledgments

First of all, I would like to thank all my friends and colleagues for their assistance. A special thank-you to all my friends in the Thursday evening DPS (Dropped Packet Society). Thank you for your help during and after our "meetings." There are too many of you to list, but Mark Boolootian, Dave Barnett, and Jim Warner, thanks for the many years of discussing technologies and answering questions. We've drawn a lot of topologies on a lot of napkins over the years.

Jim Bailey at Cisco Systems deserves much more credit than the brief mention as a technical reviewer for this book. He made me look a lot smarter than I am. Jim did an incredibly thorough job in making sure that this book was as accurate and up to date as possible. His expertise and background were invaluable in helping me author this book. He is definitely the unsung hero of this project. Thank you Jim for an amazing job.

Thank you Yenu Gobena at Cisco Systems for doing such a great job on the technical review. You made this book more accurate by filling in a lot of the blanks. You helped improve this book for the reader.

I owe a great deal of gratitude to Gerlinde Brady, Sue Nerton, and Jim Griffin for your friendship and support. You made sure that the CS/CIS departments at Cabrillo College continued to run smoothly while I was engaged in the writing process. I feel very fortunate to work with you and all our other friends in the CS/CIS department.

Writing this book has been one of many privileges, all of which have been because of Dennis Frezzo, Jeremy Creech, Karen Alderson, Sonya Stott, Wayne Lewis, Bob Vachon, and many others who work for the Cisco Networking Academy. Thank you all for the honor and opportunity to be part of a program that has changed the lives of thousands of students around the world. More than colleagues, you are all friends, for which I am grateful.

Thank you Pat Farley for making sure that I still got my surf sessions in. For those who surf, you know how important this is.

Special thanks to Mary Beth Ray, Executive Editor for Cisco Press and friend. Thank you for your patience and understanding through this long process. You always have that calm assurance and guidance, not to mention being a terrific dancer.

Thank you, Marianne Bartow at Cisco Press, for working with me on a daily basis—weekdays and weekends, editing, formatting, and orchestrating the entire process. You were a pleasure to work with, and I am very grateful for all the hard work you put into this book. You make me look as if I am actually a better writer than I am.

To Chris Cleveland, Mandie Frank, John Edwards, Tim Wright, Mark Shirar, Sandra Schroeder, and everyone else at Cisco Press, I am extremely grateful for everything you have done. I am constantly amazed at the level of cooperation and teamwork required to produce a technical book, and I am very thankful for all your help.

Thank you Luigi. Waking me up early every morning to go to the beach has been beneficial for both of us. Good dog!

Finally, I want to thank all my students over the many years. I am humbled by the opportunity to teach such wonderful people. You make my job fun and are the reason I love to go to work every day.

Contents at a Glance

Contents

Icons Used in This Book

File
Server

Router

Workgroup
Switch

PC

Cloud

Command Syntax Conventions

The conventions used to present command syntax in this book are the same conventions used in the IOS Command Reference. The Command Reference describes these conventions as follows:

- **Boldface** indicates commands and keywords that are entered literally as shown. In actual configuration examples and output (not general command syntax), boldface indicates commands that are manually input by the user (such as a **show** command).
- *Italics* indicate arguments for which you supply actual values.
- Vertical bars (|) separate alternative, mutually exclusive elements.
- Square brackets [ ] indicate optional elements.
- Braces { } indicate a required choice.
- Braces within brackets [{ }] indicate a required choice within an optional element.

Introduction

This book focuses on the basics of IPv6. There is a great deal to learn about IPv6. It is much more than just becoming familiar with a larger address.

My approach to writing this book was to do my best to explain each concept in a simple, step-by-step approach, as well as to include the critical details. It was a challenging balance between providing as much information as possible without overwhelming the reader. IPv6 is not difficult to learn but involves multiple protocols and processes that might be new to the reader.

Don't be overwhelmed by all the details. For example, although I have included a brief description for each field in the protocols discussed in the book, it isn't necessarily important that you understand the details of each one. I mention this throughout the book. But I did feel it necessary not to leave out or hide these details from the reader.

RFCs are cited throughout the book. It was important to include these references for two reasons. First of all, I wanted to give you the authoritative source for the material in this book so that you have a resource for more information. Second, IPv6 is currently and will continue to be a moving target for quite some time. Although it has been around for many years, there is still additional development and fine-tuning that is taking place. If you are not familiar with reading RFCs, don't be intimidated. Most of them are not difficult to read and do their best to explain the topic clearly.

At times I will introduce a technology or concept, but state that it is "beyond the scope of this book." I feel it is better to revisit some of the more advanced topics after you have a more complete understanding of the entire IPv6 topic. I do suggest resources for those who might be interested in learning more about those topics.

The objective of this book is to explain IPv6 as clearly as possible. At times it was like herding cats, trying to decide which topic to cover first.

Readers are welcome to use the resources on my website for IPv6, CCNA, or CCNP information, www.cabrillo.edu/~rgraziani. You can email me, graziani@cabrillo.edu, to obtain the username and password for all my materials.

Goals and Methods

The most important goal of this book is to provide a thorough yet easy-to-understand introduction to IPv6. This book is also intended to provide a foundation in IPv6 that will allow you to build on it. This includes explaining topics that might be a little more challenging to grasp.

Another goal of this book is to be a resource for IPv6. I have included command syntax, RFCs, and links to Cisco white papers to help guide you toward a further understanding of many of the topics.

Who Should Read This Book

This book is intended for anyone seeking a solid understanding of the fundamentals of IPv6, such as network engineers, network designers, network technicians, technical staff, and networking students, including those who are part of the Cisco Networking Academy. The reader should have a basic familiarity with IPv4 and IPv4 routing protocols equivalent to a CCNA certification or the applicable Cisco Network Academy courses.

Professionals planning to use Cisco technology to deploy IPv6 networks, provide IPv6 connectivity, and use IPv6 within their network will find this book useful. You will find examples, figures, IOS commands, and tips for configuring Cisco IOS IPv6 technology.

How This Book Is Organized

If you are new to IPv6, this book should be read from cover to cover. However, if you have some knowledge of IPv6, it is designed to be flexible and allows you to easily move between chapters and sections of chapters to cover just the material that you want to review.

Chapters 1 through 5 provide an introduction to IPv6, the protocol, addressing types, and ICMPv6 Neighbor Discovery Protocol. These chapters also include Cisco IOS commands and configuration examples. Chapters 6 through 9 use a common topology to implement the IPv6 addressing in the previous chapters and also introduce IPv6 routing protocols. DHCPv6 and other upper-layer protocols are also discussed. The last two chapters, Chapters 10 and 11, cover methods of transitioning from IPv4 to IPv6. If you do intend to read all the chapters, the order in the book is sequential.

The following list highlights the topics covered in each chapter and the book's organization:

- **Chapter 1, "Introduction to IPv6":** This chapter discusses how the Internet of today requires a new network layer protocol, IPv6, to meet the demands of its users. It also examines the limitations of IPv4 and describes how IPv6 resolves these issues while offering other advantages as well. This chapter examines the rationale of IPv6 and concerns regarding IPv4 address depletion. It presents a brief history of both IPv4 and IPv6. A review of the IPv4 migration technologies CIDR and NAT are also discussed.

- **Chapter 2, "The IPv6 Protocol":** This chapter examines the IPv6 protocol and its fields. The IPv4 protocol is first reviewed to provide a basis of comparison and to highlight the changes with IPv6. It also explores how fragmentation is handled. The IPv6 extension headers are discussed as well.

- **Chapter 3, "IPv6 Addressing":** This chapter introduces IPv6 addressing and address types. It begins with an explanation of the hexadecimal number system. Representation of IPv6 addresses is discussed along with the different formats of representing IPv6 addresses and the rules for compressing the IPv6 notation. This chapter provides an introductory look at the different types of IPv6 addresses. Subnetting IPv6 addresses is discussed, including subnetting on a nibble boundary and within the nibble boundary.

- **Chapter 4, "IPv6 Address Types":** This chapter examines the different types of IPv6 addresses in detail. Global unicast configuration methods, both manual and dynamic, are described. It explains and provides examples of enabling IPv6 on router interfaces using static, EUI-64, IPv6 unnumbered, Stateless Address Autoconfiguration (SLAAC), and DHCPv6. (DHCPv6 and SLAAC are examined in detail in later chapters.) Link-local addresses are described using static and dynamic IOS configuration examples. Loopback and unspecified unicast addresses are also discussed. Assigned and solicited node multicast addresses, along with anycast addresses, are described as well.

- **Chapter 5, "ICMPv6 and Neighbor Discovery Protocol":** This chapter examines ICMPv6. There are similarites between ICMPv6 and ICMPv4, but ICMPv6 is a much more robust protocol. ICMPv6 error messages are discussed, including Destination Unreachable, Packet Too Big, Time Exceeded, and Parameter Problem. ICMPv6 informational messages Echo Request and Echo Reply are covered along with Multicast Listener Discovery messages. Neighbor Discovery Protocol, Router Solicitation, Router Advertisement, Neighbor Solicitation, Neighbor Advertisement, and Redirect messages are examined in detail. Not only does IPv6 resolve larger address space issues, but ICMPv6 and Neighbor Discovery Protocol also present a major change in the network operatons, including link-layer address resolution (ARP in IPv4), Duplicate Address Detection (DAD), Stateless Address Autoconfiguration (SLAAC), and Neighbor Unreachability Detection (NUD). The IPv6 Neighbor Cache and Neighbor Cache States, similar to those of the IPv4 ARP Cache, are discussed.

- **Chapter 6, "IPv6 Configuration":** This chapter illustrates the configuration of IPv6 addressing using a common topology. Global unicast and link-local addresses are configured using different options. This chapter includes examples of the Neighbor Cache and modification of Router Adveristement messages for tuning the Neighbor Discovery parameters. This chapter also explores IPv6 access control lists, with configuration examples using the common topology.

- **Chapter 7, "Introduction to Routing IPv6":** This chapter examines the IPv6 routing table and changes in the configurations pertaining to IPv6. It also discusses the configuration of IPv6 static routes that are similar to static routes for IPv4. CEF for IPv6 is also covered.

- **Chapter 8, "IPv6 IGP Routing Protocols":** This chapter discusses three routing protocols: RIPng, EIGRP for IPv6, and OSPFv3. Differences between each protocol and their IPv4 counterpart are examined. A common topology is used to configure and verify each of the routing protocols.

- **Chapter 9, "DHCPv6 (Dynamic Host Configuration Protocol version 6)":** This chapter examines DHCP for IPv6, or DHCPv6. Stateful and stateless DHCPv6 services are discussed. DHCPv6 terminology and message types are covered along with the DHCPv6 process between the client and server. The Rapid Commit Option and relay agents are also explained. Other upper-layer protocols are discussed: DNS, TCP, and UDP.

- **Chapter 10, "Dual-Stack and Tunneling":** This chapter covers two of three strategies for IPv4 and IPv6 integration and coexistence: dual-stack and tunneling. Dual-stack is used when devices will implement both IPv4 and IPv6 protocols, enabling them to coexist in the same network. Tunneling is the encapsulation of one IP packet inside another IP packet. Basic tunneling terminology is discussed as well as an examination and configuration of three tunneling technologies: manual, 6to4, and ISATAP.

- **Chapter 11, "Network Address Translation IPv6 to IPv4 (NAT64)":** This chapter discusses the third technique for transition from IPv4 and IPv6: Network Address Translation, or NAT. Similar to NAT for IPv4, the use of NAT for IPv6 is a translation between the IPv4 and IPv6 protocols. NAT64 is a replacement for NAT-PT (NAT – Protocol Translation). NAT-PT is included in this chapter to provide continuity between the newer NAT64 and the previous technology that is still in use.

Chapter 1

Introduction to IPv6

Internet Protocol version 6 (IPv6) is designed to be the successor to IPv4. This chapter discusses how the Internet of today requires a new network layer protocol to meet the demands of its users. It also examines the limitations of IPv4 and describes how IPv6 solves these issues while offering other advantages as well.

IPv4

Internet Protocol version 4 (IPv4) is the current Layer 3 protocol used on the Internet and most networks. IPv4 has survived for over 30 years and has been an integral part of the Internet evolution. It was originally described in RFC 760 (January 1980) and obsoleted by RFC 791 (September 1981).

Can you imagine what the Internet was like in those early years? Even with the advent of the World Wide Web in the early 1990s, there were only about 16 million users on the Internet worldwide compared to over 2 billion by 2011 (reference Internet World Statistics, www.internetworldstats.com). The actual number of devices increases dramatically when taking into account that today's users usually have multiple Internet-enabled devices such as smart phones, tablets, and laptops.

The reasons to migrate from IPv4 to IPv6 are discussed later in this chapter. For now, just recognize that presently the Internet is a much different place than it was 30, 10, or even 5 years ago. Today's Internet is much more than just web pages, email, and file transfers. With the explosive growth of mobile devices and peer-to-peer networking, along with the potential impact of Internet-ready consumer goods, we have gone from just an *Internet of computers* to an *Internet of things*. The phrase *Internet of things* has been an evolving concept. Originally it centered around daily objects having radio-frequency identification (RFID) tags for identification and inventory purposes. It has since evolved into a more general connotation including smart grids, smart and connected cities, home automation, automotive computing, and more.

Imagine the impact of devices on a network that allows users the ability to communicate with one another. For example, your boss schedules an early-morning meeting on your calendar for the next morning. This data is communicated to your alarm clock to activate the alarm ten minutes earlier and initiate brewing in your coffee maker. Five minutes before you leave for the office, your car automatically warms up to melt the ice on your windshield, recognizes your driving schedule, and informs you that you will need to refuel on the way home.

This all might seem a little far-fetched, but think of all the possibilities when *things* can begin to communicate with each other. Internet-ready devices can be anything from TVs and webcams to sensors in critical automobile engine components and digestible monitors for medical diagnoses. Internet-ready sensors can be used to alert a driver that he has low tire pressure or be monitored from a central location to measure and adjust heating and cooling systems in real time, decreasing the use of power and the associated costs.

Later in this chapter, the depletion of current IPv4 address space is discussed. But in spite of all the efforts such as NAT (Network Address Translation) to extend the life of IPv4, it is obvious that we are quickly coming to the point where we need something new. NAT and its effect on preserving IPv4 address space will be discussed later in this chapter.

Early Years of the Internet

Although the Internet known as ARPANET was born in 1969, many of the protocols and technologies employed today are relatively recent. RFC 2235, Hobbes Internet Timeline, chronicles some of the early events that occurred between 1957 and 1997:

- **1957:** The USSR launches Sputnik, the first artificial earth satellite. In response, the United States forms the Advanced Research Projects Agency (ARPA) within the Department of Defense (DoD) to establish a U.S. lead in science and technology.
- **1962:** Paul Baran publishes the paper "On Distributed Communications Networks," a predecessor to the concept of packet-switching networks.
- **1969:** ARPANET is commissioned by the DoD for research into networking. The first node (a mainframe computer) is at the University of California Los Angeles (UCLA) Network Measurements Center. The next three nodes consisted of Stanford Research Institute (SRI), the University of California Santa Barbara (UCSB), and the University of Utah. The first router is an Information Message Processor (IMP), a Honeywell 516 mini-computer with 12K of memory developed by Bolt Beranek and Newman, Inc. (BBN).
- **1969:** The first Request for Comments (RFC) is written: "Host Software," by Steve Crocker.
- **1971:** Fifteen nodes (23 hosts) are on the ARPANET: UCLA, SRI, UCSB, University of Utah, BBN, Massachusetts Institute of Technology (MIT), RAND Corporation, System Development Corporation (SDC), Harvard University, MIT's Lincoln Lab, Stanford University, University of Illinois at Urbana-Champaign, Case Western Reserve University, Carnegie-Mellon University, and NASA/Ames Research Center.

- **1971:** Ray Tomlinson of BBN invents an email program to send messages across a distributed network.
- **1973:** Bob Metcalfe's Harvard Ph.D. thesis outlines the idea for Ethernet.
- **1973:** The File Transfer Protocol (FTP) specification is written (RFC 454).
- **1974:** Vint Cerf and Bob Kahn publish the paper "A Protocol for Packet Network Intercommunication," which specified in detail the design for Transmission Control Protocol (TCP).
- **1982:** ARPA establishes TCP/IP as the protocol suite for the ARPANET. This leads to one of the first definitions of an "Internet" as a connected set of networks that use TCP/IP.
- **1982:** The External Gateway Protocol (RFC 827) specification is written. EGP is used as the routing protocol between networks and is later replaced by Border Gateway Protocol (BGP) in 1994 (RFC 1656).
- **1983:** The Internet transitions from Network Control Protocol (NCP) to TCP/IP on January 1.
- **1984:** The Domain Name System (DNS) is introduced with RFC 920.
- **1984:** The number of hosts on the Internet breaks 1000.
- **1986:** The National Science Foundation Network (NSFNET) initiates operations with a backbone speed of 56 kbps.
- **1987:** The number of hosts on the Internet breaks 10,000.
- **1988:** The NSFNET backbone is upgraded to T1 (1.544 Mbps).
- **1988:** Internet Relay Chat (IRC) is developed by Jarkko Oikarinen.
- **1989:** The number of hosts on the Internet breaks 100,000.
- **1989:** *Cuckoo's Egg*, written by Clifford Stoll, tells the real-life tale of a German cracker group that infiltrated numerous U.S. facilities.
- **1990:** The first remotely operated machine to be hooked up to the Internet, the Internet Toaster, makes its debut at Interop (IT Expo and Conference).
- **1991:** The World Wide Web (WWW) is released by CERN; it was developed by Tim Berners-Lee.
- **1991:** The NSFNET backbone is upgraded to T3 (44.736 Mbps).
- **1992:** The number of hosts on the Internet breaks 1,000,000.
- **1992:** The term "surfing the Internet" is coined by Jean Armour Polly.

- **1993:** The U.S. White House comes online with www.whitehouse.gov. President Bill Clinton: president@whitehouse.gov and Vice President Al Gore: vice-president@whitehouse.gov.
- **1994:** Shopping on the Internet begins.
- **1994:** Pizza from Pizza Hut can be ordered using the World Wide Web.
- **1995:** WWW surpasses FTP as the service with the greatest amount of traffic on the Internet.
- **1995:** Online dialup providers Compuserve, America Online, and Prodigy begin to provide Internet access.
- **1995:** The Vatican comes online.
- **1996:** Internet phones catch the attention of U.S. telecommunication companies, which request the U.S. Congress to ban the technology.
- **1996:** The controversial U.S. Communications Decency Act (CDA) becomes law in the United States to prohibit distribution of indecent materials over the Internet. A few months later, a three-judge panel imposes an injunction against its enforcement. The U.S. Supreme Court unanimously rules most of it unconstitutional in 1997.
- **1996:** MCI upgrades its Internet backbone, bringing the effective speed from 155 Mbps to 622 Mbps.
- **1996:** The WWW browser war, fought primarily between Netscape and Microsoft, rushes in a new age in software development, whereby new releases are made quarterly with the help of Internet users eager to test upcoming (beta) versions.
- **1996:** Restrictions are put in place for Internet use around the world (Source: Human Rights Watch):
  - China requires users and Internet service providers (ISP) to register with the police.
  - Germany cuts off access to some newsgroups carried on Compuserve.
  - Saudi Arabia confines Internet access to universities and hospitals.
  - Singapore requires political and religious content providers to register with the state.
  - New Zealand classifies computer disks as "publications" that can be censored and seized.
- **1997:** 101,803 Name Servers are in the "whois" database.
- **1997:** The number of hosts on the Internet breaks 19,000,000.

The Internet is a dynamic environment. IPv4, and its 4.3 billion possible addresses, was introduced in 1983 when there were less than 600 hosts on the Internet. Although many of the same concepts of packet switching apply today, the number of users on the Internet and how it is used are vastly different today.

Note To learn more about the creation of the Internet and those who were responsible for its development, I highly recommend the national best-selling book *Where Wizards Stay Up Late: The Origins of the Internet*, by Katie Lyons.

IPv5

What about IPv5? In the late 1970s, a family of experimental protocols was developed known as Internet Stream Protocol (ST) and later ST2. Originally defined in Internet Engineering Note IEN-119 (1979), it was later revised in RFC 1190 and RFC 1819.

ST was an experimental resource reservation protocol intended to provide quality of service (QoS) for real-time multimedia applications such as video and voice. ST consisted of two protocols—ST (Internet Stream Protocol) and Stream Control Message Protocol (SCMP). Internet Stream Protocol version 2 (ST-II or ST2) was not designed as a replacement for IPv4. The idea was that a multimedia application would use both protocols—IPv4 for the transfer of traditional packets and ST-II for packets carrying real-time data.

Although it was never recognized as IPv5, when encapsulated in IP, ST uses IP Protocol Number 5 (RFC 1700). In other words, although it was never implemented, the designation "IP version 5" was already taken. Today's standard for resource reservation is the transport layer protocol Resource Reservation Protocol (RSVP), which can be used to provide receiver-initiated setup over IPv4. RSVP is described in RFC 2205.

History of IPv6

The Internet Engineering Task Force (IETF) began development of a successor to IPv4 in the early 1990s. In 1994, the IETF formed a working group, IP Next Generation, to establish the standards to be used for IPv6:

- An address architecture and assignment plan
- Supporting larger packet sizes
- Tunneling IPv6 packets over IPv4
- Security and autoconfiguration

The size of the Internet routing tables increasing rapidly and the explosion of the number of Internet users generated a consensus that it was time to begin designing and testing a new network layer protocol as the successor to IPv4. Figure 1-1 shows the number of networks in the Internet routing table from 1989 to 2012. As shown, in the early 1990s, there was explosive growth in the number of networks in Internet routing. Various projections, including a study done by the IETF in the early 1990s, predicted that the Internet would run out of IPv4 address space somewhere between 2005 and 2011.

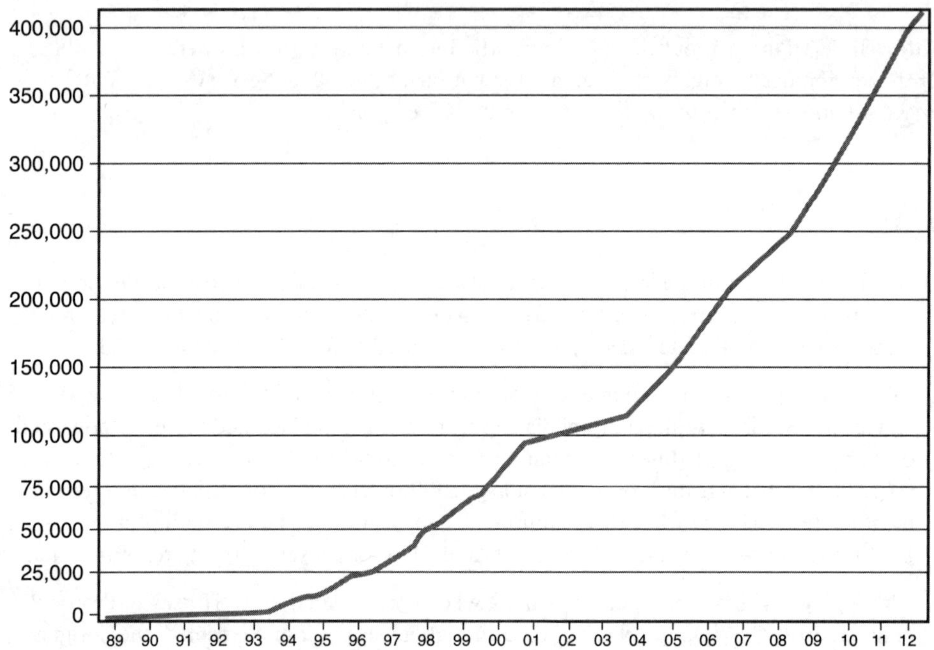

Figure 1-1 *BGP Table Size (1989–2011)*

In addition to increasing the size of the address space, this was also a unique opportunity to fix the limitations of IPv4 and develop a protocol to ensure reliable growth and enhanced performance for the future. In 1993, IETF announced a call for white papers with RFC 1550 IP: Next Generation (IPng) White Paper Solicitation. The details of these proposals are available at RFC 1752, The Recommendation for the IP Next Generation Protocol.

The three proposals were as follows:

- **Common Architecture for the Internet (CATNIP):** CATNIP proposed integrating IP, Internetwork Packet Exchange (IPX), and Connectionless Network Layer Protocol (CLNP). IPX was part of the Internetwork Packet Exchange/Sequenced Packet Exchange (IPX/SPX) suite of protocols used primarily on networks employing the Novell NetWare operating systems. CLNP is an OSI standard defined in ISO 8473 and is the equivalent of IPv4 for the OSI suite of protocols. CATNIP is defined in RFC 1707.
- **Simple Internet Protocol Plus (SIPP):** SIPP recommended increasing the IPv4 address size from 32 bits to 64 bits, along with additional improvements to the IPv4 header for more efficient forwarding. SIPP is defined in RFC 1710.
- **TCP/UDP over CLNP-Addressed Networks (TUBA):** TUBA requested minimizing the risk associated with migration to a new IP address by replacing IP with CLNP and its address size of 20 bytes (160 bits). TCP, UDP, and the traditional TCP/IP

applications would run on top of CLNP. TUBA is defined in RFCs 1347, 1526, and 1561.

IETF chose SIPP, written by Steve Deering, Paul Francis, and Bob Hinden, but with an address size of 128 bits. The IETF working group IP Next Generation was formed in 1993 (http://datatracker.ietf.org/wg/ipngwg/charter). In 1995, IETF published RFC 1883, Internet Protocol, Version 6 (IPv6) Specification, which later became obsolete and was replaced by RFC 2460 in 1998. In 2001, the IPng working group was renamed to the IPv6 working group.

In 1996, the IETF formed an IPv6 test bed network known as *6bone*. The 6bone network started out using IPv6 over IPv4 tunneling/encapsulation, operating over the IPv4-only Internet to support IPv6 transport. Later it migrated to native links for IPv6. 6bone was phased out in 2006.

Regional Internet Registries (RIR) began allocating IPv6 addresses to their customers in 1999. Adoption was slow at first, but in 2007, RIRs began receiving significantly more requests for IPv6 address space. This was because RIRs supported more widespread deployment of IPv6. For further information on IPv6 address allocation by RIRs, go to https://labs.ripe.net/Members/mirjam/interesting-graph-ipv6-allocations-since-1999 and http://en.wikipedia.org/wiki/IPv6_deployment.

In 2000, many vendors began adding IPv6 support to their mainstream products. Cisco Systems added IPv6 support with Cisco IOS Software Release 12.2(2)T. Linux vendors started supporting IPv6 in 2000, and Microsoft announced IPv6 support with Windows XP in 2001. In September 2010, the U.S. federal government committed to the operational deployment and use of IPv6. In a memorandum from Vivek Kundra, Federal Chief Information Officer, all public-/external-facing servers and services (for example, web, email, DNS, ISP services) will be IPv6 ready by the end of fiscal year 2012.

Today, there are several forums and organizations that promote and support the migration to IPv6:

- **International IPv6 Forum (www.ipv6forum.com):** A worldwide consortium of Internet vendors aiming to promote IPv6.
- **North American IPv6 Task Force (www.nav6tf.org):** A subchapter of the IPv6 Forum dedicated to the advancement and propagation of IPv6 on the North American continent.
- **The IPv6 Portal (www.ipv6tf.org):** Hosted by Consulintel, a website that helps with the deployment and support of IPv6 through forums, trainings, workshops, and labs.

Benefits of IPv6

This section discusses some of the advantages of IPv6. It includes a brief overview of several of the main benefits and features of IPv6:

- **Extended address space:** IPv6 provides 128-bit source and destination addresses compared to 32-bit addresses with IPv4. This represents an enormous number of addresses: 2^{128}, or about 340 trillion trillion trillion addresses, enough for every grain of sand on earth.
- **Stateless autoconfiguration:** IPv6 provides a configuration mechanism where hosts can self-generate a routable address. IPv4-autoconfigured addresses (RFC 3330 and RFC 5735) are usable only on the local subnet (link-local) and are never forwarded by a router. Stateful autoconfiguration using DHCPv6 is an option in IPv6.
- **Eliminates the need for NAT/PAT:** Because of the large number of public IPv6 addresses, there is no longer a need for Network Address Translation / Port Address Translation (NAT/PAT). Customer sites, from the largest enterprises to single households, can get a public IPv6 network address. This avoids some of the NAT-induced application problems experienced by applications such as Voice over IP (VoIP), videoconferencing, and other peer-to-peer applications. Although the concept of "no longer implementing NAT" is touted as one of the benefits of IPv6, NAT64 is currently an important tool used for backward compatibility with IPv4. Another issue surrounding NAT is that many organizations hide their IPv4 network behind a NAT device. This security model will have to change with publicly accessible IPv6 addresses. NAT is discussed in Chapter 11, "Network Address Translation IPv6 to IPv4 (NAT64)."
- **Eliminates broadcasts:** IPv6 does not use Layer 3 broadcast addresses. However, IPv6 does employ solicited node multicast addresses, a more efficient and selective technique for processes such as address resolution. Whereas in IPv4, Address Resolution Protocol (ARP) uses broadcasts, IPv6 employs solicited node multicasts to accomplish this same purpose. There is also an all-node multicast address that essentially has the same effect as an IPv4 broadcast. Multicast addresses and address resolution are discussed in later chapters.
- **Transition tools:** IPv6 has a variety of tools to help with the transition from IPv4 to IPv6, including tunneling and NAT. Tunneling encapsulates the IPv6 packet into an IPv4 packet so that it can be delivered over IPv4-only networks. NAT provides a mechanism to translate an IPv4 address to an IPv6 address or an IPv6 address to an IPv4 address. IPv4 can also be tunneled over IPv6. Tunneling is discussed later in Chapter 10, "Dual-Stack and Tunneling."

IPv6: When?

When will the world transition to IPv6, and is there a date to switch from IPv4 to IPv6? First of all, there is no deadline for conversion to IPv6. The transition from IPv4 to IPv6 is in progress and will continue. The Internet Society (ISOC) organizes World IPv6 Day, with the inaugural event held in June 2011. The goal during the first World IPv6 Day was for service and content providers to test their IPv6 implementations. The second-year goal of World IPv6 Day, in June 2012, was to have these same providers permanently provide IPv6 deployment for their services. As you can see, the transition to IPv6 is beginning.

However, IPv4 and IPv6 will most likely coexist for many years. Some of these transition strategies are discussed in Chapter 10.

When you ask most people what they know about IPv6, they will probably refer to the larger address space. IPv4 address depletion and IPv6 address space are discussed in much more detail throughout the book. But IPv6 is much more than just 128-bit source and destination addresses compared to 32-bit addresses in IPv4. IPv6 is a more efficient and elegant protocol, as explained later, with autoconfiguration and neighbor discovery.

IPv4 Address Depletion

Why do you need to start thinking about migrating to IPv6 now if your network runs just fine with IPv4? It's similar to considering buying a new car when the old one is running perfectly. Although there isn't a single killer-application that propels everyone to immediately move to IPv6, there are several compelling reasons, as introduced in the previous list, for network administrators to at least begin preparing for the migration. The most notable of these reasons is that we are simply running out of IPv4 address space. It is said that the killer-application for IPv6 is preserving the Internet and allowing it to move forward.

IPv4 has a theoretical maximum of 4.3 billion addresses. There is some inefficiency in the allocation of these addresses over the years. Even if it were possible to reassign the entire IPv4 address space in a more efficient manner, it would not only be impractical but would also only act as a very short-term solution.

The proponents of IPv4 continue to find ways to extend the use of IPv4 without preparing to migrate to IPv6. It is a little like rearranging deck chairs on the Titanic. It might make things a little more comfortable for a while, but sooner or later, you must come to the realization that you're in trouble.

When Bob Kahn and Vint Cerf first developed the TCP/IP suite of protocols including IPv4 and its 32-bit addresses, they never envisioned that the Internet would be what it is today. The idea that a person in his or her 70s is on the Internet several hours a day using Facebook verifies that today's Internet is no longer just for the younger generation.

The eventual exhaustion of IPv4 address space was recognized in the early 1990s. With the advent of the World Wide Web, there was an explosion in the size and diversity of the Internet population. The people using the Internet were no longer limited to a relatively small group of computer-savvy users who could navigate this unknown global network using slightly cumbersome and less-than-intuitive tools such as FTP, newsgroups, and Unix-to-Unix Copy (UUCP). With Tim Berners-Lee's development of the Hypertext Transfer Protocol (HTTP) at CERN in Geneva, followed by the first web browser, Mosaic, created by Marc Andreessen and his team at the National Center for Supercomputing Applications at the University of Illinois at Urbana-Champaign, all of a sudden the people who never owned a personal computer were accessing the Internet. It was becoming clear that 4.3 billion addresses were not going to last for long.

So, in the early 1990s, IETF began development of a new version of IP known as IP Next Generation, or IPng, which later became IPv6. This, however, was a long-term solution, and a short-term solution was needed immediately. Several steps were taken, including NAT, private IP address space, and classless interdomain routing (CIDR).

CIDR

In the early years, IPv4 network addresses were allocated using one of three classes—Class A, Class B, or Class C, as shown in Table 1-1.

Table 1-1 *Classful Unicast IP Addresses*

Address Class	First Octet Range	Number of Possible Networks	Number of Hosts per Network
Class A	0 to 127	128 (2 are reserved)	16,777,214
Class B	128 to 191	16,384	65,534
Class C	192 to 223	2,097,152	254

There were a total of five different classes:

- **Class A:** Has a subnet mask of 255.0.0.0, or a /8
- **Class B:** Has a subnet mask of 255.255.0.0, or a /16
- **Class C:** Has a subnet mask of 255.255.255.0, or a /24
- **Class D:** Used for multicast
- **Class E:** Experimental

Class A networks, with a /8 mask, can each have a total of 16,777,214 hosts (subtract two addresses for the network and broadcast addresses). The 126 Class A networks and the enormous number of hosts per network account for 50 percent of the total IPv4 address space, as shown in Figure 1-2.

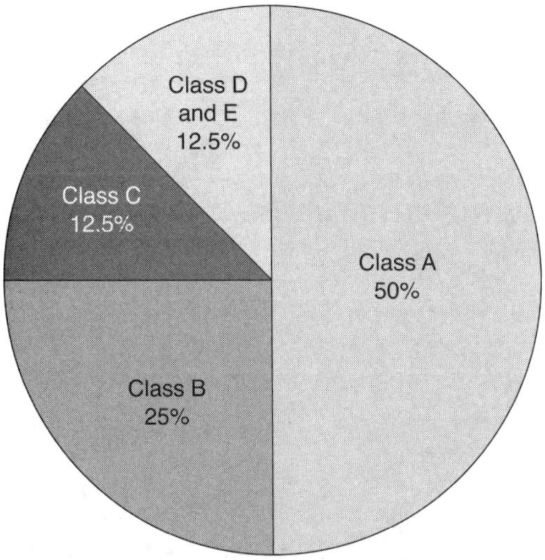

Figure 1-2 *Classful IP Address Allocation*

Class B networks have a /16 mask, which means that they can have a total of 65,534 hosts per network. The 16,384 Class B networks represent 25 percent of all IPv4 addresses.

Class C networks, with a /24 mask, can have a maximum of only 254 hosts for each Class C network address. Even though there are 2,097,152 Class C networks available, this represents only 12.5 percent of the total available IPv4 address space.

Because network administrators could only obtain a network address from one of these three classes, it made for a very inefficient method of allocating addresses. Most Class A and B networks had enormous numbers of unused addresses, while most Class C networks had comparatively very few.

In 1992, the IETF changed this method and replaced it with classless interdomain routing, or CIDR (pronounced *cider*), RFC 1338, and was later obsoleted by RFC 1519. Network addresses were no longer allocated based on one of three classes. The addresses could be assigned with any size mask, as shown in Figure 1-3. (Figure 1-3 shows the total number of possible host addresses and does not subtract two addresses for the network and broadcast addresses.) This gave RIRs and ISPs more flexibility in allocating addresses to customers and made for a much more efficient distribution of the limited IPv4 address space.

Class	Binary Mask	Prefix (Mask)	Host Addresses
Class A	11111111.00000000.00000000.00000000	/8(255.0.0.0)	16,777,216 host addresses
	11111111.10000000.00000000.00000000	/9(255.128.0.0)	8,388,608 host addresses
	11111111.11000000.00000000.00000000	/10(255.192.0.0)	4,194,304 host addresses
	11111111.11100000.00000000.00000000	/11(255.224.0.0)	2,097,152 host addresses
	11111111.11110000.00000000.00000000	/12(255.240.0.0)	1,048,576 host addresses
	11111111.11111000.00000000.00000000	/13(255.248.0.0)	524,288 host addresses
	11111111.11111100.00000000.00000000	/14(255.252.0.0)	264,144 host addresses
	11111111.11111110.00000000.00000000	/15(255.254.0.0)	131,072 host addresses
Class B	11111111.11111111.00000000.00000000	/16(255.255.0.0)	65,536 host addresses
	11111111.11111111.10000000.00000000	/17(255.255.128.0)	32,768 host addresses
	11111111.11111111.11000000.00000000	/18(255.255.192.0)	16,384 host addresses
	11111111.11111111.11100000.00000000	/19(255.255.224.0)	8,192 host addresses
	11111111.11111111.11110000.00000000	/20(255.255.240.0)	4,096 host addresses
	11111111.11111111.11111000.00000000	/21(255.255.248.0)	2,048 host addresses
	11111111.11111111.11111100.00000000	/22(255.255.252.0)	1,024 host addresses
	11111111.11111111.11111110.00000000	/23(255.255.254.0)	512 host addresses
Class C	11111111.11111111.11111111.00000000	/24(255.255.255.0)	256 host addresses
	11111111.11111111.11111111.10000000	/25(255.255.255.128)	128 host addresses
	11111111.11111111.11111111.11000000	/26(255.255.255.192)	64 host addresses
	11111111.11111111.11111111.11100000	/27(255.255.255.224)	32 host addresses
	11111111.11111111.11111111.11110000	/28(255.255.255.240)	16 host addresses
	11111111.11111111.11111111.11111000	/29(255.255.255.248)	8 host addresses
	11111111.11111111.11111111.11111100	/30(255.255.255.252)	4 host addresses
	11111111.11111111.11111111.11111110	/31(255.255.255.254)	2 host addresses
	11111111.11111111.11111111.11111111	/32(255.255.255.255)	"Host Route"

Figure 1-3 *Class IP Address Allocation*

NAT and Private Addresses

Network Address Translation (NAT) allows multiple hosts to share one or several reserved or public IPv4 addresses. Combined with private IP addresses, this becomes an extremely useful method of preserving IPv4 address space. The Internet Assigned Numbers Authority (IANA) allocated three ranges of addresses that are considered private IPv4 addresses as specified in RFC 1918. These private network addresses can be assigned to devices within private networks but are not routable in the global Internet. The private IPv4 addresses must therefore be translated to a public IP address before being forwarded by an Internet-facing router.

> **Note** Although this is by far the most common use, NAT is not utilized only for the translation between private and public IP addresses. It can occur between any pair of addresses.

The private IP addresses as defined by RFC 1918 are

10.0.0.0–10.255.255.255 (10.0.0.0/8)

172.16.0.0–172.31.255.255 (172.16.0.0/12)

192.168.0.0–192.168.255.255 (192.168.0.0/16)

You will most likely recognize the 192.168.0.0 address used by many home routers that perform NAT.

Note A new RFC 6598, IANA-Reserved IPv4 Prefix for Shared Address Space, assigns another block of shared address space, 100.64.0.0/10. Shared address space is distinct from RFC 1918 private address space because it is intended for use on service provider networks. However, it can be used in a manner similar to an RFC 1918 private address space.

Port Address Translation (PAT) is a form of dynamic NAT that maps multiple IP addresses to a single IP address using different TCP/UDP port numbers. PAT is also known as NAT overloading, single address NAT, or port-level multiplexed NAT. With PAT, each computer on the private network can be translated to the same public IP address but with a different source port number assigned. NAT/PAT is sometimes called just NAT. Whenever the term NAT is mentioned in this book, it also includes PAT.

Figure 1-4 shows an example of a network using NAT. Company XYZ has the public IP address of 209.165.200.248/29. This gives the company only six usable host addresses: 209.165.200.249 through 209.165.200.254. Company XYZ has hundreds of hosts, all of which might need access to the Internet at any given time. Because the company has only six public IP addresses, it will need to use private IP address space and NAT to meet its Internet access needs.

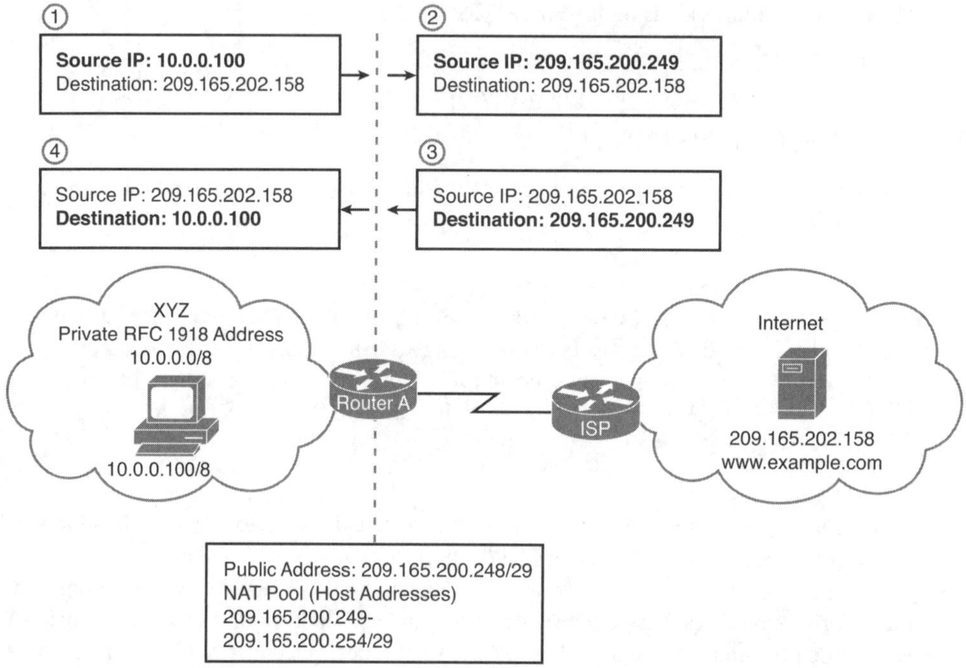

Figure 1-4 *Example of NAT*

Company XYZ's network administrator has chosen to use the private network address of 10.0.0.0/8. This provides more than enough host IP addresses to meet the company's needs. RouterA is Company XYZ's router, which connects the private network to the Internet by forwarding packets to the ISP router. The steps in Figure 1-4 show how NAT translates a private IP address to and from a public IP address. For simplification, the port translations that are part of PAT have not been included.

STEP 1. HostA on Company XYZ's network sends a packet with its source IP address of 10.0.0.100 and a destination IP address of 209.165.202.158 to the www.example.com web server.

STEP 2. RouterA receives the packet and performs the NAT/PAT translation before forwarding the packet to the ISP router. RouterA replaces the packet's private source IP address of 10.0.0.100 with the public address 209.165.200.249. The router would most likely also change the source TCP/UDP port number as part of PAT. Again, the Port Address Translation has not been included in this discussion to keep it simple. RouterA maintains a NAT table to keep track of all the addresses and port assignments that it modifies so that it can position the original address and port numbers back for the return traffic in Step 4.

STEP 3. The www.example.com web server returns the packet to the host with a source IP address of 209.165.202.158 and a destination IP address of 209.165.200.249.

STEP 4. RouterA receives the return traffic for HostA. Using its NAT table, Router A identifies the destination IP address and destination port number, and modifies these with the original address of 10.0.0.100 and the original port number.

The combination of NAT with RFC 1918 private addresses has been instrumental in slowing the depletion of IPv4 addresses. However, NAT has certain limitations. Because of the uncertainty of the actual destination IPv4 address and a public address that can be shared among multiple users, the ability for peer-to-peer communications becomes severely limited or problematic at best. Just think of the issues when two devices, both behind NAT, are trying to communicate with each other. What public IP address do they send the packets to? What if that public IP address is shared by more than one device in their network? Pure peer-to-peer communication only involves the two devices communicating with one another. NAT makes this more challenging to accomplish. Many services like Skype use publicly accessible servers that act as a relay point between users.

For those of you who might know something about Internet Protocol Security (IPsec), you are probably aware that NAT invites complications when using IPsec in transport mode. If an IPsec AH (Authentication Header) is used, the NAT translation breaks the integrity check because the packet was modified during transport. NAT modifies the TCP/UDP checksum. This will cause the integrity check to fail at the other end. Therefore, NAT cannot be used with IPsec in transport mode. Although it might work in tunnel mode, there can be issues there as well.

For most users, NAT has not been a problem as the Internet has been comprised of mainly client-server networks. Generally, the Internet has been employed by users or consumers that download content such as web pages, email, and music.

During the first decade of the 2000s, the Internet was used more as a two-way medium. People were beginning to collaborate and interact with each other, with more adopting social media sites such as Myspace and Facebook. Users were no longer just consumers of information but were becoming more the producers of content-engaging sites like YouTube and blogs. They were sharing content with each other using peer-to-peer applications like Napster and BitTorrent.

What all this means is that the way people use the Internet today is different than it was a few years ago. The Internet of tomorrow will have new applications and demands that have not yet been conceived. It is becoming more about two-way communications, where a device can be a client, a server, or both. In many cases, this can require public addresses at both ends, and NAT might not be able to work in conjunction with those applications.

Exhaustion of IPv4 Address Space

The number of people accessing the Internet is increasing dramatically. Even with short-term solutions like NAT, we are in the final stages of public IPv4 address availability. The world Internet usage and population statistics in Table 1-2 reveal some interesting facts regarding IPv4 address allocation. Notice that North America has a penetration rate of about 78 percent. "The Internet Penetration Rate corresponds to the percentage of the total population of a given country or region that uses the Internet." (Source: Internet World Stats, www.internetworldstats.com/surfing.htm.) This means that the majority of people in North America use the Internet. Compare that to another region like Asia, where they have a penetration rate of only about 29 percent. This becomes even more alarming when you compare the two populations. Notice that North America has a population of about 272 million compared to Asia at 922 million. As Asia, Africa, and other areas of the world become increasingly connected to the Internet, there just aren't enough IPv4 addresses to accommodate this kind of growth, even with NAT.

Table 1-2 *World Internet Usage and Population Statistics as of March 2011*

World Region	Population (2011 Est.)	Internet Users, Dec. 31, 2000	Internet Users, Latest Data	Penetration (% Population)	Growth, 2000–2011 (%)	Users, % of Table
Africa	1,037,524,058	4,514,400	118,609,620	11.4	2,527.4	5.7
Asia	3,879,740,877	114,304,000	922,329,554	23.8	706.9	44.0
Europe	816,426,346	105,096,093	476,213,935	58.3	353.1	22.7
Middle East	216,258,843	3,284,800	68,553,666	31.7	1,987.0	3.3
North America	347,394,870	108,096,800	272,066,000	78.3	151.7	13.0
Latin America/ Caribbean	597,283,165	18,068,919	215,939,400	36.2	1,037.4	10.3
Oceania/ Australia	35,426,995	7,620,480	21,293,830	60.1	179.4	1.0
World Total	6,930,055,154	360,985,492	2,095,006,005	30.2	480.4	110.0

The information in Table 1-2 was obtained from www.internetworldstats.com, Copyright © 2001–2011, Miniwatts Marketing Group. All rights reserved worldwide.

The phenomenal growth of the wireless industry, both cellular and wireless networks such as WLAN, 3G, 4G, WiMAX, and Mobile Wireless (MBWA), is further increasing the number of devices that need access to the Internet. One network engineer at a major U.S. university stated that each year the wireless usage on its network increases by 25 percent after students return from holiday break. This is because of students returning to school with new laptops, cell phones, iPads, and other wireless devices.

So when will we run out of IPv4 addresses? The Internet Assigned Numbers Authority (IANA) assigns IPv4 addresses to the five Regional Internet Registries in /8 address blocks. Using this address space, RIRs then redistribute these IPv4 network addresses to Internet service providers (ISP) and other end customers. The five Regional Internet Registries and the areas they manage are as follows:

- **African Network Information Centre (AfriNIC):** Africa
- **American Registry for Internet Numbers (ARIN):** United States, Canada, some parts of the Caribbean region, and Antarctica
- **Asia-Pacific Network Information Centre (APNIC):** Asia, Australia, New Zealand, and neighboring countries
- **Latin America and Caribbean Network Information Centre (LACNIC):** Central America, South America, and most of the Caribbean region
- **Réseaux IP Européens Network Coordination Centre (RIPE):** Europe, the Middle East, and Central Asia

On Monday, January 31, 2011, IANA allocated the last two blocks of IPv4 address space, 39.0.0.0/8 and 106.0.0.0/8, to APNIC, the RIR for the Asia-Pacific region. This triggered an IANA policy that the remaining five /8 addresses would be distributed equally between the five RIRs. At this point, IANA had run out of IPv4 addresses.

Does this mean that IPv4 addresses are no longer available for end customers? No. ISPs and others can still try to obtain IPv4 addresses from the RIRs, and most end users can in turn get addresses from their ISP. However, there are projections for when the RIRs might run out of IPv4 addresses. One such projection is the RIR IPv6 Address Run-Down Model, which can be found at www.potaroo.net/tools/ipv4/index.html. You can also download an IPv4 Exhaustion Counter for various platforms from Hurricane Electric, http://ipv6.he.net/statistics, showing the number of available /24 addresses by RIR. In the wake of all this IPv4 address depletion, a "grey market" for IPv4 addresses has emerged. Several websites are serving as brokers for organizations that want to sell or lease IPv4 address space. ISOC has stated that buyers and sellers should make sure that any transfers use the appropriate RIR processes so that they don't compromise network operations or security.

With the inherent limitation of 4.3 billion IPv4 addresses, an increasing Internet population, changes in how people use the Internet, and issues with NAT, the time to begin to transition to or at least become familiar with IPv6 is now.

Migrating to IPv6

The golden rule in networking, as in most things in life, is "If it's not broken, don't fix it." So, why migrate to IPv6 when your IPv4 network is working just fine? What is the killer-application that will drive IPv6 adoption?

As stated previously, the killer-application for IPv6 is the Internet itself. The Internet cannot sustain itself with IPv4. It can't continue to grow and evolve without more addresses, so the solution is IPv6. As the IPv4 Internet reaches its maximum potential, it will begin to experience performance and availability problems. The number of Internet-capable devices in our homes, businesses, and elsewhere in our lives is increasing all the time. It is no longer just our home computer but also our televisions, smart phones, tablet devices, webcams, security cameras, and so much more.

The rest of the world will eventually transition to IPv6; it is inevitable. Unless a company wants to exclude itself from the global Internet community, there is no choice but to prepare and eventually implement IPv6 on its network. There isn't a single date or timeline that applies to everyone to move to IPv6, but there are things we can do now to get ready.

Now is the best time for IT departments to begin preparation for IPv6, before there is a pressing need or immediate requirement. This gives IT organizations time to learn about IPv6, train/educate their workforce, and test/verify their implementations of IPv6. Preparation should focus on aspects of the IT department such as network operations, security, application developers, content developers, and the data center, just to name a few. Here are some of the things that can be done to start that migration:

- **Include IPv6 in your IT strategy:** IPv6 needs to be a part of your IT strategic planning for both the short-term and the long-term. IPv6 needs to be integrated in your IT planning processes, status meetings, training, and purchasing plans.
- **Training:** The optimum time to begin training about IPv6 or at least becoming familiar with it is before you have a requirement to implement it. Education/training is the best way for an IT staff to lose their fear and intimidation of IPv6. Training can also include non-IT staff as well, such as sales. A friend of mine who's been a network engineer for over 25 years told me he was hoping to have retired by the time he had to learn IPv6. As we go through this book together, you will see that IPv6 is not as complicated as you might think, and in many ways, it's easier to deal with than IPv4. For example, subnetting doesn't require any bitmapping, so IPv6 subnets can be easier to configure and identify.
- **Inventory equipment:** Develop a list of devices on your network (or use an existing inventory list) to see whether they currently support IPv6 or what upgrade/replacement is necessary. This includes
  - Clients and servers
  - Routers and multilayer switches
  - Layer 2 switches
  - Firewalls and other security devices
  - Printers, webcams, phones, and any other device with an IP address on your network
  - Applications, operating systems, and software services
- **Purchasing:** Make sure that your purchasing plan confirms that any new equipment purchased is IPv6 compatible. Ask vendors whether their hardware/software supports IPv6. If it doesn't, ask them what their product implementation plan is for including IPv6 support.

- **Test lab:** One of the best places to begin is by creating a lab, which is off the production network, to learn and play with IPv6. Then, as you become more comfortable with IPv6, you can introduce it into your network as you continue to run IPv4.

Summary

After reading this chapter, you should have a better understanding of the limitations of IPv4 and know why it is necessary to begin migrating to IPv6. Although it is discussed in more detail throughout this book, you should begin to have a basic understanding of the benefits of IPv6.

Here are some of the key items discussed in this chapter:

- How we use the Internet today is much different than it was when IPv4 was developed, with more users, more devices, and new demands. We have moved from just an *Internet of computers* to an *Internet of things*.
- Although no one knows exactly when, we will eventually run out of IPv4's 4.3 billion addresses, but the fact is that the Internet is in the final stages of public IPv4 address availability.
- IPv6, with its 128-bit address scheme, provides more than enough globally unique addresses to support the growth of the Internet.
- IPv4 and IPv6 will coexist for the foreseeable future. IPv6 includes tools and migration strategies that allow both protocols to coexist.
- The combination of CIDR, NAT, and private addressing has helped slow the depletion of IPv4 address space. However, NAT complicates many applications, including peer-to-peer networking, and with an emerging global Internet community, these enhancements to IPv4 are no longer sufficient.
- In addition to a larger address space, IPv6 offers additional enhancements such as stateless autoconfiguration and expanded address space without NAT.
- Now is the best time for IT departments to begin familiarizing themselves with IPv6 before an ordered mandate. The Internet is the killer-application for IPv6.

IPv6 is the successor to IPv4 to ensure the growth of the Internet.

References

RFCs:

RFC 1, *Host Software*, Steve Crocker, UCLA, www.ietf.org/rfc/rfc1.txt, April 1969

RFC 454, *File Transfer Protocol*, A. McKenzie, BBN, IETF, www.ietf.org/rfc/rfc454.txt, February 1973

RFC 827, *Exterior Gateway Protocol*, Eric C. Rosen, BBN, IETF, www.ietf.org/rfc/rfc827.txt, October 1982

RFC 760, *DoD Standard, Internet Protocol*, USC, IETF, www.ietf.org/rfc/rfc760.txt, January 1980

RFC 791, *Internet Protocol, DARPA Internet Program Protocol Specification*, USC, www.ietf.org/rfc/rfc791.txt, September 1981

RFC 920, *Domain Requirements*, J. Postel, J. Reynolds, ISI, IETF, www.ietf.org/rfc/rfc920.txt, October 1984

RFC 1190, *Experimental Internet Stream Protocol, Version 2 (ST-II)*, CIP Working Group, IETF, www.ietf.org/rfc/rfc1190.txt, October 1990

RFC 1338, *Supernetting: An Address Assignment and Aggregation Strategy*, V. Fuller, BARRNet, IETF, www.ietf.org/rfc/rfc1338, June 1992

RFC 1347, *TCP and UDP with Bigger Addresses (TUBA), A Simple Proposal for Internet Addressing and Routing*, Ross Callon, DEC, IETF, www.ietf.org/rfc/rfc1347.txt, June 1992

RFC 1519, *Classless Inter-Domain Routing (CIDR): An Address Assignment and Aggregation Strategy*, V. Fuller, BARRNet, IETF, www.ietf.org/rfc/rfc1519.txt, September 1993

RFC 1526, *Assignment of System Identifiers for TUBA/CLNP Hosts*, D. Piscitello, Bellcore, IETF, www.ietf.org/rfc/rfc1526.txt, September 1993

RFC 1550, *IP: Next Generation (IPng) White Paper Solicitation*, S. Bradner, Harvard University, IETF, www.ietf.org/rfc/rfc1550.txt, December 1993

RFC 1561, *Use of ISO CLNP in TUBA Environments*, D. Piscitello, Core Competence, IETF, www.ietf.org/rfc/rfc1561.txt, December 1993

RFC 1656, *BGP-4 Protocol Document Roadmap and Implementation Experience*, P. Traina, Cisco Systems, IETF, www.ietf.org/rfc/rfc1656.txt, July 1994

RFC 1700, *Assigned Numbers*, J. Reynolds, ISI, IETF, www.ietf.org/rfc/rfc1700.txt, October 1994

RFC 1707, *CATNIP: Common Architecture for the Internet*, M. McGovern, Sunspot Graphics, IETF, www.ietf.org/rfc/rfc1707.txt, October 1994

RFC 1710, *Simple Internet Protocol Plus White Paper*, R. Hinden, Sun Microsystems, IETF, www.ietf.org/rfc/rfc1710.txt, October 1994

RFC 1752, *The Recommendation for the IP Next Generation Protocol*, S. Bradner, Harvard University, IETF, www.ietf.org/rfc/rfc1752.txt, January 1995

RFC 1819, *Internet Stream Protocol Version 2 (ST2) Protocol Specification - Version ST2+*, ST2 Working Group, IETF, www.ietf.org/rfc/rfc1819.txt, August 1995

RFC 1883, *Internet Protocol, Version 6 (IPv6) Specification*, S. Deering, Xerox PARC, IETF, www.ietf.org/rfc/rfc1883.txt, December 1995

RFC 1918, *Address Allocation for Private Internets*, Y. Rekhter, Cisco Systems, IETF, www.ietf.org/rfc/rfc1918.txt, February 1996

RFC 2205, *Resource ReSerVation Protocol (RSVP) - Version 1 Functional Specification*, R. Braden, ISI, IETF, www.ietf.org/rfc/rfc2205.txt, September 1997

RFC 2235, *Hobbes' Internet Timeline*, R. Zakon, MITRE, IETF, www.ietf.org/rfc/rfc2235.txt, November 1997

RFC 2460, *Internet Protocol, Version 6 (IPv6) Specification*, S. Deering, Cisco Systems, IETF, www.ietf.org/rfc/rfc2460.txt, December 1998

RFC 3330, *Special-Use IPv4 Addresses*, IANA, IETF, www.ietf.org/rfc/rfc3330.txt, September 2002

RFC 3927, *Dynamic Configuration of IPv4 Link-Local Addresses*, S. Cheshire, Apple Computer, IETF, www.ietf.org/rfc/rfc3927.txt, May 2005

Websites:

International IPv6 Forum, www.ipv6forum.com

Internet World Stats, www.internetworldstats.com

IPv4 Address Report, www.potaroo.net/tools/ipv4/index.html

North American IPv6 Task Force, www.nav6tf.org

The IPv6 Portal, www.ipv6tf.org

The top 500 sites on the web, www.alexa.com/topsites

Global IPv6 Deployment Progress Report, http://bgp.he.net/ipv6-progress-report.cgi

Internet Protocol Version 6 Address Space, www.iana.org/assignments/ipv6-address-space/ipv6-address-space.xml

Comparison of IPv6 application support, http://en.wikipedia.org/wiki/Comparison_of_IPv6_application_support

Comparison of IPv6 support in operating systems, http://en.wikipedia.org/wiki/Comparison_of_IPv6_support_in_operating_systems

Chapter 2

The IPv6 Protocol

This chapter describes the IPv6 protocol. It examines the fields in the IPv4 header and explores both the similarities and the differences. It explains how IPv6 offers much more than just a larger address space. It's a new protocol designed to be more flexible and more efficient.

The structure of the IPv6 header is discussed in RFC 2460, Internet Protocol, Version 6 (IPv6) Specification. In addition to the main IPv6 header, a new type of IPv6 header known as an Extension header is also examined. The end of this chapter contains a summary that includes the differences between the IPv4 and IPv6 headers.

IPv4 Header

To help you better understand the IPv6 header, we will first take a look at the IPv4 header. This can be a review for you, or it can provide a better understanding of the IPv4 header. In either case, it will clarify the differences in the IPv6 header. Figure 2-1 shows the structure of the IPv4 header as defined in RFC 791, Internet Protocol, DARPA Internet Program, Protocol Specification. The IPv6 header is shown in Figure 2-2, later in this chapter. A quick comparison of the two reveals that the IPv6 header is a simpler protocol—with fewer fields. This makes for a leaner protocol and more efficient processing.

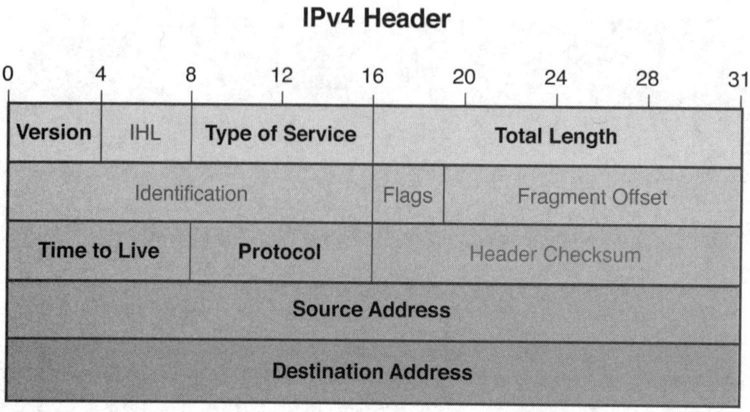

Figure 2-1 *IPv4 Header*

Note The next section examines the individual fields in the IPv4 header and is included for continuity. This section serves as a reference and a review of IPv4 for those who might need this data. This information can be helpful during the comparison of the IPv4 and IPv6 headers discussed later in this chapter.

The fields in the IPv4 header are as follows:

- **Version (4 bits):** This field contains the version number of the IP (Internet Protocol) header. In IPv4, this field is always the value of 4.
- **Internet Header Length (4 bits):** This is the length of the IP header in 32-bit words, including any optional fields. In effect, this points to where the IP header ends and the data or payload begins. The minimum value is 5 (5 * 32-bit words = 160 bits or 20 octets [bytes]). This is equal to the minimum size of an IPv4 header, excluding any options or padding.
- **Type of Service (8 bits):** The Type of Service, or ToS, field specifies what type of treatment the packet should receive from routers. The ToS information helps provide quality of service (QoS) features by offering different degrees of precedence. When multiple packets are queued to be transmitted out the same interface, the ToS value can be used to decide which is sent first. The ToS field was not widely used as originally designed, so in 1998, the Internet Engineering Task Force (IETF) redefined it further in RFC 2474 using a technique called Differentiated Services (DS). Differentiated Services Code Point (DSCP) is discussed in more detail later in this chapter, but ToS and DS are beyond the scope of this book.
- **Total Length (16 bits):** This is the length of the IP packet, measured in octets (bytes), including the IP header and the data. This is a 16-bit field, so the maximum size of an IPv4 packet is 65,535 bytes. Most IPv4 packets are much smaller.

The next three fields are used for packet fragmentation and reassembly. IP was designed for a wide variety of transmission links. Most transmission links enforce a maximum packet length known as the MTU (maximum transmission unit). The design of IP accommodates MTU differences by allowing routers to fragment IP packets when an MTU along the path is smaller than the sender's MTU. If a router receives an IPv4 packet that is larger than the MTU of the outgoing interface, this packet can be fragmented depending upon the options in the IPv4 header. Sometimes packets are fragmented into multiple packets at the source. The final destination of the IP packet is responsible for reassembling the fragments into the original full-size IP packet.

- **Identification (16 bits):** Most messages sent over the network consist of many packets. Each packet within the message has a unique value using this 16-bit Identification field. When a packet needs to be fragmented into two or more packets, this Identification field is common in all the fragmented packets to help the receiver in reassembling these fragments.
- **Flags (3 bits):** The first bit is 0, which means it is reserved or not used. The second bit is known as the DF, or Don't Fragment, bit. When set to 1, it means that this packet should not be fragmented. However, most protocols don't care about the fragmentation process and set this flag to 0, which means that this packet can be fragmented if needed. The third bit is the More Fragments Flag and is used to indicate whether this is the last fragment (0 bit) or whether there are more fragments to follow (1 bit). If a packet is not fragmented, there is only one fragment—the entire packet—and this flag is set to 0.

Note The DF flag is very useful when testing the MTU of a path between the source and the destination. If the DF flag is set to 1, the packet should not be fragmented. Any router along the path whose MTU is smaller than the packet will drop the packet and send an Internet Control Message Protocol (ICMP) "Destination Unreachable" message back to the source. The ICMP message will include the MTU of the router's egress interface. Path MTU Discovery for IPv4 is beyond the scope of our discussion. RFC 1191, Path MTU Discovery, explains this process if you are interested in learning more. Path MTU Discovery for IPv6 is discussed later in this chapter.

- **Fragment Offset (13 bits):** When a packet is fragmented, this field specifies the offset or position where this data goes in units of 8 octets (64 bits). Basically the fragment offset field notifies the receiver where to align this fragmented packet in relation to the other fragmented packets. The first fragment has offset zero. If the packet is not fragmented, this value is 0.
- **Time to Live (8 bits):** The Time to Live (TTL) field ensures that packets do not live in the network for an indefinite period of time as in the case of a routing loop. The TTL is decremented by 1 each time a router receives the packet. When the field contains the value of 0, the packet is discarded and an ICMPv4 (Internet Control Message

Protocol version 4) Time Exceeded (Type 11) message is sent to the source of the packet.

Note The Time to Live field was originally intended to represent the actual maximum amount of time that the packet is allowed to traverse the network and not the necessarily the number of router hops. RFC 791 stated, "Even if no local information is available on the time actually spent, the field must be decremented by 1. The time is measured in units of seconds (i.e., the value 1 means one second). Thus, the maximum time to live is 255 seconds or 4.25 minutes." Instead of calculating the amount of time, routers just decrement the TTL by 1, in effect making it the number of hops.

- **Protocol (8 bits):** This field indicates the protocol carried in the data portion of the IP packet. The values for various protocols are specified in RFC 1700, Assigned Numbers, and were later replaced by an online database maintained by IANA at www.iana.org/assignments/protocol-numbers/protocol-numbers.xml. Some of the more common values are 1 for ICMP, 6 for TCP, and 17 for UDP.

Note At times this field is referred to as carrying an upper-layer protocol. This can be misleading because the protocol being carried as the data or payload might be another Layer 3 protocol such as ICMP or even IP.

- **Header Checksum (16 bits):** A checksum for the IP header is provided for protection against any corruption in transit. This is not the more complex CRC (Cyclic Redundancy Check) used by Ethernet but a much simpler 16-bit checksum performed only on the IP header. Each router along the path verifies and recomputes this field. If the checksum fails, the router discards the packet.
- **Source Address (32 bits):** This is the 32-bit IP address of the originator of the packet.
- **Destination Address (32 bits):** This is the 32-bit IP address of the final destination or recipient of the packet. This address is used by routers to forward the packet along its path toward its ultimate destination.

Note Network Address Translation (NAT) can change either the source or destination address to one of the translator's addresses, typically an RFC 1918 private IP address. NAT is outside the scope of this book. See RFC 4787 for more information.

- **Options (variable length):** This field is optional, so it might or might not appear in the IP packet. It is variable in size and not included in most packets. Some of the options contain record route, timestamp, and traceroute used as an enhancement to the traceroute utility and described in RFC 1393, Traceroute Using an IP Option.

- **Padding (variable length):** If one or more options are used, and the size of the IP header is no longer a multiple of 32 bits, 0 bits are added to pad out the header so that it ends on a 32-bit boundary.
- **Data (variable length):** This is the data to be transmitted in the IP packet and identified by the Protocol field. The data can be another Layer 3 protocol such as ICMP, or a higher-layer protocol such as TCP or UDP.

IPv6 Header

IPv6 is defined in RFC 2460, Internet Protocol, Version 6 (IPv6) Specification. Figure 2-2 shows the basic structure of the IPv6 header or what is sometimes referred to as the main IPv6 header. The main IPv6 header can also include one or more IPv6 extension headers. Extension headers are explained later in this chapter.

The IPv6 header and its fields are examined in Figure 2-2.

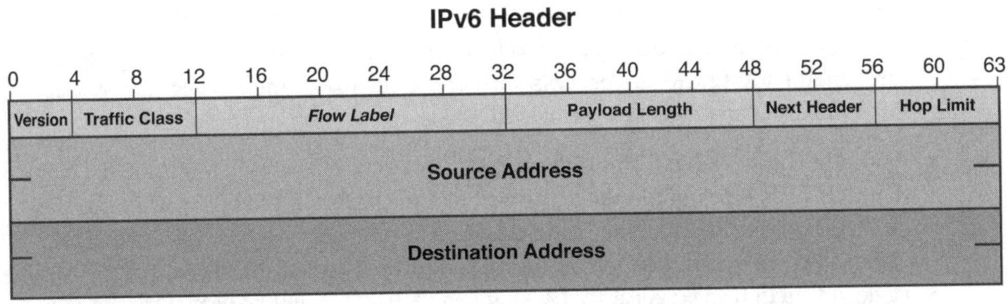

Figure 2-2 *IPv6 Header*

The IPv6 main header is required and consists of the following fields:

- **Version (4 bits):** This field contains the version number of the IP (Internet Protocol) header. In IPv6, this field is always the value of 6.
- **Traffic Class (8 bits):** This field has similar functions to the Type of Service (ToS) field in the IPv4 header. It is the same size as the IPv4 ToS field; only the name has changed. The Traffic Class field is used to identify and distinguish between different classes or priorities of IPv6 packets. IPv6 uses the Differentiated Services technique specified in RFC 2474, Definition of the Differentiated Services Field (DS Field) in the IPv4 and IPv6 Headers. Using 6 bits for the DSCP (Differentiated Services Code Point) allows a possibility of 64 markings. This provides much more granularity in priority selection than the original 3 bits for IPv4 Precedence, with its 8 values.

Note DSCP and IP Precedence are beyond the scope of this book. One interesting note is that the IP Precedence value is actually the first 3 bits of the DSCP value, as shown in Figure 2-3. Therefore, both values cannot be used simultaneously. If DSCP with its additional 3 bits is used, it supersedes IP Precedence.

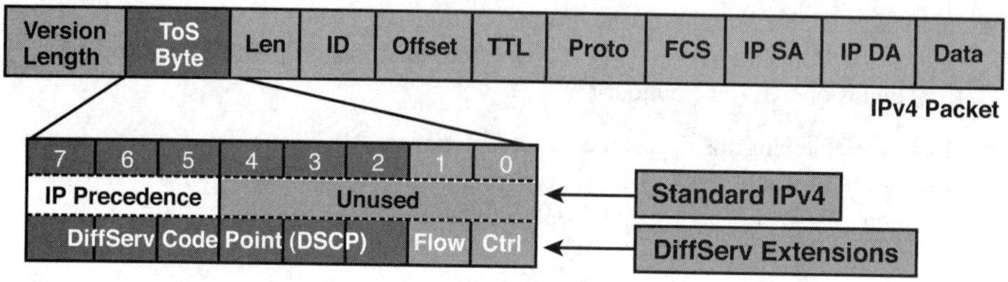

Figure 2-3 *IPv4 ToS Byte*

- **Flow Label (20 bits):** The Flow Label field is used to tag a sequence or flow of IPv6 packets sent from a source to one or more destination nodes. This flow can be used by a source to label sequences of packets for which it requests special handling by the IPv6 routers, such as "real-time" service. The Flow Label field is used to help identify all the packets within the same flow to ensure that all the packets receive the same type of handling by the IPv6 routers. Flow Label usage is described in RFC 6437, IPv6 Flow Label Specification. Routers keep track of these individual packet flows. Because routers do not have to independently process each packet's header, these multipacket flows are processed more efficiently. At the time of this writing, this field is still somewhat experimental.

- **Payload Length (16 bits):** This is the length in octets of the payload following the main IP header or, in other words, the data portion of the packet. If the IPv6 packet has one or more extension headers, they are included in the number of bytes contained in the Payload Length field. Extension headers are considered part of the payload. The IPv6 Payload Length field is similar to the Total Length field in the IPv4 header, except for one important difference. IPv4's Total Length field includes both the IPv4 header and the data, whereas the IPv6 Payload Length field only specifies the number of bytes of data; it does not include the main IPv6 header. The IPv4 header can vary in length because of Padding and Options fields, whereas the IPv6 header is fixed at 40 bytes.

  The Payload Length field is 16 bits, allowing a maximum payload size of 65,535 bytes. IPv6 has a Jumbogram extension header to support larger packet sizes if needed. RFC 2675, IPv6 Jumbograms, specifies an additional 32-bit field to allow the transmission of IPv6 packets with payloads between 65,536 and 4,294,967,295 bytes. Extension headers along with the Jumbo Payload Options are discussed later in this chapter.

- **Next Header (8 bits):** This field has two benefits. In a situation when there is only the main IPv6 header and no extension headers, the Next Header field specifies the protocol carried in the data portion of the IPv6 packet. This is similar to the Protocol field in the IPv4 header. The same values used in the IPv4 Protocol field are used in the IPv6 Next Header field along with additional values. Table 2-1 shows some of the significant IPv6 Next Header values. A complete listing can be found at www.iana.org/assignments/protocol-numbers/protocol-numbers.xml. You might recognize some of these, as many are the same values used by the Protocol field in IPv4 such as 6 for TCP and 17 for UDP. Figure 2-4 shows several examples including the Next Header field, indicating that the data portion of the IPv6 packet is a TCP segment.

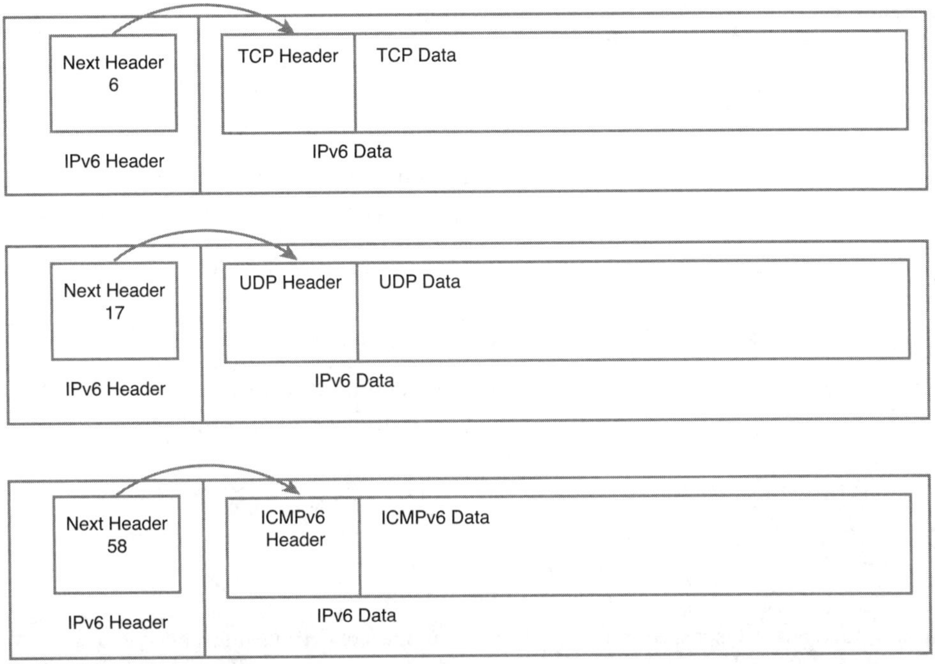

Figure 2-4 *Next Header Field*

Table 2-1 *Significant IPv6 Next Header Values*

Next Header Value (Decimal)	Next Header Value (Hexadecimal)	Description
0	0	Hop-by-hop options extension header for IPv6
1	1	Internet Control Message Protocol version 4 (ICMPv4)
2	2	Internet Group Management Protocol version 4 (IGMPv4)
4	4	IPv4 encapsulation
5	5	Internet Stream Protocol (ST)
6	6	Transmission Control Protocol (TCP)
8	8	Exterior Gateway Protocol (EGP)
17	11	User Datagram Protocol (UDP)
41	29	IPv6 encapsulation
43	2B	Routing extension header for IPv6
44	2C	Fragment header for IPv6

Next Header Value (Decimal)	Next Header Value (Hexadecimal)	Description
46	2E	Resource Reservation Protocol (RSVP)
47	2F	Generic Routing Protocol (GRE)
50	32	Encapsulation Security Protocol (ESP)
51	33	Authentication Header (AH)
58	3A	Internet Control Message Protocol version 6 (ICMPv6)
59	3B	No Next Header for IPv6
60	3C	Destinations options extension header for IPv6
88	58	Enhanced Interior Gateway Routing Protocol (EIGRP)
89	58	Open Shortest Path First (OSPF)

Note Tunneling is discussed in Chapter 10, "Dual-Stack and Tunneling," but for now, notice that an IP packet can encapsulate another IP packet. The Next Header field contains the value 4 when the following header is an IPv4 header, and 41 to indicate another IPv6 header.

- **Hop Limit (8 bits):** The Hop Limit field is equivalent to the Time to Live (TTL) field in the IPv4 header. Its name in IPv6 is more reflective of the way that routers treat this field by decrementing the hop limit by 1. Just as with the IPv4 TTL field, if the router decrements the hop limit from 1 to 0, the packet is discarded. In IPv6, an ICMPv6 Time Exceeded message (Type 3, Code 0) is sent to notify the source of the packet that the packet has been dropped. I will discuss ICMPv6 in Chapter 5, "ICMPv6 and Neighbor Discovery Protocol."

- **Source Address (128 bits):** This field contains the 128-bit IP address of the originator of the IPv6 packet. As with IPv4, this is the address of the node that originally sent the packet. The source address must be a unicast address.

- **Destination Address (128 bits):** This is the 128-bit IP address of the intended final destination or recipient of the IPv6 packet. It represents the ultimate destination, which can be a unicast or multicast address. Unlike IPv4, there is no broadcast address; however, there is an all-nodes multicast address. The details of IPv6 addresses are discussed in Chapter 3, "IPv6 Addressing," and Chapter 4, "IPv6 Address Types."

Packet Analysis Using Wireshark

Let's take a look at an IPv6 packet using a packet analyzer such as Wireshark. Based on the network setup shown in Figure 2-5, we will do a simple ping from PC1 to PC2.

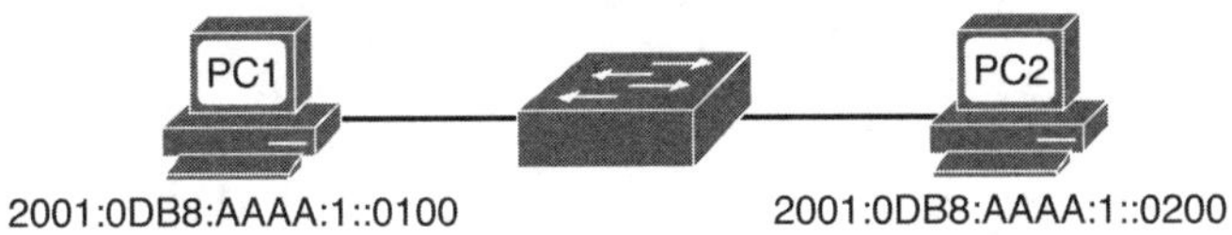

Figure 2-5 *PC1 Pinging an IPv6 Address on PC2*

```
PC1> ping 2001:0db8:aaaa:0001::0200

Pinging 2001:db8:aaaa:1::200 from 2001:db8:aaaa:1::100 with 32 bytes of data:
Reply from 2001:db8:aaaa:1::200: time<1ms
Reply from 2001:db8:aaaa:1::200: time<1ms
Reply from 2001:db8:aaaa:1::200: time<1ms
Reply from 2001:db8:aaaa:1::200: time<1ms

Ping statistics for 2001:db8:aaaa:1::200:
    Packets: Sent = 4, Received = 4, Lost = 0 (0% loss),
Approximate round trip times in milli-seconds:
    Minimum = 0ms, Maximum = 0ms, Average = 0ms

PC1>
```

Notice that some of the 0s in the addresses have been omitted in the output. IPv6 addresses and compressed formats are also discussed in Chapter 3. For now, be assured that these are the same addresses.

The IPv6 addresses are 128-bit addresses and written in hexadecimal. They might look a little strange right now, but don't worry, you will become very familiar with these addresses beginning in Chapter 3. Figure 2-6 shows the Wireshark capture of the ICMPv6 Echo Request (ping), which is further described in Table 2-2. ICMPv6 will be explained in more detail in Chapter 5.

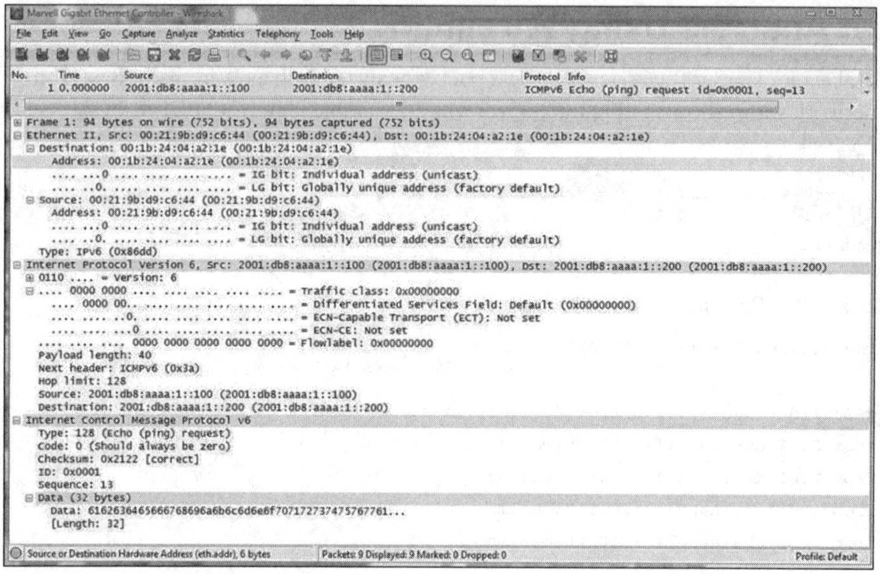

Figure 2-6 *Wireshark Capture of an IPv6 Packet*

Table 2-2 *Analysis of an IPv6 Packet*

	Field Name	Size (Bits)	Value – Description
IPv6 Header (40 Bytes)	Version	4	6 – Indicates IP version 6
	Traffic Class	8	0 – Default of 0
	Flow Label	20	0 – Default of 0
	Payload Length	16	40 bytes – This indicates the size of the data, which in this case is an ICMPv6 message. Notice that the ICMPv6 message has a length of 40 bytes.
	Next Header	8	58 – This identifies the following header as an ICMPv6 header. See Table 2-1 for a partial listing of IPv6 Next Header values.
	Hop Limit	8	128 – The maximum number of routers that this packet can traverse before being discarded.
	Source Address	128	2001:0db8:aaaa:1::100 – The source IPv6 address in hexadecimal.
	Destination Address	128	2001:0db8:aaaa:1::200 – The destination IPv6 address in hexadecimal.

	Field Name	Size (Bits)	Value – Description
ICMPv6 Header (40 Bytes)	Type	8	128 – Identifies this as an ICMPv6 Echo Request message.
	Code	8	0 – Not used; default is 0.
	Checksum	16	0x2122 – 16-bit checksum that is used to verify the integrity of the ICMPv6 header.
	ID	16	0x0001 – Used to help match ICMPv6 Echo Request and Echo Reply messages.
	Sequence	16	13 – Used to help match ICMPv6 Echo Request and Echo Reply messages.
	Data	256	Optional data of variable length depending upon the type of ICMPv6 message.

Note Wireshark is a network protocol analyzer for both IPv4 and IPv6. Wireshark is available for several operating systems and is a free downloaded at www.wireshark.org.

Extension Headers

Extension headers can be difficult to understand, so this chapter guides you with a step-by-step process. Some of them are fairly easy to grasp while others can be a little more difficult. So, don't be too concerned if some of this seems a little vague. The purpose of this section is to familiarize you with the concept of what extension headers are and how they are used.

Extension headers are optional and follow the main IPv6 header. As discussed previously, the IPv6 header includes a Next Header field, which has one of two purposes:

- To identify the protocol carried in the data portion of the packet
- To identify the presence of an extension header

As explained previously, the Next Header field can indicate which protocol is being carried in the data portion of the IPv6 packet, similar to IPv4's Protocol field and illustrated in Figure 2-5.

The second purpose is one of the more important additions to the IPv6 header, the indication of an additional header known as an extension header. Immediately following the mandatory main IPv6 header, there can be zero, one, or several extension headers. A field common in all extension headers is another Next Hop field, which indicates whether another extension header is to follow, or the protocol of the data (payload) like a TCP segment. Therefore, the last extension header will always specify which protocol is encapsulated as the data or payload—again, similar to the Protocol field in IPv4.

The intention of extension headers is to provide flexibility to the main IPv6 header for future enhancements without having to redesign the entire protocol. This also allows the main IPv6 header to have a fixed size for more efficient processing.

There are currently six extension headers as defined in RFC 2460 and summarized in Table 2-3. If you remember, in IPv4 there is a little-used Options field of variable length to provide some additional flexibility. Two of the extension headers in IPv6 provide a similar function: the Hop-by-Hop Options and the Destination Options headers. Figure 2-7 shows an example of an IPv6 packet using two extension headers.

- The main IPv6 header has all the fields we have discussed, including the source and destination addresses. The Next Hop field is also in this header with the value of 0, indicating that a Hop-by-Hop extension header immediately follows.
- The Hop-by-Hop extension header follows the main IPv6 header. Extension headers will be explained in more detail in the next section, but for now, notice that this field also contains its own Next Header field. Its value of 51 signifies that there is yet another extension header to follow, the Authentication Header (AH).
- The final extension header is the Authentication Header. Its Next Header field has a value of 6, indicating that a TCP upper-layer header is to follow. This also means that there are no more extension headers in this packet.

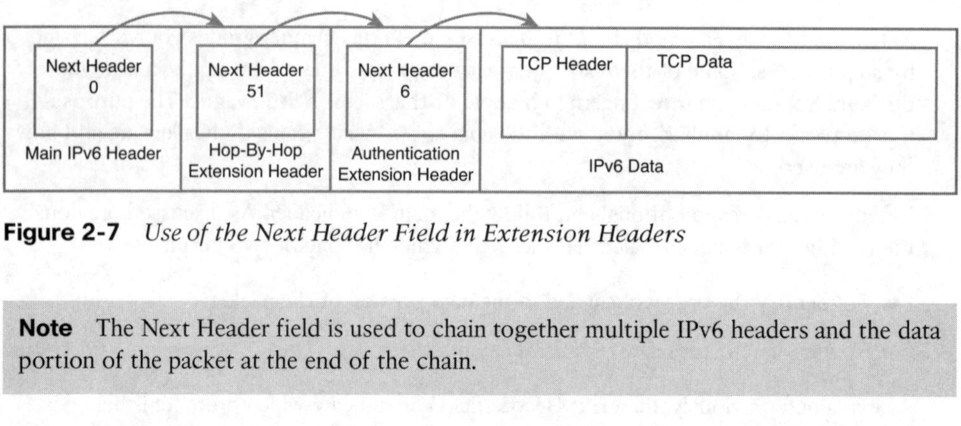

Figure 2-7 *Use of the Next Header Field in Extension Headers*

Note The Next Header field is used to chain together multiple IPv6 headers and the data portion of the packet at the end of the chain.

Table 2-3 IPv6 Extension Headers

Next Header Value (Decimal)	Extension Header Name	Extension Header Length (Bytes)	Variable-Length Options (TLV) Used?	Extension Header Description
0	Hop-by-Hop Options	Variable	Yes	Used to carry optional information, which must be examined by every router along the path of the packet.
43	Routing	Variable	No	Allows the source of the packet to specify the path to the destination.
44	Fragment	8	No	Used to fragment IPv6 packets.
50	Encapsulating Security Payload (ESP)	Variable	No	Used to provide authentication, integrity, and encryption.
51	Authentication Header (AH)	Variable	No	Used to provide authentication and integrity.
60	Destination Options	Variable	Yes	Used to carry optional information that only needs to be examined by a packet's destination node(s).

RFC 2460 recommends that when multiple extension headers are used in the same packet, those headers appear in the following order:

1. Main IPv6 header
2. Hop-by-Hop Options header
3. Destination Options header
4. Routing header
5. Fragment header
6. Authentication header
7. Encapsulating Security Payload header
8. Destination Options header
9. Upper-layer protocol header

Hop-by-Hop Options Extension Header

The Hop-by-Hop Options header is used to carry optional information that must be examined by every router along the path of the packet. The Hop-by-Hop Options header is one of two extension headers that contains a variable-length options field similar to IPv4. As the name implies, this type of option is to be examined by every router, at every hop along the path.

Note The Destination Options is the other extension header that uses options. And as its name implies, it contains information intended only for the final destination. Destination Options are discussed at the end of this section.

Let's examine the use of these options. Options provide flexibility, allowing IPv6 packets to be supplemented with sets of values that are not defined in the standard group of extension headers. These sets of values are also referred to as Type-Length-Value (TLV) triplets. It has already been established that two extension headers use these options, Hop-by-Hop Options and Destination Options. As shown in Figure 2-8, these two types of extension headers have a Next Header and a Header Extension Length field, followed by one or more sets of options. Each option contains a set of Options Type, Options Length, and Options Data field (Type, Length, Value, or TVL).

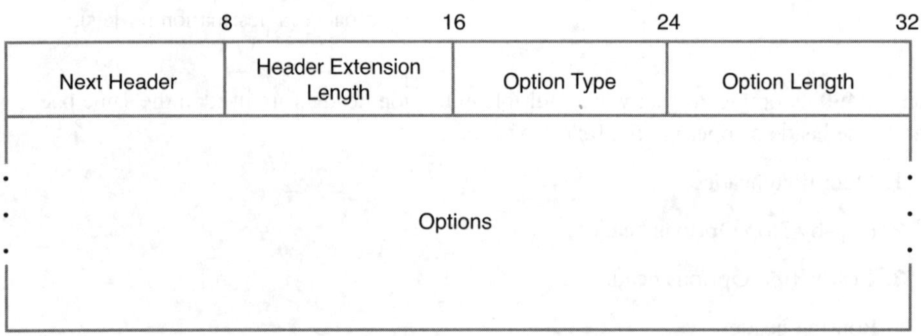

Figure 2-8 *Extension Header Options*

Figure 2-9 shows a Hop-by-Hop extension header referencing a Jumbo Payload Option. The Jumbo Payload Option is used to indicate that the size of this IPv6 packet is larger than 65,535 bytes. Because it is a Hop-by-Hop Option, this information is to be examined by each router along the path.

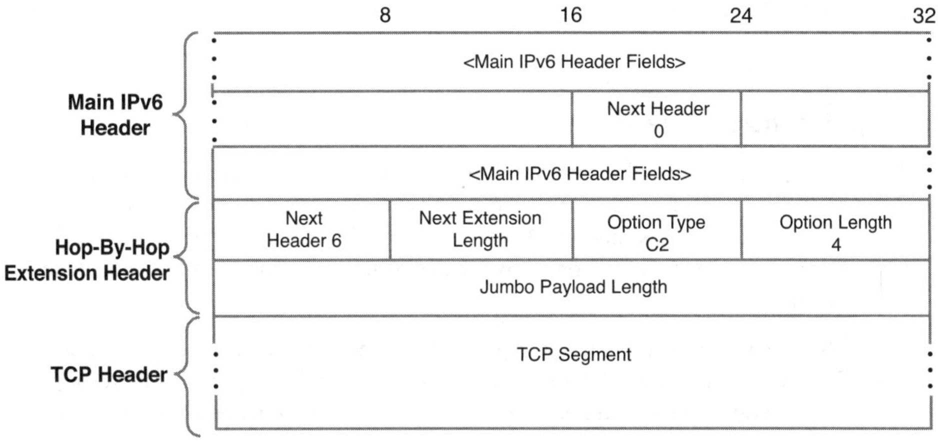

Figure 2-9 *Hop-by-Hop Extension Header with Jumbo Payload Option*

The following describes the fields associated with the Hop-by-Hop extension header:

- **The main IPv6 header: Next Header (8 bits):** Along with other information in the main IPv6 header, there is a Next Header field with the value of 0. This indicates that a Hop-by-Hop Options extension header follows this main header.
- **The Hop-by-Hop extension header:**
  - **Next Header (8 bits):** The value of 6 in the Next Header field indicates that a TCP header follows this header and that there are no other extension headers.
  - **Header Extension Length (8 bits):** This is the length of the Hop-by-Hop Options header in 8-octet units, not including the first 8 octets. There can be multiple options, with each option consisting of a TLV (Options Type, Options Length, and Options Data field).
  - **Option Type (8 bits):** This is the type of option carried in this header. A hexadecimal value of C2 indicates that this is a Jumbo Payload Option.
  - **Option Data Length (8 bits):** This is the number of bytes in the Option Data field. A value of 4 indicates that the Option data is 4 bytes (32 bits) long.
  - **Option Data (variable-length):** The data in this example is the Jumbo Payload Length. The Jumbo Payload Length is a 32-bit field indicating the size of the IPv6 packet in bytes, excluding the IPv6 header but including the Hop-by-Hop Options header and any other extension headers present. Jumbo Payload Length must be greater than 65,535 and can be up to 4,294,967,295 bytes.
- **TCP Segment:** Because there was only one option and no other extension headers, a TCP segment follows as indicated by the Next Header value of 6 in the previous Hop-by-Hop extension header.

If a Hop-by-Hop Options extension header is used, it will immediately follow the main IPv6 header.

Routing Extension Header

The Routing extension header allows the source of the packet to specify the path to the destination. This header contains a list of one or more intermediate routers on the way to a packet's destination. This function is very similar to the Loose Source option used in IPv4. The Routing header is identified by a Next Header value of 43 in the immediately preceding header.

Figure 2-10 shows the structure of a Type 2 Routing header used for mobility support in IPv6. This extension header allows the packet to be routed directly from a correspondent to the mobile node's care-of address, which provides information about the mobile node's current location.

The following describes the fields associated with the Routing Extension Header:

- **Next Header (8 bits):** Identifies the type of header immediately following the Routing header. This will be either another extension header or the protocol of the payload.
- **Header Extension Length (8 bits):** This is the length of the Routing header in 8-octet units, not including the first 8 octets.
- **Routing Type (8 bits):** This value is 2.
- **Segments Left (8 bits):** This value is 1.
- **Reserved (32 bits):** This field is reserved. Initialized to 0 for transmission and ignored on reception.
- **Home Address (128 bits):** This is the Home Address of the destination mobile node.

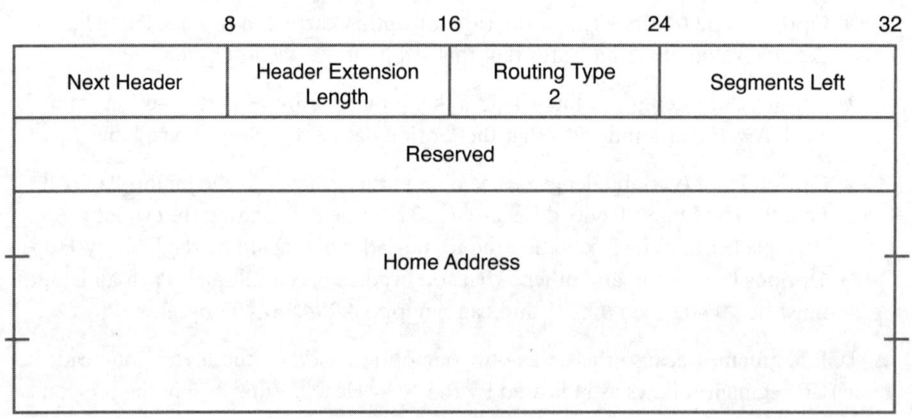

Figure 2-10 *Type 2 Routing Header*

> **Note** The details of how the Routing extension header is processed by each router are beyond the scope of this book. If you are interested, refer to RFC 2460 or the Cisco Press book *Cisco Self-Study: Implementing Cisco IPv6 Networks*. Many ISPs cast a suspicious eye if the source node offers to help with packet next-hop selection, and it is common for packets containing routing extensions to be administratively blocked. Currently the only valid routing header is a Type 2, which is used for mobility in IPv6.

Fragment Extension Header

The Fragment extension header, as shown in Figure 2-11, is similar to that in IPv4 fields used for fragmentation. This method is used when the source of the IPv6 packet needs to divide the packet into fragments and send each fragment as a separate packet. The recipient of the packet reassembles the fragments, each with its own main IPv6 header and a Fragment extension header.

Unlike IPv4, IPv6 routers do not fragment packets unless it is the source of the packet. Intermediate nodes do not perform fragmentation. Only the source of the packet can fragment it. If a router receives an IPv6 packet that is larger than the MTU of the egress interface, the router will discard the packet and send an ICMPv6 Packet Too Big error message back to the source.

Similar to IPv4, for every packet to be fragmented, the source generates a unique Identification value. This value is included in each of the fragment packets. The Identification value ensures that fragments from the original packet are properly reassembled. If the source needs to fragment additional packets within the same message, different Identification values are used.

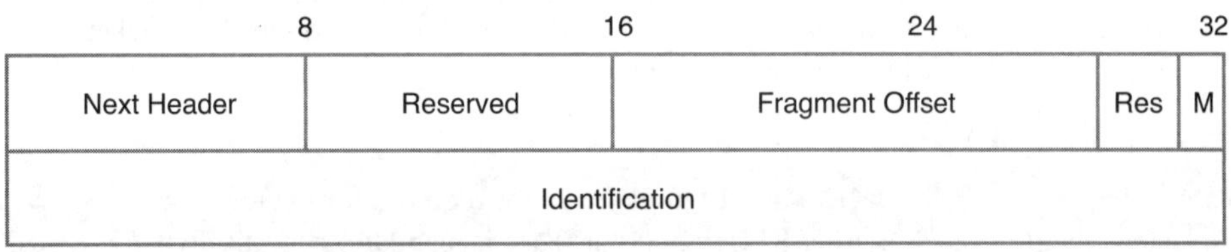

Figure 2-11 *Fragment Header*

The following fields are part of the Fragment header, as shown in Figure 2-11:

- **Next Header (8 bits):** Identifies the protocol number of the data, the fragmented part of the original packet.
- **Reserved (8 bits):** This field is reserved. Initialized to 0 for transmission and ignored on reception.
- **Fragment Offset (13 bits):** This is the relative offset or position, in 8-octet units, of the fragmented data following this header, relative to the original packet. Similar to the Fragment Offset field in IPv4, this informs the receiver where to align this fragmented packet in relation to the other fragmented packets.

- **Res (2 bits):** This field is reserved. Initialized to 0 for transmission and ignored on reception.
- **M flag (1 bit):** The M, or More Fragments, flag is used to indicate whether this is the last fragment (0 bit) or whether there are more fragments to follow (1 bit). This is similar to IPv4's More Fragments flag.
- **Identification (32 bits):** Similar to the same field in the IPv4 header, this is used to uniquely identify all fragmented packets within the same original packet. This field has been expanded from 16 bits in IPv4 to 32 bits in IPv6.

IPsec: AH and ESP Extension Headers

The following extension headers are used to implement two core security protocols in IPsec:

- Authentication Header (AH)
- Encapsulating Security Payload (ESP)

IPsec

Before examining the AH and ESP extension headers, I'll briefly discuss IPsec and the function of these two security protocols. This is not meant to give you a thorough understanding of IPsec, AH, and ESP, but will give you enough information to understand their importance and use in IPv6.

IPsec is a suite of protocols for securing delivery of packets of IP networks. Authentication Header (AH) and Encapsulating Security Payload (ESP) are two main protocols used to provide authentication and integrity for all or part of an IPv6 packet. ESP includes the additional feature of encryption.

> **Note** IPsec is part of both IPv4 and IPv6. IPsec is not required for devices that implement the IPv4 stack. Earlier RFCs state that IPsec is mandatory for all IPv6 implementations, stating that IPsec "must be supported." RFC 6434, IPv6 Node Requirements, relaxes this requirement by declaring that IPsec "should be implemented."

The Authentication Header (AH) is used to guarantee the authenticity and integrity of the packet. *Authentication* means that it ensures that the sender and receiver of the packet are really who they say they are. *Integrity* guarantees that the data was not altered in transit. The Authentication Header provides authentication and integrity but does not provide encryption. *Encryption* is the process of transforming information (usually in plain text) by using an algorithm (called a cipher) to make it unreadable to anyone except those possessing special information (usually referred to as a key).

The Encapsulating Security Payload (ESP) provides authentication integrity *and* encryption. ESP not only protects the packet from being altered by intermediate devices but also protects the content of the packet from being viewed. ESP has its own authentication scheme, or it can be used in conjunction with AH. In summary, AH only provides authentication and integrity, while ESP provides both of these and encrypts the packet as well.

What hasn't been discussed yet is how much of the packet is authenticated or encrypted. The answer to that depends on whether transport mode or tunnel mode is used in IPsec.

Transport and Tunnel Modes

As the name suggests, Transport mode protects the transport layer and higher. The initial IP header is still used. Because the original source and destination IP addresses are in the main IP header intermediate devices, routers recognize the IPsec participants. Transport mode is typically used for host-to-host communications.

Tunnel mode is employed to protect the entire contents of the IP packet, including the IP header. This is accomplished by encapsulating the original IP packet, including the IP header, in a new IP header with the tunnel endpoints used as the new source and destination IP addresses. The tunnel endpoints can be routers or can be the hosts themselves. Tunnel mode protects the entire IP packet while Transport mode does not. Figure 2-12 illustrates the differences between Transport and Tunnel mode.

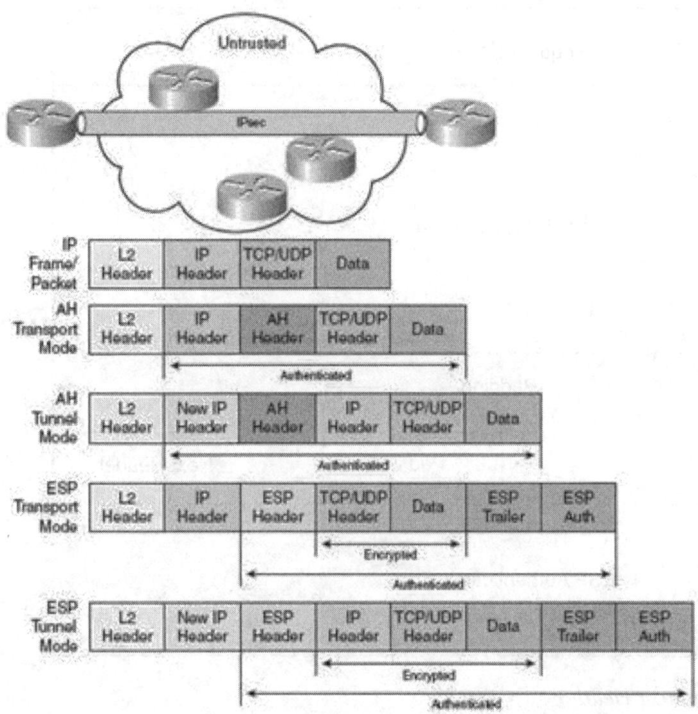

Figure 2-12 *Transport and Tunnel Mode*

Let's return to the extension headers used for AH and ESP. If you are new to IPsec, it is perfectly understandable if some of the details of AH and ESP are a not perfectly clear.

Encapsulating Security Payload (ESP) Extension Header

The Encapsulating Security Payload (ESP) is a variable-length extension header. As discussed previously, this header is used to provide authentication, integrity, and encryption. The ESP extension header is identified by a Next Header value of 50 in the immediately preceding header.

Figure 2-13 shows the ESP extension header. The ESP header can be divided into four parts:

- **ESP Header:** SPI and Sequence Number fields
- **Payload:** ESP Payload Data field
- **ESP Trailer:** Padding, Pad Length, and Next Header fields
- **ESP Authentication Data**

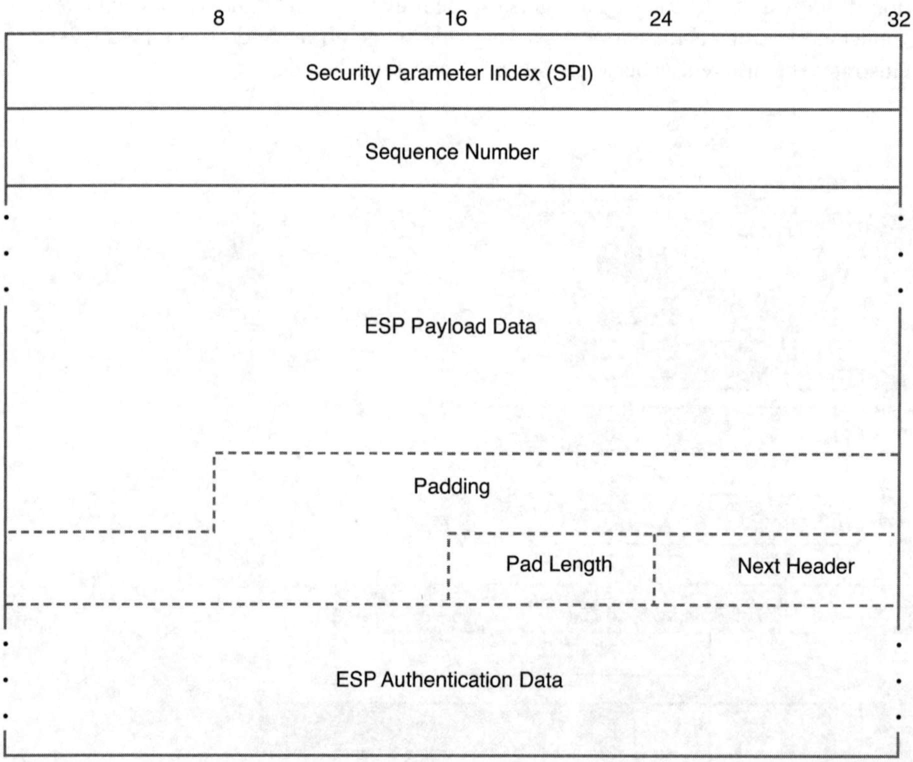

Figure 2-13 *ESP Extension Header*

Figure 2-13 illustrates the fields in the ESP extension header. ESP is viewed as end-to-end communications; in other words, it is not processed by routers along the path. Remember, ESP provides authentication integrity and confidentiality of the original packet. Therefore, the ESP extension header is encapsulated after the main IPv6 header, and after the Hop-by-Hop, Routing, and Fragment extension headers, as shown in Figure 2-14. For IPv6, encryption covers the entire transport-level segment plus the ESP trailer and the Destination Options extension header if it occurs after the ESP header. The Destination Options extension header could appear before or after the ESP header, depending upon the intent desired.

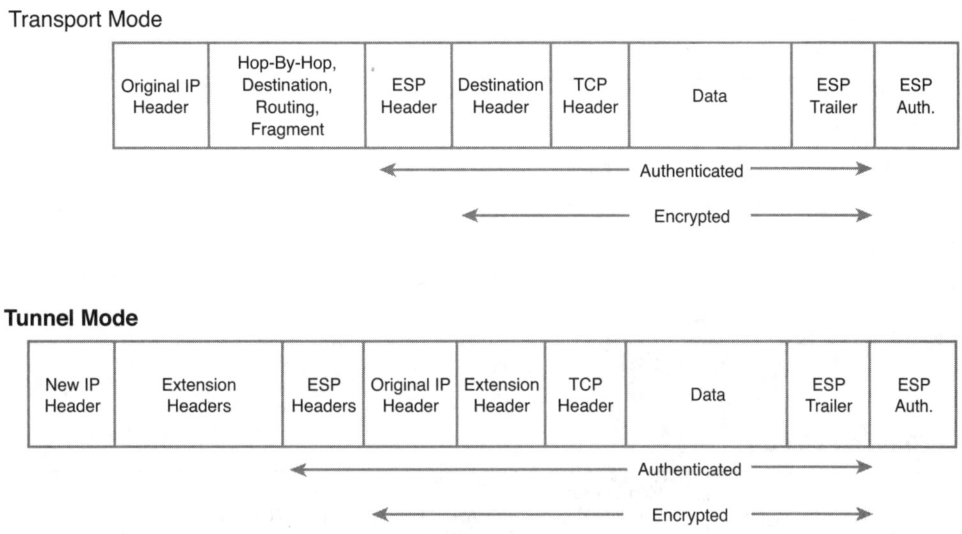

Figure 2-14 *ESP – Transport and Tunnel Modes*

Unlike the previous extension headers, the details of each field are beyond the scope of this book and require a better understanding of IPsec. If you are new to IPsec, it is understandable if some of this might be a little vague. For more information about IPsec, the Cisco Press book *IPsec Virtual Private Network Fundamentals*, by James Henry Carmouche, is an excellent resource.

Authentication Header (AH) Extension Header

The Authentication Header (AH) is also a variable-length extension header. Unlike the ESP, AH only provides authentication and integrity, and does not use encryption to provide confidentiality. The AH extension header is identified by a Next Header value of 51 in the preceding header.

Figure 2-15 illustrates the fields in the Authentication Header. Like ESP, AH is viewed as end-to-end communications. Remember, AH only provides data integrity, a feature to ensure that the participants are who they say they are and that any alteration in the packet's content in transit is detected by the recipient. Similar to ESP, the Authentication Header is encapsulated after the main IPv6 header, and after the Hop-by-Hop, Routing, and Fragment extension headers, as shown in Figure 2-16. The Destination Options extension header can appear before or after the AH header, depending upon the intent desired.

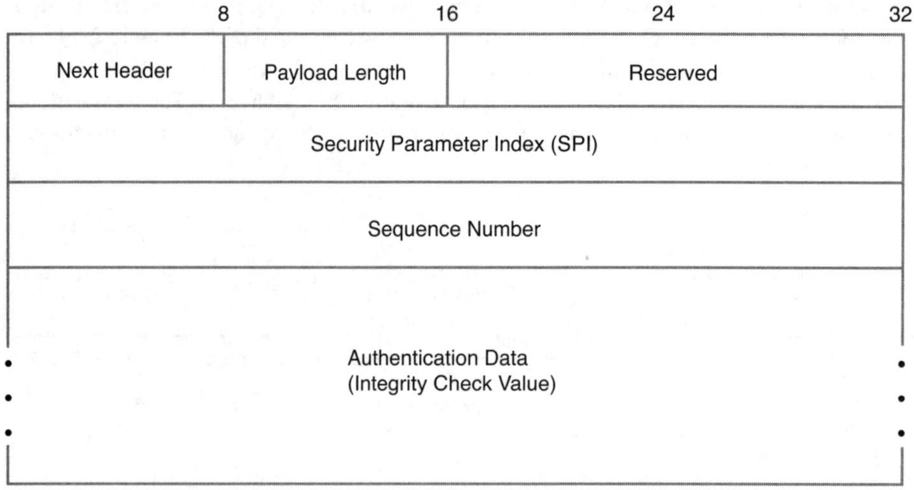

Figure 2-15 *AH Extension Header*

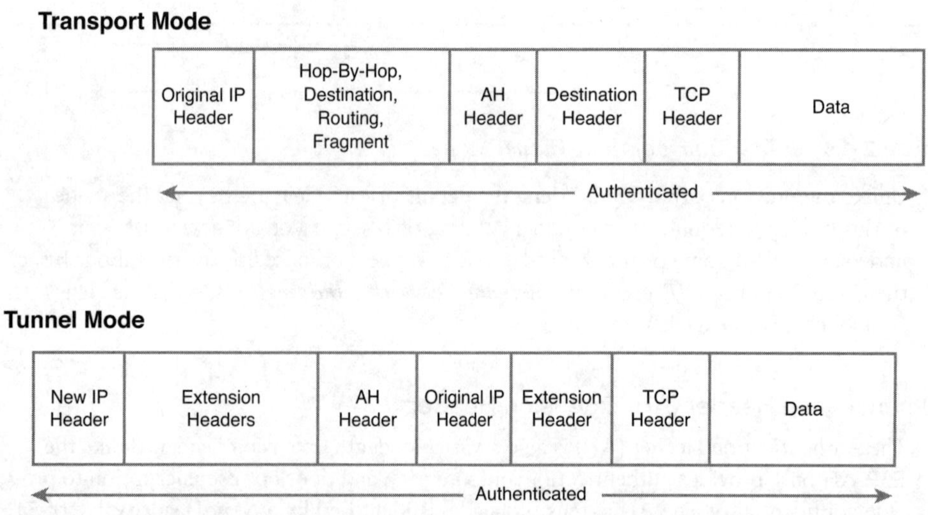

Figure 2-16 *AH – Transport and Tunnel Modes*

As with the other IPsec extension header, the details of AH and these fields are beyond the scope of this book and require a more thorough understanding of IPsec.

Destination Options Extension Header

The Destination Options header is used to carry optional information that only needs to be examined by a packet's destination node(s). The Destination Options header is the other extension header that uses options. (The Hop-by-Hop header is the other one.) The Destination Options header is identified by a Next Header value of 60 in the preceding header. As illustrated in Figure 2-17, the Destination Options header has the following format:

- **Next Header (8 bits):** Identifies the type of header immediately following the Destination Options header. This will be either another extension header or the protocol of the payload.
- **Header Extension Length (8 bits):** This is the length of the Destination Options header in 8-octet units, not including the first 8 octets.
- **Options (variable-length):** This field contains one or more TLV-encoded options, Option Type, Option Data Length, and Option Data:
  - **Option Type (8 bits):** This is the type of option carried in this header.
  - **Option Data Length (8 bits):** This signifies the number of bytes of the Option Data field.
  - **Option Data (variable-length):** This is the data content depending upon the use of this field.

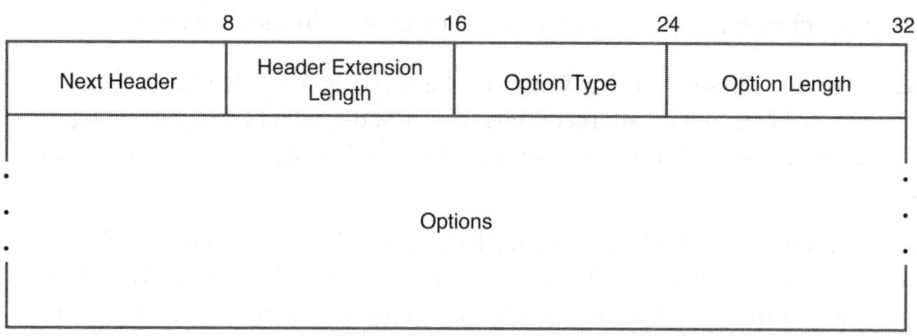

Figure 2-17 *Destination Options Extension Header*

> **Note** One of the proposed uses for the Destination Options extension header is mobility support, as described in RFC 6275, Mobility Support in IPv6:
>
> "Each mobile node is always identified by its home address, regardless of its current point of attachment to the Internet. While situated away from its home, a mobile node is also associated with a care-of address, which provides information regarding the mobile node's current location. IPv6 packets addressed to a mobile node's home address are transparently routed to its care-of address. The protocol enables IPv6 nodes to cache the binding of a mobile node's home address with its care-of address, and to then send any packets destined for the mobile node directly to it at this care-of address. To support this operation, Mobile IPv6 defines a new IPv6 protocol and a new destination option. All IPv6 nodes, whether mobile or stationary, can communicate with mobile nodes."

No Next Header

The Next Header value of 59 indicates that there is no data following this header. This is just a placeholder indicating that there is nothing after this header. If the payload length indicates that there are additional bytes beyond the header, those bytes will be ignored.

Comparing IPv4 and IPv6

After examining the details of the IPv4 and IPv6 headers, it's easy to miss some of the important differences between the two protocols. There was a lot of information to digest, so let's summarize some of these differences, referring back to Figures 2-1 and 2-2.

IPv4 and IPv6 Header Comparisons

These IPv4 field names are the same as those in IPv6:

- **Version (IPv4 and IPv6):** This is an easy one; the value is 4 in IPv4 and 6 in IPv6.
- **Source Address and Destination Address (IPv4 and IPv6):** Probably the most noticeable differences are the 32-bit IPv4 source and destination addresses, which have been increased to 128 bits in IPv6.

IPv4 field names changed in IPv6 with functional differences in some cases:

- **Type of Service (IPv4) → Traffic Class (IPv6):** IPv4 can use either the 3-bit IP Precedence field along with another 3 bits for delay, throughput, and reliability, or the 6-bit Differentiated Services technique. IPv6 was designed to use the 6-bit DS method.
- **Total Length (IPv4) → Payload Length (IPv6):** IPv4's Total Length field includes both the IPv4 header and the data, whereas the IPv6 Payload Length field only specifies the number of bytes of data (payload), including any extension headers, and does not include the main IPv6 header.
- **Time to Live (IPv4) → Hop Limit (IPv6):** This has the same function in both IPv4 and IPv6, with the name being more reflective of its actual use in IPv6.
- **Protocol (IPv4) → Next Header (IPv6):** In IPv4, this indicates the protocol being carried in the IPv4 data or payload. This same function exists in the Next Header field in IPv6 but can also indicate the existence of an extension header following the main IPv6 header.

IPv4 fields removed from IPv6:

- **Internet Header Length (IPv4):** This field is not needed in IPv6 because the main IPv6 header has a fixed length of 40 bytes. Any additional headers are linked as indicated in the Next Header field.

- **Identification (IPv4), Flags (IPv4), and Fragment Offset (IPv4):** These fields are used for fragmentation in IPv4. Fragmentation is handled differently in IPv6 using the Fragment extension header.
- **Header Checksum (IPv4):** Layer 2 data link layer technologies such as Ethernet perform their own checksum and error control. Upper-layer protocols such as TCP and UDP also have their own checksums and therefore a checksum at Layer 3 becomes redundant and unnecessary. A UDP checksum, which is optional in IPv4, is mandatory in IPv6.
- **Options (IPv4):** Options in IPv4 are now handled using extension headers in IPv6. Two IPv6 extension headers, Hop-by-Hop Options and Destination Options, contain their own set of TLV options.
- **Padding (IPv4):** Because IPv6 has a fixed length of 40 bytes, it is unnecessary to extend the header to make sure that it falls on a 32-bit boundary.

New field in IPv6:

- **Flow Label (IPv6):** This is a new field to IPv6, and the specifications of its use are still being determined by the IETF. RFC 2460 does discuss using the Flow Label field to label sequences of packets for needing special handling by IPv6 routers for "real-time" service. RFC 6437, IPv6 Flow Label Specification, contains additional details on the Flow Label field.

Other Differences

There are several other important differences in the two protocols. The uses of the Hop-by-Hop extension header and the Jumbo Payload Options increase the potential size of an IP packet from 65,535 bytes in IPv4 to 4,294,967,295 bytes in IPv6.

Larger Maximum Transmission Unit (MTU)

IPv4 requires that every node must be able to forward an IP packet of 68 bytes without any further fragmentation. This is because an IPv4 header can be as large as 60 bytes in length or have a minimum fragment size of 8 bytes. Every IPv4 node that is the final destination of the IPv4 packet must be able to receive an IPv4 packet of a minimum size of 576 bytes, which can be all or fragments of the original packet.

IPv6 requires that every link have a minimum MTU of 1280 bytes, with a recommended MTU of 1500 bytes, compared to 68 bytes in IPv4.

Note RFC 1981, Path MTU Discovery for IP version 6, suggests that IPv6 devices should perform PTMU (Path Maximum Transmission Unit) discovery to avoid fragmentation.

User Datagram Protocol (UDP)

The User Datagram Protocol (UDP) Checksum field in IPv4 is optional. Although the protocol remains the same in IPv6, the Checksum field is mandatory. This is because the IPv4 header has its own Checksum field but has been removed in the IPv6 header. The Checksum field is used to verify the integrity of the UDP header and data.

> **Note** The Checksum field in Transmission Control Protocol (TCP) is mandatory for both IPv4 and IPv6. TCP and UDP run on top of IPv6 without any structural modifications to these protocols. TCP, UDP, and other upper-layer protocols are examined in Chapter 9, "DHCPv6 (Dynamic Host Configuration Protocol version 6)."

Fragmentation

When the Fragment extension header was discussed earlier, it was noted that unlike IPv4, IPv6 routers do not fragment packets unless the router is the source of the packet. Only the source node of the IPv6 packet can perform fragmentation. If an intermediate node such as a router receives an IPv6 packet that needs to be fragmented, it will discard the packet and send an ICMPv6 Packet Too Big error message back to the source. Fragmentation and Path MTU discovery are discussed in Chapter 5.

Summary

This chapter examined both the IPv4 header and the IPv6 header. It compared the similarities and the differences between the two protocols. The IPv6 header has fewer fields, and in many respects, IPv6 is a simpler protocol. Some of the fields moving from IPv4 to IPv6 remained the same, some had name changes with functional differences, others were removed completely, and there was a new Flow Label field added.

Extension headers were introduced. They provide more flexibility and better efficiency for IPv6. The impact of IPv6 on User Datagram Protocol (UDP) and maximum transmission unit (MTU) was explained.

Chapter 3 allows you to become familiar with IPv6 notation and the general structure of an IPv6 unicast address.

References

RFCs:

RFC 791, *Internet Protocol, DARPA Internet Program Protocol Specification*, USC, www.ietf.org/rfc/rfc791.txt, September 1981

RFC 1191, *Path MTU Discovery*, J. Mogul, Stanford University, www.ietf.org/rfc/rfc1191.txt, November 1990

RFC 1393, *Traceroute Using an IP Option*, G. Malkin, Xylogics, Inc., www.ietf.org/rfc/rfc1393.txt, January 1993

RFC 1700, *Assigned Numbers*, J. Reynolds, ISI, IETF, www.ietf.org/rfc/rfc1700.txt, October 1994

RFC 1981, *Path MTU Discovery for IP version* 6, J. McCann, Digital Equipment Corporation, www.ietf.org/rfc/rfc1981, August 1996

RFC 2460, *Internet Protocol, Version 6 (IPv6) Specification*, S. Deering, Cisco Systems, IETF, www.ietf.org/rfc/rfc2460.txt, December 1998

RFC 2474, *Using a Technique Called Differentiated Services (DS)*, K. Nichols, Cisco Systems, www.ietf.org/rfc/rfc2474.txt, December 1998

RFC 2675, *IPv6 Jumbograms*, D. Borman, Berkeley Software Design, www.ietf.org/rfc/rfc2675.txt, August 1999

RFC 3775, *Mobility Support in IPv6*, D. Johnson, Rice University, www.ietf.org/rfc/rfc3775.txt, June 2004

RFC 6434, *IPv6 Node Requirements*, E. Jankiewicz, SRI International, www.ietf.org/rfc/rfc6434, December 2011

RFC 6437, *IPv6 Flow Label Specification*, S. Amante, Level 3, www.ietf.org/rfc/rfc6437, November 2011

Website:

www.iana.org/assignments/protocol-numbers/protocol-numbers.xml

Chapter 3

IPv6 Addressing

The most recognizable difference between IPv4 and IPv6 is the address space. An IPv4 address is 32 bits and expressed in dotted-decimal notation, whereas an IPv6 address is 128 bits in length and written in hexadecimal. IPv6 addressing is defined in RFC 4291, IP Version 6 Addressing Architecture.

In this chapter, you will become familiar with reading IPv6 addresses and recognizing the different parts. You will take a brief look at the different types of IPv6 addresses and the basic structure of a global unicast address. You will configure a router's interface with an IPv6 address and verify reachability with the **ping** command. This chapter also examines how to subnet an IPv6 address, which in most cases, is much easier than subnetting in IPv4.

At first, the longer, hexadecimal IPv6 address can look intimidating. This does not have to be the case—as a matter of fact, IPv6 addresses can be easier to read and much simpler to subnet than their IPv4 counterparts. By the end of this book, you might actually prefer working with IPv6 addresses than with IPv4 addresses! I begin by making sure that you understand the hexadecimal number system and IPv6 address notation.

Hexadecimal Number System

This section is intended for people who are unfamiliar with the hexadecimal number system. If you are comfortable with hexadecimal numbers, you might want to skip this section. An IPv6 address is 128 bits in length, and you will see that hexadecimal is the ideal number system for representing long strings of bits.

If you understand the decimal, or base 10, number system, you can understand any number system, including the hexadecimal, or base 16, number system. Let's assume that you are already familiar with binary or base 2, but if you're not, you will still be able to understand base 16. The same general rules apply to all number systems.

When looking at integer-based number systems, there are three general rules:

Rule #1: Base n number systems have *n* number of digits:

- Base 10 (decimal) number system has 10 digits.
- Base 2 (binary) number system has 2 digits.
- Base 16 (hexadecimal) number system has 16 digits.

Rule #2: All number systems begin with 0.

Combining Rule #1 and Rule #2, we get:

- Base 10 has ten digits starting with 0: 0, 1, 2, 3, 4, 5, 6, 7, 8, 9.
- Base 2 has two digits starting with 0: 0, 1.
- Base 16 has 16 digits starting with 0: 0, 1, 2, 3, 4, 5, 6, 7, 8, 9, A, B, C, D, E, F (I discuss the alphanumeric digits in a moment).

Rule #3: The first column, the rightmost column or least significant digit, is always the column of 1s (ones). Each preceding column is *n* times the previous column. (*n* is the base n number system.) Using base 10 as an example, the first column is the column of 1s; the next column is 10 times the 1s column, resulting in a column of 10s; the next column is 10 times the 10s column, resulting in a column of 100s; and so on. This makes it very easy when converting other number systems to base 10. This is illustrated in Table 3-1.

Table 3-1 *Number Systems*

Base n Number System	n^3	n^2	n^1	n^0
Base 10	1000	100	10	1
Base 2	8	4	2	1
Base 16	4096	256	16	1

- Base 10: 10,000s, 1000s, 100s, 10s, 1s
- Base 2: 128s, 64s, 32s, 16s, 8s, 4s, 2s, 1s
- Base 16: 256s, 16s, 1s

If you understand the three rules, it is time to examine the hexadecimal number system more closely. The hexadecimal number system, base 16, has 16 digits beginning with 0. Table 3-2 shows these 16 digits and their equivalence in decimal and binary.

Table 3-2 *Decimal, Hexadecimal, and Binary*

Decimal (Base 10)	Hexadecimal (Base 16)	Binary (Base 2)
0	0	0000
1	1	0001
2	2	0010
3	3	0011
4	4	0100
5	5	0101
6	6	0110
7	7	0111
8	8	1000
9	9	1001
10	A	1010
11	B	1011
12	C	1100
13	D	1101
14	E	1110
15	F	1111

Applying the three rules to the hexadecimal number system:

- **Rule #1:** The hexadecimal number system has 16 digits.
- **Rule #2:** Table 3-2 illustrates the 16 hexadecimal digits and their decimal and binary equivalents starting with 0. Notice that you needed unique alphanumeric digits, A through F, to represent the decimal values 10 through 15.
- **Rule #3:** For representing IPv6 addresses in hexadecimal, you only need to use the first column or column of 1s.

So, why use hexadecimal numbers to represent IPv6 addresses? Hexadecimal is a very common number system used in computer science, computer networking, and other areas of computer technology. This is because any 4 bits (half of a byte or half of an octet) can be represented as a single hexadecimal digit. In other words, there are 16 unique combinations of 4 bits, and there are also 16 digits in a hexadecimal number system, so it is a perfect match. Because one hexadecimal digit can represent 4 bits, this means that two hexadecimal digits can represent a single byte or octet.

> **Note** 4 bits is half a byte or half an octet, and is also known as a *nibble*. You will sometimes see the alternative spellings of *nybble* or *nyble*.

Representation of IPv6 Addresses

IPv6 addresses are 128 bits in length and written as a string of hexadecimal digits. Every 4 bits are represented by a single hexadecimal digit, for a total of 32 hexadecimal values (4 * 32 = 128). The alphanumeric characters used in hexadecimal are not case sensitive; therefore, uppercase and lowercase characters are equivalent.

> **Note** RFC 5952, A Recommendation for IPv6 Address Text Representation, recommends that IPv6 addresses be represented in lowercase. Throughout this book, you will see many cases where I have used uppercase characters. I have done this to make it easier for you to visualize and differentiate the different types of addresses.

As described in RFC 4291, the preferred format is x:x:x:x:x:x:x:x. Each *x* is a 16-bit section that can be represented using up to four hexadecimal digits separated by a colon. This results in eight 16-bit sections (for a total of 128 bits) of the address, as shown in Figure 3-1.

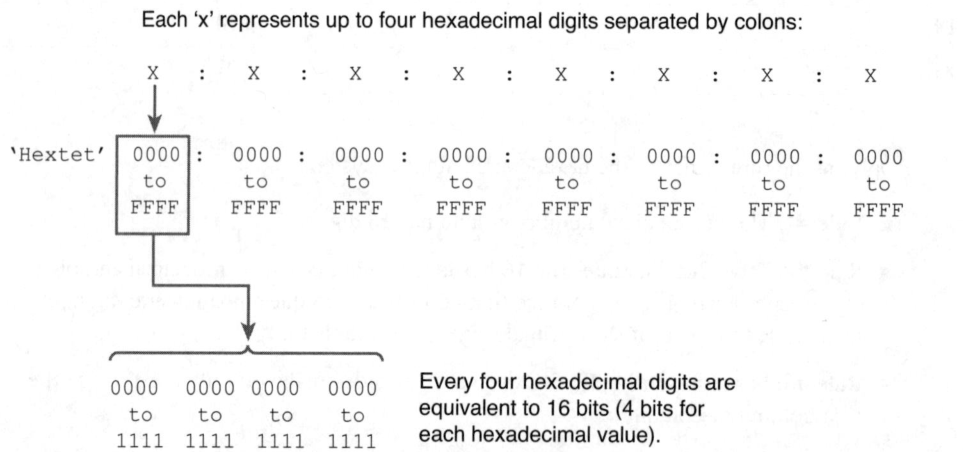

Figure 3-1 *Preferred Format of IPv6 Address*

The preferred format is the longest representation of an IPv6 address. A total of 32 hexadecimal values are used. A colon separates every group of four hexadecimal digits. Once again, each hexadecimal digit is equivalent to 4 bits.

Note The unofficial term for a section of four hexadecimal values is a *hextet*, similar to the term *octet* used in IPv4 addressing. Therefore, an IPv6 address consists of eight hextets separated by colons. As Figure 3-1 illustrates, each hextet with its four hexadecimal digits is equivalent to 16 bits. For clarity, the term *hextet* will be used throughout this book when referring to individual 16-bit segments. Table 3-3 shows several examples of IPv6 addresses using the preferred format. Notice that the last two addresses are the IPv6 addresses of PC1 and PC2 in the topology from Chapter 2, "The IPv6 Protocol."

Table 3-3 *Examples of IPv6 Addresses Using the Preferred Format*

Preferred Format of IPv6 Addresses
0000:0000:0000:0000:0000:0000:0000:0000
0000:0000:0000:0000:0000:0000:0000:0001
FF02:0000:0000:0000:0000:0000:0000:0001
FC00:0001:A000:0B00:0000:0527:0127:00AB
2001:DCBA:1111:000A:00B0:0000:9000:0200
2001:0000:0000:0000:ABCD:0000:0000:1234
2001:0DB8:AAAA:0001:0000:0000:0000:0100
2001:0DB8:AAAA:0001:0000:0000:0000:0200

At first glance, these addresses can look overwhelming. Don't worry; later in this chapter, you will be introduced to a technique to bolster your confidence in reading and using IPv6 addresses. Besides the preferred format, RFC 2373 and RFC 5952 provide two helpful rules in reducing the notation of these addresses.

Rule 1: Omission of Leading 0s

Leading 0s (zeroes) in any hextet, 16-bit section, can be omitted. This applies only to leading 0s and not to trailing 0s; otherwise, the address would be ambiguous. Using a list of preferred IPv6 addresses, Table 3-4 shows how the leading 0s can be removed.

Table 3-4 *Examples of Omitting Leading 0s in a Hextet*

Format	IPv6 Address
Preferred	0000:0000:0000:0000:0000:0000:0000:0000
Leading 0s omitted	0: 0: 0: 0: 0: 0: 0: 0 or 0:0:0:0:0:0:0:0

Format	IPv6 Address
Preferred	0000:0000:0000:0000:0000:0000:0000:0001
Leading 0s omitted	0: 0: 0: 0: 0: 0: 0: 1 or 0:0:0:0:0:0:0:1
Preferred	FF02:0000:0000:0000:0000:0000:0000:0001
Leading 0s omitted	FF02: 0: 0: 0: 0: 0: 0: 1 or FF02:0:0:0:0:0:0:1
Preferred	FC00:0001:A000:0B00:0000:0527:0127:00AB
Leading 0s omitted	FC00: 1:A000: B00: 0: 527: 127: AB or FC00:1:A000:B00:0:527:127:AB
Preferred	2001:0DB8:1111:000A:00B0:0000:9000:0200
Leading 0s omitted	2001: DB8:1111: A: B0: 0:9000: 200 or 2001:DB8:1111:A:B0:0:9000:200
Preferred	2001:0DB8:0000:0000:ABCD:0000:0000:1234
Leading 0s omitted	2001: DB8: 0: 0:ABCD: 0: 0:1234 or 2001:DB8:0:0:ABCD:0:0:1234
Preferred	2001:0DB8:AAAA:0001:0000:0000:0000:0100
Leading 0s omitted	2001: DB8:AAAA: 1: 0: 0: 0: 100 or 2001:DB8:AAAA:1:0:0:0:100
Preferred	2001:0DB8:AAAA:0001:0000:0000:0000:0200
Leading 0s omitted	2001: DB8:AAAA: 1: 0: 0: 0: 200 or 2001:DB8:AAAA:1:0:0:0:200

Note In Table 3-4, the 0s to be omitted are in bold. Spaces remain to better visualize where the 0s were removed.

It is important to remember that only leading 0s can be removed; otherwise, it will make the address ambiguous. For example, if trailing 0s were also permitted, you wouldn't know what the correct address was. There can only be one correct interpretation; therefore, only leading 0s can be omitted:

■ Zeroes omitted:	2001:1944:100:A:0:BC:ABCD:D0B
■ Incorrect (trailing 0s):	2001:1944:100**0**:A**000**:**000**0:BC**00**:ABCD:D0B**0**
■ Correct (leading 0s):	2001:1944:**0**100:**000**A:**000**0:**00**BC:ABCD:**0**D0B

Rule 2: Omission of all-0s hextets

A double colon (::) can represent any single, contiguous string of one or more hextets (16-bit segments) consisting of all 0s. This will help further reduce the size of an IPv6 address. Table 3-5 illustrates the use of the double colon.

Table 3-5 *Example of Omitting a Single Contiguous String of All-0 Hextets*

Format	IPv6 Address
Preferred	**0000:0000:0000:0000:0000:0000:0000:0000**
(::) All-0 segments	::
Preferred	**0000:0000:0000:0000:0000:0000:0000**:0001
(::) All-0 segments	::0001
Preferred	FF02:**0000:0000:0000:0000:0000:0000**:0001
(::) All-0 segments	FF02::0001
Preferred	FC00:0001:A000:0B00:**0000**:0527:0127:00AB
(::) All-0 segments	FC00:0001:A000:0B00::0527:0127:00AB
Preferred	2001:DCBA:1111:000A:00B0:**0000**:9000:0200
(::) All-0 segments	2001:DCBA:1111:000A:00B0::9000:0200
Preferred	2001:**0000:0000:0000**:ABCD:0000:0000:1234
(::) All-0 segments	2001::ABCD:0000:0000:1234

Note: This address can also be written as 2001:0000:0000:0000:ABCD::1234.

Format	IPv6 Address
Preferred	2001:0DB8:AAAA:0001:**0000:0000:0000**:0100
(::) All-0 segments	2001:0DB8:AAAA:0001::0100
Preferred	2001:0DB8:AAAA:0001:**0000:0000:0000**:0200
(::) All-0 segments	2001:0DB8:AAAA:0001::0200

Note In Table 3-5, the 0s in bold in the preferred address are replaced by the double colon.

Only a single contiguous string of all-0 segments can be represented with a double colon; otherwise, the address would be ambiguous:

- Incorrect address using two double colons:

```
2001::ABCD::1234
```

- Possible ambiguous choices:

```
2001:0000:0000:0000:0000:ABCD:0000:1234
2001:0000:0000:0000:ABCD:0000:0000:1234
2001:0000:0000:ABCD:0000:0000:0000:1234
2001:0000:ABCD:0000:0000:0000:0000:1234
```

As you can see, if two double colons are used, there would be multiple possibilities, and you wouldn't know which address is the correct interpretation.

Note RFC 5952 suggests that the double colon should represent the longest string of 0s.

Combining Rule 1 and Rule 2

Combining both rules can reduce the address even further. Table 3-6 illustrates all three formats. Again, spaces were left to better visualize where the 0s were removed.

Table 3-6 *Combining Rule 1 and Rule 2*

Format	IPv6 Address
Preferred	0000:0000:0000:0000:0000:0000:0000:0000
No Leading 0s	0: 0: 0: 0: 0: 0: 0: 0
"::" All-0 segments	::
Preferred	0000:0000:0000:0000:0000:0000:0000:0001
No Leading 0s	0: 0: 0: 0: 0: 0: 0: 1
"::" All-0 segments	::1
Preferred	FF02:0000:0000:0000:0000:0000:0000:0001
No Leading 0s	FF02: 0: 0: 0: 0: 0: 0: 1
"::" All-0 segments	FF02::1
Preferred	FC00:0001:A000:0B00:0000:0527:0127:00AB
No Leading 0s	FC00: 1:A000: B00: 0: 527: 127: AB
"::" All-0 segments	FC00:1:A000:B00::527:127:AB
Preferred	2001:DCBA:1111:000A:00B0:0000:9000:0200
No Leading 0s	2001:DCBA:1111: A: B0: 0:9000: 200
"::" All-0 segments	2001:DCBA:1111:A:B0::9000:200
Preferred	2001:0000:0000:0000:ABCD:0000:0000:1234
No Leading 0s	2001: 0: 0: 0:ABCD: 0: 0:1234
"::" All-0 segments	2001::ABCD:0:0:1234
Note: This address can also be written as 2001:0:0:0:ABCD::1234.	
Preferred	2001:0DB8:AAAA:0001:0000:0000:0000:0100
No Leading 0s	2001: DB8:AAAA: 1: 0: 0: 0: 100
"::" All-0 segments	2001:DB8:AAAA:1::100
Preferred	2001:0DB8:AAAA:0001:0000:0000:0000:0200
No Leading 0s	2001: DB8:AAAA: 1: 0: 0: 0: 200
"::" All-0 segments	2001:DB8:AAAA:1::200

Table 3-7 shows the preferred IPv6 address format that you began with and the final compressed format implementing both rules.

Table 3-7 *IPv6 Preferred and Compressed Format*

Preferred Format of IPv6 Addresses	Compressed Format
0000:0000:0000:0000:0000:0000:0000:0000	::
0000:0000:0000:0000:0000:0000:0000:0001	::1
FF02:0000:0000:0000:0000:0000:0000:0001	FF02::1
FC00:0001:A000:0B00:0000:0527:0127:00AB	FC00:1:A000:B00::527:127:AB
2001:DCBA:1111:000A:00B0:0000:9000:0200	2001:DCBA:1111:A:B0::9000:200
2002:0000:0000:0000:ABCD:0000:0000:1234	2002::ABCD:0:0:1234
2001:0DB8:AAAA:0001:0000:0000:0000:0100	2001:DB8:AAAA:1::100
2001:0DB8:AAAA:0001:0000:0000:0000:0200	2001:DB8:AAAA:1::200

Even with these rules to compress the format, an IPv6 address can still look unwieldy. Soon, you will look at a technique that is called the "3-1-4." It will help you recognize the segments of an IPv6 address.

Prefix Notation

In IPv4, the prefix or network portion of the address can be identified by a dotted-decimal netmask, commonly referred to as a subnet mask. For example, 255.255.255.0 indicates that the network portion or prefix length of the IPv4 address is the leftmost 24 bits.

As defined in RFC 4291, IP Version 6 Addressing Architecture, the representation of IPv6 address prefixes is similar to the way that IPv4 address prefixes are written in classless interdomain routing (CIDR) notation. An IPv6 address prefix (network portion of the address) is represented using the following format:

ipv6-address/prefix-length

The *prefix length* is a decimal value indicating the number of leftmost contiguous bits of the address. The prefix length identifies the prefix or the network portion of the address.

Let's look at an example using the address 2001:0DB8:AA AA:1111:0000:0000:0000:0000/64. Figure 3-2 illustrates how the /64 prefix length identifies the prefix or network portion of the address. The /64 prefix length leaves us with another 64 bits, which is the Interface ID portion of the address, known as the host portion in IPv4. I discuss the Interface ID in the next section.

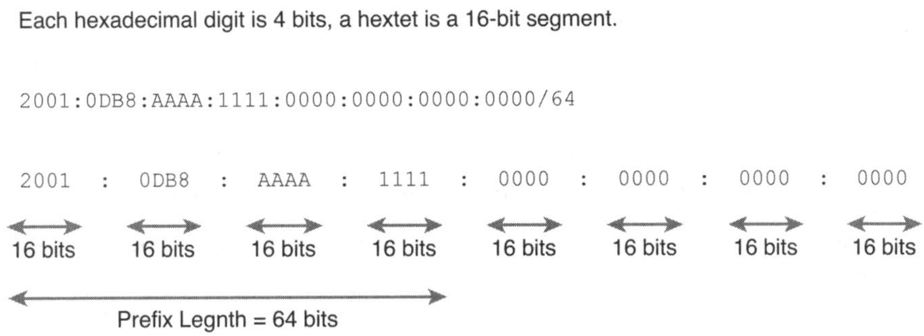

Figure 3-2 *IPv6 Prefix*

Using the rules learned for reducing the notation of an address, other valid representations of this address could also be written as

2001:0DB8:AAAA:1111:0:0:0:0/64

2001:0DB8:AAAA:1111::/64

2001:DB8:AAAA:1111::/64

Devices such as host computers would have an IPv6 address that is part of this prefix or network address, as shown in Figure 3-3. Using the topology from Chapter 2, two valid host addresses would be

2001:0DB8:AAAA:1111:0000:0000:0000:0100/64

or

2001:DB8:AAAA:1111::100/64

2001:0DB8:AAAA:1111:0000:0000:0000:0200/64

or

2001:DB8:AAAA:1111::0200/64

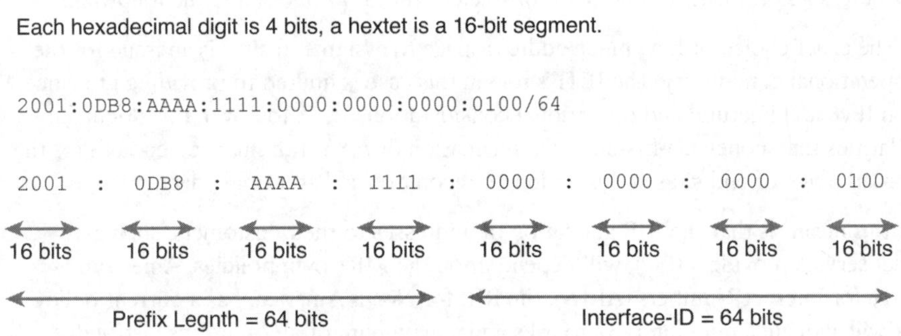

Figure 3-3 *IPv6 Prefix Length and Interface ID*

In IPv6, just as in IPv4, the number of devices you can have on your network depends on the prefix length. As discussed in Chapter 1, "Introduction to IPv6," as the Internet grew, the limited IPv4 address space was quickly becoming depleted. A customer request for an IPv4 address and a prefix length (subnet mask) to accommodate his network requirements must be justified by the customer. Most sites rely heavily on Network Address Translation (NAT) to accommodate the number of internal IPv4 hosts in their networks.

With IPv6, this is no longer the case. There is plenty of IPv6 address space. Many people have become accustomed to limiting the allocation of IPv4 addresses in networks. It's very common to use a /30 for point-to-point serial links on IPv4 networks. This is not a concern with IPv6, and it can be a difficult habit to break.

The Internet Architecture Board (IAB) and the Internet Engineering Steering Group (IESG) published a set of recommendations for IPv6 address allocations in RFC 3177, IAB/IESG Recommendations on IPv6 Address Allocations to Sites. This is a recommendation from the IAB and IESG to the five Regional Internet Registries (RIR). It is helpful to note that in their RFC, they state the following:

> "The technical principles that apply to address allocation seek to balance healthy conservation practices and wisdom with a certain ease of access. On one hand, when managing a potentially limited resource, one must conserve wisely to prevent exhaustion within an expected lifetime. On the other hand, the IPv6 address space is in no sense as limited a resource as the IPv4 address space, and unwarranted conservatism acts as a disincentive in a marketplace already dampened by other factors. So from a market development perspective, we would like to see it be very easy for a user or an ISP to obtain as many IPv6 addresses as they really need without a prospect of immediate renumbering or of scaling inefficiencies."

In RFC 3177, the IESG and the IAB recommended using specific prefix lengths for different size networks. One of their recommendations was that in general, all sites should get a /48, including home networks and small to large enterprise networks. The RIRs adopted that recommendation in 2002, but began reconsidering the policy in 2005. In 2011, RFC 6177, IPv6 Address Assignments to End Sites, obsoleted RFC 3177 and stated the following:

> "The exact choice of how much address space to assign end sites is an issue for the operational community. The IETF's role in this case is limited to providing guidance on IPv6 architectural and operational considerations. . . . Moreover, this document clarifies that a one-size-fits-all recommendation of /48 is not nuanced enough for the broad range of end sites and is no longer recommended as a single default."

What this means is that the RIR allocation of addresses to their customers, such as Internet service providers (ISP), will depend upon the RIR's own policies. American Registry for Internet Numbers (ARIN), the RIR for North America, has a current policy that it will allocate a minimum /32 to ISPs and a maximum of a /24, unless justified otherwise. End sites should get at least a /48 or a larger assignment if it can be justified. Because a /48 still seems to be the normal allocation for end sites, this will be used in these examples. RFC 6177 suggests that home sites might not need a /48, but something more like a /56. This gives ISPs more addresses to allocate, and the only difference to the home site is the number of subnets per home site network.

Note There are two types of addresses that can be assigned to an end-user organization: provider-independent (PI) and provider-aggregatable (PA). Provider-independent address space is assigned by an RIR directly to the end-user organization. Provider-independent address space allows organizations to change service providers without obtaining new address space. Provider-aggregatable address space is assigned by the RIR to the ISP. This allows the ISP to aggregate its address space for more efficient routing. These addresses belong to the ISP. Unlike PI addresses, if an end user changes providers, PA addresses cannot migrate with the end user.

As discussed in the next section, the typical host portion of an IPv6 unicast address is 64 bits, known as the Interface ID. If a site receives a /48 prefix, this allows 65,535 subnets, with 18,446,744,073,709,551,616 (18 quintillion) interface addresses (hosts) for each subnet! A /56 prefix for a home site means the same number of hosts per subnet but with only 256 subnets. This is still more than adequate for most homes.

Note A single host can have multiple interfaces, with each interface having one or more IPv6 addresses.

Brief Look at IPv6 Address Types

The following sections review the basic types of IPv6 addresses. They are examined in more detail in Chapter 4, "IPv6 Address Types." With IPv4, there are unicast, multicast, and broadcast addresses. In IPv6, there are no broadcast addresses. The three types of addresses in IPv6 are

- Unicast
- Anycast
- Multicast

Unicast Addresses

A unicast address uniquely identifies an interface on an IPv6 device. A packet sent to a unicast address is delivered to the interface identified by that address. An IPv6 address more accurately identifies an interface on a host rather than the host itself. A single interface can have multiple IPv6 addresses and an IPv4 address in as well.

There are several types of unicast addresses in IPv6, in particular

- Global unicast
- Unique local unicast (site-local was deprecated in September 2004)

- Link-local unicast
- Unspecified address
- Loopback address

There are also some special-purpose subtypes of global unicast, such as IPv6 addresses with embedded IPv4 addresses. The structure of a global unicast address is discussed later in the chapter.

Anycast Addresses

An anycast address is a unicast address assigned to several devices. A packet sent to an anycast address is delivered only to one of the devices configured with that address. The anycast packet will be routed to the nearest device.

There is an anycast address in IPv4 and, like IPv6, it is a common unicast address assigned to multiple devices. In both IPv4 and IPv6, an anycast address is syntactically indistinguishable from a unicast address. In IPv6, the devices to which the anycast address is assigned are explicitly configured to recognize that it is an anycast address. This is not necessarily the case in IPv4.

Multicast Addresses

A multicast address identifies a group of interfaces, typically belonging to different devices. A packet sent to a multicast address is delivered to all the devices identified by that address. All members of the multicast group process the packet. So, the difference between an anycast and a multicast address is that an anycast packet is only delivered to a single device, whereas multiple devices can receive a multicast packet.

There are no broadcast addresses in IPv6. In its place is an all-nodes multicast address.

Structure of a Global Unicast Address

The following sections examine the basic structure of a global unicast address. Global unicast addresses are also known as *aggregatable global unicast addresses*. These are addresses that are globally routable and reachable on the IPv6 Internet. They are equivalent to public IPv4 addresses.

Figure 3-4 shows the structure of a global unicast address for a typical site.

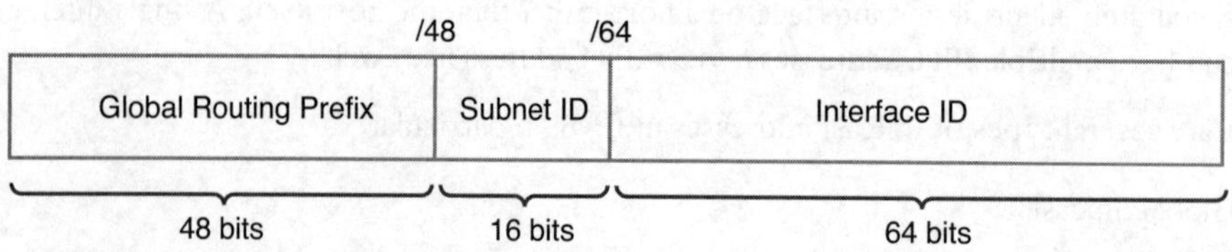

Figure 3-4 *Structure of a Global Unicast Address for a Typical Site*

Global Routing Prefix

The global routing prefix is the prefix or network portion of the address assigned by the provider, such as an ISP, to a customer or site. Although the IESG and IAB no longer recommend specific prefix lengths for different-size networks, it is still common for RIRs such as ARIN to have the policy for end sites to use a 48-bit prefix (/48). Figure 3-4 shows a typical /48 global routing prefix.

Note RFC 4291 does not specify the size of the Subnet ID. The 16-bit Subnet ID in Figure 3-4 results from a site receiving a /48 global routing prefix. With a 128-bit Interface ID, this leaves 16 bits for the Subnet ID. See RFC 3587, IPv6 Global Unicast Address Format, for more information.

Subnet ID

A big difference between IPv4 and IPv6 addresses is the location of the subnet portion of the address. In IPv4, bits are borrowed from the host portion of the address to create subnets. With IPv6, the Subnet ID is a separate field and is not part of the host portion of the address, known as the Interface ID in IPv6.

As shown in Figure 3-4, the IPv6 address has a 16-bit Subnet ID. This allows 65,536 individual subnets. Just in case you're wondering—yes, you can use the all 0s and the all 1s subnets. Subnetting is discussed in the next section.

Interface ID

The Interface ID uniquely identifies the interface on the subnet. As shown earlier, the 64-bit Interface ID allows 18,446,744,073,709,551,616 (18 quintillion) addresses for each subnet! The term *Interface ID* is used rather than *Host ID* because, as mentioned previously, a single host can have multiple interfaces, each having one or more IPv6 addresses.

Another important difference between the IPv6 and IPv4 addresses is that the all-0s and all-1s addresses are legal IPv6 interface addresses. An IPv6 Interface ID can contain all 0s or all 1s. In IPv4, all 0s in the host portion of the address are reserved for the network or subnet address. All 1s in the host portion of an IPv4 address indicate a broadcast address. Remember, there is no broadcast address in IPv6.

3-1-4 Rule

IPv6 global unicast addresses can look complicated, and it can be difficult to recognize all the parts. A simple technique that I created to quickly break it down is my 3-1-4 rule, as shown in Figure 3-5. Each number refers to the number of hextets, or 16-bit segments, of that portion of the address. Perhaps an easy way to remember these numbers is to call it the *pi rule* (pi = 3.14).

- **3:** This indicates the three hextets, or 48 bits, of the Global Routing Prefix.
- **1:** This indicates the one hextet, or 16 bits, of the Subnet ID.
- **4:** This indicates the four hextets, or 64 bits, of the Interface ID.

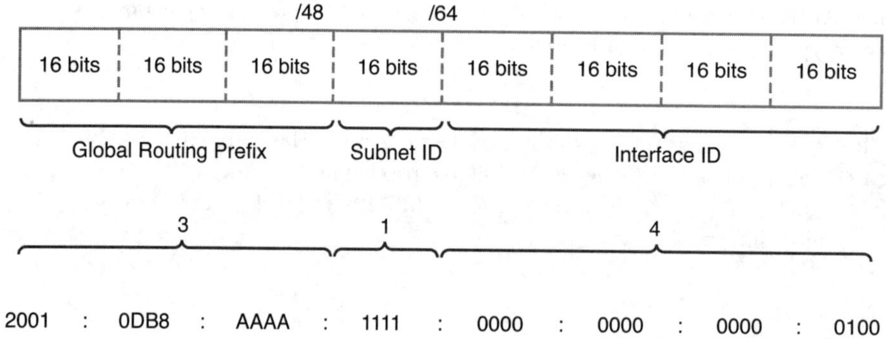

Figure 3-5 *Global Unicast Addresses and the 3-1-4 Rule*

> **Note** This technique is useful whenever the global unicast address has a /48 global routing prefix and a 64-bit Interface ID, which is a common prefix allocation. As discussed later in this chapter and later in the book, Global Routing Prefixes and Interface IDs do not necessarily have to be 48 bits and 64 bits, respectively.

Table 3-8 shows several examples of /48 global unicast addresses using the 3-1-4 technique. Although the double colon compresses the notation of the address, it can sometimes make it more difficult to recognize the three parts of the address. Sometimes it can be easier to start from the Interface ID, or from both ends toward the middle Subnet ID.

Table 3-8 *Examples of /48 Global Unicast Addresses with the 3-1-4 Technique*

/48 Global Unicast Address	Global Routing Prefix 3	Subnet ID 1	Interface ID 4
2001:0DB8:AAAA:1234:1111:2222:3333:4444	2001:0DB8:AAAA	1234	1111:2222:3333:4444
2001:0DB8:BBBB:4321:AAAA:BBBB:CCCC:DDDD	2001:0DB8:BBBB	4321	AAAA:BBBB:CCCC:DDDD
2001:0DB8:AAAA:0001:0000:0000:0000:0100	2001:0DB8:AAAA	0001	0000:0000:0000:0100
2001:0DB8:AAAA:9:0:0:0:A	2001:0DB8:AAAA	0009	0000:0000:0000:000A
2001:0DB8:AAAA:0001::0200	2001:0DB8:AAAA	0001	0000:0000:0000:0200
2001:DB8:AAAA::200	2001:0DB8:AAAA	0000	0000:0000:0000:0200

/48 Global Unicast Address	Global Routing Prefix 3	Subnet ID 1	Interface ID 4
2001:DB8::ABC:0	2001:0DB8:0000	0000	0000:0000:0ABC:0000
2001:DB8:ABC::	2001:0DB8:0ABC	0000	0000:0000:0000:0000
2001:DB8:ABC::FFFF:FFFF:FFFF:FFFF	2001:0DB8:0ABC	0000	FFFF:FFFF:FFFF:FFFF
2001:DB8::FFFF:FFFF:FFFF:FFFF:FFFF	2001:0DB8:0000	FFFF	FFFF:FFFF:FFFF:FFFF

Notice that both of the following addresses are legal interface (host) addresses in IPv6:

- **All 0s address:** 2001:DB8:ABC:: or 2001:0DB8:0ABC:0000:0000:0000:0000:0000
- **All 1s address:** 2001:DB8::FFFF:FFFF:FFFF:FFFF:FFFF or 2001:DB8:0000:FFFF:FFFF:FFFF:FFFF:FFFF

Putting It Together

You should now have a basic understanding of IPv6 global unicast addresses. Figure 3-6 illustrates your IPv6 network.

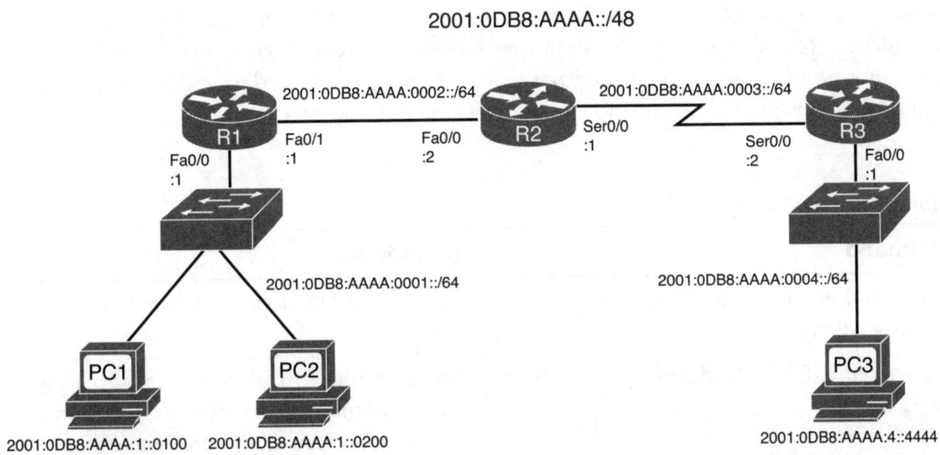

Figure 3-6 *IPv6 Topology*

Begin with using the 2001:0DB8:AAAA::/48 address. These first three hextets identify the global routing prefix or, in other words, the IPv6 network addresses that have been received from the provider. The /48 network is divided into four /64 subnets—0001, 0002, 0003, and 0004. The four subnets are

- 2001:0DB8:AAAA:0001::/64
- 2001:0DB8:AAAA:0002::/64

- 2001:0DB8:AAAA:0003::/64
- 2001:0DB8:AAAA:0004::/64

Using the 3-1-4 technique, you can quickly see that the first three hextets comprise the Global Routing Prefix (2001:0DB8:AAAA) and the fourth hextet is the Subnet ID.

Note 2001:0DB8:AAAA::/48 is part of the 2001:0DB8::/32 block of addresses reserved for examples and documentation.

Configuring an IPv6 address on a router's interface is very similar to that of IPv4. As shown throughout this book, most of the commands are identical, except the parameter **ipv6** is used in place of **ip**.

Table 3-9 illustrates the commands necessary to manually configure an IPv6 address on a router's interface. Chapter 4 explains some of the optional parameters for the **ipv6 address** command.

Note IPv6 address configuration is discussed in Chapter 4. The **ipv6 address** interface command is only included here to show the similarity between IPv6 and IPv4 commands. The global configuration command **ipv6 unicast-routing** is required to enable a router to route IPv6 packets. This command is also discussed in Chapter 4.

Table 3-9 *ipv6 address Command*

Command	Description
Router(config)# **interface** *interface-type interface-number*	Specifies the interface type and interface number.
Router(config-if)# **ipv6 address** *ipv6-address/ prefix-length*	Specifies the IPv6 address and prefix length to be assigned to the interface. To remove the address from the interface, use the **no** form of this command.

Now configure the devices for the first subnet. Using the 3-1-4 technique and the topology shown in Figure 3-6, all three components of the address are easily recognizable, as shown in Table 3-10.

Table 3-10 *IPv6 Address Chart for 2001:0DB8:AAAA:0001::/64*

Device	Global Routing Prefix 3	Subnet ID 1	Interface ID 4
Router R1	2001:0DB8:AAAA	0001	0000:0000:0000:0001
PC1	2001:0DB8:AAAA	0001	0000:0000:0000:0100
PC2	2001:0DB8:AAAA	0001	0000:0000:0000:0200

Example 3-1 shows the commands for configuring Router R1's Fast Ethernet 0/0 interface with the IPv6 address 2001:0DB8:AAAA:0001::0100 and the prefix length /64.

Example 3-1 *Cisco Router IPv6 Interface Configuration*

```
R1(config)# interface fastethernet 0/0
R1(config-if)# ipv6 address 2001:0db8:aaaa:0001::1/64
R1(config-if)# no shutdown
R1(config-if)# end
R1#
```

Note When configuring an IPv6 address in Cisco IOS, there is not a space between the IPv6 address and the prefix length.

Figure 3-7 shows PC1's IPv6 address configuration. Router R1's IPv6 address is being used for the PC's default gateway. You can verify the configuration on both Windows PCs by using the **ipconfig** command. In this example, the IPv6 address is configured manually. It is more likely that end devices will receive their IPv6 address configuration dynamically using Stateless Address Autoconfiguration or a DHCPv6 server. Both of these techniques are discussed in Chapter 4.

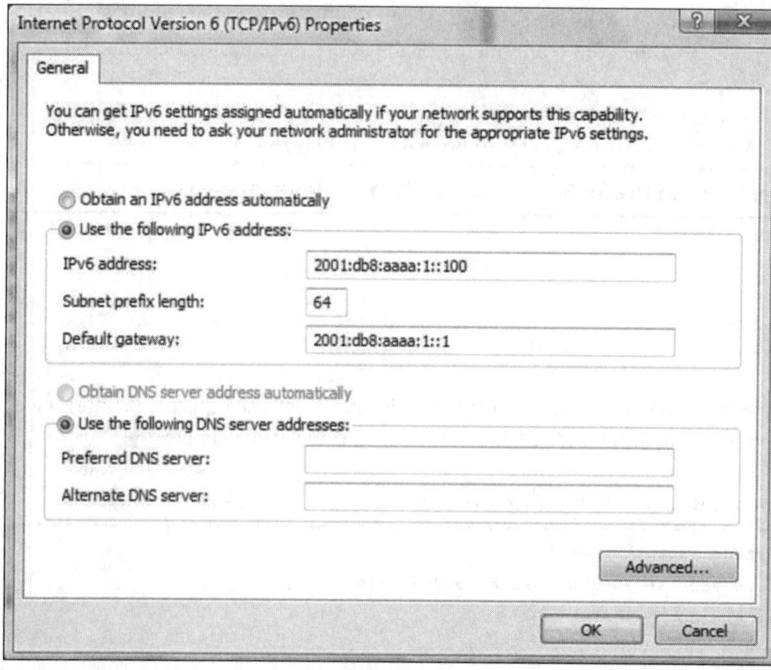

Figure 3-7 *PC1 IPv6 Interface Configuration*

In Example 3-2, IPv6 communications are verified by pinging PC1 and PC2. Notice that the same **ping** command is used as with IPv4. The only difference is that the destination is an IPv6 address. The **ping** command sends ICMPv6 Echo Request messages to the IPv6 destination address. The ! indicates that the ICMPv6 Echo Reply messages from the destination interface have been received, therefore verifying end-to-end communications. ICMPv6 is discussed in more detail in Chapter 5, "ICMPv6 and Neighbor Discovery Protocol."

Example 3-2 *Router R1 Pinging PC1 and PC2*

```
R1# ping 2001:db8:aaaa:0001::0100

Type escape sequence to abort.
Sending 5, 100-byte ICMP Echos to 2001:DB8:AAAA:1::100, timeout is 2 seconds:
!!!!!
Success rate is 100 percent (5/5), round-trip min/avg/max = 1/2/4 ms
R1# ping 2001:db8:aaaa:0001::0200

Type escape sequence to abort.
Sending 5, 100-byte ICMP Echos to 2001:DB8:AAAA:1::200, timeout is 2 seconds:
!!!!!
Success rate is 100 percent (5/5), round-trip min/avg/max = 1/1/4 ms
R1#
```

Subnetting

Depending on the size of environment, developing an IPv6 addressing can require substantial planning. However, basic subnetting of an IPv6 address is very straightforward. In many ways, it is much simpler than subnetting an IPv4 address. Unless you are subnetting on a natural octet boundary in IPv4, the specific subnets are not always obvious.

Note RFC 5375, IPv6 Unicast Address Assignment Considerations, offers guidelines for subnet prefix considerations. Many RIRs also offer guidelines to assist in developing an IPv6 addressing plan:

- ARIN's IPv6 Addressing Plans: www.getipv6.info/index.php/IPv6_Addressing_Plans
- RIPE's Preparing an IPv6 Addressing Plan: https://labs.ripe.net/Members/steffann/preparing-an-ipv6-addressing-plan

It is important to clarify a couple of terms. As illustrated in Figure 3-8, there is both a Subnet ID and a Subnet Prefix. The term *Subnet ID* refers to the contents of the 16-bit field used to allocate individual subnets. Subnet Prefix refers to the Global Routing Prefix and the Subnet ID addressing bits.

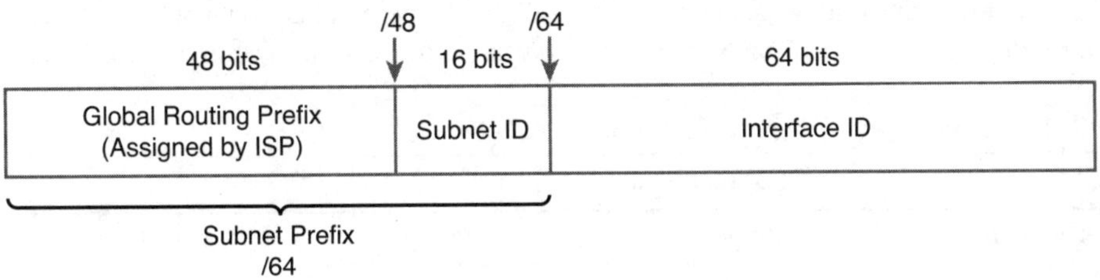

Figure 3-8 *Subnet Prefix*

A typical IPv6 site prefix will have a /48 assigned by its provider, usually from an ISP. This creates a 16-bit Subnet ID, allowing 2^{16}, or 65,536, subnets. The all-0s and all-1s subnets are valid subnets. This leaves 64 bits for the Interface ID, giving us 2^{64}, or 18 quintillion, interfaces (hosts) per subnet. Site prefixes and subnetting are examined later in Chapter 4.

Using the topology in Figure 3-6, the /48 network has been segmented into four /64 subnets, as shown in Table 3-11.

Table 3-11 *IPv6 Address Chart for 2001:0DB8:AAAA:0001::/64*

Subnet Prefix	
Global Routing Prefix	**Subnet ID**
2001:0DB8:AAAA:	0001
2001:0DB8:AAAA:	0002
2001:0DB8:AAAA:	0003
2001:0DB8:AAAA:	0004

Valid abbreviations for the four subnets are

- 2001:DB8:AAAA:1::/64
- 2001:DB8:AAAA:2::/64
- 2001:DB8:AAAA:3::/64
- 2001:DB8:AAAA:4::/64

With a 16-bit Subnet ID, the values can range from 0000 to FFFF, which provides 65,536 total subnets. Subnetting is painless because you can start with 0000 and increment by 1. Remember that this is in hexadecimal, so after 0009, the next Subnet ID would be 000A. Subnetting by using the 16-bit Subnet ID is easy to perform, as illustrated in Table 3-12.

Table 3-12 *Subnetting Using the 16-bit Subnet ID*

Range	**Subnet ID**
First 16 subnets	0000
	0001
	0002
	through . . .
	0009
	000A
	000B
	000C
	000D
	000E
	000F

Range	Subnet ID
Next 16 subnets	0010
	0011
	0012
	through . . .
	001F
Next 16 subnets	0020
	0021
	0022
	through . . .
	002F
And so on	0030
	0031
	Etc.

Extending the Subnet Prefix

Subnetting is not limited to a 16-bit Subnet ID. Any number of subnet bits can be chosen for the Subnet ID. Just as with IPv4, if you want to extend the number of subnets or more likely to reduce the number of hosts per subnet, you must borrow bits from the Interface ID. It is important to note that best practice dictates that this should only be done on network infrastructure links. Any segment that includes end systems should stay with a /64 prefix. A /64 prefix length is required for supporting Stateless Address Autoconfiguration.

As shown in Figure 3-9, you can use a /112 prefix length, extending the original /48 prefix by 64 bits (four hextets), giving it a prefix of /112.

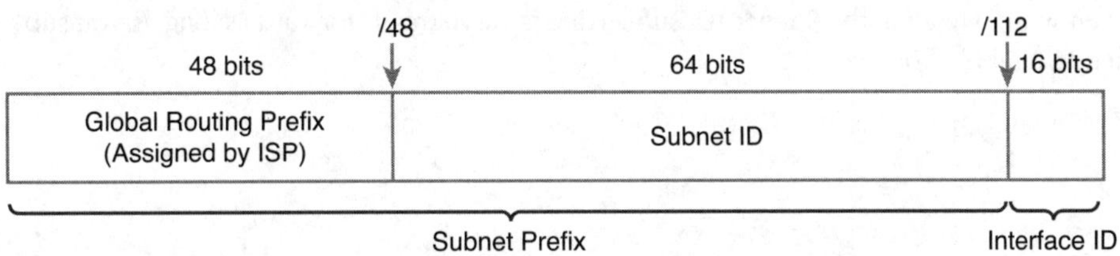

Figure 3-9 */112 Subnet Prefix*

The first four subnets would be

- 2001:0DB8:AAAA:0000:0000:0000:0000::/112
- 2001:0DB8:AAAA:0000:0000:0000:0001::/112
- 2001:0DB8:AAAA:0000:0000:0000:0002::/112
- 2001:0DB8:AAAA:0000:0000:0000:0003::/112

Figure 3-10 shows the range of subnet prefixes using a /112 prefix length.

```
                              Subnet Prefix

Global Routing Prefix                   Subnet-ID                      Interface ID

2001 : 0DB8 : AAAA : FFFF : 0000 : 0000 : 0000 : 0000 : 0000
2001 : 0DB8 : AAAA : FFFF : 0000 : 0000 : 0000 : 0001 : 0000
2001 : 0DB8 : AAAA : FFFF : 0000 : 0000 : 0000 : 0002 : 0000
2001 : 0DB8 : AAAA : FFFF : 0000 : 0000 : 0000 : 0003 : 0000
2001 : 0DB8 : AAAA : FFFF : 0000 : 0000 : 0000 : 0004 : 0000
       thru
2001 : 0DB8 : AAAA : FFFF : FFFF : FFFF : FFFF : FFFF : 0000
2001 : 0DB8 : AAAA : FFFF : FFFF : FFFF : FFFF : FFFF : 0000
```

Figure 3-10 *Range of /112 Subnet Prefixes*

> **Note** SURFnet, a nonprofit organization that forms partnerships between Dutch higher-education and research institutions in Information Technology, held a workshop with its customers on IPv6. From this workshop, an IPv6 addressing plan was developed. The document, Preparing an IPv6 Addressing Plan, can be downloaded from the Regional Internet Registry RIPE's website:
>
> https://labs.ripe.net/Members/steffann/preparing-an-ipv6-addressing-plan

Even with extending the Subnet ID, subnetting is very straightforward as long as you subnet on a nibble boundary.

Subnetting on a Nibble Boundary

If you are going to extend the Subnet ID, which means using bits from the Interface ID, it is best practice to subnet on a nibble boundary. A nibble is 4 bits, as shown in Table 3-13.

Table 3-13 *Decimal, Hexadecimal, and Binary Chart*

Decimal	Hexadecimal	Binary (Nibble)
0	0	0000
1	1	0001
2	2	0010
3	3	0011
4	4	0100
5	5	0101
6	6	0110
7	7	0111
8	8	1000
9	9	1001
10	A	1010
11	B	1011
12	C	1100
13	D	1101
14	E	1110
15	F	1111

In Figure 3-11, you are extending the /64 subnet prefix by 4 bits, one nibble, to a /68. This increases the Subnet ID from 16 bits to 20 bits. By doing so, this will allow more subnets but reduce the size of the Interface ID. In this case, there isn't any practical reason for doing this except to illustrate the concept. By extending the Subnet Prefix by 4 bits, or one full nibble, you are implementing the best practice of subnetting on a nibble boundary. Using 20 bits, a factor of 4 bits makes it very easy to list the subnets. This is illustrated in Figure 3-11.

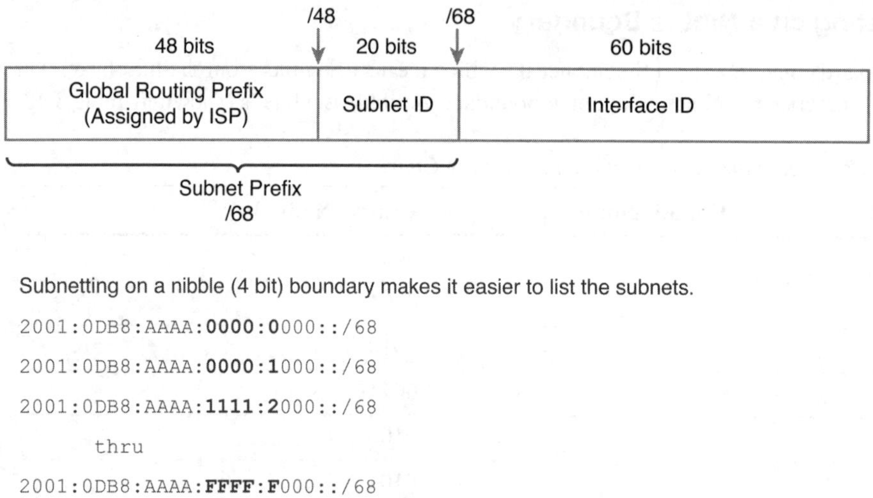

Figure 3-11 *Subnetting on a Nibble Boundary*

Subnetting Within a Nibble

For most customer networks, subnetting within a nibble is not recommended. It provides little if any benefits and only makes implementation and troubleshooting more difficult. However, there can be cases when subnetting on a nibble is potentially wasteful and it is beneficial to subnet within the 4-bit nibble. The addressing plans discussed previously help address some of those instances.

When you subnet within a nibble, life becomes a little more problematic. In Figure 3-12, you are using a /70 subnet prefix, extending the simple /68 to a more difficult /70. Because it is extended by only 2 bits instead of a nibble (4 bits), it makes the conversion a little more troublesome. Of course it is perfectly valid; it just makes it more cumbersome to convert.

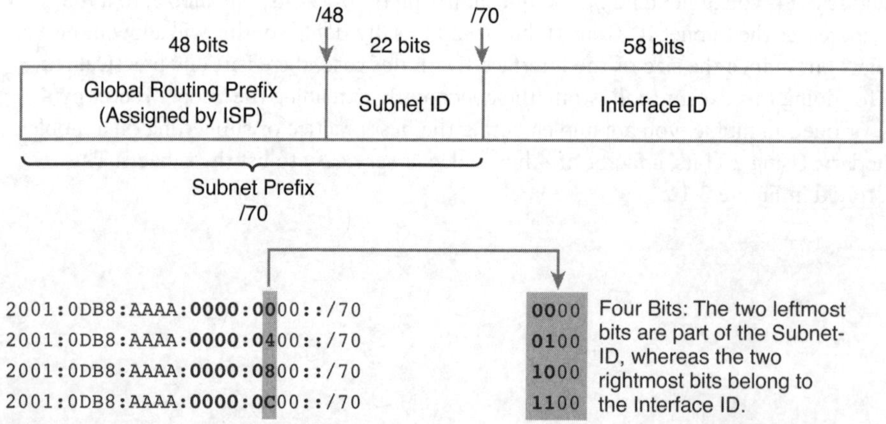

Figure 3-12 *Subnetting Within a Nibble*

Looking at the first four subnets, you get

- 2001:0DB8:AAAA:**0000:00**00::/70
- 2001:0DB8:AAAA:**0000:04**00::/70
- 2001:0DB8:AAAA:**0000:08**00::/70
- 2001:0DB8:AAAA:**0000:0C**00::/70

The first subnet is easy enough to figure out, but right away, you can see that the second subnet requires a little more thinking. IPv6 addresses use hexadecimal values to represent each 4 bits. Because a /70 subnet prefix was chosen, the first half of the last hexadecimal digit belongs to the Subnet ID and the other half belongs to the Interface ID. So, only the first 2 bits of the last digit of the Subnet ID are modified, as shown in Table 3-14.

Table 3-14 *Subnetting Within a Nibble*

Subnetting Within a Nibble	Last Digit of Subnet ID Binary to Hexadecimal
2001:0DB8:AAAA:0**000:00**00::/70	0000 = 0
2001:0DB8:AAAA:**0000:04**00::/70	0100 = 4
2001:0DB8:AAAA:**0000:08**00::/70	1000 = 8
2001:0DB8:AAAA:**0000:0C**00::/70	1100 = C

Limiting the Interface ID Space

Although IPv6 address space is plentiful, there can be reasons for limiting the size of the Interface ID within a network infrastructure. There is much debate on this issue. This section includes a brief explanation for a basic understanding of the topic.

RFC 6164, Using 127-Bit IPv6 Prefixes on Inter-Router Links, recommends employing 127-bit IPv6 prefixes (/127) on inter-router point-to-point links, for security and other reasons. This is similar to the use of 31-bit (/31) prefixes in IPv4. An issue of considerable debate centers around what is known as an NDP (Neighbor Discovery Protocol) exhaustion attack.

A 64-bit Interface ID allows an abundance of interface addresses, more than 18 quintillion interfaces (hosts) per subnet. IPv4 hosts have Address Resolution Protocol (ARP) caches to maintain a list of IPv4 addresses and their relative Layer 2 MAC addresses. In IPv6, there is something similar known as a Neighbor Cache, which is also explained in Chapter 5.

There is concern that with such a large IPv6 Interface ID space, an attacker could send a continuous stream of packets to routers or other devices on the subnet from hundreds of millions of fake source IPv6 addresses. This would cause the recipient to create a Neighbor Cache for each address, consuming large amounts of memory. Depending upon the type of packet sent, it might cause the recipient to respond with a large number of Neighbor Solicitation packets that will never receive replies, thereby consuming large amounts of memory and processing. (Neighbor Solicitation messages are part of NDP and will also be discussed in Chapter 5.) This is the equivalent to filling a device's ARP cache in IPv4.

RFC 3756, IPv6 Neighbor Discovery (ND) Trust Models and Threats, propose some techniques to address the NDP exhaustion attack issue such as Secure Neighbor Discover (SeND). The ultimate resolution is the source of much debate and beyond the scope of an IPv6 Fundamentals book. For more information on this topic, read "IPv6 NDP Table Exhaustion Attack," by Jeff S Wheeler. His presentation can be downloaded from http://inconcepts.biz/~jsw/IPv6_NDP_Exhaustion.pdf.

There are also reasons for using the larger 64-bit Interface ID. As shown in Chapter 4, Stateless Address Autoconfiguration (SLAAC) used on segments with end systems requires a /64 prefix and a 64-bit Interface ID.

Summary

This chapter explained the basics of IPv6 addressing. The preferred format of an IPv6 128-bit address is written as eight 16-bit segments (hextets) and separated by colons. The notation of the address can be reduced by omitting leading 0s and by using the double colon to replace contiguous hextets of 0s.

The IPv6 prefix length was discussed as well as the recommended size of the global routing prefix for different organizations. There was an introduction to the different IPv6 address types: unicast, anycast, and multicast.

The basic structure of a global unicast address has three parts: the Global Routing Prefix, Subnet ID, and Interface ID. Using the 3-1-4 technique can help to recognize the hextets in a /48 global unicast address.

The simplicity of subnetting an IPv6 address using the Subnet ID or extending the Subnet ID on a nibble boundary was also acknowledged. Subnetting within a nibble can be done, but it is a little more difficult and not recommended.

References

RFCs:

RFC 2374, *An IPv6 Aggregatable Global Unicast Address Format*, R. Hinden, Nokia, IETF, www.ietf.org/rfc/rfc2374.txt, July 1998

RFC 2460, *Internet Protocol, Version 6 (IPv6) Specification*, S. Deering, Cisco Systems, IETF, www.ietf.org/rfc/rfc2460.txt, December 1998

RFC 3177, *IAB/IESG Recommendations on IPv6 Addresses*, IAB, IESG, www.ietf.org/rfc/rfc3177.txt, September 2001

RFC 3587, *IPv6 Global Unicast Address Format*, R. Hinden, Nokia, IETF, www.ietf.org/rfc/rfc3587.txt, August 2003

RFC 3756, *IPv6 Neighbor Discovery (ND) Trust Models and Threats*, P. Nikander, Ericsson Research Nomadic Lab, IETF, www.ietf.org/rfc/rfc3756.txt, May 2004

RFC 4291, *IP Version 6 Addressing Architecture*, R. Hinden, Nokia, IETF, www.ietf.org/rfc/rfc4291.txt, February 2006

RFC 5453, *Reserved IPv6 Interface Identifiers*, S. Krishnan, www.ietf.org/rfc/rfc5453.txt, February 2009

RFC 6164, *Using 127-Bit IPv6 Prefixes on Inter-Router Links*, M. Kohno, Juniper Networks, www.ietf.org/rfc/rfc6164.txt, April 2011

RFC 6177, *IPv6 Address Assignment to End Sites*, IAB, IESG, www.ietf.org/rfc/rfc6177.txt, March 2011

Websites:

IPv6 NDP Table Exhaustion Attack, Jeff S Wheeler, http://inconcepts.biz/~jsw/IPv6_NDP_Exhaustion.pdf

AfriNIC IPv6 Resource website: www2.afrinic.net/IPv6/index.htm

ARIN IPv6 Resource website: http://ipv6.com/articles/general/ipv6-the-next-generation-internet.htm

APNIC IPv6 Resource website: http://icons.apnic.net/display/IPv6/home

LACNIC IPv6 Resource website: http://portalipv6.lacnic.net

RIPE NCC IPv6 Resource website: www.ripe.net/internet-coordination/ipv6

Chapter 4

IPv6 Address Types

This chapter further examines the three types of IPv6 addresses that were introduced in Chapter 3, "IPv6 Addressing:"

- Unicast
- Multicast
- Anycast

Figure 4-1 diagrams the three types of addresses in more detail. This chapter begins with unicast addresses. Don't be intimidated by all the different types of unicast addresses. The most significant are global unicast addresses, which were introduced in Chapter 3. They are equivalent to IPv4 public addresses, and much of this chapter is dedicated to learning the different ways to configure a global unicast address.

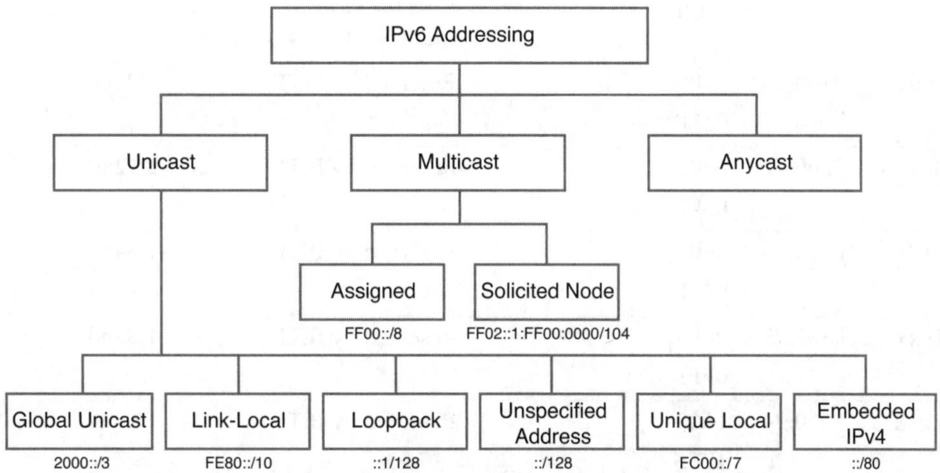

Figure 4-1 *IPv6 Address Types*

The next type of address covered is link-local. These unicast addresses are confined to a single link. IPv6 routing protocols use link-local addresses to exchange updates and other routing messages. The remaining unicast addresses—loopback, unspecified, unique local, and embedded IPv4—will also be discussed. They do not have as many options as global unicast and will require little explanation. Embedded IPv4 unicast addresses are discussed further in Chapter 10, "Dual-Stack and Tunneling."

This chapter also explores multicast addresses, in both assigned and solicited nodes. Chapter 5, "ICMPv6 and Neighbor Discovery Protocol," discusses the protocol's (ND or NDP) use of multicast addresses. Routing protocols rely heavily on assigned multicast addresses, which are examined in more detail in Chapter 8, "IPv6 IGP Routing Protocols."

Finally, there is a brief discussion on anycast addresses. An anycast address is indistinguishable from a unicast address other than how it is assigned. A unicast address is assigned to a single interface, whereas an anycast address can be assigned to interfaces on multiple devices.

IPv6 Address Space

Table 4-1 shows the Internet Assigned Numbers Authority's (IANA's) allocation of IPv6 address space. Notice the allocations for global unicast, unique local unicast, link-local unicast, and multicast addresses shown in bold. Each of these allocations is discussed independently later in this chapter. Figure 4-2 charts the makeup of the IPv6 address space.

Table 4-1 *IANA's Allocation of IPv6 Address Space*

Leading Bits	Address	Range of First Hextet	Allocation	Fraction of Space	
000x					
0000 0000	**0000::/8**	**0000 00FF**	**Unspecified, Loopback, Embedded IPv4**	1/8th	**1/256th**
0000 0001	0100::/8	0100 01FF	Reserved by IETF		1/256th
0000 001x	0200::/7	0200 03FF	Reserved by IETF		1/128th
0000 010x	0400::/6	0400 05FF	Reserved by IETF		1/64th
0000 1xxx	0800::/5	0800 0FFF	Reserved by IETF		1/32nd
0001 xxxx	1000::/4	1000 1FFF	Reserved by IETF		1/16th

Leading Bits	Address	Range of First Hextet	Allocation	Fraction of Space	
001x	**2000::/3**	**2000 3FFF**	Global Unicast	1/8th	
010x	4000::/3	4000 5FFF	Reserved by IETF	1/8th	
011x	6000::/3	6000 7FFF	Reserved by IETF	1/8th	
100x	8000::/3	8000 9FFF	Reserved by IETF	1/8th	
101x	A000::/3	A000 BFFF	Reserved by IETF	1/8th	
110x	C000::/3	C000 DFFF	Reserved by IETF	1/8th	
111x					
1110 xxxx	E000::/4	E000 EFFF	Reserved by IETF	1/8th	1/16th
1111 0xxx	F000::/5	F000 F7FF	Reserved by IETF		1/32nd
1111 10xx	F800::/6	F800 FBFF	Reserved by IETF		1/64th
1111 110x	**FC00::/7**	**FC00 FDFF**	**Unique Local Unicast**		**1/128th**
1111 1110 0	FE00::/9	FE00 FE74	Reserved by IETF		1/512th
1111 1110 10	**FE80::/10**	**FE80 FEBF**	**Link-Local Unicast**		**1/1024th**
1111 1110 11	FEC0::/10	FEC0 FEFF	Reserved by IETF; previously Site-Local (deprecated)		1/1024th
1111 1111	**FF00::/8**	**FF00 FFFF**	**Multicast**		**1/256th**

In Table 4-1, it is important to note that the Range of the First Hextet column does not show the complete range of the address space. For example, the actual range of the global unicast address space would be 2000:: through 3FFF:FFFF:FFFF:FFFF:FFFF:FFFF:FFFF:FFFF.

In both Table 4-1 and Figure 4-2, the IPv6 address space is divided into eighths using the leading 3 bits (000, 001, 010, 011, 100, 101, 110, and 111). This information might be a little overwhelming right now, but by the end of this chapter, you will understand it.

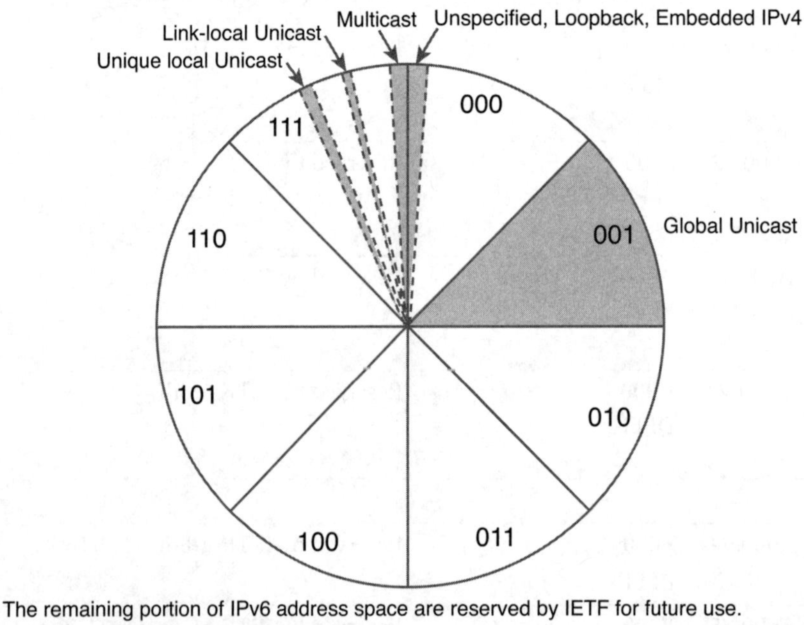

Figure 4-2 *IANA's Allocation of IPv6 Address Space in 1/8th Sections*

Unicast Address

A unicast address uniquely identifies an interface on an IPv6 device. A packet sent to a unicast address is received by the interface that is assigned to that address. Similar to IPv4, source IPv6 addresses must be a unicast address.

This section covers the different types of unicast addresses, as illustrated in Figure 4-1. The following is a quick preview of each type of unicast address:

- **Global unicast:** A routable address in the IPv6 Internet, similar to public IPv4 addresses.
- **Link-local:** Used only to communicate with devices on the same local link.
- **Loopback:** An address not assigned to any physical interface and can be used for a host to send an IPv6 packet to itself.

- **Unspecified address:** Only used as a source address and indicates the absence of an IPv6 address.
- **Unique local:** Similar to private addresses in IPv4 (RFC 1918), these addresses are not intended to be routable in the IPv6 Internet. However, unlike RFC 1918 addresses, unique local prefixes have an extremely high probability of being globally unique.
- **IPv4 embedded:** An IPv6 address that carries an IPv4 address in the low-order 32 bits of the address.

Global Unicast Address

Global unicast addresses, also known as an *aggregatable global unicast addresses*, are globally routable and reachable in the IPv6 Internet. They are equivalent to public IPv4 addresses. They play a significant role in the IPv6 addressing architecture. One of the main motivations for transitioning to IPv6 is the exhaustion of its IPv4 counterpart.

Figure 4-3 shows the generic structure of a global unicast address. In Chapter 3, Figure 3-4 showed a /48 format that is typical for most sites. Figure 4-3 illustrates the more general structure without the specific size of the global routing prefix.

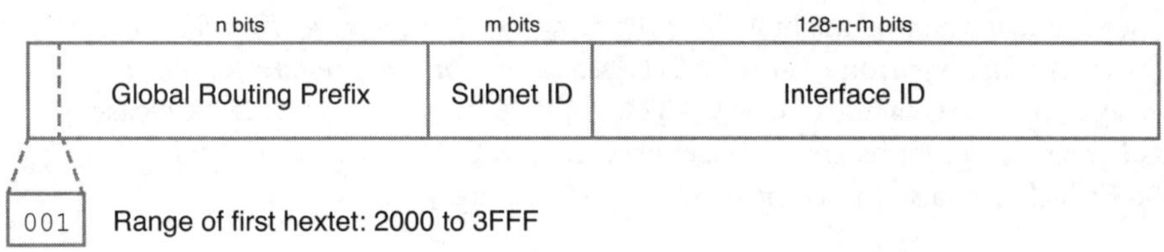

Figure 4-3 *Structure of a Global Unicast Address*

> **Note** Although the interface can be any length, a 64-bit Interface ID is required for SLAAC (Stateless Address Autoconfiguration). SLAAC is covered later in this chapter.

Figure 4-4 shows how address space can be allocated to the Regional Internet Registries (RIR) and Internet service providers (ISP). These are minimum allocations, which means that an RIR will get a /23 or shorter, an ISP will get a /32 or shorter, and a site will get a /48 or shorter. A shorter prefix length allows more available address space. For example, a site could get a /40 instead of a /48, giving it more addresses if it can be justified it to its ISP. Figure 4-4 shows a provider-aggregatable model where the end customer obtains his IPv6 address from the ISP. The end customer can also choose a provider-independent address space by going straight to the RIR. In this case, it is not uncommon for an end customer to be able to justify a /32 prefix.

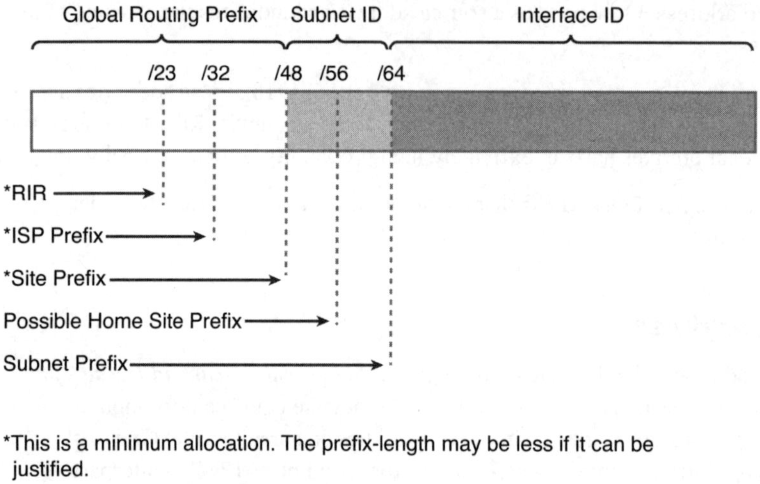

Figure 4-4 *Global Routing Prefix Sizes*

> **Note** Some documentation might include the terms *top-level aggregation identifier (TLA)*, *next-level aggregation identifier (NLA)*, and *site-level aggregation identifier (SLA)*. These terms originated from RFC 2374, An IPv6 Aggregatable Global Unicast Address Format. These terms are no longer used, and RFC 2374 has been obsoleted by RFC 3587, which uses a simpler format, as shown in Figure 4-3.

Internet Corporation for Assigned Names and Numbers (ICANN), the operator for IANA, allocates IPv6 address blocks to the five RIRs. The current global unicast address assignment from IANA begins with binary value 001 or the prefix 2000::/3. This results in a range of global unicast addresses of 2000::/3 through 3FFF::/3, as shown in Table 4-1.

How do you get this range of addresses using the 2000::/3 prefix? The /3 prefix length implies that only the first 3 bits are significant in matching the prefix 2000. The first 3 bits of the first hexadecimal value 2 are 001x. The fourth bit, x, is insignificant and can be either a 0 or a 1. This results in the first hextet being a 2 (0010) or a 3 (0011). The remaining 24 bits in the hextet (16-bit segment) can be a 0 or a 1. This is illustrated in Table 4-2.

Table 4-2 *Range of Global Unicast Addresses*

Global Unicast Address (Hexadecimal)	Range of First Hextet	Range of First Hextet in Binary
2000::/3	2000	**0010** 0000 0000 0000
	3FFF	**0011** 1111 1111 1111

Revisit Figure 4-2. Note that the IPv6 unicast space encompasses the entire IPv6 address range with the exception of FF00::/8, which is reserved for multicast addresses. Currently, IANA limits global unicast address assignments to the range of 2000::/3. IANA assignments from this block are registered in the IANA registry, IPv6 Global Unicast Address Assignments; see www.iana.org/assignments/ipv6-unicast-address-assignments/ipv6-unicast-address-assignments.xml. Notice that many of the RIRs have prefixes shorter than a /23, giving them more addresses to allocate to ISPs.

It was mentioned earlier that a global unicast address is configured on an interface. An interface can be configured with multiple global unicast addresses, which can be on the same or different subnets.

An interface does not have to be configured with a global unicast address, but at a minimum, it must be assigned with a link-local address. In other words, if an interface has a global unicast address, it must have a link-local address. However, if an interface has a link-local address, it does not necessarily have to have a global unicast address. Link-local addresses are discussed in the next section.

Similar to IPv4, a device, or more accurately an interface, can be assigned a global unicast address manually or dynamically. Figure 4-5 shows the various configuration options. Each will be discussed beginning with manual configuration.

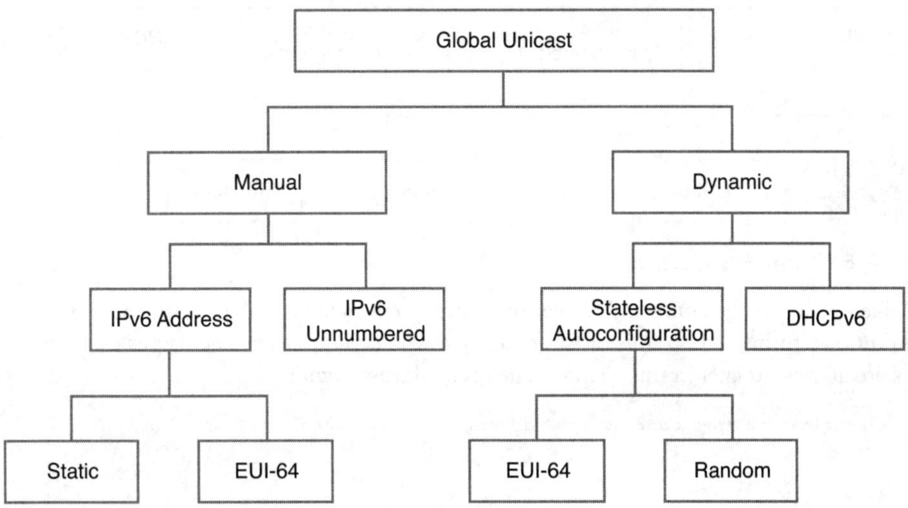

Figure 4-5 *Unicast Addresses*

Manual Global Unicast Configuration

Manually configuring a global unicast address has several options. This section discusses the following ways to manually configure a global unicast address:

- **Static:** Static configuration is similar to configuring a static IPv4 address. The IPv6 address and the prefix length are both configured on the interface.

- **EUI-64:** This type of configuration allows you to specify the prefix and prefix length, while the Interface ID is created automatically.
- **IP unnumbered:** IP unnumbered is the same in IPv6 as it is with IPv4. It allows an interface to use the IP address of another interface from the same device.

Static Configuration

As shown in Chapter 3, the static configuration of a global unicast address on a Cisco router is similar to the configuration of an IPv4 address. Figure 4-6 illustrates the global unicast addressing technique that will be examined in this section.

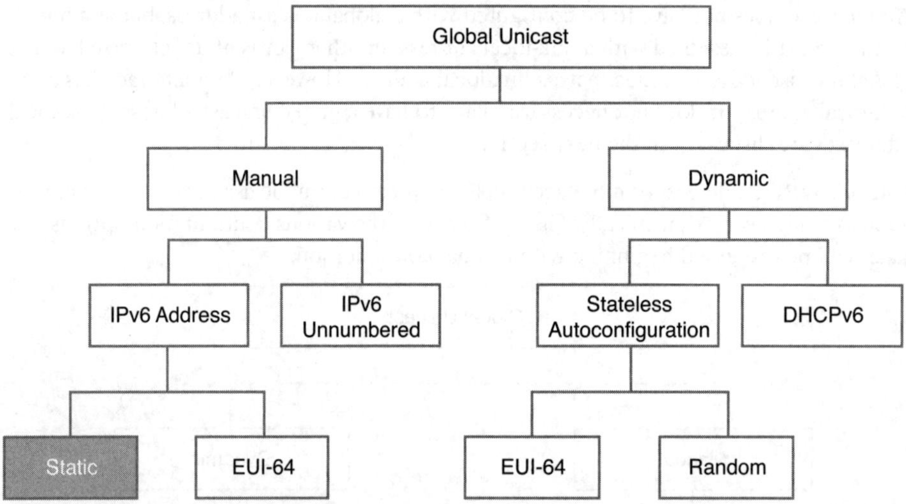

Figure 4-6 *Static IPv6 Address*

Table 4-3 shows the command format to statically configure a global unicast address. Additional forms and options of this command when configuring other types of addresses are addressed later in this chapter. The **ipv6 address** command is

```
Router(config-if)# ipv6 address ipv6-address/prefix-length
```

Table 4-3 *IPv6 Address Command*

Command	Description
Router(config)# **interface** *interface-type interface-number*	Specifies the interface type and interface number.
Router(config-if)# **ipv6 address** *ipv6-address/prefix-length*	Specifies the IPv6 address and prefix length to be assigned to the interface. To remove the address from the interface, use the **no** form of this command.

Similar to IPv4, it is typically best practice to manually configure IPv6 addresses on router interfaces and servers.

Figure 4-7 shows the topology that was introduced in Chapter 3.

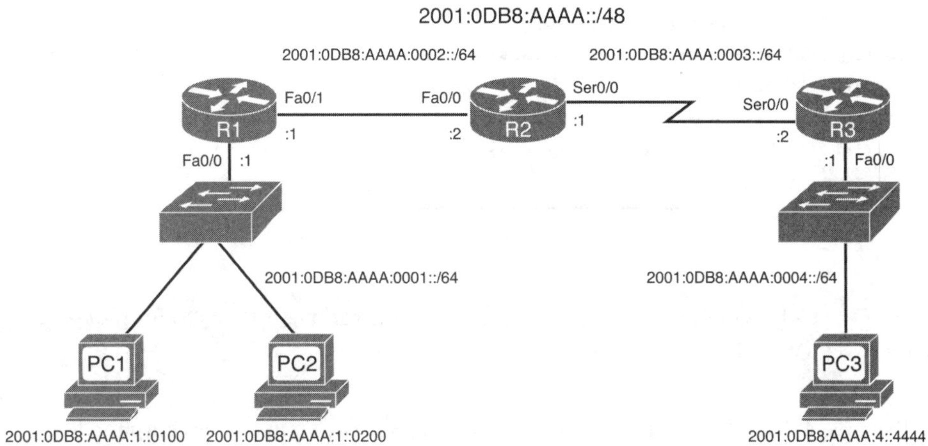

Figure 4-7 *IPv6 Topology*

As mentioned earlier, there is a 2001:0DB8:AAAA::/48 network subnetted into four /64 subnets:

- 2001:0DB8:AAAA:0001::/64
- 2001:0DB8:AAAA:0002::/64
- 2001:0DB8:AAAA:0003::/64
- 2001:0DB8:AAAA:0004::/64

Example 4-1 shows the commands for configuring the global unicast addresses for Routers R1, R2, and R3 (although any necessary **clock rate** and **no shutdown** commands are not shown). Notice that there is not a space between the prefix and the prefix length when configuring the IPv6 address.

Example 4-1 *Configuring Global Unicast Addresses on Routers R1, R2, and R3*

```
R1(config)# interface fastethernet 0/0
R1(config-if)# ipv6 address 2001:db8:aaaa:1::1/64
R1(config-if)# exit
R1(config)# interface fastethernet 0/1
R1(config-if)# ipv6 address 2001:db8:aaaa:2::1/64
R1(config-if)# exit
----------------------------------------------------
R2(config)# interface fastethernet 0/0
R2(config-if)# ipv6 address 2001:db8:aaaa:2::2/64
R2(config-if)# exit
```

```
R2(config)# interface serial 0/0
R2(config-if)# ipv6 address 2001:db8:aaaa:3::1/64
R1(config-if)# exit
```

```
R3(config)# interface fastethernet 0/0
R3(config-if)# ipv6 address 2001:db8:aaaa:4::1/64
R3(config-if)# exit
R3(config)# interface serial 0/0
R3(config-if)# ipv6 address 2001:db8:aaaa:3::2/64
R3(config-if)# exit
```

Note The global configuration command **ipv6 unicast-routing** is required for the router to route IPv6 packets.

Example 4-2 shows the running config for Router R1. The no ip address output refers to the lack of an IPv4 address. Even if you do not use an abbreviated IPv6 address when configuring the interface, the running config will use the compressed format. You can have both an IPv6 address and an IPv4 address configured on the same interface. This is known as "dual stack" and will be discussed in Chapter 10.

Example 4-2 *show running-config Command on Router R1*

```
R1# show running-config
<output omitted for brevity>
interface FastEthernet0/0
 no ip address
 duplex auto
 speed auto
 ipv6 address 2001:DB8:AAAA:1::1/64
!
interface FastEthernet0/1
 no ip address
 duplex auto
 speed auto
 ipv6 address 2001:DB8:AAAA:2::1/64
```

Most of the verification commands that are implemented in IPv4 can be used with IPv6 by substituting **ip** with **ipv6**. Example 4-3 shows the output from the **show ipv6 interface brief** command. The output is similar, but there are differences from the **show ip interface brief** command that is used for IPv4 addresses. Note that the line protocol and state of both of the interfaces are up and up.

Example 4-3 *show ipv6 interface brief Command on Router R1*

```
R1# show ipv6 interface brief
FastEthernet0/0             [up/up]
    FE80::203:6BFF:FEE9:D480    ! Link-local unicast address
    2001:DB8:AAAA:1::1          ! Global unicast address
FastEthernet0/1             [up/up]
    FE80::203:6BFF:FEE9:D481
    2001:DB8:AAAA:2::1
R1#
```

Although only one IPv6 address was configured per interface, each interface has two IPv6 addresses. The address that begins with FE80 is known as a link-local unicast address. It is automatically configured on the interface whenever a global unicast address is assigned. Link-local addresses can only communicate with other devices on the same link. Link-local addresses are discussed later in this chapter.

The output from the **show ipv6 interface fastethernet 0/0** command is shown in Example 4-4. Focus on the global unicast address that was configured along with a link-local address. Notice that there are a group of other addresses beginning with FF02 below the header "Joined group address(es)." These are multicast addresses that the router is automatically a member of when the global unicast address was configured on at least one interface. Multicast addresses are explored later in this chapter. There are also several lines that refer to ND, or Neighbor Discovery, which is part of ICMPv6. ICMPv6 and Neighbor Discovery are explained in Chapter 5.

Example 4-4 *show ipv6 interface fastethernet 0/0 Command on R1*

```
R1# show ipv6 interface fastethernet 0/0
FastEthernet0/0 is up, line protocol is up
  IPv6 is enabled, link-local address is FE80::203:6BFF:FEE9:D480
  Global unicast address(es):
    2001:DB8:AAAA:1::1, subnet is 2001:DB8:AAAA:1::/64
  Joined group address(es):
    FF02::1
    FF02::2
    FF02::1:FF00:1
    FF02::1:FFE9:D480
  MTU is 1500 bytes
  ICMP error messages limited to one every 100 milliseconds
  ICMP redirects are enabled
  ND DAD is enabled, number of DAD attempts: 1
  ND reachable time is 30000 milliseconds
  ND advertised reachable time is 0 milliseconds
  ND advertised retransmit interval is 0 milliseconds
  ND router advertisements are sent every 200 seconds
```

```
  ND router advertisements live for 1800 seconds
  Hosts use stateless autoconfig for addresses.
R1#
```

So, as you can see, although the global unicast address is configured, which is equivalent to an IPv4 address, there is still much more to IPv6 than just a longer IP address.

EUI Configuration

Another way to manually configure an IPv6 global unicast address is in conjunction with the IEEE defined Extended Unique Identifier or *modified EUI-64* process. With the EUI-64 option, the prefix (network portion) of the address is configured manually while the EUI-64 process is used to automatically assign the Interface ID. The modified EUI-64 process uses the interface's Ethernet MAC address to generate a 64-bit Interface ID (host portion of the address) and therefore requires a /64 prefix. Combined with a manually configured prefix, a global unicast address is generated for the interface. Figure 4-8 illustrates the EUI-64 technique as another method of manually configuring an IPv6 address.

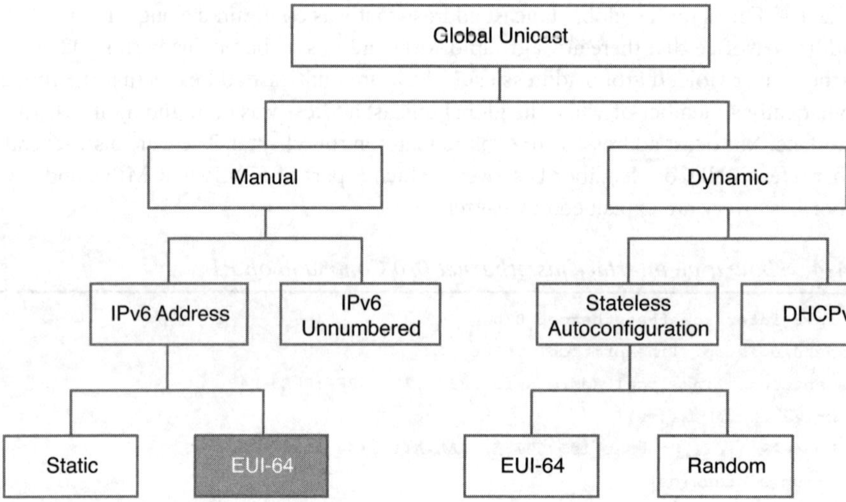

Figure 4-8 *EUI-64*

An Ethernet MAC address is 48 bits. There is also a standard for 64-bit MAC addresses. As shown in Figure 4-9, an Ethernet 48-bit MAC address is a combination of a 24-bit Organizational Unique Identifier (OUI) and a 24-bit device identifier, written in hexadecimal. Manufacturers of Ethernet network interface cards (NIC) have one or more OUI or vendor codes. Each 24-bit OUI has a 24-bit device identifier that uniquely identifies the Ethernet NIC. In other words, appending a 24-bit device identifier to a 24-bit OUI uniquely identifies an Ethernet NIC.

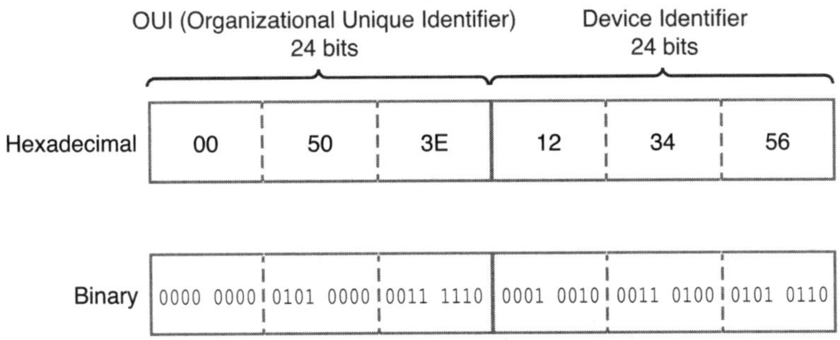

Figure 4-9 *Ethernet MAC Address*

Note For a list of IEEE OUI codes, go to http://standards.ieee.org/develop/regauth/oui/oui.txt.

Modified EUI-64 is a concatenation of the 24-bit OUI with the U/L OUI bit *flipped*, a 16-bit value of FFFE, and the 24-bit device identifier. This process is accomplished in three simple steps, as illustrated in Figure 4-10.

Step 1. After converting the MAC address to binary, the MAC address is split in the middle with the 24-bit OUI on the left and the 24-bit device identifier on the right.

Step 2. FFFE is inserted between the OUI and the device identifier. The binary equivalent of FFFE is 1111 1111 1111 1110. FFFE is an IEEE-reserved value that indicates the EUI-64 address was generated from a 48-bit MAC address.

Step 3. The Universally/Locally (U/L) bit, also known as the Local/Global bit, is the seventh bit of the first byte and is used to determine whether the address is universally or locally administered. If this bit is 0, IEEE, through the designation of a unique company ID, has administered the address. If the U/L bit is a 1, the address is locally administered. The network administrator has overridden the manufactured address and specified a different address.

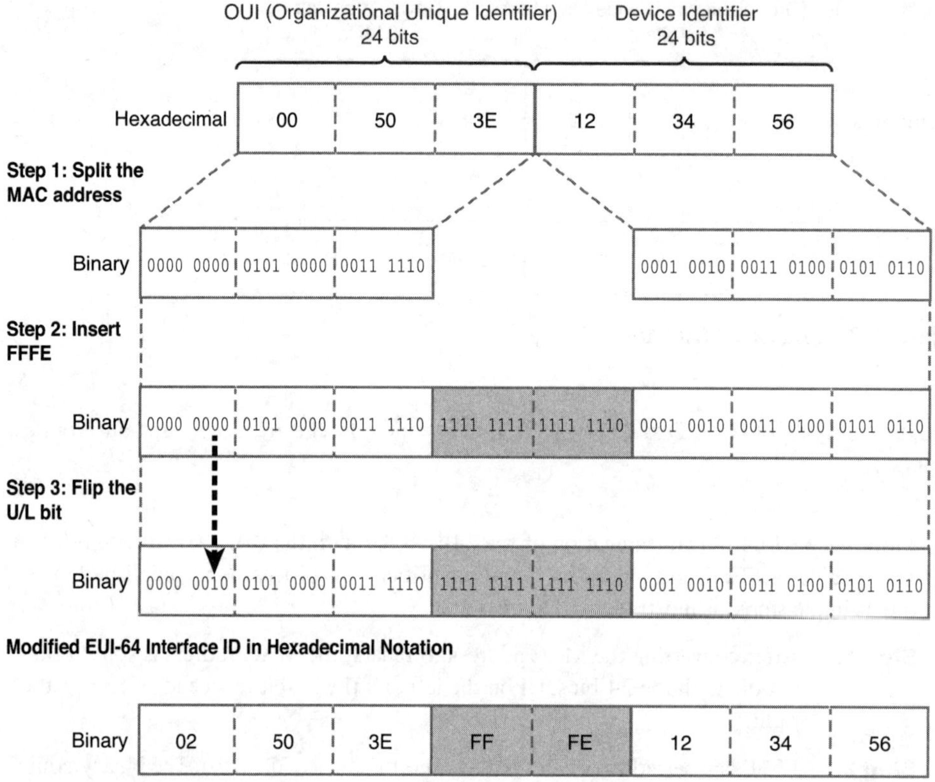

Figure 4-10 *Modified EUI-64 Format*

There seems to be some conflict as to whether this bit should be flipped, from 0 to 1 or 1 to 0. Some documentation states that the U/L bit should only be modified if it is a 0, flipping it to a 1. (However, it seems that Cisco devices will flip this bit regardless of its value.) As shown in Figure 4-10, flipping the U/L bit will modify the second hexadecimal value in the Interface ID.

> **Note** RFC 5342, IANA Considerations and IETF Protocol Usage for IEEE 802 Parameters, discusses the logic behind flipping the U/L bit. The decision was to invert the U/L bit to make it easier for network operators to type in local-scope identifiers.

Using the EUI-64 process, the 48-bit MAC address was used to create a 64-bit IPv6 Interface ID. The MAC address of 00-50-3E-12-34-56 was translated into the EUI-64 format of 02-50-3E-FF-FE-12-34-56. EUI-64 inserted FFFE into the middle of the address, and the modification of the seventh bit altered the second hexadecimal value from 0 to 2.

Note The IPv6 Interface ID is 64 bits, which accommodates longer 64-bit MAC addresses. The modified EUI-64 format is used when the interface has a 48-bit MAC address, which is the current standard.

Table 4-4 shows the command for configuring an IPv6 address using the modified EUI-64 format. Notice that only the prefix (network address) portion of the address is specified along with the prefix length. The Interface ID (host portion) is determined by the EUI-64 process. The **ipv6 address** command with **eui-64** is shown here:

```
Router(config-if)# ipv6 address ipv6-prefix/prefix-length eui-64
```

Table 4-4 *IPv6 EUI-64 Interface*

Command	Description
Router(config)# **interface** *interface-type interface-number*	Specifies the interface type and interface number.
Router(config-if)# **ipv6** *address ipv6-prefix/prefix-length* **eui-64**	Specifies the IPv6 prefix and prefix length to be assigned to the interface. The address is configured using an EUI-64 Interface ID in the lower-order 64 bits of the address.

In Example 4-5, we configure R1's Fast Ethernet 0/0 interface using the EUI-64 format. Notice that the command only includes the prefix 2001:0db8:aaaa:0001:: and the prefix length /64, followed by the **eui-64** option. Had the **eui-64** option not been included, the Interface ID would have consisted of all 0s, which is a valid IPv6 interface address.

Example 4-5 *Configuring an EUI-64 Address on Router R1*

```
R1(config)# interface fastethernet 0/0
R1(config-if)# ipv6 address 2001:0db8:aaaa:0001::/64 ?
  eui-64  Use eui-64 interface identifier
  <cr>

R1(config-if)# ipv6 address 2001:0db8:aaaa:0001::/64 eui-64
R1(config-if)#
```

Using the **show ipv6 fastethernet 0/0** command, shown in Example 4-6, notice the addition of a second global unicast address on this interface, 2001:DB8:AAAA:1:203:6BFF:FEE9:D480. The Interface ID portion was created with the EUI-64 format, which uses the interface's Ethernet MAC address 0003.6BE9.D480. The Ethernet MAC address can be verified with the **show interface fastethernet 0/0** command.

Example 4-6 *R1's show ipv6 interface fastethernet 0/0 Command*

```
R1# show ipv6 interface fastethernet 0/0
FastEthernet0/0 is up, line protocol is up
  IPv6 is enabled, link-local address is FE80::203:6BFF:FEE9:D480
  Global unicast address(es):
    2001:DB8:AAAA:1::1, subnet is 2001:DB8:AAAA:1::/64
    ! Address using EUI-64 format
    2001:DB8:AAAA:1:203:6BFF:FEE9:D480, subnet is  2001:DB8:AAAA:1::/64
Joined group address(es):
    FF02::1
    FF02::2
    FF02::1:FF00:1
    FF02::1:FFE9:D480
<output omitted for brevity>

R1# show interface fastethernet 0/0
FastEthernet0/0 is up, line protocol is up
  Hardware is AmdFE, address is 0003.6be9.d480 (bia 0003.6be9.d480)
! Ethernet MAC Address
  MTU 1500 bytes, BW 100000 Kbit, DLY 100 usec,
     reliability 255/255, txload 1/255, rxload 1/255
<output omitted for brevity>
```

Figure 4-11 shows how EUI-64 transformed R1's Ethernet MAC address into the Interface ID.

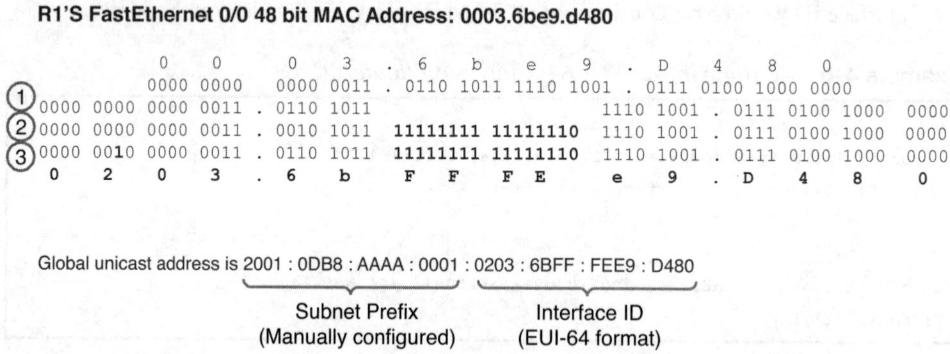

Figure 4-11 *EUI-64 Format for R1's Fast Ethernet 0/0 Interface*

The three-step process is as follows:

Step 1. The 48-bit MAC address of Fast Ethernet 0/0 is split into two 24-bit segments.

Step 2. FFFE (1111 1111 1111 1110) is inserted in the middle.

Step 3. The seventh bit (U/L bit) is flipped from a 0 to a 1, changing the second hextet from 0 to 2.

To summarize, in Example 4-5, the subnet prefix was manually configured and used the **eui-64** option to create an Interface ID. By prepending the manually configured subnet prefix (2001:DB8:AAAA:1::/64) to the EUI-64-generated Interface ID (6BFF:FEE9:D480), you get the global unicast address of 2001:DB8:AAAA:1:203:6BFF:FEE9:D480.

Looking once again at the **show ipv6 fastethernet 0/0** output in Example 4-6, notice that this interface has two global unicast addresses: the statically configured address 2001:DB8:AAAA:1::1 address from Example 4-1 and 2001:DB8:AAAA:1:203:6BFF:FEE9:D480 that was just configured using EUI-64. Notice that both addresses on this interface are on the same 2001:DB8:AAAA:1::/64 subnet.

So, which of these addresses is used as the source address on packets originating from the router when the interface has multiple addresses on the same subnet? This issue is addressed in RFC 3484, Default Address Selection for Internet Protocol version 6 (IPv6). If you are going to assign multiple global unicast addresses within the same subnet to an interface, you should have a reason for doing so and also be familiar with the selection process. RFC 3484 also applies to having both global unicast and link-local unicast addresses on the same interface. Because these are two different types of addresses, it is easier to see which address get used, depending upon the application or protocol. Link-local addresses are examined later in this chapter.

To keep things simple, remove the EUI-64-created address on R1, as shown in Example 4-7. The **no ipv6 address** command with the IPv6 address/prefix length removes the specific address. Unlike IPv4, using the **ipv6 address** command does not overwrite an existing IPv6 address. IPv6 accepts multiple IPv6 addresses on the same interface. The **show ipv6 interface brief** command is used to verify that there is only one global unicast address on the Fast Ethernet 0/0 interface.

Example 4-7 *show ipv6 interface brief Command on R1*

```
R1(config)# interface fastethernet 0/0
R1(config-if)# no ipv6 address 2001:DB8:AAAA:1:203:6BFF:FEE9:D480/64
R1(config-if)# end
R1# show ipv6 interface brief
FastEthernet0/0            [up/up]
    FE80::203:6BFF:FEE9:D480    ! Link-local unicast address
    2001:DB8:AAAA:1::1          ! Global unicast address
Serial0/0                  [administratively down/down]
    unassigned
FastEthernet0/1            [up/up]
    FE80::203:6BFF:FEE9:D481
    2001:DB8:AAAA:2::1
Serial0/1                  [administratively down/down]
    unassigned
R1#
```

> **Note** The practice in which the modified EUI-64 process is used with Stateless Address Autoconfiguration (SLAAC) will be discussed shortly.

IPv6 Unnumbered Configuration

Another form of manual configuration for global unicast addresses is the **ipv6 unnumbered** command. The **ipv6 unnumbered** command enables IPv6 processing on an interface by assigning it a global unicast address from another interface. Figure 4-12 illustrates the IPv6 unnumbered technique as another method of manually configuring IPv6 addresses.

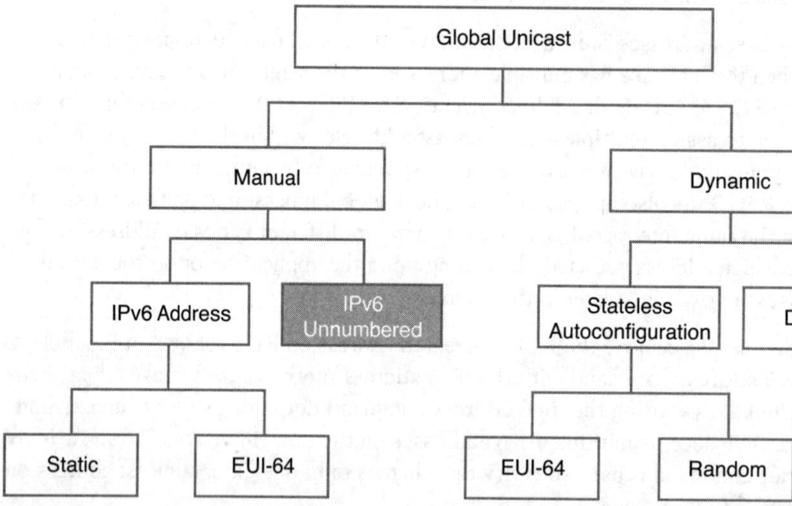

Figure 4-12 *IPv6 Unnumbered*

The **ipv6 unnumbered** *interface* command is shown in Table 4-5, which is used to specify the source address that the interface will use when originating IPv6 packets. The **ipv6 unnumbered** command is shown here:

```
Router(config-if)# ipv6 unnumbered interface-type interface-number
```

Table 4-5 *ipv6 unnumbered Command*

Command	Description
Router(config)# **interface** *interface-type interface-number*	Specifies the interface type and interface number.
Router(config-if)# **ipv6 unnumbered** *interface-type interface-number*	Specifies the interface type and number of the source address that the unnumbered interface uses when it originates IPv6.

Note The **ip unnumbered** command in IPv4 is used to help conserve IPv4 address space. Obviously, address space is not a concern in IPv6 networks, so this command will have more limited uses.

Example 4-8 demonstrates using the **ipv6 unnumbered** command on a router that is not part of the topology. The router's serial 0/1 interface is configured as unnumbered. IPv6 packets that are sent on serial 0/1 will use the IPv6 address of Fast Ethernet 0/0 as their source address.

Example 4-8 *Example of Using the **ipv6 unnumbered** Command*

```
Router(config)# interface fastethernet 0/0
Router(config-if)# ipv6 address 2001:0DB8:ABCD:1234::1/64
Router(config)# interface serial 0/1
Router(config-if)# ipv6 unnumbered fastethernet 0/0
```

Dynamic Configuration

Global unicast addresses can also be configured dynamically, without any manual configuration. Two ways to dynamically configure global unicast addresses are as follows:

- **Stateless Address Autoconfiguration (SLAAC):** Using this method, the Interface ID is created using EUI-64 while the prefix and prefix length are determined from ND Router Advertisement messages.
- **DHCPv6:** Dynamic Host Configuration Protocol (DHCP) for IPv6 is similar to that of DHCP for IPv4. A device can automatically receive its addressing information by using the services of a DHCPv6 server.

Stateless Address Autoconfiguration

Stateless Address Autoconfiguration (SLAAC) is the first of two automatic methods discussed for assigning global unicast addresses to interfaces. SLAAC is defined in RFC 4862, IPv6 Stateless Address Autoconfiguration. Figure 4-13 illustrates the first dynamic addressing technique, Stateless Autoconfiguration.

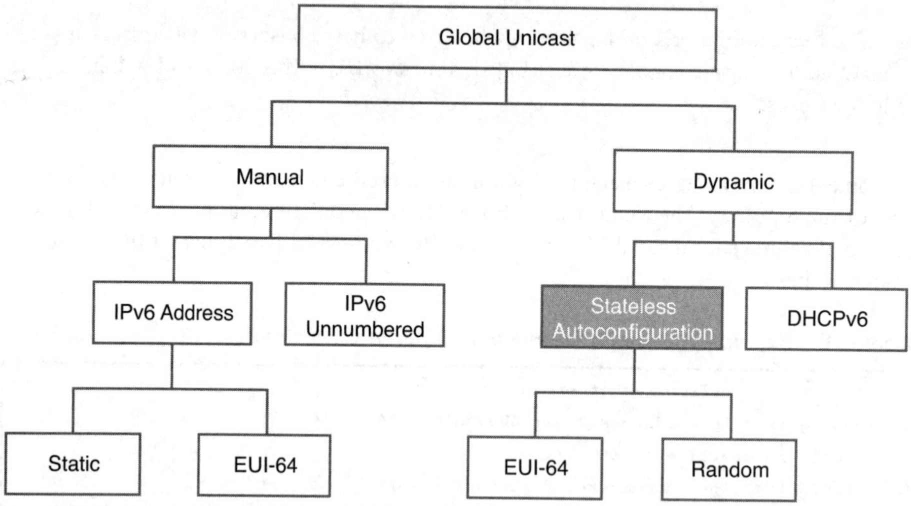

Figure 4-13 *Stateless Address Autoconfiguration*

SLAAC uses the IEEE-modified EUI-64 format shown earlier. By using its Ethernet MAC address, this process allows a device to create its own Interface ID (host portion) of its address. Combined with another process, Neighbor Discovery Protocol, a host can determine its entire global unicast address without any manual configuration or the services of a DHCPv6 server. ND (Neighbor Discovery) and SLAAC are discussed in more detail in Chapter 5. ND is introduced here for a basic understanding of SLAAC.

ND is defined in RFC 4861, Neighbor Discovery in IPv6. ND uses ICMPv6 to exchange the messages necessary for its functions, specifically, five new ICMPv6 messages:

- Router Advertisement (RA) messages
- Router Solicitation (RS) messages
- Neighbor Solicitation (NS) messages
- Neighbor Advertisement (NA) messages
- Redirect messages

ICMPv6 is a much more robust protocol than the ICMP for IPv4. ICMPv6 contains new functionality and improvements. Only the first four messages are relevant to the introductory discussion on SLAAC. As stated throughout this chapter, the main objective is to understand these messages as they relate to the address types. ND and each of these messages will be explored in more detail in Chapter 5.

IPv6 Neighbor Discovery Protocol does exactly what it says—discover neighbors. Devices can receive ND messages to automatically determine their prefix, prefix length, default gateway, and other information. Except for its Interface ID, a device will obtain its network configuration from these messages originated by the router. How is this different than a server or router configured to provide DHCP services? DHCP can be a stateless or a *stateful* service. A stateful service remembers client data (state) from one request to the next. A stateless service does not keep any state information. A stateful DHCP server must maintain an accurate listing of available addresses so that it does not give out duplicates. As the name indicates, SLAAC is *stateless*. After the host creates its own unique address without the services of a stateful DHCPv6 server, it will need to verify that its address is indeed unique.

Figure 4-14 shows that the host, PC-B, has been configured to obtain its IPv6 address automatically. This means, PC-B will get IPv6 address either from a DHCPv6 server or in our scenario using SLAAC.

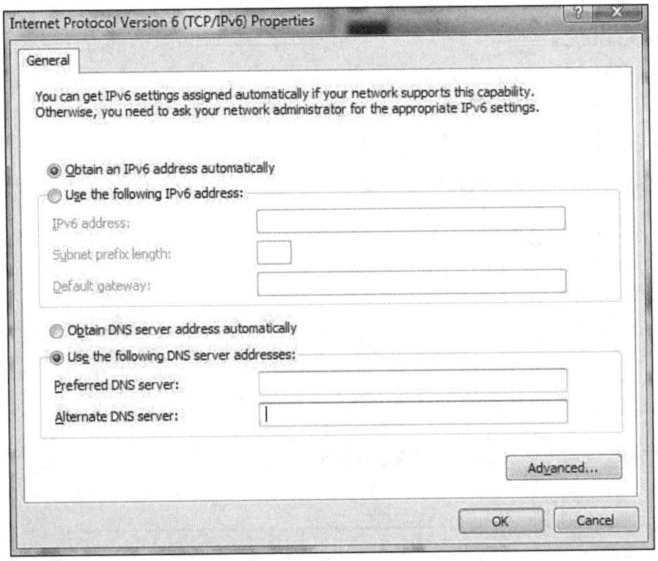

Figure 4-14 *Obtaining an IPv6 Address Automatically on PC-B*

Autoconfigured (SLAAC) addresses are in one or more of the following states:

- **Tentative:** The uniqueness of the address is in the process of being verified. A tentative address is not considered to be assigned to an interface. An interface discards received packets addressed to a tentative address, but accepts Neighbor Discovery packets related to Duplicate Address Detection for the tentative address.
- **Preferred:** The interface address has been verified as unique. The device can send and receive traffic using this address. The period of time that an address can remain in the tentative and preferred states is included in the Router Advertisement message.
- **Deprecated:** The address assigned to an interface is still valid but implementation is discouraged. A deprecated address should no longer be used as a source address in new communications, but packets sent from or to deprecated addresses are delivered as expected. A deprecated address can continue to be used as a source address in existing communications where changing to a preferred address might cause a problem with specific upper-layer activity such as an existing TCP connection.

- **Valid:** The address is a preferred or deprecated address. A valid address can be the source or destination address of a packet. The amount of time that an address remains in the tentative and valid states is included in the Router Advertisement message. The valid lifetime must be greater than or equal to the preferred lifetime. Router Advertisement messages are introduced next. Valid lifetimes and preferred lifetimes are discussed in Chapter 5.
- **Invalid:** A valid address becomes invalid when its valid lifetime expires. Invalid addresses should not appear as the destination or source address of a packet.

Figure 4-15 illustrates the five autoconfigured address states.

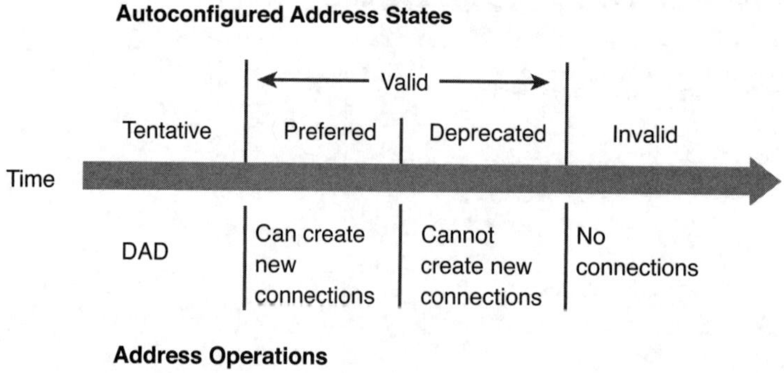

Figure 4-15 *Autoconfigured Address States*

Figure 4-16 shows a simplified version of the SLAAC process.

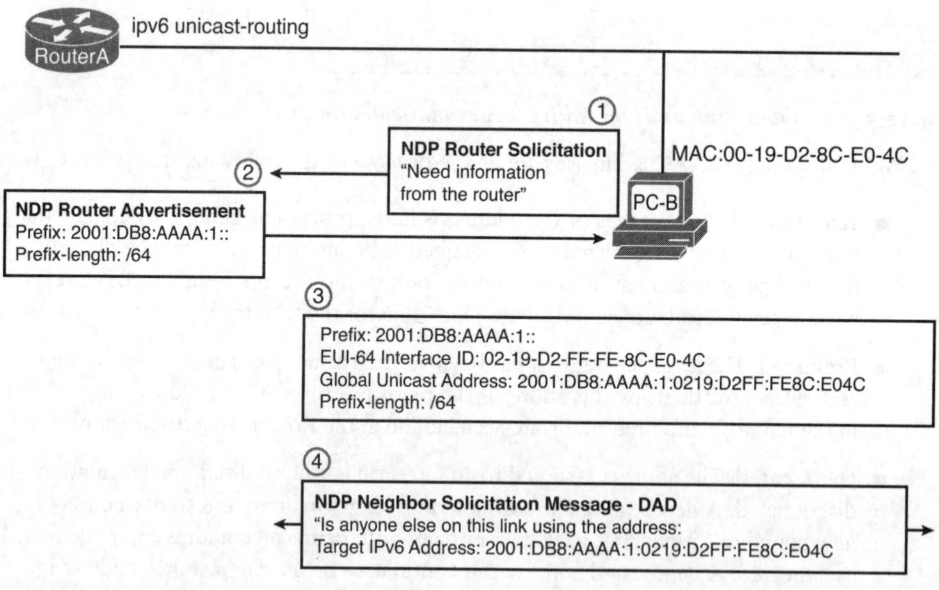

Figure 4-16 *NDP Router Advertisement and Router Solicitation Messages*

RouterA periodically sends out ND Router Advertisement (RA) messages. RA messages are originated by routers to advertise their presence and link-specific parameters such as the link prefix, prefix length, default gateway, and link maximum transmission unit (MTU). Router Advertisements are sent to the *all-nodes multicast* address (FF02::1), which is essentially the same as a broadcast. Multicast addresses are discussed later in this chapter. Router Advertisements are sent periodically and also in response to a Router Solicitation (RS) message.

RS messages are originated by hosts to request that a router send a Router Advertisement. RS messages are sent to the all-routers multicast address (FF02::2), which is processed by any IPv6 routers on the link and configured with the **ipv6 unicast-routing** command.

For a router to send Router Advertisement messages and as shown later to run an IPv6 routing protocol, it must be configured with **ipv6 unicast-routing** command:

```
RouterA(config)# ipv6 unicast-routing
```

As displayed in Figure 4-16, the SLAAC process includes the following steps:

Step 1. As noted in Figure 4-14, PC-B is configured to obtain its IP addressing automatically. Since booting up, PC-B has not seen a Router Advertisement message, so it sends out a Router Solicitation message to inform the local IPv6 router that it needs an RA message.

Step 2. RouterA receives the Router Solicitation message and responds with a Router Advertisement. Included in the RA message are the prefix and prefix length of the link, along with its own address as the default gateway. The default gateway address that RouterA propagates is actually its link-local address, not its global unicast address as you might expect. This is discussed in more detail in Chapter 5.

Step 3. PC-B receives the Router Advertisement, which includes the prefix and prefix length for the local network, 2001:DB8:AAAA:1::/64.

PC-B's Ethernet MAC address is 00-19-D2-8C-E0-4C. Using modified EUI-64, FF-FE is inserted between the OUI and the device identifier of the MAC address. The seventh bit is flipped from 0 to 1, which changes the second hexadecimal value from 0 to 2. As a result, the Interface ID is assigned the 64-bit value 02-19-D2-FF-FE-8C-E0-4C.

PC-B prepends the prefix 2001:DB8:AAAA:1:: from the Router Advertisement to create its global unicast address of 2001:DB8:AAAA:1:02-19-D2-FF-FE-8C-E0-4C. The address is in the tentative state until its uniqueness is verified in the next step.

Step 4. Because SLAAC is a stateless process, there isn't any device keeping track of all the global unicast addresses on the link to prevent duplication. So, it is up to the host itself to make sure that it didn't create itself an address that is already used by another device. This ND process is known as Duplicate

Address Detection (DAD).DAD is explored in more detail in Chapter 5, but the process is fairly straightforward. It's nothing more than a device sending its address out to everyone on the link to see whether anyone else is using it. This is similar to a gratuitous ARP request in IPv4. PC-B sends a Neighbor Solicitation (NS) message—similar to an IPv4 ARP request—with its own global unicast address 2001:DB8:AAAA:1:02-19-D2-FF-FE-8C-E0-4C as the target address. If another device has this address, it will respond with a Neighbor Advertisement message, similar to an ARP reply in IPv4. The NS message is sent to a *solicited node multicast* address. The purpose of solicited node multicast address is similar to that of a broadcast address but is much more efficient. Solicited node multicast addresses are discussed later in this chapter.If PC-B does not hear a response to its Neighbor Solicitation message in the form of a Neighbor Advertisement, it can rest assured that its global unicast address is unique. The address is now in the preferred state.

Whether a host that is configured to obtain its addressing information automatically uses SLAAC or DHPv6 depends upon the configuration of the router's Router Advertisement message. The RA message can be configured to instruct devices in the link to use stateful, DHCPv6 autoconfiguration rather than stateless autoconfiguration.

The ability for a device to dynamically determine its own global unicast address without the need of a DHCPv6 server is a significant advantage in IPv6. In an "Internet of things," IPv6 devices such as webcams and sensors can just be powered on and can obtain all their addressing information from the router and the EUI-64 process.

Note There are some privacy concerns with using a device's Ethernet MAC address as the Interface ID. Packets could potentially be traced back to the actual source device. Therefore, not all operating systems utilize the EUI-64 process as described previously. Windows operating systems, Windows XP, and Windows Server 2003 use EUI-64, while Windows Vista and newer versions do not. Instead, these operating systems create a random 64-bit Interface ID when using SLAAC.

Dynamic Host Configuration Protocol for IPv6

Dynamic Host Configuration Protocol for IPv6 (DHCPv6) is similar to DHCP for IPv4. DHCPv6 provides stateful and stateless autoconfiguration for IPv6 devices. When devices are configured to obtain their IPv6 addressing information automatically, as shown in Figure 4-14, they will use one of the following methods:

- Stateless addressing using Router Advertisements
- Stateful addressing using DHCPv6

Figure 4-17 illustrates DHCPv6 as one of the techniques for dynamically assigning IPv6 addresses.

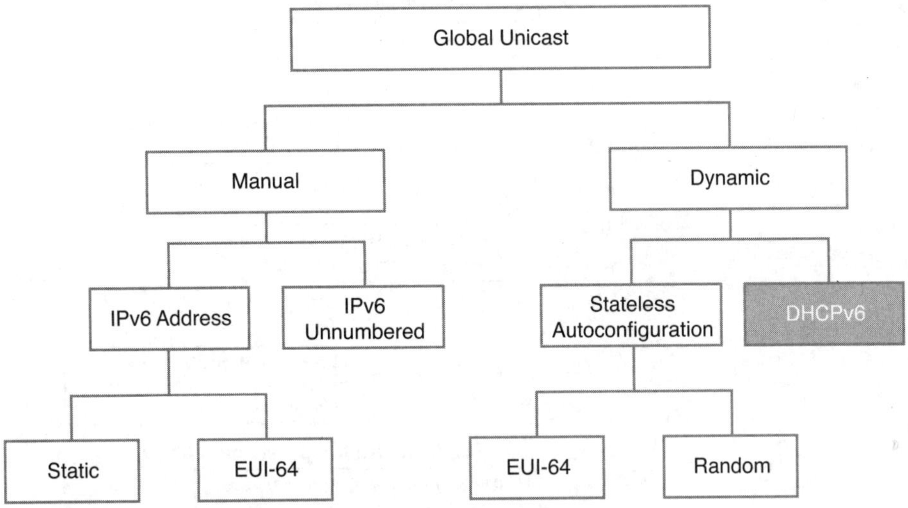

Figure 4-17 *DHCPv6*

DHCPv6 is defined in RFC 3315, Dynamic Host Configuration Protocol for IPv6 (DHCPv6), and is explored further in Chapter 9, "DHCPv6 (Dynamic Host Configuration Protocol version 6)." This section examines the DHCPv6 process and describes how a device determines whether to use stateless or stateful addressing.

Figure 4-18 illustrates this progression in steps beginning with PC-B to determine whether *stateless* or *stateful* autoconfiguration will be used.

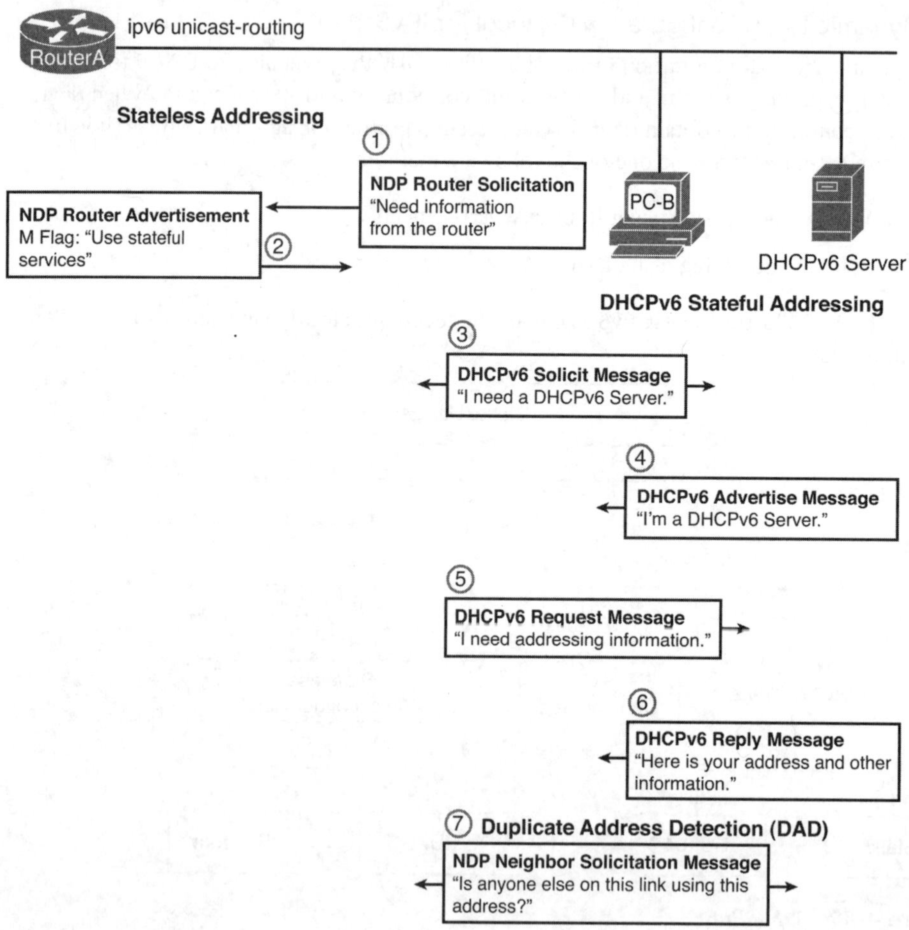

Figure 4-18 *Stateful DHCPv6*

Step 1. PC-B sends out a Router Solicitation message unless a Router Advertisement message has already been received.

Step 2. Router Advertisements have a 1-bit field known as the *Managed address configuration flag*, or *M flag*:

- When this flag is set to 0, it informs the devices to use Stateless Address Autoconfiguration (SLAAC).
- If the flag is set to 1, it indicates that the device needs to use stateful autoconfiguration (DHCPv6), as shown in Figure 4-18.

Now that PC-B recognizes that it must use stateful autoconfiguration, it begins the process to obtain its addressing information from a DHCPv6 server.

Step 3. PC-B sends out a DHCPv6 Solicit message to a special multicast address specifically for DHCPv6 servers—FF02::1:2. (Multicast addresses are discussed later in this chapter.)

Step 4. One or more DHCPv6 servers respond with a DHCPv6 Advertise message, indicating that they are available for DHCPv6 service. If PC-B receives multiple Advertise messages, there is a process that generates a Server Preference value that it will use to select the appropriate DCHPv6 server (as discussed in Chapter 9).

Step 5. PC-B will respond to the selected server by sending a Request message asking for configuration parameters, including IP addresses.

Step 6. The DHCPv6 server responds with a Reply message containing the assigned addresses and other configuration parameters similar to those used with DHCP for IPv4.

Even though PC-B obtained its address from DHCPv6, a stateful service, it will still use the Duplicate Address Detection (DAD) process to ensure that there aren't any other devices on the link with this address.

Step 7. PC-B sends out a Neighbor Solicitation (NS) message with its newly obtained global unicast address to all devices on the link. The source address is an unspecified address, "::" because PC-B's global unicast address is tentative until proven to be unique. The destination address is a solicited node multicast address, which as mentioned earlier, is similar to that of a broadcast address. If any devices on the link have the same address, that device will respond with a Neighbor Advertisement message.

Link-local Unicast

Link-local addresses are unicast addresses that are confined to a single link. Their uniqueness must be confirmed on that link because these packets are not routable off the link. In other words, routers will not forward any packets with link-local source or destination addresses. Figure 4-19 illustrates link-local addresses as a type of unicast address.

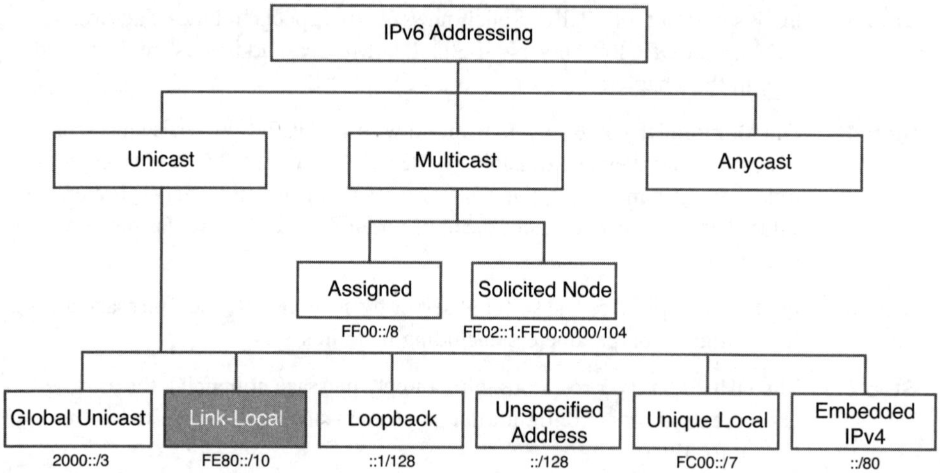

Figure 4-19 *Link-local Unicast*

Link-local addresses are configured in one of three ways:

- Dynamically, using EUI-64
- Random-generated Interface ID
- Statically, entering the link-local address manually

Link-local addresses provide a unique benefit in IPv6. A device can create its own link-local address completely on its own, without the service of a DHCPv6 server or a Router Advertisement message. This solves the "Which came first, the chicken or the egg?" problem with IPv4. That is, "How do I ask a server for an IP address when I need to first have an IP address before I can communicate with it?"

Figure 4-20 shows the format of a link-local unicast address. Link-local unicast addresses are in the range from FE80::/10.

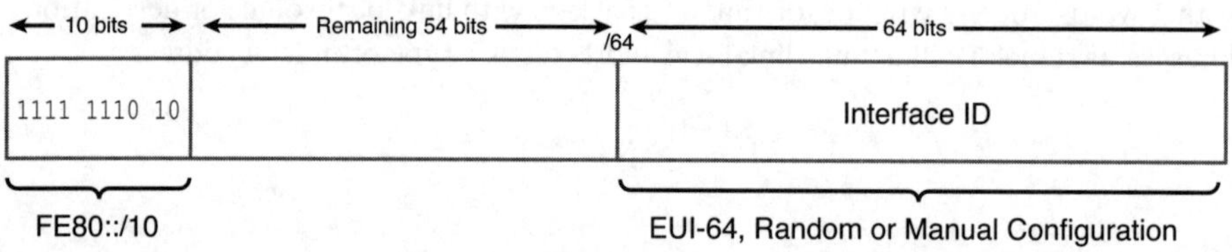

Figure 4-20 *Link-local Unicast Address*

Using this prefix and prefix length gives the range of addresses from FE80::/10 to FEBF::/10, as illustrated in Table 4-6.

Table 4-6 *Range of Link-local Unicast Addresses*

Link-local Unicast Address (Hexadecimal)	Range of First Hextet	Range of First Hextet in Binary
FE80::/10	FE80	**1111 1110 10**00 0000
	FEBF	**1111 1110 10**11 1111

The /10 indicates that the first 10 bits are the significant bits, the bits that must match the prefix. The prefix is FE80, or 1111 1110 10 in binary. So, as long as these first 10 bits match, the remaining 54 bits can be of any value. Therefore, the first hextet could be any value in the range FE80 through FEBF.

As explained later in this book, IPv6 link-local addresses are used in the following ways:

- Routers use their link-local address as the default gateway address in their Router Advertisements.
- Routers running protocols such as Enhanced Interior Gateway Routing Protocol (EIGRP) for IPv6 and Open Shortest Path First version 3 (OSPFv3) employ their link-local addresses to establish adjacencies.
- Dynamic routes in IPv6 routing tables use the link-local address as their next-hop addresses.

Dynamic Link-local Address: EUI-64

By default, devices automatically create their own link-local unicast address without the assistance of another device such a DHCP server or a router. As shown in Figure 4-20, the prefix/prefix length will typically be FE80::/64. The 64-bit Interface ID is automatically assigned either randomly or using the EUI-64 format; Cisco devices use EUI-64. Randomly generated Interface IDs are examined in the next section.

Example 4-9 shows Router R1's link-local address on Fast Ethernet 0/0 using the **show ipv6 interface** command. Because a link-local address was not manually configured on this interface, one was created automatically using the EUI-64 format. Notice in the output that the MAC address of Fast Ethernet 0/0 was used to generate the link-local Interface ID using EUI-64.

Example 4-9 *Link-local Unicast Address*

```
R1# show ipv6 interface fastethernet 0/0
FastEthernet0/0 is up, line protocol is up
  ! Link-local address using EUI-64 format
  IPv6 is enabled, link-local address is FE80::203:6BFF:FEE9:D480
Global unicast address(es):
    2001:DB8:AAAA:1::1, subnet is 2001:DB8:AAAA:1::/64
  Joined group address(es):
    FF02::1
```

```
    FF02::2
    FF02::1:FF00:1
    FF02::1:FFE9:D480
<output omitted for brevity>

R1# show interface fastethernet 0/0
FastEthernet0/0 is up, line protocol is up
  ! Ethernet MAC Address
  Hardware is AmdFE, address is 0003.6be9.d480 (bia 0003.6be9.d480)
  MTU 1500 bytes, BW 100000 Kbit, DLY 100 usec,
     reliability 255/255, txload 1/255, rxload 1/255
<output omitted for brevity>
```

The MAC address of R1's Fast Ethernet 0/0 interface is 0003.6BE9.D480. Using modified EUI-64, FF-FE is inserted between the OUI and the device identifier of the MAC address. The seventh bit is flipped from 0 to 1, which changes the second hexadecimal value from 0 to 2. As a result, the Interface ID is assigned the 64-bit value 02-03-6B-FF-FE-E9-D4-80. The link-local prefix of FE80::/10 is prepended to the Interface ID, resulting in a link-local address for R1's Fast Ethernet 0/0 interface of FE80::0203:6BFF:FEE9:D480.

It was explained earlier in this chapter how the EUI-64 was used to create the Interface ID for a global unicast address on this same interface. Compare the link-local address in Example 4-9 to the global unicast address in Example 4-6. Because the same MAC address is used in both of these addresses using EUI-64, both addresses will have the same Interface ID. Only the prefix, the leading 64 bits, will be different.

Randomly Generated Interface IDs

EUI-64 is a convenient technique for automatically creating a 64-bit Interface ID from a 48-bit MAC address. However, this introduces a concern for some users: the ability to trace an IPv6 address to the actual device using the 48-bit MAC address used to create the Interface ID. To alleviate this privacy concern, devices can use randomly generated 64-bit Interface IDs.

Note Privacy extensions are addressed in RFC 5375, IPv6 Unicast Address Assignment Considerations, and RFC 4941, Privacy Extensions for Stateless Address Autoconfiguration in IPv6.

Whether a device uses EUI-64 or randomly generated Interface IDs is dependent upon the operating system. Cisco routers use EUI-64. Windows operating systems later than XP use a random number for the Interface ID. Prior Windows operating systems used EUI-64. The trend seems to be for host operating systems to generate their Interface ID randomly by default.

Example 4-10 shows the link-local addresses for PC1 and PC2, two of the hosts in the topology shown in Figure 4-7. Both of the Windows hosts generated their own link-local addresses. Because these hosts are running a Windows OS later that XP, a random number was generated for the Interface ID instead of using EUI-64.

Example 4-10 *IPv6 Link-local Addresses for PC1 and PC2*

```
PC1> ipconfig

Windows IP Configuration

Ethernet adapter Local Area Connection:

   Connection-specific DNS Suffix  . :
   IPv6 Address. . . . . . . . . . . : 2001:db8:aaaa:1::100
   Link-local IPv6 Address . . . . . : fe80::50a5:8a35:a5bb:66e1%11
   Default Gateway . . . . . . . . . : 2001:db8:aaaa:1::1
```

```
PC2> ipconfig

Windows IP Configuration

Ethernet adapter Local Area Connection:

   Connection-specific DNS Suffix  . :
   IPv6 Address. . . . . . . . . . . : 2001:db8:aaaa:1::200
   Link-local IPv6 Address . . . . . : fe80::1c00:3ea4:74ff:a8cf%8
   Default Gateway . . . . . . . . . : 2001:db8:aaaa:1::1
```

The %value following the link-local address is a Windows Zone ID and not part of IPv6.

Note Example 4-10 shows the link-local addresses followed by %n, where n represents a Zone ID. This information is not particularly relevant for this discussion, but if you are interested, you can read more about Zone IDs at http://technet.microsoft.com/en-us/library/bb726952.aspx and in RFC 4007, IPv6 Scoped Address Architecture.

Static Link-local Address

Dynamically assigned link-local addresses are ideal for most devices such as hosts. The disadvantage is the lengthy Interface ID, which can be difficult to recognize or remember when troubleshooting or verifying network operations. Because dynamic routing protocols such as EIGRP for IPv6 and OSPFv3 use link-local addresses for establishing adjacencies and other messages, its easier to use manually configured link-local addresses that are more recognizable.

The command for configuring a static link-local unicast address is as follows:

```
Router(config-if)# ipv6 address ipv6-address link-local
```

Table 4-7 shows the command for configuring a static link-local unicast address.

Table 4-7 *Configuring a Static Link-local Unicast Address*

Command	Description
Router(config)# **interface** *interface-type interface-number*	Specifies the interface type and interface number.
Router(config-if)# **ipv6 address** *ipv6-address* **link-local**	Specifies the IPv6 link-local address. The **link-local** parameter is required.

Note Some Cisco documentation states that the interface command is *ipv6-address/prefix-length* **link-local**; however, this is not the case with the IOS used in this example.

Figure 4-21 shows the topology with static link-local addresses assigned to each interface. Example 4-11 shows the configuration of these addresses on Routers R1, R2, and R3. The same link-local address for each interface was configured for each router. This makes it easy to recognize the link-local addresses on each router. R1 has the Interface ID ::1 on all its interfaces, R2 has the Interface ID ::2 on all its interfaces, and Router R3 has the Interface ID ::3 on all its interfaces. Remember, a link-local address only has to be unique for that link because it is not routable off the link.

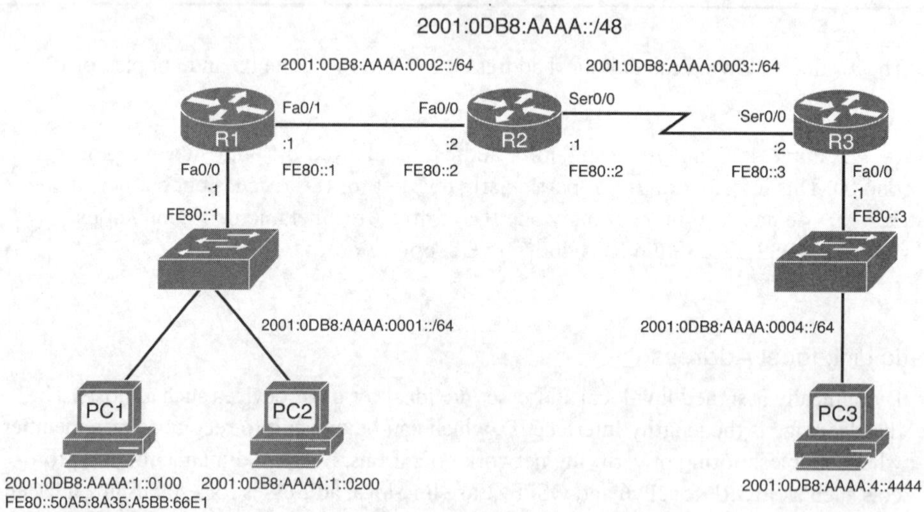

Figure 4-21 *IPv6 Topology with Static Link-local Addresses*

Example 4-11 *Configuring Static Link-local Unicast Addresses on R1, R2, and R3*

```
R1(config)# interface fastethernet 0/0
R1(config-if)# ipv6 address fe80::1 ?
  link-local  Use link-local address

R1(config-if)# ipv6 address fe80::1 link-local
R1(config-if)# exit
R1(config)# interface serial 0/0
R1(config-if)# ipv6 address fe80::1 link-local
```

```
R2(config)# interface fastethernet 0/0
R2(config-if)# ipv6 address fe80::2 link-local
R2(config-if)# exit
R2(config)# interface serial 0/0
R2(config-if)# ipv6 address fe80::2 link-local
```

```
R3(config)# interface fastethernet 0/0
R3(config-if)# ipv6 address fe80::3 link-local
R3(config-if)# exit
R3(config)# interface serial 0/0
R3(config-if)# ipv6 address fe80::3 link-local
```

In Example 4-12, the configuration is verified using the **show ipv6 interface brief** command. Again, notice that for each router, you must configure the same link-local address on each interface. Chapter 7, "Introduction to Routing IPv6," demonstrates an uncomplicated approach to configuring IPv6 routing protocols.

Example 4-12 *Verifying the Static Link-local Unicast Addresses on R1, R2, and R3*

```
R1# show ipv6 interface brief
! Notice that highlighted link-local unicast addresses are the same
FastEthernet0/0             [up/up]
    FE80::1
    2001:DB8:AAAA:1::1
FastEthernet0/1             [up/up]
    FE80::1
    2001:DB8:AAAA:2::1
R1#
```

```
R2# show ipv6 interface brief
! Notice that highlighted link-local unicast addresses are the same
FastEthernet0/0             [up/up]
    FE80::2
    2001:DB8:AAAA:2::2
```

```
Serial0/0                    [up/up]
    FE80::2
    2001:DB8:AAAA:3::1
R2#
```

```
R3# show ipv6 interface brief
! Notice that highlighted link-local unicast addresses are the same
FastEthernet0/0              [up/up]
    FE80::3
    2001:DB8:AAAA:4::1
Serial0/0                    [up/up]
    FE80::3
    2001:DB8:AAAA:3::2
R3#
```

Link-local Addresses and Duplicate Address Detection

As discussed previously with global unicast addresses, devices use Duplicate Address Detection (DAD) to see whether another device on the link is using an address it is about to use. Whether the link-local address is created automatically or manually configured, before a device uses its link-local address, it will perform DAD to make sure that it is unique on the link. This is shown in Figure 4-22.

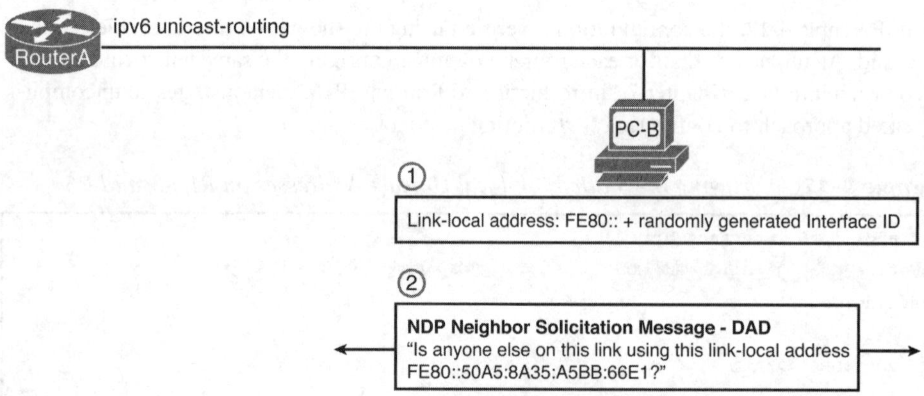

Figure 4-22 *Link-local Addresses and Duplicate Address Detection*

For example, if you configure a router with a link-local address that already exists on the link, you will receive a warning message displaying the link-local address and interface with the duplicate address, as shown here:

```
*%IPV6-4-DUPLICATE: Duplicate address FE80::3 on Serial0/0
```

Although the address will still be accepted, the interface detects that the address it wants to use is a duplicate and will deem the address unusable. Link-local unicast addresses must be unique on the link.

Duplicate Address Detection is discussed in more detail in Chapter 5.

Link-local Addresses and Default Gateways

Neighbor Discovery Protocol (ND or NDP) was discussed earlier. Using ND Router Solicitation and Router Advertisement messages, hosts can obtain IP addressing information automatically, such as prefix, prefix length, and a default gateway address. In Figure 4-23, PC1 in the topology has been configured to obtain its IP address automatically. PC1 sends out an ND Router Solicitation message, and Router R1 responds with a Router Advertisement. Because PC1 is running Windows Vista, instead of using EUI-64, it uses a random number for its Interface ID and prepends the prefix from the Router Advertisement.

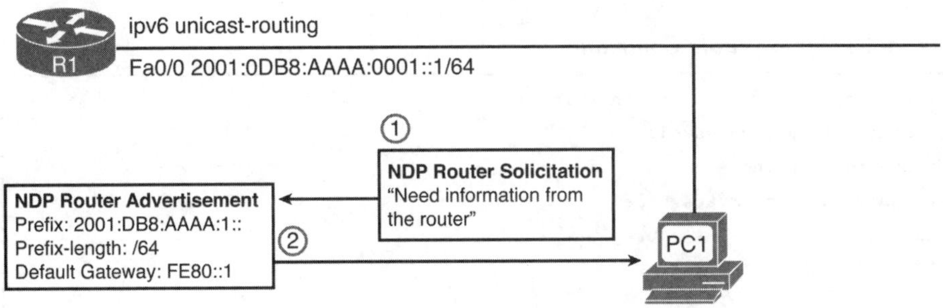


```
PC1> ipconfig

Windows IP Configuration

Ethernet adapter Local Area Connection:

    Conneciton-specific DNS Suffix  . :
    IPv6 Address. . . . . . . . . . . : 2001: db8:aaaa:1:50a5:8a35:a5bb:66e1
    Link-local IPv6 Address . . . . . : fe80::50a5:8a35:a5bb:66e1%11
    Default Gateway . . . . . . . . . : fe80::1% 11
```

Figure 4-23 *Windows ipconfig with Link-local Address for Default Gateway*

The interesting point here is the default gateway address. Notice that Router R1 uses its link-local address FE80::1 as the default gateway in its Router Advertisement instead of its global unicast address of 2001:0DB8:AAAA:0001::1. Router Solicitation and Router Advertisement messages are discussed in more detail in Chapter 5.

Isolated Link-local Address

A link-local address is created automatically whenever IPv6 is enabled on an interface. This can be the result of a global unicast or unique local unicast address configured on an interface or the use of the **ipv6 enable** command. If all occurrences of these addresses are removed, the interface's link-local address is also deleted. To enable an interface so that it can have a link-local address without a global unicast or unique local unicast address, the **ipv6 enable** command is used as shown here:

```
Router(config-if)# ipv6 enable
```

Example 4-13 illustrates how this command can be employed to create a link-local address without configuring a unicast address. After this command is configured on an interface, the router immediately creates a link-local address using the EUI-64 format. In Example 4-13, the link-local address FE80::20C:30FF:FE10:92E1 was automatically created for the Fast Ethernet 0/1 interface.

Example 4-13 *ipv6 enable Command*

```
Router(config)# interface fastethernet 0/1
Router(config-if)# ipv6 enable
Router(config-if)# end
Router# show ipv6 interface brief
FastEthernet0/1            [up/up]
    FE80::20C:30FF:FE10:92E1
Router#
```

Loopback Address

Another type of unicast address is a loopback address, as illustrated in Figure 4-24. An IPv6 loopback address is an all-0s address except for the last bit, which is set to a 1. It is equivalent to the IPv4 loopback address 127.0.0.1.

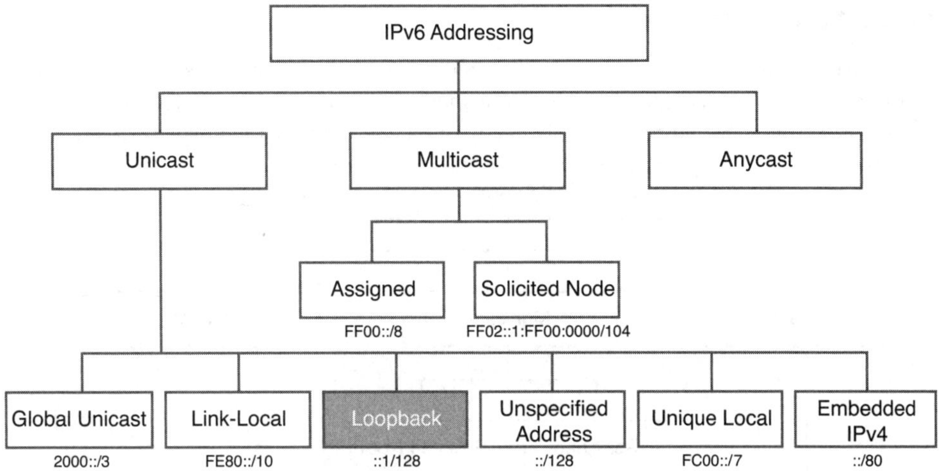

Figure 4-24 *Loopback Address*

Table 4-8 shows the different formats for representing an IPv6 loopback address.

Table 4-8 *IPv6 Loopback Address Representations*

Representation	IPv6 Loopback Address
Preferred	0000:0000:0000:0000:0000:0000:0000:0001
No leading 0s	0:0:0:0:0:0:0:1
Compressed	::1

The loopback address can be used by a node to send an IPv6 packet to itself, typically when testing the TCP/IP stack. This is equivalent to the 127.0.0.0/8 address in IPv4. Loopback addresses have the following characteristics:

- A loopback address cannot be assigned to a physical interface.
- A loopback address can only be a source address if the packet is not sent outside the device.
- A loopback address can only be a destination address if the packet is not sent outside the device.
- A router can never forward a packet with a destination address that is a loopback address.
- The device must drop a packet received on an interface that has a destination address of a loopback address.

Unspecified Address

An unspecified unicast address is an all-0s address. It cannot be assigned to an interface. An unspecified unicast address is used as a source address to indicate the absence of an address. Figure 4-25 illustrates another type of unicast address, the unspecified address.

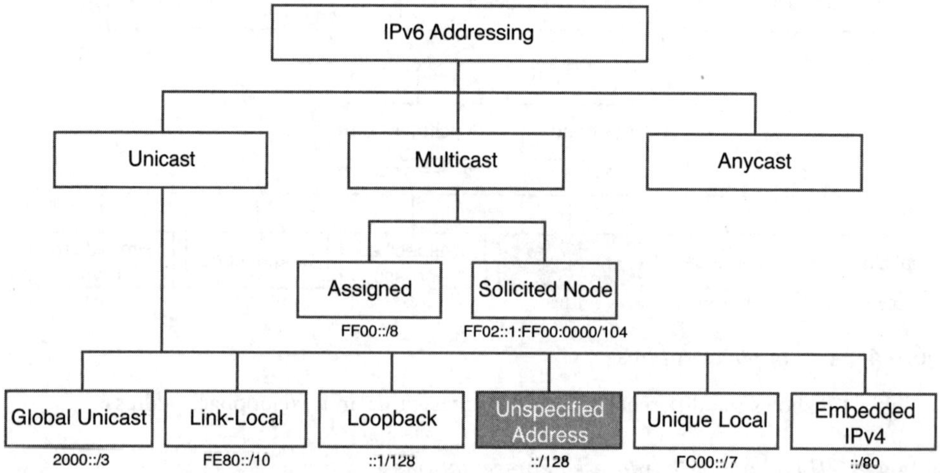

Figure 4-25 *Unspecified Address*

As mentioned earlier, Duplicate Address Detection (DAD) is the process where a device sends out an all-nodes multicast (similar to a broadcast in IPv4) to all devices on the link to ensure that no one else is using the same address that it wants to assign to itself. For example, in Figure 4-22, PC1 uses DAD before implementing its newly created link-local address. The source IPv6 address of PC1's Neighbor Solicitation message is an unspecified address because it does not yet have a valid IPv6 address to use.

Table 4-9 shows the different formats for representing an IPv6 unspecified address.

Table 4-9 *IPv6 Unspecified Address Representations*

Representation	IPv6 Loopback Address
Preferred	0000:0000:0000:0000:0000:0000:0000:0000
No leading 0s	0:0:0:0:0:0:0:0
Compressed	::

Unspecified addresses have the following characteristics:

- An unspecified address cannot be assigned to a physical interface.
- An unspecified source address indicates the absence of an address.
- An unspecified address cannot be used as a destination address.
- A router will never forward a packet with an unspecified source address.

Unique Local Address

The original IPv6 specification allocated address space for site-local addresses, similar to RFC 1918, Private Address Space in IPv4. Site-local addresses were defined in RFC 3513 and given the prefix range FEC0::/10. (You will most likely come across this prefix in older documentation.) The problem was that the term *site* was ambiguous. No one could really agree on what a site really meant. The other issue was that there was no guarantee that two sites within the same organization wouldn't end up using the same or overlapping site-local addresses, which kind of defeats the purpose of IPv6 and all this extra address space. So, site-local addresses have since been deprecated and replaced with unique local addresses. Figure 4-26 illustrates the unicast address type unique local address.

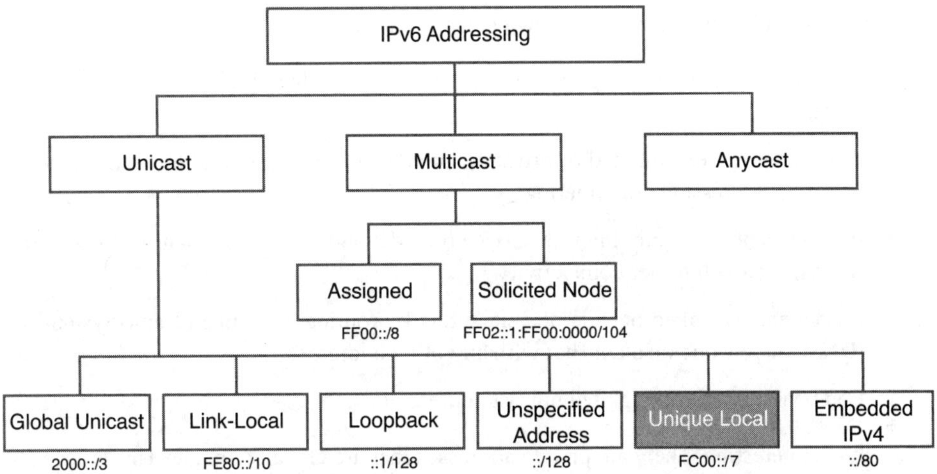

Figure 4-26 *Unique Local Address*

Unique local addresses (ULA) are defined in RFC 4193, Unique Local IPv6 Unicast Addresses. Figure 4-27 illustrates the format of a unique local unicast address.

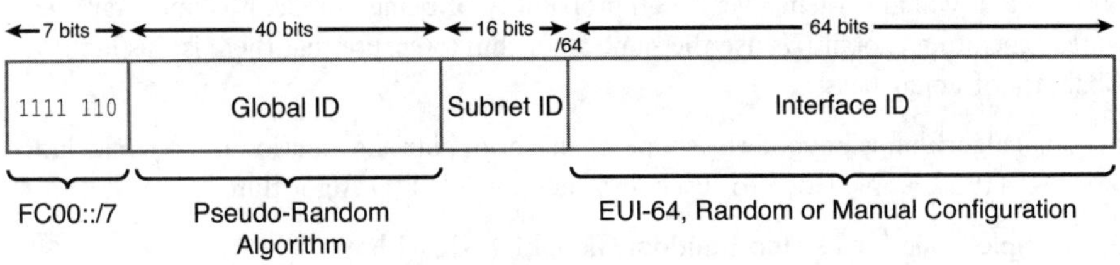

Figure 4-27 *Unique Local Unicast Address*

Unique local addresses have the prefix FC00::/7, which results in the range of addresses from FC00::/7 to FDFF::/7, as shown in Table 4-10.

Table 4-10 *Range of Unique Local Unicast Addresses*

Unique Local Unicast Address (Hexadecimal)	Range of First Hextet	Range of First Hextet in Binary
FC00::/7	FC00	**1111 110**0 0000 0000
	FDFF	**1111 110**1 1111 1111

Unique local addresses and are also known as *local IPv6 addresses*. These addresses are expected to be globally unique but should not be routable in the global Internet. They are to be used in a more limited area such as within a site or routed between a limited number of sites.

Unique local addresses have the following characteristics:

- Possess a globally unique prefix or at least have a very high probability of being unique.
- Allow sites to be combined or privately interconnected without address conflicts or requiring addressing renumbering.
- Are independent of any Internet service provider and can be used within a site without having any Internet connectivity.
- If accidentally leaked outside of a site either by routing or Domain Name System (DNS), there won't be a conflict with any other addresses.
- Can be used just like a global unicast address.

So, this is interesting. There are private addresses that are globally unique. This is accomplished so that there won't be any conflicts when combining two sites using ULAs or just in case they get leaked out into the Internet. The trick is that the global IDs must somehow be unique without being administered by a central authority. RFC 4193 defines a process where locally assigned Global IDs can be generated using a pseudorandom algorithm that will give them a very high probability of being unique. It is important that all sites generating Global IDs use the same algorithm to ensure that there is this high probability of uniqueness.

The actual algorithm is beyond the scope of this book, but information has been included from RFC 4193, Sample Code for Pseudo-Random Global ID Algorithm:

3.2.2. Sample Code for Pseudo-Random Global ID Algorithm

> The algorithm described below is intended to be used for locally assigned Global IDs. In each case the resulting global ID will be used in the appropriate prefix as defined in Section 3.2.
>
> 1. Obtain the current time of day in 64-bit NTP format [NTP].
>
> 2. Obtain an EUI-64 identifier from the system running this algorithm. If an EUI-64 does not exist, one can be created from a 48-bit MAC address as specified in

[ADDARCH]. If an EUI-64 cannot be obtained or created, a suitably unique identifier, local to the node, should be used (e.g., system serial number).

3. Concatenate the time of day with the system-specific identifier in order to create a key.

4. Compute an SHA-1 digest on the key as specified in [FIPS, SHA1]; the resulting value is 160 bits.

5. Use the least significant 40 bits as the Global ID.

6. Concatenate FC00::/7, the L bit set to 1, and the 40-bit Global ID to create a Local IPv6 address prefix.

This algorithm will result in a Global ID that is reasonably unique and can be used to create a locally assigned local IPv6 address prefix. The following website can be used to generate and register your ULA space: www.sixxs.net/tools/grh/ula.

IPv4 Embedded Address

The final unicast address types are IPv4 embedded addresses, as illustrated in Figure 4-28. IPv4 embedded addresses are IPv6 addresses used to help the transition from IPv4 to IPv6. IPv4 embedded addresses carry an IPv4 address in the low-order 32 bits. These addresses are used to represent an IPv4 address inside an IPv6 address. RFC 4291 defines two types of IPv4 embedded addresses:

- IPv4-compatible IPv6 addresses (deprecated)
- IPv4-mapped IPv6 addresses

Special techniques such as tunnels are used to provide communications between islands of IPv6 devices over an IPv4-only network. To support this compatibility, IPv4 addresses can be embedded within an IPv6 address. This is easy to do because a 128-bit IPv6 address has plenty of room for the 32-bit IPv4 address. Basically, IPv6 just puts it at the end of the address and pads the front end. IPv4 and IPv6 packets are not compatible. Features such as NAT-PT and NAT64 are required to translate between the two address families. This is discussed later in Chapter 10.

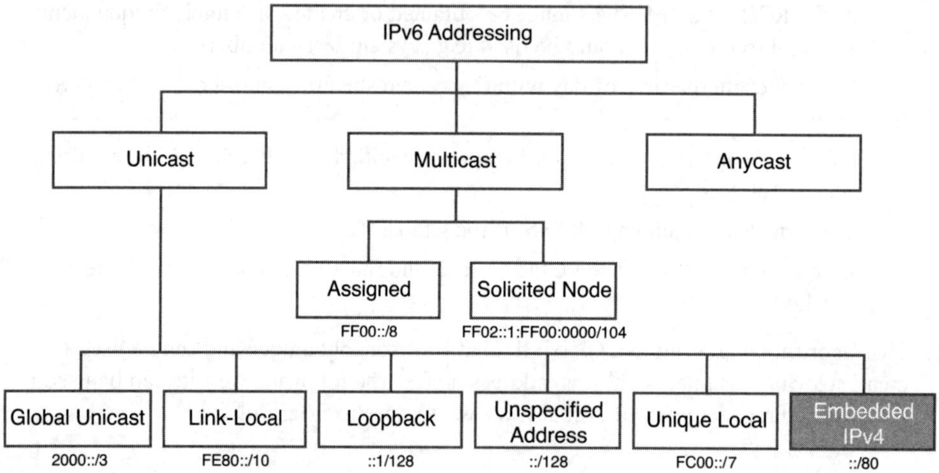

Figure 4-28 *IPv4 Embedded Address*

IPv4-Compatible IPv6 Addresses

IPv4-compatible IPv6 addresses are used by dual-stack devices that support both IPv4 and IPv6. As shown in Figure 4-29, the first 96 bits are set to all 0s, which include a 16-bit segment, used to differentiate it from an *IPv4-mapped IPv6 address*. The last 32 bits is the IPv4 address are represented in dotted-decimal notation. So, the first 96 bits are represented in hexadecimal with last 32 bits containing the IPv4 address in dotted-decimal notation.

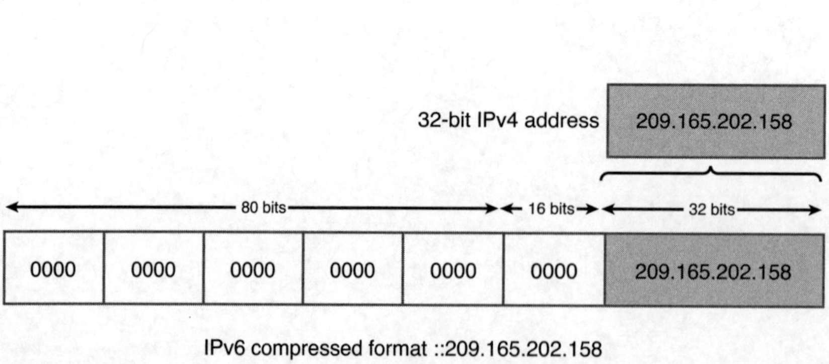

Figure 4-29 *IPv4-Compatible IPv6 Address (Deprecated)*

Table 4-11 shows the various formats for representing an IPv4-compatible IPv6 address using the IPv4 address 209.165.202.158.

Table 4-11 *IPv4-Compatible IPv6 Address Representations*

Representation	IPv6 Loopback Address
Preferred	0000:0000:0000:0000:0000:0000:0000:209.165.202.158
No leading 0s	0:0:0:0:0:0:209.165.202.158
Compressed	::209.165.202.158

The IPv4 address used in the "IPv4-compatible IPv6 address" must be a globally unique IPv4 unicast address. The "IPv4-compatible IPv6 address" was rarely used and is now deprecated. Current IPv6 transition mechanisms no longer use this address type.

IPv4-Mapped IPv6 Addresses

IPv4-mapped IPv6 addresses are similar to IPv4-compatible IPv6 addresses. IPv4-mapped IPv6 addresses are used to represent addresses of IPv4-only devices. An IPv6 device can use this address to send a packet to an IPv4-only device.

An IPv4-mapped IPv6 address is almost identical to an IPv4-compatible IPv6 address, except the 16-bit segment preceding the 32-bit IPv4 address is all 1s. Figure 4-30 illustrates the structure of an IPv4-mapped IPv6 address. The IPv4 address does not have to be globally unique.

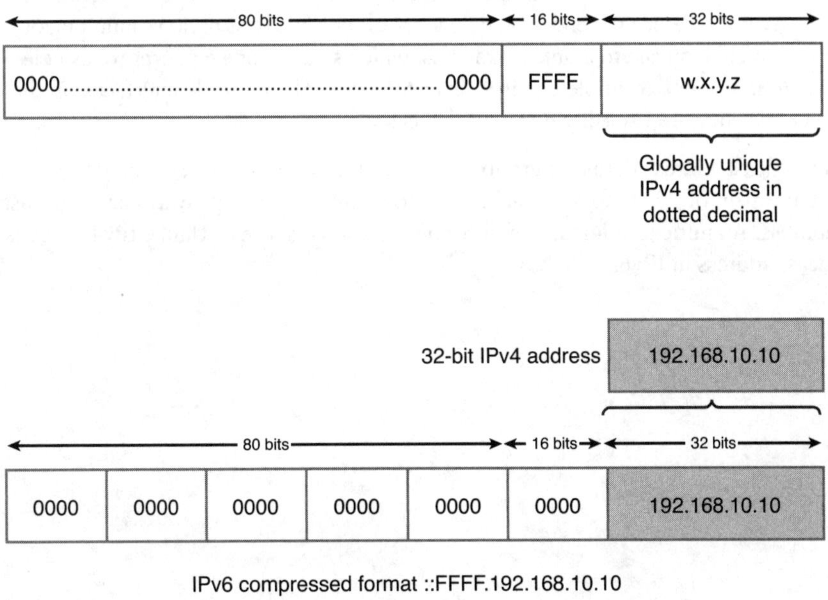

Figure 4-30 *IPv4-Mapped IPv6 Address*

Table 4-12 shows the various formats for representing an IPv4-mapped IPv6 address using the IPv4 address 192.168.10.10.

Table 4-12 *IPv4-Mapped IPv6 Address Representations*

Representation	IPv6 Loopback Address
Preferred	0000:0000:0000:0000:0000:0000:FFFF:192.168.10.10
No leading 0s	0:0:0:0:0:FFFF:192.168.10.10
Compressed	::FFFF:192.168.10.10

IPv4-compatible IPv6 addresses and IPv4-mapped IPv6 addresses are used by transition mechanisms on hosts and routers to create IPv4 tunnels that deliver IPv6 packets over IPv4 networks. These addresses and the transition mechanisms that use them will be discussed in more detail in Chapter 10.

Note Chapter 10 discusses transition and coexistence strategies, along with more common tunneling mechanisms such as 6to4 and ISATAP.

Multicast

The next address type is a multicast address, as illustrated in Figure 4-31. Multicast is a technique used for a device to send a single packet to multiple destinations simultaneously (one-to-many) in contrast to a unicast address, which sends a single packet to a single destination (one-to-one). Multiple destinations can actually be multiple interfaces on the same device but they are typically different devices.

An IPv6 multicast address defines a group of devices known as a *multicast group*. It is the IPv4 equivalent of 224.0.0.0/4. A packet sent to a multicast group always has a unicast source address. A multicast address can never be the source address. Unlike IPv4, there is no broadcast address in IPv6.

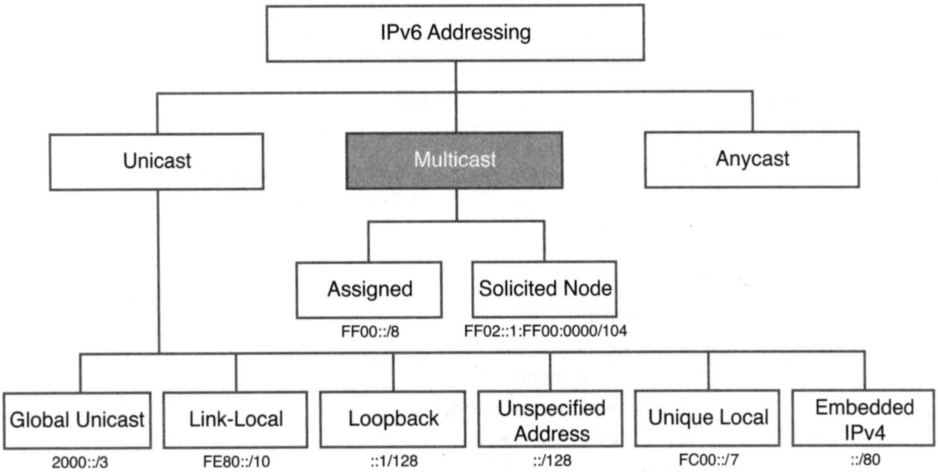

Figure 4-31 *Multicast Addresses*

IPv6 multicast addresses have the prefix FF00::/8. Table 4-13 shows the various representations.

Table 4-13 *IPv6 Multicast Address Representations*

Representation	IPv6 Loopback Address
Preferred	FF00:0000:0000:0000:0000:0000:0000:0000/8
No leading 0s	FF00:0:0:0:0:0:0:0/8
Compressed	FF00::/8

Figure 4-32 shows the structure of an IPv6 multicast address. The first 8 bits are 1 bits (FF), followed by a 4-bit Flag and a 4-bit Scope. The next 112 bits represent the Group ID.

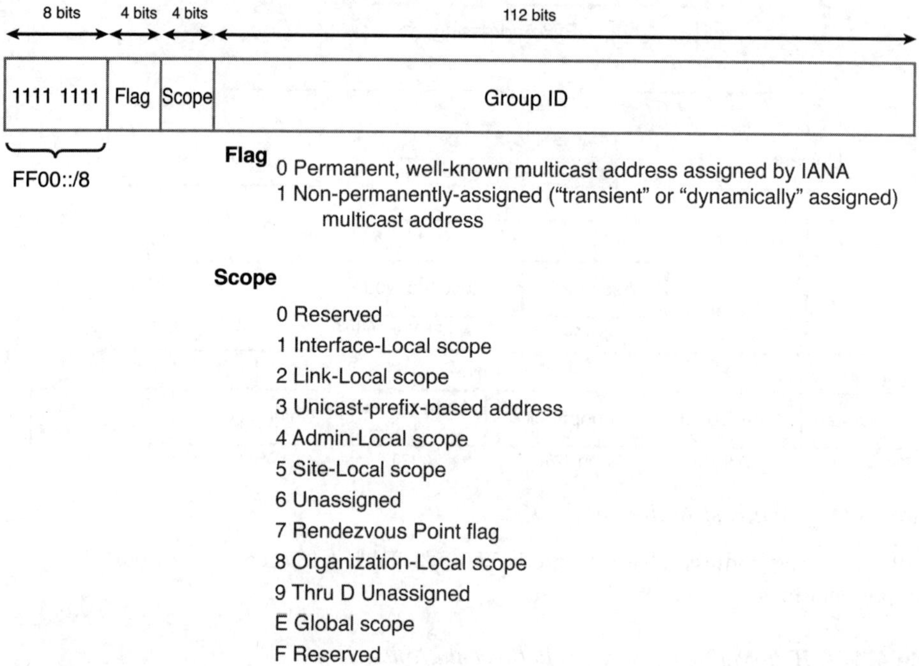

Figure 4-32 *IPv6 Multicast Address*

The Flag field indicates the type of multicast address. The two types of multicast addresses are

- **Permanent (0):** These are well-known multicast addresses assigned by the Internet Assigned Numbers Authority (IANA), which are discussed in the next section.
- **Nonpermanent (1):** These are "transient" or "dynamically" assigned multicast addresses.

Scope is a 4-bit field used to define the range of the multicast packet. The possible values for scope are

- **0:** Reserved
- **1:** Interface-Local scope
- **2:** Link-Local scope
- **3:** Unicast-Prefix-based address
- **4:** Admin-Local scope
- **5:** Site-Local scope
- **6:** Unassigned
- **7:** Rendezvous Point flag

- **8:** Organization-Local scope
- **9:** Unassigned
- **A:** Unassigned
- **B:** Unassigned
- **C:** Unassigned
- **D:** Unassigned
- **E:** Global scope
- **F:** Reserved

RFC 4007, IPv6 Scoped Address Architecture, specifies the characteristics, expected behavior, and usage of IPv6 addresses of different scopes. A more graphical representation of these scopes is illustrated in Figure 4-33. The Scope field allows devices to define the range of the multicast packet and allows routers to immediately determine how broadly to propagate it. This improves efficiency by eliminating traffic from being sent outside the intended area.

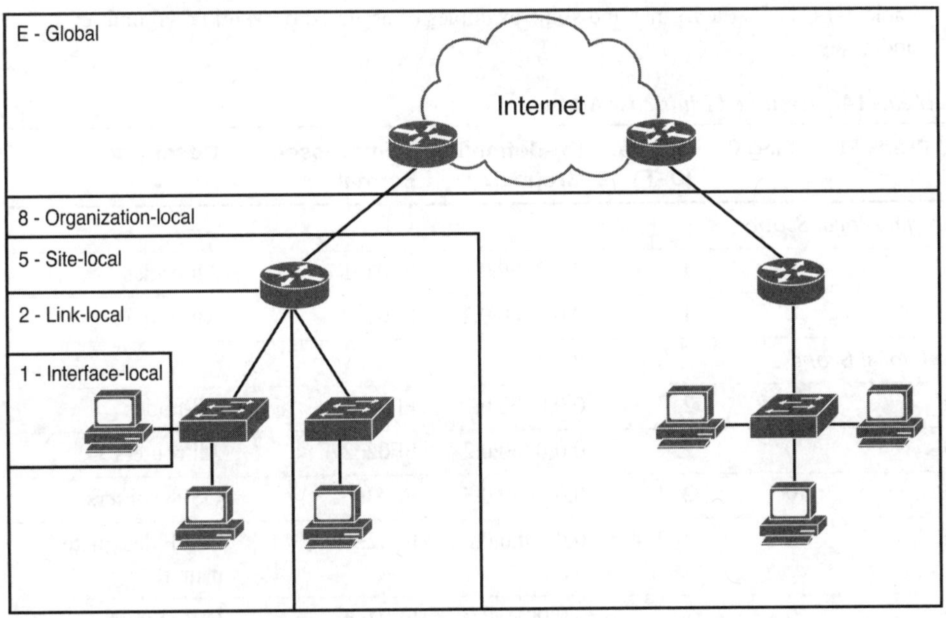

Figure 4-33 *Multicast Scope*

Assigned Multicast Addresses

RFC 2375, IPv6 Multicast Address Assignments, defines the initial assignment of IPv6 multicast addresses that have permanently assigned Global IDs. In other words, these are reserved multicast addresses for predefined groups of devices. Assigned multicast addresses have a prefix of FF00::/8 and are shown in Figure 4-34.

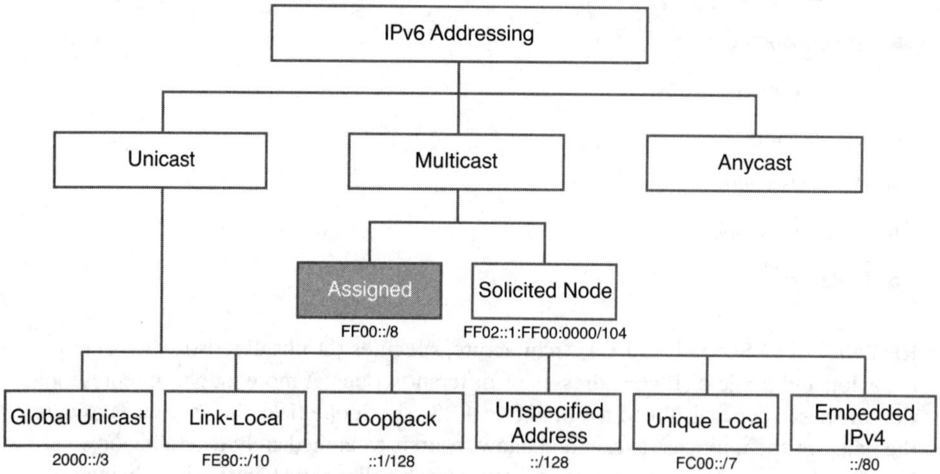

Figure 4-34 *Assigned Multicast Addresses*

Table 4-14 shows the format and some examples of assigned or well-known multicast addresses.

Table 4-14 *Assigned Multicast Addresses*

/8 Prefix FF	Flag 0	Scope (0–F)	Predefined Group ID	Compressed Format	Description
Interface-local Scope					
FF	0	1	0:0:0:0:0:0:1	FF01::1	All-nodes
FF	0	1	0:0:0:0:0:0:2	FF01::2	All-routers
Link-local Scope					
FF	0	2	0:0:0:0:0:0:1	FF02::1	All-nodes
FF	0	2	0:0:0:0:0:0:2	FF02::2	All-routers
FF	0	2	0:0:0:0:0:0:5	FF02::5	OSPF routers
FF	0	2	0:0:0:0:0:0:6	FF02::6	OSPF designated routers
FF	0	2	0:0:0:0:0:0:9	FF02::9	RIP routers
FF	0	2	0:0:0:0:0:0:A	FF02::A	EIGRP routers
FF	0	2	0:0:0:0:0:1:2	FF02::1:2	All DHCP agents
Site-local Scope					
FF	0	5	0:0:0:0:0:0:2	FF05::2	All-routers
FF	0	5	0:0:0:0:0:1:3	FF05::1:3	All DHCP servers

Looking at Table 4-14, notice that the same predefined Group ID can have various scopes or ranges. Depending upon the scope, a packet sent to the all-routers Group ID of 0:0:0:0:0:0:2 can be confined to a single link (FF02::2) or for an entire site (FF05::2).

Assigned multicast addresses are used in context with specific protocols such as Neighbor Discovery Protocol and EIGRP for IPv6, which are examined in more detail in the following chapters. We can examine which multicast groups Router R1 is a member of by using the **show ipv6 interface fastethernet 0/0** command. Example 4-14 shows that the R1's Fast Ethernet 0/0 interface is a member of four multicast groups. Router R1 will listen for and process any packets with a destination address of these assigned multicast addresses:

- **FF02::1:** All-nodes multicast group for this link.
- **FF02::2:** All-routers multicast group for this link.
- **FF02::1:FF00:1:** This is the solicited-node multicast address for R1's global unicast address on this interface. The next section discusses solicited-node multicast addresses.
- **FF02::1:FFE9:D480:** This is the solicited-node multicast address for R1's link-local address on this interface.

Example 4-14 *R1 Multicast Groups*

```
R1# show ipv6 interface fastethernet 0/0
FastEthernet0/0 is up, line protocol is up
  IPv6 is enabled, link-local address is FE80::203:6BFF:FEE9:D480
  Global unicast address(es):
    2001:DB8:AAAA:1::1, subnet is 2001:DB8:AAAA:1::/64
  Joined group address(es):   ! Multicast Groups
    FF02::1                   ! All-nodes on this link
    FF02::2                   ! All-routers on this link
    FF02::1:FF00:1            ! Solicited-node multicast address
                              ! for Global Unicast Address
    FF02::1:FFE9:D480         ! Solicited-node multicast address for
                              ! Link-local Address
<output omitted for brevity>
```

Note It is easy to confuse link-local unicast addresses with multicast addresses with link-local scope. A link-local unicast address identifies a device or interface, which is unique only on that link. An IPv6 packet with a destination address of a link-local unicast address is intended for a *single device on that link.* An IPv6 packet with a destination address containing a multicast address with link-local scope is intended for *one or more devices on that link.*

Solicited-Node Multicast Addresses

In addition to every unicast address assigned to an interface, a device will also have a special multicast address known as a solicited-node multicast address, as shown in Figure 4-35. These multicast addresses are automatically created using a special mapping of the device's unicast address with the solicited-node multicast prefix FF02:0:0:0:0:1:FF00::/104.

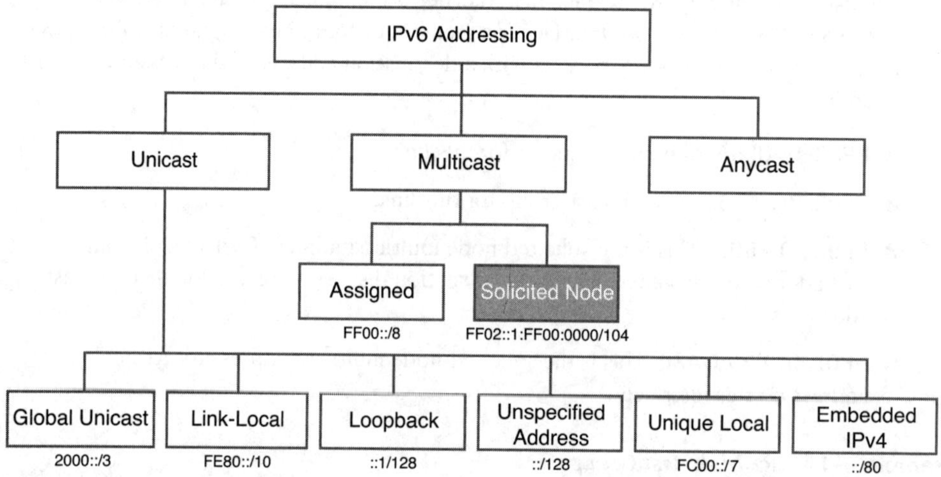

Figure 4-35 *Solicited-Node Multicast Addresses*

You might recall that unlike IPv4, IPv6 does not have a broadcast address. IPv4's ARP process sends out a Layer 2 broadcast to all devices on the network when it is only trying to reach a single device—the device with the target IPv4 address. Although an all-nodes multicast address is essentially the same thing in IPv6, the intent is to make IPv6 a more efficient protocol. Why make every device on the network process the contents of an ARP request when there is only a single device that needs to reply?

IPv6's solicited-node multicast address provides a more efficient solution. Solicited-node multicast addresses can reach every device on the link but without most of those devices having to process the contents of the packet. Illustrated in Figure 4-36, solicited-node multicast addresses are used for two essential IPv6 mechanisms, both part of Neighbor Discovery Protocol (NDP):

- **Address resolution:** Equivalent to ARP in IPv4, an IPv6 device sends a Neighbor Solicitation message to a solicited-node multicast address to learn the link layer (typically Ethernet) address of a device on the same link. The device recognizes the IPv6 address of the destination on that link but needs to know its data-link (Ethernet) address.
- **Duplicate Address Detection (DAD):** DAD allows a device to verify that its unicast (or anycast) address, created using Stateless Address Autoconfiguration (SLAAC), is unique on the link. A Neighbor Solicitation message is sent to the device's own solicited-node multicast address to determine whether anyone else has this same address.

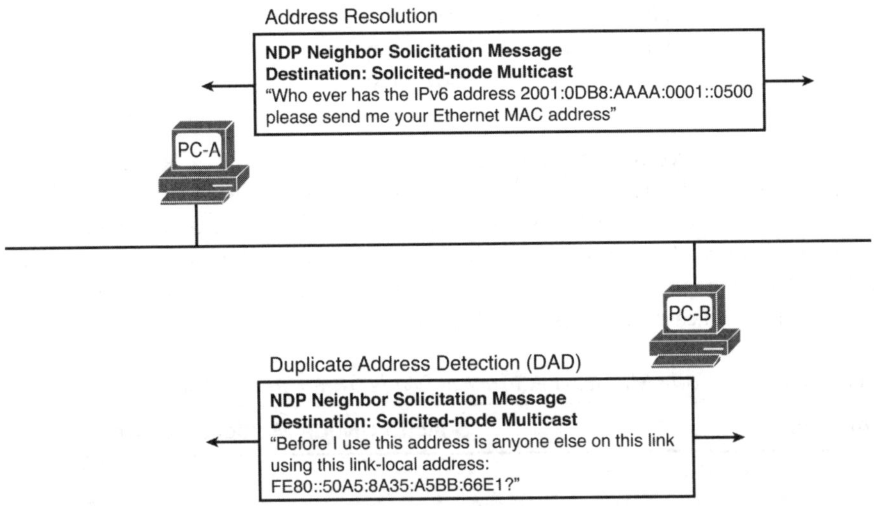

Figure 4-36 *Use of Solicited-Node Multicasts with Address Resolution and DAD*

ND, DAD, and address resolution are discussed in detail in Chapter 5.

As shown in Table 4-15, an IPv6 solicited-node multicast address has the prefix FF02:0:0:0:0:1:FF00::/104. Figure 4-37 shows the structure of a solicited-node multicast address.

Table 4-15 *IPv6 Solicited-Node Multicast Address Representations*

Representation	IPv6 Loopback Address
Preferred	FF02:0000:0000:0000:0000:0001:FF00::/104
Compressed	FF02:0:0:0:0:1:FF00::/104

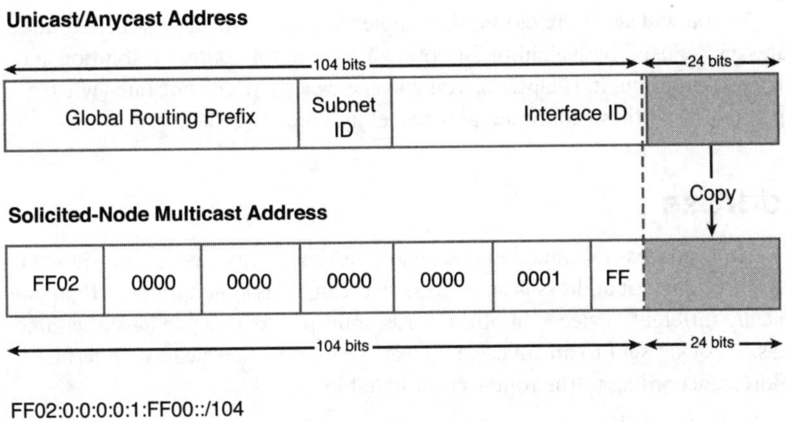

Figure 4-37 *Solicited-Node Multicast Address*

As mentioned earlier, solicited-node multicast addresses are automatically created for every unicast address on a device. The solicited-node multicast prefix FF02:0:0:0:0:1:FF00::/104 is appended to the low-order 24 bits of the unicast address, as illustrated in Figure 4-37.

Looking at the **show ipv6 interface** output in Example 4-14, notice that Router R1 has two solicited-node multicast addresses: one for its global unicast address and one for its link-local unicast address. Table 4-16 shows how both of these solicited-node multicast addresses were created from its respective unicast addresses with the low-order 24 bits in bold. Table 4-16 also includes the solicited-node multicast addresses for the global unicast and link-local unicast addresses of PC1 and PC2.

Table 4-16 *Solicited-Node Multicast Addresses Made from Unicast Addresses*

Unicast Address		Solicited-Node Multicast Address
Router R1		
Global	2001:DB8:AAAA:1::**1**	FF02::1:FF00:**1**
Link-local	FE80::203:6BFF:FE**E9:D480**	FF02::1:FF**E9:D480**
PC1		
Global	2001:DB8:AAAA:1::**100**	FF02::1:FF00:**100**
Link-local	FE80::50A5:8A35:A5**BB:66E1**	FF02::1:FF**BB:66E1**
PC2		
Global	2001:DB8:AAAA:1::**200**	FF02::1:FF00:**200**
Link-local	FE80::1C00:3EA4:74**FF:A8CF**	FF02::1:FF**FF:A8CF**

What this means is that these devices will not only process packets with the destination address of its unicast addresses but also those with their respective solicited-node multicast addresses. As you will see more closely in Chapter 5, these respective solicited-node multicast addresses are used by Neighbor Discovery Protocol for address resolution and Duplicate Address Detection. In Chapter 5, you will see exactly what transpires when a host boots up and how all these addresses and processes come together.

Anycast Address

The last type of IPv6 address examined in this chapter is the anycast address, as shown in Figure 4-38. An IPv6 anycast address is an address that can be assigned to more than one interface (typically different devices). In other words, multiple devices can have the same anycast address. A packet sent to an anycast address is routed to the "nearest" interface having that address, according to the router's routing table.

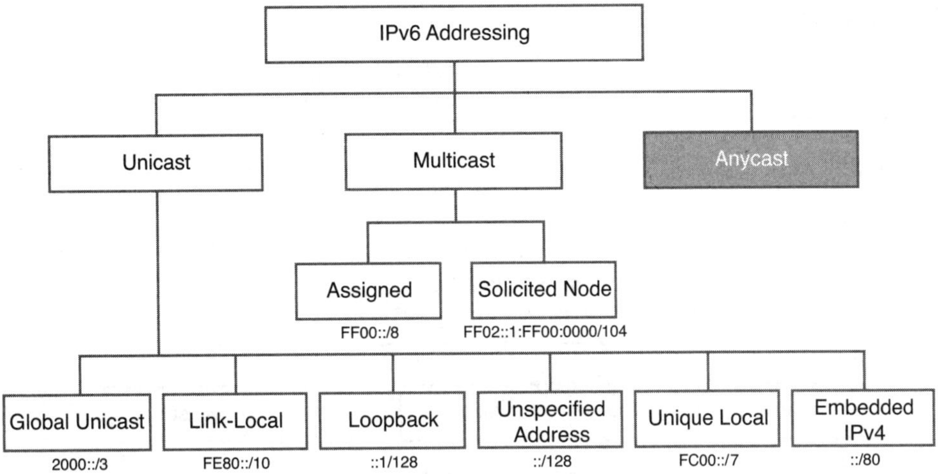

Figure 4-38 *Anycast Addresses*

Anycast addresses are available for both IPv4 and IPv6, initially defined in RFC 1546, Host Anycasting Service. Anycast was meant to be used for services such as DNS and HTTP but was never really implemented as designed.

There is no special prefix for an IPv6 anycast address. An IPv6 anycast address uses the same address range as global unicast addresses. Each participating device will be configured to have the same anycast address, as shown in Figure 4-39.

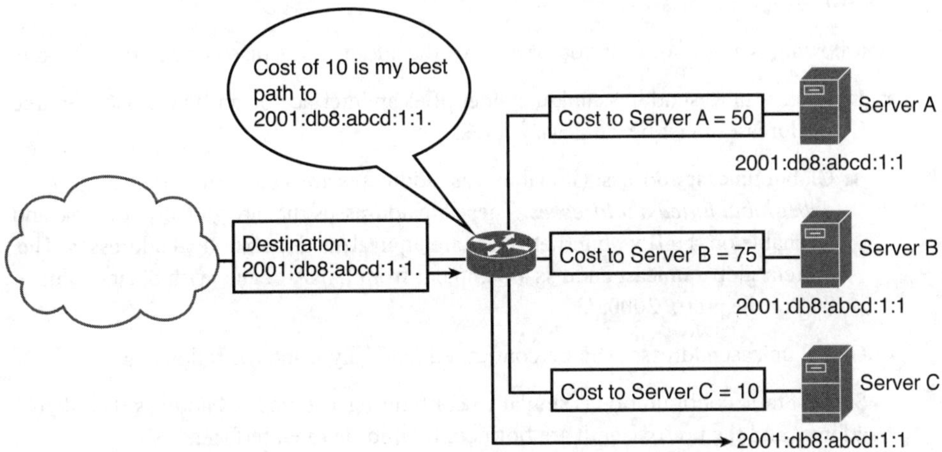

Figure 4-39 *Example of Anycast Addressing*

There are some reserved anycast address formats such as the subnet-router anycast address defined in RFC 4291 and RFC 2526. IPv6 anycast addressing is still somewhat in the experimental stage and beyond the scope of this book.

Summary

As illustrated in Figure 4-40, this chapter introduced the three types of IPv6 addresses:

- Unicast
- Multicast
- Anycast

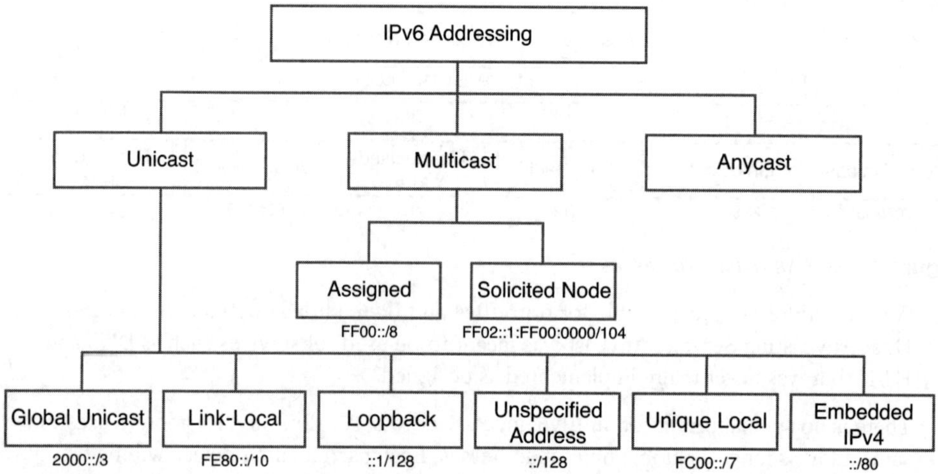

Figure 4-40 *IPv6 Address Types*

The following is a brief description of each of the addresses as discussed in this chapter:

- **Unicast:** A unicast address uniquely identifies an interface on an IPv6 device. Source IPv6 addresses must be a unicast address.
  - **Global unicast address:** Global unicast addresses are also known as an *aggregatable global unicast addresses*. These are addresses that are globally routable and reachable on the IPv6 Internet. They are equivalent to public IPv4 addresses. The current global unicast address assignment from IANA begins with binary value 001 or the prefix 2000::/3.

  Global unicast addresses can be configured manually using the following:

  Static: Static configuration is similar to configuring a static IPv4 address. The IPv6 address and the prefix length are both configured on the interface.

  EUI-64: This type of configuration allows you to configure the prefix and prefix length, while the Interface ID is created automatically. Modified EUI-64 is a concatenation of the 24-bit OUI with the U/L OUI bit *flipped*, a 16-bit value of FFFE, and the 24-bit device identifier.

  IP unnumbered: IP unnumbered is the same in IPv6 as it is with IPv4. It is a way to use the IP of different interface on the same device.

Global unicast address can be configured dynamically using the following:

Stateless Address Autoconfiguration (SLAAC): Using this method, the Interface ID is created using EUI-64 while the prefix and prefix length are determined using ND Router Advertisement messages from the router.

DHPCv6 (Stateful): DHCP for IPV6 is similar to that of DHCP for IPv4. Using the services of a DHCPv6 server, a device can automatically receive its addressing information.

- **Link-local address:** Link-local unicast addresses are unicast addresses that are confined to a single link. Their uniqueness only has to be assured on that link because these packets are not routable off the link. Link-local unicast addresses are configured either
  - Dynamically, using EUI-64 (or a random-generated Interface ID)
  - Statically, entering the link-local address manually
- **Loopback address:** A loopback address is an all-0s address except for the last bit, which is set to a 1. It is equivalent to the IPv4 loopback address 127.0.0.1.
- **Unspecified address:** An unspecified unicast address is an all-0s address. It cannot be assigned to an interface. An unspecified unicast address is used as a source address to indicate the absence of an address.
- **Unique local address:** A unique local address is similar to the RFC 1918 private address space in IPv4. Site-local addresses were defined in RFC 3513 and given the prefix range FEC0::/10 but later deprecated. Unique local addresses are expected to be globally unique but should not be routable in the global Internet. They are to be used in more limited areas such as within a site or routed between a limited number of sites.
- **IPv4 embedded addresses:** IPv6 addresses help the transition from IPv4 to IPv6. IPv4 embedded addresses carry an IPv4 address in the low-order 32 bits. These addresses are used to represent an IPv4 address inside an IPv6 address. Two types of IPv4 embedded addresses are
  - IPv4-compatible IPv6 addresses (deprecated)
  - IPv4-mapped IPv6 addresses

- **Multicast:** Multicast is a technique used for a device to send a single packet to multiple destinations simultaneously:
  - **Assigned or well-known multicast:** These are reserved multicast addresses for predefined groups of devices such as all-nodes and all-routers. The Scope field within the multicast address allows devices to define the range of the multicast packet and allows routers to immediately determine how broadly to propagate it. This improves efficiency by eliminating traffic from being sent outside the intended area.

- **Solicited-node:** Every unicast address assigned to an interface will also have a special multicast address known as a solicited-node multicast address. These multicast addresses are automatically created using a special mapping by prepending the solicited-node multicast prefix FF02:0:0:0:0:1:FF00::/104 to the last 24 bits of the unicast address. IPv6's solicited-node multicast address provides a way to reach every device on the link without all those devices needing to process the contents of the packet.

- **Anycast:** An IPv6 anycast address is an address that can be assigned to more than one interface (typically different devices). In other words, multiple devices can have the same anycast address. A packet sent to an anycast address is routed to the "nearest" interface having that address, according to the router's routing table.

References

RFCs:

RFC 1546, *Host Anycasting Service*, C. Partridge, BBN, IETF, www.ietf.org/rfc/rfc1546.txt, November 1993

RFC 1918, *Address Allocation for Private Internets*, Y. Rekhter, Cisco Systems, IETF, www.ietf.org/rfc/rfc1918.txt, February 1996

RFC 2373, *IP Version 6 Addressing Architecture*, R. Hinden, Nokia, IETF, www.ietf.org/rfc/rfc2373.txt, July 1998

RFC 2374, *An IPv6 Aggregatable Global Unicast Address Format*, R. Hinden, Nokia, IETF, www.ietf.org/rfc/rfc2374.txt, July 1998

RFC 2375, *IPv6 Multicast Address Assignments*, R. Hinden, Ipsilon Networks, IETF, www.ietf.org/rfc/rfc2375.txt, July 1998

RFC 3306, *Unicast-Prefix-Based IPv6 Multicast Addresses*, B. Haberman, Consultant, IETF, www.ietf.org/rfc/rfc3306.txt, August 2002

RFC 3956, *Embedding the Rendezvous Point (RP) Address in an IPv6 Multicast Address*, P. Savola, CSC/FUNET, IETF, www.ietf.org/rfc/rfc3956.txt, November 2004

RFC 3315, *Dynamic Host Configuration Protocol for IPv6 (DHCPv6)*, R. Droms, Cisco Systems, IETF, www.ietf.org/rfc/rfc3315.txt, July 2003

RFC 3513, *Internet Protocol Version 6 (IPv6) Addressing Architecture*, R. Hinden, Nokia, IETF, www.ietf.org/rfc/rfc3513.txt, April 2003

RFC 3484, *Default Address Selection for Internet Protocol version 6 (IPv6)*, R. Draves, Microsoft Research, IETF, www.ietf.org/rfc/rfc3484.txt, February 2003

RFC 3587, *IPv6 Global Unicast Address Format*, R. Hinden, Nokia, IETF, www.ietf.org/rfc/rfc3587.txt, August 2003

RFC 3972, *Cryptographically Generated Addresses (CGA)*, T. Aura, Microsoft Research, www.ietf.org/rfc/rfc3972.txt, March 2005

RFC 4007, *IPv6 Scoped Address Architecture*, S. Deering, Cisco Systems, IETF, www.ietf.org/rfc/rfc4007.txt, March 2005

RFC 4193, *Unique Local IPv6 Unicast Addresses*, R. Hinden, Nokia, IETF, www.ietf.org/rfc/rfc4193.txt, October 2005

RFC 4291, *IP Version 6 Addressing Architecture*, R. Hinden, Nokia, IETF, www.ietf.org/rfc/rfc4291.txt, February 2006

RFC 4861, *Neighbor Discovery for IP version 6 (IPv6)*, Y. Narten, IMB, IETF, www.ietf.org/rfc/rfc4861.txt, September 2007

RFC 4862, *IPv6 Stateless Address Autoconfiguration*, S. Thomon, Cisco Systems, IETF, www.ietf.org/rfc/rfc4862.txt, September 2007

Websites:

Internet Protocol Version 6 Address Space: www.iana.org/assignments/ipv6-address-space/ipv6-address-space.txt

IPv6 Global Unicast Address Assignments: www.iana.org/assignments/ipv6-unicast-address-assignments/ipv6-unicast-address-assignments.xml

Chapter 5

ICMPv6 and Neighbor Discovery Protocol

If you are familiar with Internet Control Message Protocol (ICMP) for IPv4, you will find ICMPv6 very similar; however, ICMPv6 is more than just ICMP for IPv6. ICMPv6 is a more robust protocol, containing new features and improving upon similar functionality found in ICMPv4.

ICMP is one of the core protocols of the TCP/IP suite of protocols. It is employed by operating systems to send messages between devices. The types of messages can be either informational and/or error messages such as an Echo Request for a **ping** command or informing the sender that the router was unable to forward the packet. ICMP is used with applications such a ping and traceroute to test network connectivity between two devices.

ICMPv6 is described in RFC 4443, Internet Control Message Protocol (ICMPv6) for the Internet Protocol Version 6 (IPv6) Specification. ICMPv6 is much more robust than ICMPv4, containing new functionality and improvements.

This chapter explores the general message format for ICMPv6 using the similar Type and Code fields found in ICMPv4. It examines two types of ICMPv6 messages, error messages and informational messages.

The ICMPv6 error messages discussed are

- Destination Unreachable
- Packet Too Big
- Time Exceeded
- Parameter Problem

The following ICMPv6 informational messages used by the **ping** command are also discussed:

- Echo Request
- Echo Reply

This is followed by an explanation of the following ICMPv6 informational messages used for Multicast Listener Discovery (RFC 2710 and RFC 3810):

- Multicast Listener Query
- Multicast Listener Report
- Multicast Listener Done

The chapter concludes with a discussion of ICMPv6 informational messages with coverage messages used by Neighbor Discovery (RFC 4861):

- Router Solicitation message
- Router Advertisement message
- Neighbor Solicitation message
- Neighbor Advertisement message
- Redirect message

Topology and Wireshark will be implemented for a closer look at many of these messages. In the Neighbor Discovery section, address resolution (similar to ARP in IPv4), Duplicate Address Detection (DAD), and Neighbor Unreachability Detection (NUD) are covered.

General Message Format

The general format of an ICMPv6 message is similar to that of ICMPv4. As shown in Figure 5-1, an IPv6 header with a Next Header value of 58 precedes every ICMPv6 message. (In IPv4, the Protocol field is set to 1 to indicate an ICMPv4 message.) The preceding header does not have to be the main IPv6 header. It could also be one of the IPv6 extension headers that were discussed in Chapter 3, "IPv6 Addressing."

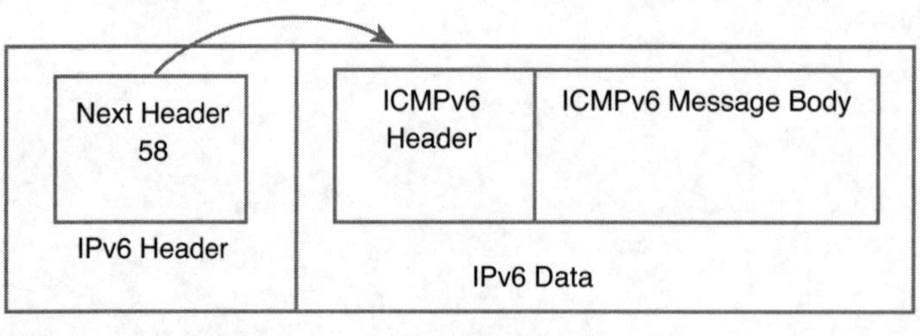

Figure 5-1 *ICMPv6 Next Header Value 58*

All ICMPv6 messages have the same general format, as shown in Figure 5-2.

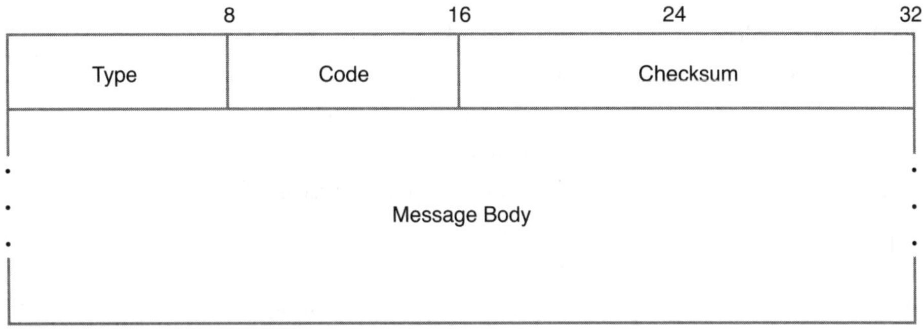

Figure 5-2 *ICMPv6 General Message Format*

The three fields in the message are as follows:

- **Type (8 bits):** Indicates the type of ICMPv6 message, such as Echo Request, Destination Unreachable, or Packet Too Big.
- **Code (8 bits):** Provides more granularity for the Type field. Its meaning will depend upon the message type. For example, if the message type is Destination Unreachable, the Code field will give the specific reason why the packet was not able to reach its destination, for example, the host could not be reached or a router did not have a route to a host's network in its routing table.
- **Checksum (16 bits):** Used to detect data corruption in the ICMPv6 message and parts of the IPv6 header.

The Type field is used to group ICMPv6 messages into two classes:

- Error messages (Type = 0 to 127)
- Informational messages (Type = 128 to 255)

Error messages are identified by a high-order bit of 0 (0xxxxxx) in the message Type field. This results in an error message having a Type value from 0 to 127. Thus, informational messages with a high-order bit of 1 will have a Type value of 128 to 255.

ICMPv6 error messages notify a device as to why a packet it sent could not be delivered, such as the hop limit was reached, decremented to 0, and then dropped by the router.

ICMP informational messages are not employed to report errors but provide information required for various testing, diagnostics, and support functions. Two common informational messages found in both ICMP for IPv4 and IPv6 are the Echo Request and Echo Reply messages used by the **ping** command.

Table 5-1 provides an overview of the different types of ICMPv6 error messages, and Table 5-2 provides an overview of the different types of ICMPv6 informational messages.

Table 5-1 *ICMPv6 Error Messages*

Type	Type Description	Code and Code Description
1	Destination Unreachable	0: No route to destination 1: Communication with destination administratively prohibited 2: Beyond scope of source address 3: Address unreachable 4: Port unreachable 5: Source address failed ingress/egress policy 6: Reject route to destination
2	Packet Too Big	0: Ignored by receiver
3	Time Exceeded	0: Hop limit exceeded in transit 1: Fragment reassembly time exceeded
4	Parameter Problem	0: Erroneous header field encountered 1: Unrecognized Next Header type encountered 2: Unrecognized IPv6 option encountered
101	Private Experimentation	—
107	Private Experimentation	—
127	Reserved for expansion of ICMPv6 error messages	—

Table 5-2 *ICMPv6 Informational Messages*

Type	Type Description	Code and Code Description
Used by the **ping** *command (RFC 4443)*		
128	Echo Request	0: Ignored by receiver
129	Echo Reply	0: Ignored by receiver
Used for Multicast Listener Discovery (RFC 2710)		
130	Multicast Listener Query	0: Ignored by receiver
131	Multicast Listener Report	0: Ignored by receiver
132	Multicast Listener Done	0: Ignored by receiver

Type	Type Description	Code and Code Description
Used by Neighbor Discovery (RFC 4861)		
133	Router Solicitation message	0: Ignored by receiver
134	Router Advertisement message	0: Ignored by receiver
135	Neighbor Solicitation message	0: Ignored by receiver
136	Neighbor Advertisement message	0: Ignored by receiver
137	Redirect message	0: Ignored by receiver

The following ICMPv6 informational messages, shown in Table 5-3, are beyond the scope of this book but are included here for completeness and to give you a better idea of how ICMPv6 is used.

Table 5-3 *ICMPv6 Informational Messages*

Type	Description
Type 138 Router Renumbering	Used for router renumbering, the mechanisms for informing a set of routers of renumbering operations they are to perform. (RFC 2894)
Type 139 Node Information Query **Type 140** Node Information Reply	Requests an IPv6 node to supply certain network information, such as its host name or fully qualified domain name. (RFC 4620)
Type 141 Inverse Neighbor Discovery Solicitation message **Type 142** Inverse Neighbor Discovery Advertisement message	Allows a node to determine and advertise an IPv6 address corresponding to a given link layer address similar to IPv4 Inverse ARP used with Frame Relay. (RFC 3122)
Type 143 Version 2 Multicast Listener Report message	MLDv2 adds the ability for a node to report interest in listening to packets with a particular multicast address only from specific source addresses or from all sources except for specific source addresses. (RFC 3810)

Type	Description
Type 144 ICMP Home Agent Address Discovery Request message **Type 145** ICMP Home Agent Address Discovery Reply message **Type 146 ICMP** Mobile Prefix Solicitation message format **Type 147** ICMP Mobile Prefix Advertisement message format	Supports mobile IPv6. (RFC 3775)
Type 148 Certification Path Solicitation message format **Type 149** Certification Path Advertisement message format	Provides security mechanisms for Neighbor Discovery Protocol.
Type 151 Advertisement Packet format **Type 152** Solicitation Packet format **Type 153** Termination Packet format	Allows the discovery of multicast routers. (RFC 4286)
Type 200 **Type 201**	Used for private experimentation. (RFC 4443)
Type 255	Reserved for expansion of ICMPv6 informational messages. (RFC 4443)

ICMP Error Messages

Layer 3 devices, such as hosts and routers, use ICMPv6 error messages to notify the sender as to why a packet could not be delivered. As shown in Table 5-1, there are four types of error messages:

- Destination Unreachable
- Packet Too Big

- Time Exceeded
- Parameter Problem

> **Note** An ICMPv6 error message must never be sent as a result of a previous ICMPv6 error message because this could lead to confusion and a never-ending exchange of error messages.

Destination Unreachable

An ICMPv6 Destination Unreachable message is sent when a packet cannot be delivered to its destination for reasons other than congestion. Instead of having a source just resend packets without any idea why they were not received, these feedback messages are used to help provide some useful information to the sender about the reason why. A router or a firewall usually generates these Destination Unreachable messages.

> **Note** It can be argued that a firewall or any security device should not send destination unreachable messages.

Figure 5-3 shows the format of a Destination Unreachable message. Notice that the Type field is set to 1.

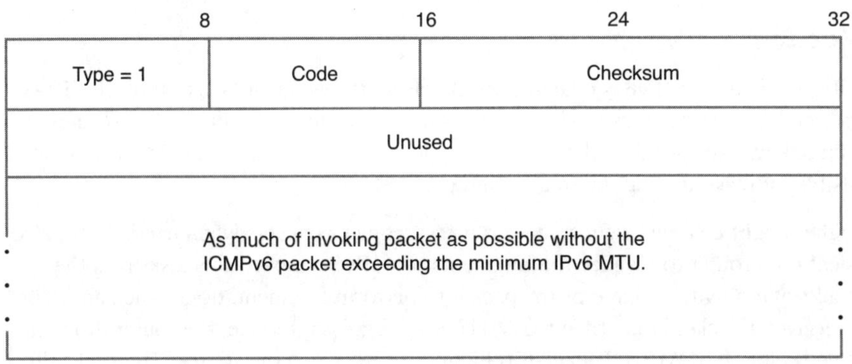

Figure 5-3 *ICMPv6 Destination Unreachable Message*

There are a several reasons why the destination might be unreachable. The Code field is used to provide more detailed information about why the packet was not delivered. There are seven codes:

- **Code = 0, No route to destination:** The packet could not be delivered because the router did not have a route to this destination. This can only occur if the router does not have a default route in its routing table. This message is equivalent to the Network Unreachable message in ICMPv4.

- **Code = 1, Communications with destination administratively prohibited:** The packet was blocked because of an access control list or other packet filtering.
- **Code = 2, Beyond scope of source address:** This error message is generated when the source address is a link-local address and the destination address is a global unicast address.
- **Code = 3, Address unreachable:** This error message indicates that there was a problem delivering the packet because the host specified in the destination address could not be reached. This can occur if the destination address could not be resolved to its corresponding data-link address (MAC address on LANs) or the destination address is incorrect. This is equivalent to the ICMPv4 Host Unreachable message.
- **Code = 4, Port unreachable:** This error message occurs because the destination port specified in the TCP or UDP header does not exist or the destination is not listening on that port. For example, if a packet is sent with a TCP destination port 80 but the receiving host is not running the HTTP web service, a Port Unreachable message will be transmitted.
- **Code = 5, Source address failed ingress/egress policy:** This error message indicates that the packet with this source address is blocked because of an access control list or other packet filtering. Code 5 is a subset of Code 1.
- **Code = 6, Reject route to destination:** This error message will occur when packets with a specific prefix are blocked by an access control list or other packet filtering. Code 6 is a subset of Code 1.

Packet Too Big

A significant change to IPv6 is related to packet fragmentation and reassembly. In IPv4, routers could fragment a packet when the maximum transmission unit (MTU) of the outgoing link was smaller than the size of the packet. The destination device would be responsible for reassembling the fragmented packets.

Although it might be convenient to have routers fragment packets when needed, it is also inefficient for a router to manage the fragmentation. IPv6 removed this task from the router, allowing only the source of the packet to perform fragmentation. When an IPv6 router receives a packet larger than the MTU of the egress interface, the router drops the packet and sends an ICMPv6 Packet Too Big message back to the source. The Packet Too Big message includes the MTU size of the link in bytes so that the source can change the size of the packet for retransmission.

Note The router can fragment an IPv6 packet if it is the source of the packet.

As shown in Figure 5-4, an ICMPv6 Packet Too Big message has the Type set to 2 and the Code equal to 0. The MTU is the maximum transmission unit of the next-hop link.

This ICMPv6 error message is also used as part of Path MTU Discovery.

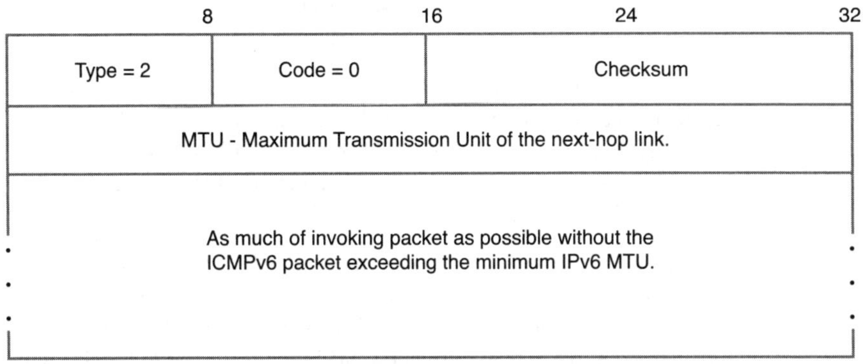

Figure 5-4 *ICMPv6 Packet Too Big Message*

Path MTU Discovery

Path MTU Discovery is defined in RFC 1981, Path MTU Discovery for IP version 6. When a device has a large number of packets to transmit, it is preferable that these packets are as large as possible, allowing fewer packets. This requires the device to know the minimum link MTU (the smallest MTU) of all the links in the path to the destination. This allows the sender to transmit the largest packet size possible without the risk of a router dropping the packet along the path because the MTU of its outgoing link was too small. The size of this packet is referred to as the Path MTU (PMTU).

> **Note** IPv6 requires that every link in the Internet have a minimum MTU of 1280 bytes compared to 68 bytes for IPv4. This improves the ratio of payload to header length and reduces the need for fragmentation by the source.

The Path MTU Discovery process works as illustrated in Figure 5-5 and described in the steps that follow.

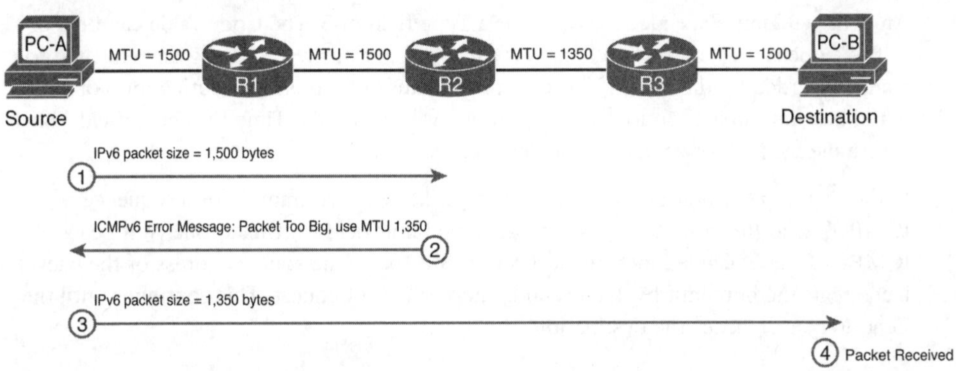

Figure 5-5 *Path MTU Discovery*

Step 1. A device assumes that the Path MTU (PMTU) size of the packet is equal to the MTU of its outgoing link to the first-hop router. In Figure 5-5, PC-A sets the PMTU to 1500 bytes, the MTU of the Ethernet link.

Step 2. If the packet size is larger than the MTU of the router's next-hop link, the packet is dropped and an ICMPv6 Packet Too Big message is sent back to the source. Included in the message is the MTU of the next-hop link. In Figure 5-5, Router R2 drops the packet and sends a Packet Too Big message back to PC-A with an MTU of 1350 bytes.

Step 3. The source device uses the information in the Packet Too Big message to reduce the packet size to match the MTU contained in the message. The source device sends further packets using this smaller MTU. PC-A in Figure 5-5 transmits further packets with the new MTU of 1350. The MTU size will never go below 1280 bytes, the minimum link MTU for IPv6.

Step 4. This process of routers sending ICMPv6 Packet Too Big messages and the source reducing its packet size continues until the packet reaches its destination. In Figure 5-5, the new MTU was sufficient for sending the packet to its destination PC-B.

Because the path from a specific source to a given destination can change, so might the PMTU. So, it is possible that source devices might have to dynamically modify the PMTU size of their packets. Devices are not required to implement Path MTU, but it is recommended in RFC 4443. Path MTU Discovery supports multicast as well as unicast destinations.

Time Exceeded

Before a router forwards an IPv6 packet, it decrements the Hop Limit field by 1. This is identical to the TTL field in IPv4 but with a name more reflective of its function. If the Hop Limit results in a 0, the packet is dropped and an ICMPv6 Time Exceeded message is sent to the source. This is an insurance mechanism in both IPv4 and IPv6 to make sure that packets don't travel endlessly throughout the networks.

An ICMPv6 Time Exceeded message has a Type field of 3. The Code value can be 0 or 1. The Code is 0 when the hop limit was exceeded in transit, eventually decremented to 0 and discarded by the router. This could be because of a possible routing loop or the initial hop limit being too low. The traceroute utility uses the Time Exceeded field to help determine the path of routers to the destination.

In the first implementation of the traceroute utility, the program sends a sequence of ICMPv6 Echo Request messages with the Hop Limit field starting at one. With each ICMPv6 Time Exceeded message it receives, it displays the source address of the packet, increments the hop limit by 1, and sends another Echo Request. This continues until the Echo Request reaches the destination.

The Cisco IOS **traceroute** command uses UDP segments with an initial destination port number of 33434 or as specified in the extended **traceroute** command. The IPv6 hop limit of the first packet is 1. As long as an ICMP Time Exceeded message is received by the source, this cycle repeats with incremental hop limits and destination port numbers. When the source receives an ICMPv6 Port Unreachable message, this indicates to the source that the destination has been reached.

Note RFC 1393, Traceroute Using an IP Option, defined a more efficient way to perform a traceroute. The source device sends a single packet to the destination, containing a special Traceroute IP option. Each router in the path recognizes the option as the test message and responds to the original source with an ICMP Traceroute message.

The Code will equal 1 when the destination device does not receive all the fragmented packets after attempting to reassemble the original message. After receiving the first fragment, instead of waiting indefinitely, a timer is set and a specific amount of time is allotted for all the fragments to reach this destination. If they do not all arrive in the appropriate time, an ICMPv6 Time Exceeded message is sent to the source.

Parameter Problem

An ICMPv6 Parameter Problem error message is generated when a device processing a packet finds a problem with a field in the main IPv6 header or an extension header. This means that the receiving device didn't understand the information in the IPv6 header and had to discard it. This occurs if the arguments in the extension header are invalid or if the extension header is unsupported by this device.

ICMP Informational Messages

Devices use ICMPv6 error messages to let the sender know why a packet could not be delivered. ICMPv6 informational messages are used to help devices discover and share information with each other. As shown in Table 5-2 and listed as follows, there are several types of informational messages:

Used by the **ping** command (RFC 4443):

- Echo Request
- Echo Reply

Used for Multicast Listener Discovery (RFC 2710 and RFC 3810):

- Multicast Listener Query
- Multicast Listener Report
- Multicast Listener Done

Used by Neighbor Discovery (RFC 4861) :

- Router Solicitation message
- Router Advertisement message
- Neighbor Solicitation message
- Neighbor Advertisement message
- Redirect message

Echo Request and Echo Reply

Echo Request and Echo Reply are two ICMP messages used by ping, a very common TCP/IP utility. Ping is commonly used to test network layer connectivity between two devices. Its name comes from active sonar terminology.

A device sends an Echo Request to prompt the destination to return an Echo Reply to verify network layer connectivity. If the sender does not receive a corresponding Echo Reply, it does not necessarily mean that the destination could not be reached. It is possible that internetwork devices in the path are discarding the Echo Requests or the Echo Replies. It is also possible that the destination itself is not accepting or responding the Echo Requests.

Figure 5-6 shows the format of Echo Request and Echo Reply messages. The structure of Echo Request and Echo Reply is identical except for the value in the Type field. An Echo Request has the Type field set to 128, whereas an Echo Reply has a Type value of 129. The Code field is always set to 0. The remaining fields are shown in Figure 5-6.

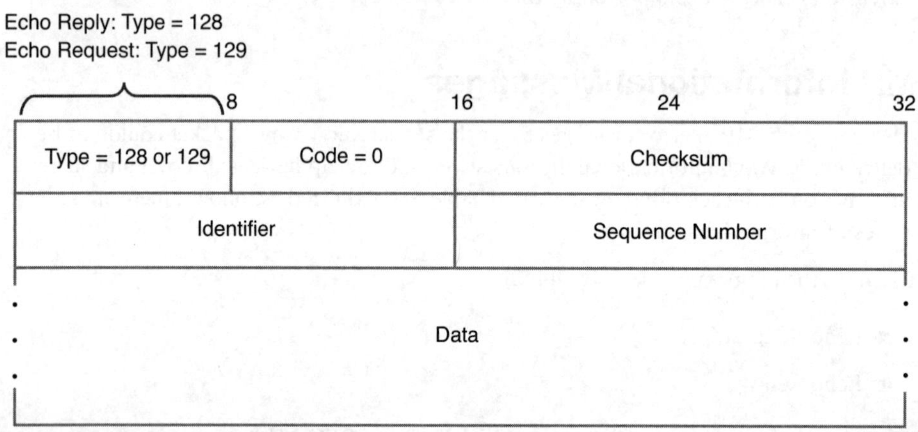

Figure 5-6 *ICMPv6 Echo Request and Echo Reply Messages*

Figure 5-7 shows the previous topology with the global unicast and link-local address of PC1 and Router R1. Using the packet analyzer Wireshark, the ICMPv6 Echo Request and Echo Reply messages are examined when pinging both a global unicast address and a link-local address.

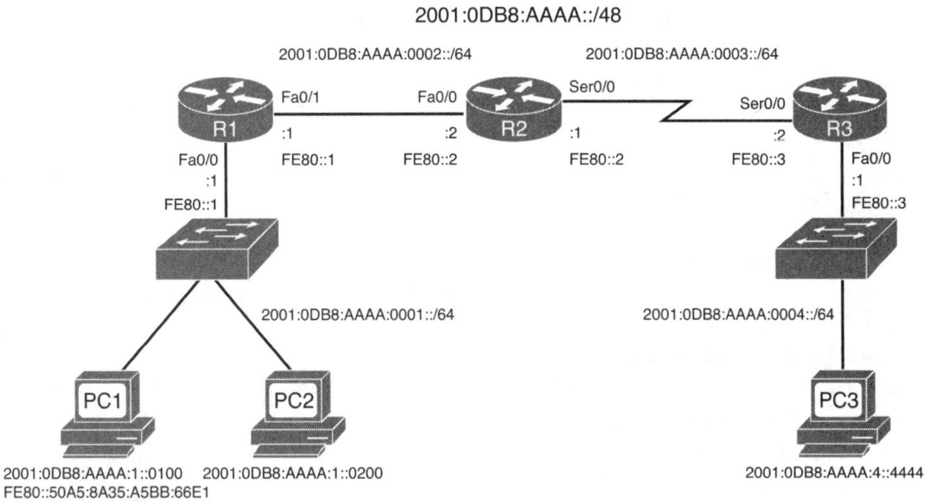

Figure 5-7 *IPv6 Topology*

Pinging a Global Unicast Address

In Example 5-1, you ping the global unicast address of Router R1 from the host, PC1. It shows the **ping** command issued from PC-1. Except for the IPv6 addresses, it looks identical to pinging an IPv4 address.

Example 5-1 *Ping Global Unicast Address from PC1 to R1*

```
PC1> ping 2001:db8:aaaa:1::1

Pinging 2001:db8:aaaa:1::1 from 2001:db8:aaaa:1:1c3f:114a:4bcb:1b9c with 32 bytes of
data:

Reply from 2001:db8:aaaa:1::1: time=1ms
Reply from 2001:db8:aaaa:1::1: time=1ms
Reply from 2001:db8:aaaa:1::1: time=1ms
Reply from 2001:db8:aaaa:1::1: time=1ms

Ping statistics for 2001:db8:aaaa:1::1:
    Packets: Sent = 4, Received = 4, Lost = 0 (0% loss),
Approximate round trip times in milli-seconds:
    Minimum = 1ms, Maximum = 1ms, Average = 1ms

PC1>
```

Example 5-2 examines the ICMPv6 Echo Request sent from PC1 to Router R1.

Example 5-2 *Echo Request from PC1 to R1*

```
Ethernet II, Src: 00:21:9b:d9:c6:44, Dst: 00:03:6b:e9:d4:80

Internet Protocol Version 6
    0110 .... = Version: 6
    .... 0000 0000 .... .... .... .... .... = Traffic class: 0x00000000
    .... .... .... 0000 0000 0000 0000 0000 = Flowlabel: 0x00000000
    Payload length: 40
    Next header: ICMPv6 (0x3a)
    Hop limit: 128
    Source: 2001:db8:aaaa:1:1c3f:114a:4bcb:1b9c
    Destination: 2001:db8:aaaa:1::1

Internet Control Message Protocol v6
    Type: 128 (Echo (ping) request)
    Code: 0 (Should always be zero)
    Checksum: 0x8f38 [correct]
    ID: 0x0001
    Sequence: 0
    Data (32 bytes)
```

Notice all the fields that were discussed previously in Chapter 3 (beginning with the IPv6 header), including the version and source and destination addresses. Because the destination address in the **ping** command was a global unicast address 2001:db8:aaaa:1::1, the source address will also be the global unicast address 2001:db8:aaaa:1:1c3f:114a:4bcb:1b9c. Example 5-3 shows similar information for the corresponding ICMPv6 Echo Reply. In both IPv6 packets, the value in the Next Header field (hexadecimal 3A, decimal 58) indicates that an ICMPv6 header follows the IPv6 header.

Example 5-3 *Echo Reply from R1 to PC1*

```
Ethernet II, Src: 00:03:6b:e9:d4:80, Dst: 00:21:9b:d9:c6:44

Internet Protocol Version 6
    0110 .... = Version: 6
    .... 0000 0000 .... .... .... .... .... = Traffic class: 0x00000000
    .... .... .... 0000 0000 0000 0000 0000 = Flowlabel: 0x00000000
    Payload length: 40
    Next header: ICMPv6 (0x3a)
    Hop limit: 64
    Source: 2001:db8:aaaa:1::1
    Destination: 2001:db8:aaaa:1:1c3f:114a:4bcb:1b9c
```

```
Internet Control Message Protocol v6
    Type: 129 (Echo (ping) reply)
    Code: 0 (Should always be zero)
    Checksum: 0x8e38 [correct]
    ID: 0x0001
    Sequence: 0
    Data (32 bytes)
```

Looking at the ICMPv6 header in both Examples 5-2 and 5-3 gives you a better understanding of these messages:

- **Type:** In the Echo Request, the Type is set to 128, and in the Echo Reply, the Type is set to 129.
- **Code:** Ignored by the receiver, the Code is always 0 for both an Echo Request and an Echo Reply.
- **Checksum:** The checksum validates the ICMPv6 header.
- **Identifier:** This field is used to help match Echo Requests with their corresponding Echo Replies. Notice that the Echo Request and the Echo Reply have the same value. This value remains constant for the entire sequence of Echo Requests and the Echo Replies that was generated by this instance of the **ping** command. In Example 5-3, the Identifier is set to 1 for the series ICMPv6 messages.
- **Sequence:** This field also helps match Echo Requests and Echo Replies, providing a little more granularity. The Echo Request is generated with a Sequence number, and its corresponding Echo Reply includes that same Sequence number. The next Echo Request increments the Sequence number by 1, and the receiver uses that same value in its returning Echo Reply. In Example 5-3, the Sequence number is 0 for both the Echo Request and the Echo Reply. The next Echo Request and Echo Reply from the same **ping** command will increment the Sequence number to 1.
- **Data:** The Echo Request adds zero or more bytes of arbitrary data. The receiving device Echo Reply copies this data into the returned Echo Request.

Pinging a Link-local Address

In Example 5-4, another **ping** command is issued, this time pinging the link-local address from Router R1 to PC1. Remember that a link-local address only has to be unique on that link and is never routed off the link.

Example 5-4 *Ping Link-local Address from R1 to PC1*

```
R1# ping fe80::50a5:8a35:a5bb:66e1
Output Interface: fastethernet 0/0
% Invalid interface. Use full interface name without spaces (e.g. Serial0/1)
R1# ping fe80::50a5:8a35:a5bb:66e1
Output Interface: fastethernet0/0
Type escape sequence to abort.
Sending 5, 100-byte ICMP Echos to FE80::50A5:8A35:A5BB:66E1, timeout is 2 seconds:
!!!!!
Success rate is 100 percent (5/5), round-trip min/avg/max = 1/2/4 ms
R1#
```

With that in mind, looking at Example 5-4, notice that you cannot ping a link-local address of PC1 without first specifying the exit interface or *output interface* of the router. As described later, destinations to link-local addresses are not included in the router's routing table, so the router doesn't know which exit interface to use. As you can see in the failure of the first **ping** command to a link-local address, Cisco IOS requires the use of the full interface name without any spaces.

Examples 5-5 and 5-6 show the Echo Request and Echo Reply using this link-local addresses.

Example 5-5 *Echo Request to Link-local Address from R1 to PC1*

```
Ethernet II, Src: 00:03:6b:e9:d4:80, Dst: 00:21:9b:d9:c6:44

Internet Protocol Version 6
    0110 .... = Version: 6
    .... 0000 0000 .... .... .... .... .... = Traffic class: 0x00000000
    .... .... .... 0000 0000 0000 0000 0000 = Flowlabel: 0x00000000
    Payload length: 60
    Next header: ICMPv6 (0x3a)
    Hop limit: 64
     Source: fe80::1
     Destination: fe80::50a5:8a35:a5bb:66e1

Internet Control Message Protocol v6
    Type: 128 (Echo (ping) request)
    Code: 0 (Should always be zero)
    Checksum: 0x0444 [correct]
    ID: 0x0a24
    Sequence: 0
    Data (52 bytes)
```

Example 5-6 *Echo Reply to Link-local Address from PC1 to R1*

```
Ethernet II, Src: 00:21:9b:d9:c6:44, Dst: 00:03:6b:e9:d4:80

Internet Protocol Version 6
    0110 .... = Version: 6
    .... 0000 0000 .... .... .... .... .... = Traffic class: 0x00000000
    .... .... .... 0000 0000 0000 0000 0000 = Flowlabel: 0x00000000
    Payload length: 60
    Next header: ICMPv6 (0x3a)
    Hop limit: 64
     Source: fe80::50a5:8a35:a5bb:66e1
     Destination: fe80::1

Internet Control Message Protocol v6
    Type: 129 (Echo (ping) reply)
    Code: 0 (Should always be zero)
    Checksum: 0x0344 [correct]
    ID: 0x0a24
    Sequence: 0
     Data (52 bytes)
```

Notice that both devices use their link-local addresses as the IPv6 source address of the packet. The remainder of the message is identical to that of the previous ICMPv6 messages. Again, link-local addresses are confined to that link. Therefore, PC1 is not able to ping the link-local address of PC3, which is on a different network or link.

Note If you ping the link-local address *from* the host, PC1, which has only a single interface, you will not have to include an exit interface.

Multicast Listener Discovery

Multicast is nothing new in IPv6. It has been available in IPv4 since 1988. Multicast addresses are used to send a single packet or more likely a single stream of packets to multiple devices simultaneously. This is much more efficient than duplicating these packets as separate unicast transmissions for each destination.

In IPv4, the management of multicast groups is accomplished by using Internet Group Management Protocol (IGMP). Hosts use IGMP to dynamically register themselves in a multicast group on a particular network. This is done by hosts sending IGMP messages to their local multicast router, informing the router as to which multicast addresses it wants to receive traffic. Routers configured for IGMP listen to IGMP messages from hosts. Routers periodically send out queries to discover which multicast groups are still active, in other words, the groups with hosts that still want to receive traffic for that multicast address. This enables the router to determine which multicast addresses are inactive and no longer have hosts requiring that traffic. With the first version of IGMP, there was no way for a host to explicitly leave a multicast group, informing the router that it wanted to leave that group. IGMPv2 included a leave mechanism for the host to inform the router that it was withdrawing from that multicast group.

IPv6 uses ICMPv6 Multicast Listener Discovery (MLD) for the same services, basing its functionality on IGMPv2. So, if you are familiar with IGMP, MLD is very similar. MLD is defined in RFC 2710, Multicast Listener Discovery for IPv6. MLD version 2 was defined in RFC 3810, Multicast Listener Discovery Version 2 (MLDv2) for IPv6. Based on IGMPv3, MLDv2 extends the first version of MLD to support Source Specific Multicast (SSM) and is backward compatible with MLDv1. SSM provides the ability for a host to request multicast packets, not only for a destination multicast address but also from a specific source address as well. MLDv2 is the default version for Cisco IOS.

Note MLD messages use an IPv6 Hop-by-Hop Header option that notifies routers to examine this packet more closely. The goal is to provide an efficient mechanism whereby routers can recognize when to intercept datagrams not addressed to them without having to extensively examine every datagram.

Note As with all IPv4 and IPv6 packets, the source address must be a unicast address.

There are three types of MLD messages:

- **Multicast Listener Query** (Type = decimal 130): The router periodically transmits host membership query messages to determine which multicast groups still have members on the router's directly attached networks. There are two subtypes of Multicast Listener Query messages:
  - **General Query:** This is used to learn which multicast addresses have listeners on an attached link. The General Query is sent to the link-scope all-nodes multicast address FF02::1, to all IPv6 devices on the link.
  - **Multicast-Address-Specific Query:** This is used to learn whether a particular multicast address (multicast group) has any listeners on an attached link. An Address-Specific Query is sent to the multicast address being queried.
- **Multicast Listener Report** (Type = decimal 131): This message is sent by the listener to register for a multicast group. The listener can send this message in response to a query or can send it unsolicited, without waiting for a query from the router. If in response to a query, only one member of the multicast group needs to send a Multicast Listener Report. In MLDv1, these Listener Reports are sent to the multicast address being reported. This was changed in MLDv2, and Listener Reports are sent to a special multicast address FF02::16, all-MLDv2-capapable routers.

- **Multicast Listener Done** (Type = decimal 132): When a listener no longer wants to receive traffic for a particular multicast group, it will send a Multicast Listener Done message to inform the router that it is leaving that multicast group. Listener Done messages are sent to the link-scope all-routers multicast address (FF02::2).

Figure 5-8 illustrates an example of MLDv2 General Query and Listener Report messages, which are described in the steps that follow.

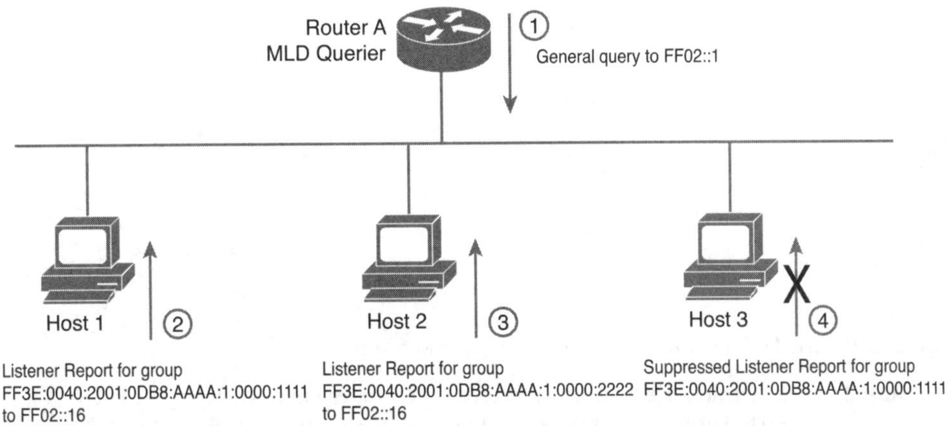

Figure 5-8 *MLDv2 General Query and Listener Reports*

Step 1. Router A, which is the MLD-designated querier on the network, periodically sends a General Query message to the link-scope all-nodes multicast address FF02::1, to discover which multicast groups hosts want to receive the groups' traffic.

Step 2. Host 1, a member of the multicast group FF3E:0040:2001:0DB8:AA AA:1:0000:1111, receives the General Query and waits a random delay interval before sending a Multicast Listener Report. Not seeing a Report from another host for this group, Host 1 transmits its Multicast Listener Report to FF02::16, all-MLDv2-capable routers. This is used to inform Router A that it still wants to receive traffic for this multicast address.

Step 3. Host 2 is a member of a different multicast group, FF3E:0040:2001:0DB8 :AAAA:1:0000:2222. Host 2 sends a separate Multicast Listener Report to FF02::16, informing Router A that it still wants to receive traffic destined for this multicast group.

Step 4. Host 3 is also a member of multicast group FF3E:0040:2001:0DB8:AA AA:1:0000:1111, but after waiting a random delay period, it sees that Host 1 has already sent a Multicast Listener Report to Router A for the group. Host 3 suppresses sending the Report because Router A only needs to hear from one member of any multicast group.

When a host no longer wants to receive traffic for a multicast group, it can inform the router buy sending a Multicast Listener Done message. Figure 5-9 illustrates the process of a host leaving a multicast group, which is described in the following steps.

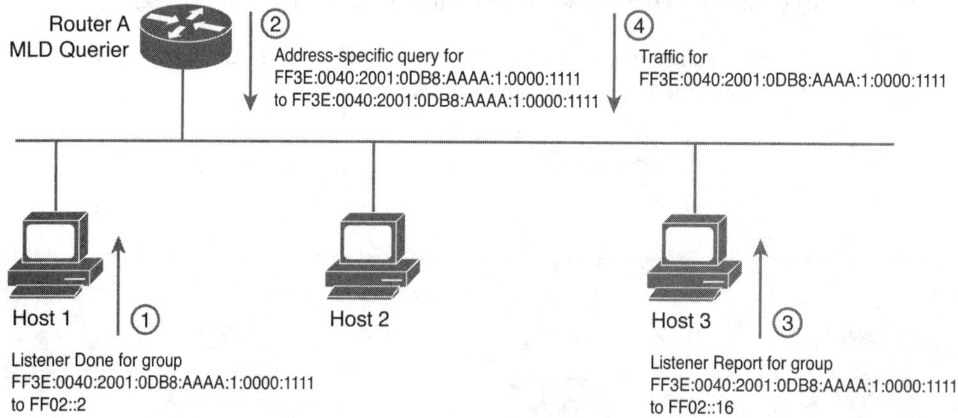

Figure 5-9 *MLDv2 Listener Done and Listener Reports*

Step 1. Host 1 no longer wants to receive traffic for the multicast group FF3E:0040:2001:0DB8:AAAA:1:0000:1111 and sends a Multicast Listener Done message to link-scope all-routers multicast address FF02::2, to inform the router that it wants to leave the group.

Step 2. Router A, the designated MLD querier for the network, receives the Listener Done message. The router maintains only a list of multicast groups on the network, not a list of the devices that are members of those groups. So when the router receives a Multicast Listener Done message, it must send a Multicast-Address-Specific Query to see whether any other devices still need to receive traffic for that multicast group. Router A sends a Multicast-Address-Specific Query specifically to the multicast group FF3E:0040:2001:0DB8:AAAA:1:0000:1111.

Step 3. Host 3 is still a member of the FF3E:0040:2001:0DB8:AAAA:1:0000:1111 multicast group. Host 3 replies with a Multicast Listener Report for that group to inform the router that it still wants to receive traffic for that group. The Multicast Listener Report is sent to FF02::16, all-MLDv2-capapable routers.

Step 4. Router A receives the Multicast Listener Report from Host 3 and continues to send traffic to that multicast address. However, if Router A, after waiting a configurable time period, has not received a Report from any host in that group, it stops forwarding traffic for that group.

Hosts communicate with routers to join and leave multicast groups, but routers also need a way to communicate with each other to route multicast traffic. A special protocol, PIM (Protocol Independent Multicast), is used for IPv4 and PIM6 for IPv6. Configuration of

MLD and PIM6 are beyond the scope of this book. If you are interested in more information on these topics, the following Cisco websites are recommended:

- www.cisco.com/en/US/docs/switches/datacenter/sw/5_x/nx-os/multicast/configuration/guide/mld.html
- www.cisco.com/en/US/docs/ios/ipv6/configuration/guide/ip6-multicast.html
- www.cisco.com/en/US/technologies/tk648/tk872/technologies_white_paper0900aecd80260049.pdf

Neighbor Discovery Protocol

Neighbor Discovery Protocol (ND or NDP) is defined in RFC 4861, Neighbor Discovery for IPv6. Neighbor Discovery includes similar processes from IPv4 such as ARP, ICMP Router Discovery, and Redirect, but with significant differences. ND also includes new functionality such as Duplicate Address Detection (DAD) and Neighbor Unreachability Detection (NUD). As described briefly in Chapter 4, "IPv6 Address Types," Neighbor Discovery plays an important role in the autoconfiguration of IPv6 address.

Devices (hosts and routers) use Neighbor Discovery for the following reasons:

- Stateless Address Autoconfiguration (SLAAC), to automatically determine network prefix, default gateway, and other configuration information.
- To determine whether a link-local or global unicast address it is about to use is already used by another device (DAD).
- To determine the Layer 2 data-link address (typically Ethernet) of a device on its network when it recognizes the destination IPv6 address.
- To keep track of which neighbors are reachable and which are not (NUD).
- When a router or the path to a router fails, a host actively searches for functioning alternates.

There are five ICMPv6 messages used by Neighbor Discovery:

- Router Solicitation message
- Router Advertisement message
- Neighbor Solicitation message
- Neighbor Advertisement message
- Redirect message

The following section examines each message type and the methods used for router and prefix discovery, address resolution, and Duplicate Address Detection.

Router Solicitation and Router Advertisement Messages

IPv6 devices can be separated into two categories, routers and hosts. Router Solicitation and Router Advertisement messages are about communications between a host and a router. Routers periodically send Router Advertisement messages or respond to a Router Solicitation message from a host on the link. Hosts send a Router Solicitation to prompt routers to immediately send a Router Advertisement.

A host sends a Router Solicitation (RS) message when it needs prefix, prefix length, default gateway, and other information for Stateless Address Autoconfiguration (SLAAC). This typically occurs when the host has just been powered on and has been configured to obtain its IP address automatically. Chapter 4 illustrated that SLAAC can use the IEEE modified EUI-64 format or randomly generate the 64-bit Interface ID of its unicast address. The host obtains its prefix and prefix length from the Router Advertisement (RA) message. The host can either wait for the next periodic RA message or send an RS message to have the router send one. Now it is time to examine the fields in both the Router Solicitation and Router Advertisement messages.

> **Note** For comprehensiveness, I have included a description of all the fields in the Router Solicitation and Router Advertisement messages.

> **Note** Some of these fields are more significant than others. Don't be overwhelmed by all the information described in these messages. You will have a better understanding of the fields that are pertinent to IPv6 when viewing the examples that follow these message descriptions.

Figure 5-10 shows the format of an ND Router Solicitation message, as described further in the list that follows.

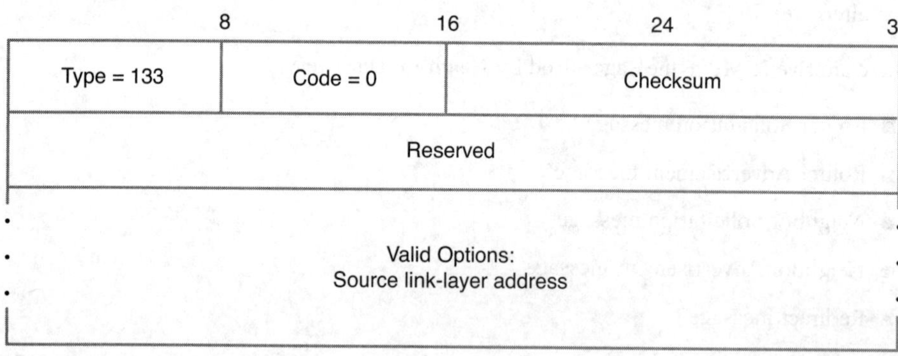

Figure 5-10 *ICMPv6 ND Router Solicitation Message*

- IPv6 header:
  - **Source address:** This is either an IPv6 address already assigned to the sending interface or an unspecified address if no address is assigned. When SLAAC is examined in more detail, note that this is typically the host's link-local address. Remember, link-local addresses are created either randomly or automatically by the device using the FE80::/10 prefix and generating the Interface ID using EUI-64.
  - **Destination address:** The destination address is typically the all-routers multicast address FF02::2.
  - **Hop limit:** The hop limit is always set to 255.
- **ICMPv6 fields:**
  - **Type:** The Type field is set to 133, indicating that this is a Router Solicitation message.
  - **Code:** The Code is set to 0 and ignored by the receiver.
  - **Checksum:** This is to validate the ICMPv6 header.
  - **Reserved:** This field is unused.
  - **Source Link Layer Address:** This is the Layer 2 link layer (or data link layer) address of the sender.

A Router Advertisement message is sent periodically or in response to a Router Solicitation message. It is used to provide hosts with addressing and other configuration information and is an important part of Stateless Address Autoconfiguration (SLAAC). There is a lot of information in Router Advertisement messages, so don't get overwhelmed by all the different fields. The most significant messages are explained in Example 5-7. The format of a Router Advertisement message is shown in Figure 5-11 and described further in the list that follows.

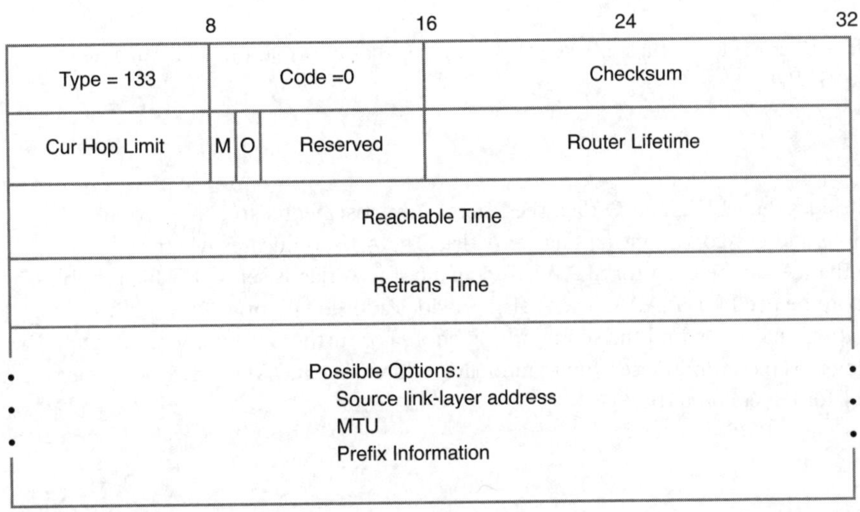

Figure 5-11 *ICMPv6 ND Router Advertisement Message*

- **IPv6 header:**
  - **Source address:** The source address is the router's link-local address assigned to the interface.
  - **Destination address:** The destination address is typically the all-nodes multicast address FF02::1.
  - **Hop limit:** The hop limit is always set to 255.
- **ICMPv6 fields:**
  - **Type:** The Type field is set to 134, indicating that this is a Router Advertisement message.
  - **Code:** The Code is set to 0 and ignored by the receiver.
  - **Checksum:** This validates the ICMPv6 header.
  - **Cur Hop Limit:** This is the number that the router recommends for hosts on the network to use as the Hop Limit field for their IP packets. A value of 0 means that the router is not recommending a hop limit and that the host should determine its own value.
  - **M Flag:** This is a *Managed Address Configuration* flag. When set to 0, the hosts on the network use Stateless Address Autoconfiguration (SLAAC). When set to 1, this informs the host to use stateful configuration (DHCPv6).
  - **O Flag:** This is an *Other Configuration* flag. When set to 0, there is no additional information available from a DHCPv6 server. When set to 1, this tells the host that additional information is available from the DHCPv6 server, such as DNS-related information.

Note If neither M nor O flags are set, this indicates that information is unavailable through DHCPv6.

Note Besides the M flag and O flag, the Router Advertisement also contains the autonomous address-configuration flag, or A flag. The A flag indicates whether the prefix in the RA can be used for SLAAC. By default, the A flag is set to 1, which enables the prefix to be used for SLAAC. The A flag provides additional options for address configurations and is beyond the scope of this book. For further information, refer to http://blogs.cisco.com/borderless/ipv6-automatic-addressing and RFC 4861, Neighbor Discovery for IP version 6 (IPv6).

- **Reserved:** Not used.
- **Router Lifetime:** Informs a host the duration, in seconds, that the router should be used as the default gateway. A lifetime of 0 indicates that the router is not a default gateway. The Router Lifetime applies only to the router's function as a default gateway. It does not apply to other information contained in other message fields or options such as prefix and prefix length. The host refreshes its own timer every time it receives Router Advertisement.
- **Reachable Time:** Tells a host how long, in milliseconds, that it can assume that a neighbor is reachable after receiving reachability confirmation. This is used by Neighbor Unreachability Detection (NUD) and is discussed in more detail later in this chapter. A value of 0 means that the router is not specifying a value.
- **Retrans Timer:** Notifies a host the period of time, in milliseconds, that it should wait before retransmitting Neighbor Solicitation messages. This is used by address resolution and Neighbor Unreachability Detection (NUD). Neighbor Solicitation messages are discussed later in this chapter.
- **Source Link Layer Address:** This is the Layer 2 link layer (or data link layer) address of the sender. In the example that follows, Example 5-9, this is the same address as the sender's Ethernet MAC address.
- **MTU:** Informs hosts of the maximum transmission unit (MTU) for the network. Hosts use this information to maximize the size of the IPv6 packet.
- **Prefix Information:** Notifies the host what the prefix (network portion of the address) and prefix length (analogous to an IPv4 subnet mask) of the network are.

That was a lot of information! Let's examine of some of the more significant fields. First of all, for a router to send Router Advertisement messages or to implement an IPv6 routing protocol, it must be configured with the **ipv6 unicast-routing** command:

```
R1(config)# ipv6 unicast-routing
```

Figure 5-12 focuses the topology on Router R1's LAN and PC1. PC1 has been configured to obtain its IP addressing automatically. This part of SLAAC is used to examine Router Solicitation and Router Advertisements using Wireshark. The SLAAC process is completed later in this chapter.

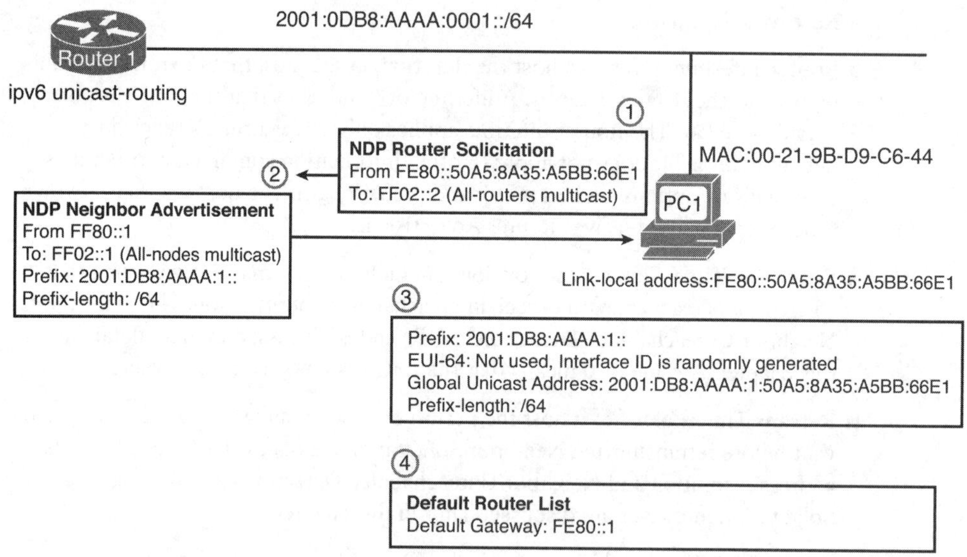

Figure 5-12 *ND Router Solicitation and Router Advertisement Messages*

Figure 5-12 illustrates the process of the Router Solicitation and Router Advertisement messages, which are described in the following steps:

Step 1. PC1 sends out a Router Solicitation message requesting a Router Advertisement from Router R1. This message is sent to the all-routers multicast address FF02::2.

Step 2. Router R1 responds with a Router Advertisement. The message includes the prefix and prefix length information that PC1 will need to configure its address using SLAAC. The Router Advertisement is not sent specifically to PC1 but as an all-nodes multicast FF02::1.

Step 3. PC1 receives the Router Advertisement and uses the prefix and prefix length to automatically configure its global unicast address.

Step 4. PC1 also uses the information in the Advertisement to update its Default Router List with the link-local address of the router. It will use this information as its default gateway address. The Default Router List is a list of default gateways that this router can use for reaching devices on networks other than its own.

Example 5-7 shows the actual Router Solicitation message from PC1.

Example 5-7 *ND Router Solicitation from PC1*

```
Ethernet II, Src: 00:21:9b:d9:c6:44, Dst: 33:33:00:00:00:02

Internet Protocol Version 6
    0110 .... = Version: 6
```

```
    .... 0000 0000 .... .... .... .... .... = Traffic class: 0x00000000
    .... .... .... 0000 0000 0000 0000 0000 = Flowlabel: 0x00000000
    Payload length: 16
    Next header: ICMPv6 (0x3a)              ! Next header is an ICMPv6 header
    Hop limit: 255
    Source: fe80::50a5:8a35:a5bb:66e1       ! Link-local address
    Destination: ff02::2                    ! All-routers multicast address


Internet Control Message Protocol v6
    Type: 133 (Router solicitation)         ! Router Solicitation message
    Code: 0
    Checksum: 0x3277 [correct]
    ICMPv6 Option (Source link-layer address)
        Type: Source link-layer address (1)
        Length: 8
        Link-layer address: 00:21:9b:d9:c6:44   ! MAC address of PC1
```

Looking first at the IPv6 header, notice that the *source* address is PC1's link-local address. The *destination* address is the all-routers multicast address FF02::2, soliciting configuration information from any router on the link. The Next Header field indicates that an ICMPv6 header immediately follows.

Looking at the ICMPv6 header, the Type field is set to 133, indicating that this ICMPv6 message is a Router Solicitation message. The *source link layer address* is the MAC address of PC1.

Next, focus on the Router Advertisement message. Router R1 has been enabled as an IPv6 router with the **ipv6 unicast-routing** command. Verify this by using the **show ipv6 interface fastethernet 0/0** command, as shown in Example 5-8.

Example 5-8 *ND Router Advertisements*

```
R1# show ipv6 interface fastethernet 0/0
FastEthernet0/0 is up, line protocol is up
  IPv6 is enabled, link-local address is FE80::1
  Global unicast address(es):
    2001:DB8:AAAA:1::1, subnet is 2001:DB8:AAAA:1::/64
  Joined group address(es):
    FF02::1
    FF02::2          ! All-routers multicast group
    FF02::1:FF00:1
  MTU is 1500 bytes
  ICMP error messages limited to one every 100 milliseconds
  ICMP redirects are enabled
  ND DAD is enabled, number of DAD attempts: 1
```

```
  ND reachable time is 30000 milliseconds
  ND advertised reachable time is 0 milliseconds
  ND advertised retransmit interval is 0 milliseconds
  ND router advertisements are sent every 200 seconds
  ND router advertisements live for 1800 seconds
  Hosts use stateless autoconfig for addresses.
R1#
```

R1 is a member of the FF02::2, the all-routers multicast group, as one of its *joined group address(es)*. This occurs only if R1 was enabled as an IPv6 router with the **ipv6 unicast-routing** command. As an IPv6 router, R1 will send Router Advertisement messages. Notice that R1 is sending out RA messages using the default of every 200 seconds. The Router Lifetime determined that this router should be used as the default gateway for 1800 seconds. If the host does not receive a Router Advertisement from this router in the next 1800 seconds, it should remove this router from its list of default gateways.

> **Note** If a router is not enabled as an IPv6 router using the **ipv6 unicast-routing** command, it will not send out ND Router Advertisement messages, but it still can be configured with IPv6 interfaces. Essentially, this turns the router into an IPv6 host. The router can send and receive IPv6 packets but it cannot route them. Output from the **show ipv6 interface** command would not display "ND advertised retransmit interval" or "ND router advertisements" information.

Example 5-9 examines Router R1's Router Advertisement.

Example 5-9 *ND Router Advertisement from Router R1*

```
Ethernet II, Src: 00:03:6b:e9:d4:80, Dst: 33:33:00:00:00:01
Internet Protocol Version 6
    0110 .... = Version: 6
    .... 1110 0000 .... .... .... .... .... = Traffic class: 0x000000e0
    .... .... .... 0000 0000 0000 0000 0000 = Flowlabel: 0x00000000
    Payload length: 64
    Next header: ICMPv6 (0x3a) ! Next header is an ICMPv6 header
    Hop limit: 255
    Source: fe80::1            ! Link-local address
                               ! Added to the Default Router List and
                               ! is the address hosts will use as
                               ! their defa`ult gateway
    Destination: ff02::1       ! All-nodes multicast group

Internet Control Message Protocol v6
    Type: 134 (Router advertisement) ! Router advertisement message
```

```
Code: 0
Checksum: 0x04d2 [correct]
Cur hop limit: 64          ! Recommended Hop Limit value for hosts
Flags: 0x00                ! M and O flags indicate that no
                           ! information is available via DHCPv6
Router lifetime: 1800      ! This router is a valid gateway for the
                           ! next 1800 seconds (3 minutes)
Reachable time: 0          ! No value specified
Retrans timer: 0           ! No value specified
ICMPv6 Option (Source link-layer address)
    Type: Source link-layer address (1)
    Length: 8
    Link-layer address: 00:03:6b:e9:d4:80  ! R1's MAC address
ICMPv6 Option (MTU)
    Type: MTU (5)
    Length: 8
    MTU: 1500              ! MTU of the link:
ICMPv6 Option (Prefix information)
    Type: Prefix information (3)
    Length: 32
    Prefix Length: 64      ! Prefix-length (/64) to be used for
                           ! autoconfiguration
    Flags: 0xc0
    Valid lifetime: 2592000
    Preferred lifetime: 604800
    Reserved
    Prefix: 2001:db8:aaaa:1::    ! Prefix of this network to
                                 ! be used for autoconfiguration
```

Look at the IPv6 header and see that the Next Header indicates an ICMPv6 header that immediately follows. The source is the link-local address of the interface. It is important to note that this is the address that a host will use as its default gateway. The destination address is an all-nodes multicast FF02::1. Although this Router Advertisement can be sent in response to a specific Router Solicitation message, it is always sent to the all-nodes multicast address.

Note A device that is not a router maintains a *Default Router List*. When it receives a Router Advertisement, it will add the link-local source address of the packet as one of the routers it can use as a default gateway. Each entry has an invalidation timer, the Router Lifetime, extracted from the Router Advertisement used to delete entries that are no longer being advertised.

The ICMPv6 header provides the addressing and configuration information that PC1 and other hosts need. The Type field is 134, indicating that this is a Router Advertisement. The Cur Hop Limit field recommends that hosts use a value of 64 for their IPv6 Hop Limit field when sending packets through this router. The flags (M and O) are both set to 0, which means that SLAAC is being used and that there is no additional information available from a DHCPv6 server. The Router Lifetime of 1800 tells autoconfigured hosts that this router is a valid default gateway for the next 1800 seconds, or 30 minutes, unless updated by another Router Advertisement. The link-local IPv6 source address is the default gateway address to be used. The Reachable Time and Retrans Timer are set to 0, which means that the router is not specifying a value for Neighbor Unreachability Detection (NUD).

The Router Advertisement includes several options. The Source link layer address is R1's MAC address. The MTU option indicates a maximum transmission unit of 1500 bytes. As we saw earlier in Path MTU Discovery, the host will use this as its Path MTU (PMTU) size of a packet unless it receives an ICMPv6 Packet Too Big message from another router in the path to the destination. The Prefix option provides several pieces of information, primarily the Prefix Length of 64 (/64) and the Prefix itself of 2001:DB8:AAAA:1::. A host such as R1 using autoconfiguration can use this information to generate its global unicast address. In Figure 5-12, Step 3 shows that PC1 uses this information to create its global unicast address, but instead of using the EUI-64 process, the Interface ID is randomly generated. Notice that the default gateway of PC1 is the link-local address of Router R1.

The Router Advertisement in Example 5-9 also includes two other lifetime fields: Preferred Lifetime and Valid Lifetime. Chapter 4 examined autoconfigured address states. Figure 5-13 shows the autoconfigured address states relative to the Preferred and Valid Lifetimes. The Preferred Lifetime is the amount of time in seconds that a device should consider addresses generated from the RA's Prefix and SLAAC as preferred. A preferred address means the device can send and receive traffic using this address. After the Preferred Lifetime has expired a device can no longer create new connections using this address. The Valid Lifetime is the amount of time in seconds that a device should consider the prefix in the Router Advertisement as valid. The Valid Lifetime extends beyond the Preferred Lifetime. If the Preferred Lifetime expires the device will not be able to create any new connections using this address, but any exisiting connections are valid until the Valid Lifetime expires. A value of all 1 bits, or 0xFFFFFFFF, is considered "infinity" for both lifetimes. The device resets its Preferred Lifetime and Valid Lifetime timers each time it receives a new Router Advertisement message.

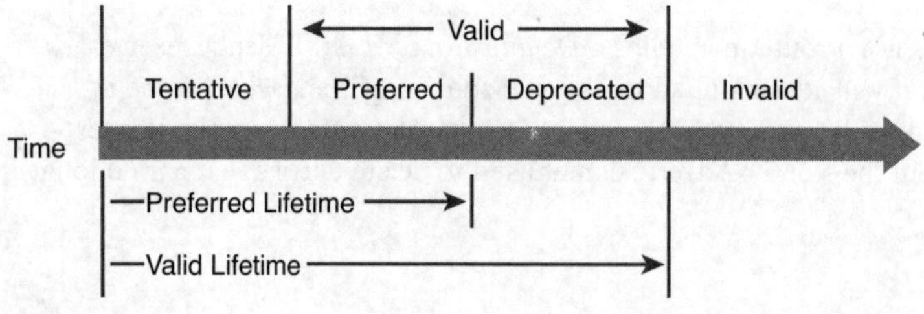

Figure 5-13 *RA Valid Lifetime and Preferred Lifetime*

Neighbor Solicitation and Neighbor Advertisement Messages

Neighbor Solicitation and Neighbor Advertisement messages are two more protocols that use ICMPv6 Neighbor Discovery. These messages are used by a device to request Layer 2, link layer address information from another device on the same network or to provide this information to the requesting device. Neighbor Solicitation and Neighbor Advertisement messages are part of three important processes:

- Address resolution
- Duplicate Address Detection (DAD)
- Neighbor Unreachability Detection (NUD)

Neighbor Solicitation and Neighbor Advertisement messages are very similar to ARP Requests and ARP Replies in IPv4. Neighbor Solicitations are sent to request the Layer 2, link layer address of a target device while also providing its own link layer address to the target. These link layer addresses are typically Ethernet MAC addresses.

Neighbor Advertisements are transmitted in response to Neighbor Solicitations and are also sent when it's necessary to propagate new information quickly. Let's look at the Neighbor Solicitation and Neighbor Advertisement message formats and see how they are used with the processes previously mentioned.

Note Once again, there is a lot of information in both of these messages, so don't worry about having a thorough understanding of every field. A description of each field is included for completeness. The most significant ones will be explained later in this section.

Figure 5-14 shows the format of an ND Neighbor Solicitation message.

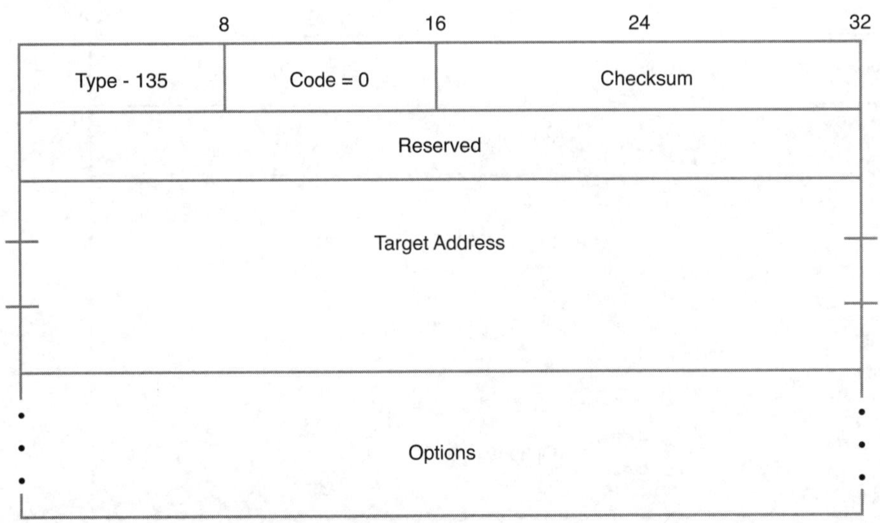

Figure 5-14 *ICMPv6 ND Neighbor Solicitation Message*

The following is a description of the fields in the IPv6 and ICMPv6 headers that encapsulate the ICMPv6 Neighbor Solicitation message. Once again, do not worry about the details of every field.

- **IPv6 header:**
  - **Source address:** Either an IPv6 address already assigned to the sending interface or, if this message is being sent as part of Duplicate Address Detection, the unspecified unicast address
  - **Destination address:** Either the solicited node multicast address corresponding to the target or the target address itself
  - **Hop limit:** Always set to 255
- **ICMPv6 fields:**
  - **Type:** Set to 135, indicating that this is a Neighbor Solicitation message.
  - **Code:** Set to 0 and ignored by the receiver.
  - **Checksum:** Validates the ICMPv6 header.
  - **Reserved:** This field is unused.
  - **Target Address:** The IPv6 address of the target, the device in which the sender knows the IPv6 address but not the Layer 2, link layer address. The address cannot be a multicast address.
  - **Source Link Layer Address:** The Layer 2, link layer address of the sender. This address must not be included when the source IPv6 address is an unspecified address.

Neighbor Advertisement messages are sent in response to Neighbor Solicitations or are unsolicited when necessary to propagate new information quickly. Figure 5-15 shows the format of an ND Neighbor Advertisement message.

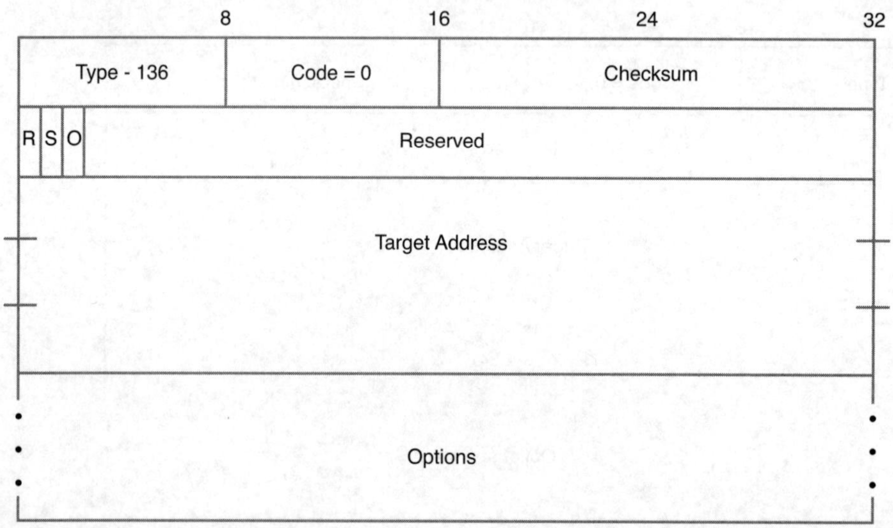

Figure 5-15 *ICMPv6 ND Neighbor Advertisement Message*

Following is a description of the fields in the IPv6 and ICMPv6 headers that encapsulate the ICMPv6 Neighbor Advertisement message. Once again, do not worry about the details of every field.

- **IPv6 header:**
  - **Source address:** An IPv6 address assigned to the sending interface.
  - **Destination address:** If the source address in the corresponding Neighbor Solicitation message was an unspecified unicast address, the destination address will be the all-nodes multicast address FF02::1. Otherwise, the destination address will be the source address used in the Neighbor Solicitation message.
  - **Hop limit:** The hop limit is always set to 255.
- **ICMPv6 fields:**
  - **Type:** Set to 136, indicating that this is a Neighbor Advertisement message.
  - **Code:** Set to 0 and ignored by the receiver.
  - **Checksum:** Validates the ICMPv6 header.
  - **R** (R-bit or Router flag): When the R-bit is set to 1, it indicates that the sender is a router. The R-bit is used by Neighbor Unreachability Detection to detect a router that changes to a host.
  - **S** (S-bit or Solicited flag): When the S-bit is set to 1, it indicates that this Neighbor Advertisement message was sent in response to a Neighbor Solicitation. The S-bit is used as a reachability confirmation during Neighbor Unreachability Detection.
  - **O** (O-bit or Override flag): When the O-bit is set to 1, it indicates that this Neighbor Advertisement should override the existing Neighbor cache entry (equivalent to an IPv4 ARP cache) by updating the cached Layer 2 address for IPv6 address. When it is not set, this advertisement will not update a cached link layer address but create one if one does not already exist.
  - **Reserved:** This field is unused.
  - **Target Address:** When the Neighbor Advertisement is in response to a Neighbor Solicitation, the target address is the IPv6 address found in the Target Address field of the solicitation. In other words, it is the IPv6 address of the device sending this advertisement. For an unsolicited advertisement, the target address is the IPv6 address whose link layer address has changed.
  - **Source Link Layer Address:** This is the Layer 2, link layer address of the sender. It must not be included when the source IPv6 address is an unspecified address.

Let's discuss two important data structures, the Neighbor Cache and Destination Cache, before using both of these messages.

Neighbor Cache and Destination Cache

The host will maintain two tables or caches for each interface:

- Neighbor Cache
- Destination Cache

The *Neighbor Cache* is equivalent to an ARP cache or table in IPv4. The Neighbor Cache maintains a list of information to which traffic has been recently sent. Entries consist of IPv6 unicast addresses and their corresponding Layer 2 addresses, typically an Ethernet MAC address. Devices maintain this cache from the information received in Neighbor Advertisement messages. The R-bit in the Neighbor Advertisement will also tell the device if this is a router. A Neighbor Cache entry can be in one of five states, which are illustrated in Figure 5-16, the state diagram for the Neighbor Cache. Although we have not examined the Neighbor Solicitation and Neighbor Advertisements in any detail, for the purpose of understanding the Neighbor Cache, Neighbor Solicitation and Neighbor Advertisement messages are equivalent to IPv4 ARP Requests and ARP Replies, respectively.

The Neighbor Cache states illustrated in Figure 5-16 are described as follows:

- **No Entry Exists:** This is not a Neighbor Cache state. There is no entry in the Neighbor Cache for an IPv6 address and its associated MAC address.
- **Incomplete:** Address resolution is in progress, and the link layer address is not yet known. A Neighbor Solicitation is sent to request the MAC address for the targeted IPv6 address. If three Neighbor Solicitation messages are sent without corresponding Neighbor Advertisements in reply, the Incomplete entry is removed because no entry exists.
- **Reachable:** Packets have recently been received providing confirmation that this device is reachable. A Neighbor Advertisement message has been received specifying the MAC address associated with the targeted IPv6 address in the previously sent Neighbor Solicitation.
- **Stale:** A certain time period, known as the Reachable time, has elapsed since a packet has been received from this address. The Neighbor Cache also transitions to this state when an unsolicited Neighbor Advertisement has been received. There is no action required by the device.
- **Delay:** Neighbor is pending reresolution, and traffic might flow to this neighbor. A packet has been sent by the device and is awaiting confirmation by means of a returning packet, such as a TCP Syn/Ack as part of the three-way handshake. If a packet is received within five seconds, the entry returns to the Reachable state; otherwise, it transitions to the Probe state.
- **Probe:** Neighbor reresolution is in progress, and traffic might flow to this neighbor. Similar to an Incomplete state, a Neighbor Solicitation is sent to once again request the MAC address for the targeted IPv6 address. If a Neighbor Advertisement is

returned by the solicited device, the entry returns to the Reachable state. If three Neighbor Advertisements are sent without corresponding Neighbor Advertisements in return, the entry is removed.

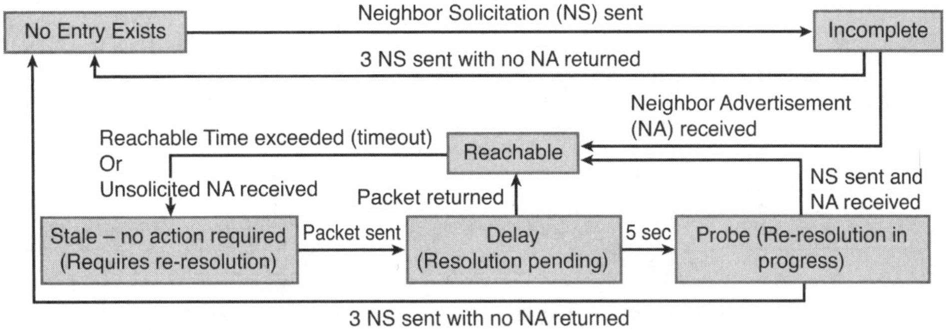

Figure 5-16 *Neighbor Cache States*

The router's Neighbor Cache can be displayed using the **show ipv6 neighbors** command. In Example 5-10, Router R1's Neighbor Cache has an entry for 2001:db8:aaaa:1::100, the address of PC1. Because the Reachable time limit has elapsed, the entry is currently in the stale state. The Age column shows the time in minutes that the entry has been in its current state. After communication is reestablished with PC1 using the **ping** command, the Neighbor Cache state transitions to Reachable.

Example 5-10 *Displaying the Neighbor Cache*

```
R1# show ipv6 neighbors
IPv6 Address                                    Age Link-layer Addr State Interface
2001:db8:aaaa:1::100                             16 0021.9bd9.c644  STALE Fa0/0

R1# ping 2001:db8:aaaa:1::100

Type escape sequence to abort.
Sending 5, 100-byte ICMP Echos to 2001:DB8:AAAA:1::100, timeout is 2 seconds:
!!!!!
Success rate is 100 percent (5/5), round-trip min/avg/max = 1/1/1 ms
R1# show ipv6 neighbors
IPv6 Address                                    Age Link-layer Addr State Interface
2001:DB8:AAAA:1::100                              0 0021.9bd9.c644  REACH Fa0/0

R1#
```

There is also another data structure known as the *Destination Cache*. Like the Neighbor Cache, it maintains a list of the destinations that traffic has been recently sent to, including those on other links or networks. In those cases, the entry will be the Layer 2 address of the next-hop router. The Destination Cache can be a subset of the Neighbor Cache.

Address Resolution

Address resolution is one of the processes in which Neighbor Solicitation and Neighbor Advertisement message are used. This is similar to the ARP process in IPv4. Figure 5-17 shows PC1 attempting to ping PC2.

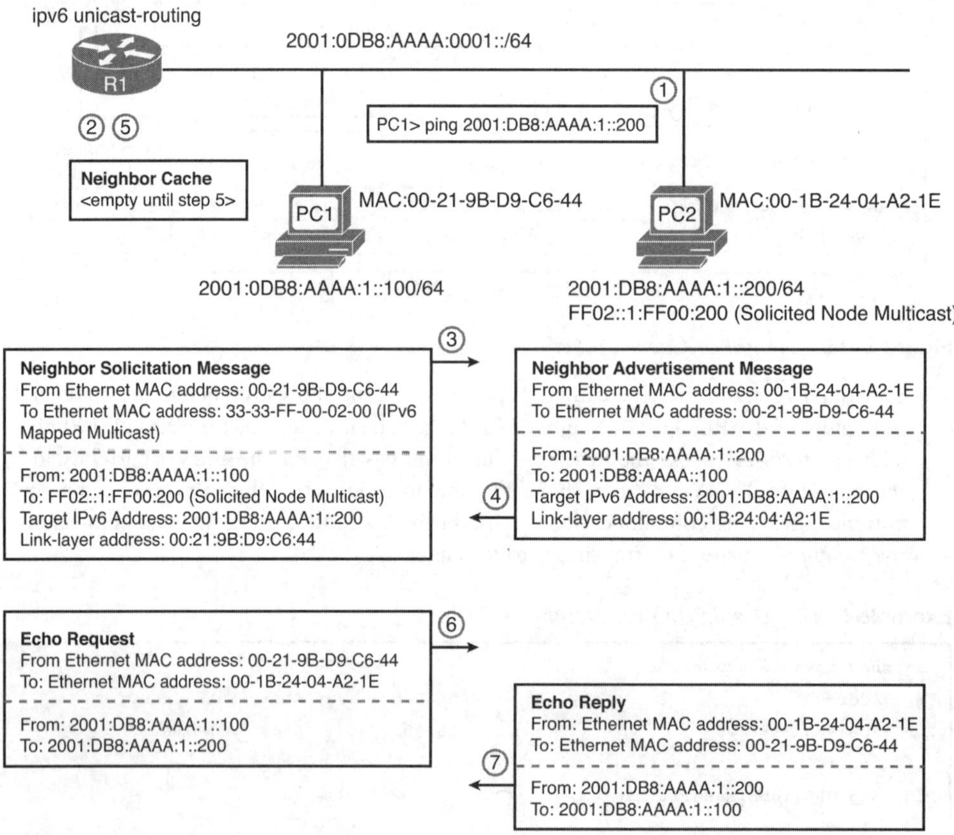

Figure 5-17 *Address Resolution*

Before PC1 can send the Echo Request, it must determine the Layer 2, link layer address of PC2 so that it can encapsulate the IPv6 packet into an Ethernet frame, as shown in the following steps:

Step 1. PC1 issues the **ping** command to PC2's address, 2001:DB8:AAAA:1::200.

Step 2. PC1 needs to encapsulate the IPv6 packet containing the Echo Request into an Ethernet frame. PC1 knows the IPv6 address of PC2 and checks its Neighbor Cache for a corresponding Layer 2 MAC Address. The entry for 2001:DB8:AAAA:1::200 does not exist.

Step 3. PC1 puts the IPv6 packet on hold and issues a Neighbor Solicitation message. The Neighbor Solicitation is sent to the solicited node multicast address that was discussed in Chapter 4. The target address in the Neighbor Solicitation is the IPv6 address issued with the **ping** command. We will examine the details of this message and the solicited-node multicast address in a moment.

Step 4. PC2 receives the Neighbor Solicitation and responds to PC1 with a Neighbor Advertisement message, providing its link layer, MAC address. The Neighbor Advertisement is sent as a unicast back to PC1. Soon you will notice how PC2 was able to extract the MAC address from the Neighbor Solicitation message so that it could reply immediately with a Neighbor Advertisement message. PC2 adds the IPv6 address and MAC address of PC1 to its own Neighbor Cache.

Step 5. PC1 receives the Neighbor Advertisement and updates its Neighbor Cache with the IPv6 address 2001:DB8:AAAA:1::200 and the newly discovered MAC address 00-1B-24-04-A2-1E of PC2.

Step 6. PC1 now has the information necessary to encapsulate the IPv6 packet with the Echo Request into and Ethernet frame and send it to PC2.

Step 7. PC2 responds with an Echo Reply.

In Example 5-11, the Neighbor Solicitation message is examined in more detail.

Example 5-11 *ND Neighbor Solicitation from PC1*

```
! Mapped multicast address for PC2
Ethernet II, Src: 00:21:9b:d9:c6:44, Dst: 33:33:ff:00:02:00

Internet Protocol Version 6
    0110 .... = Version: 6
    .... 0000 0000 .... .... .... .... .... = Traffic class: 0x00000000
    .... .... .... 0000 0000 0000 0000 0000 = Flowlabel: 0x00000000
    Payload length: 32
    Next header: ICMPv6 (0x3a)      ! Next header is an ICMPv6 header
    Hop limit: 255
    Source: 2001:db8:aaaa:1::100    ! Global unicast address
    Destination: ff02::1:ff00:200   ! Solicited-node multicast address

Internet Control Message Protocol v6
    Type: 135 (Neighbor solicitation) ! Neighbor Solicitation message
    Code: 0
    Checksum: 0xbbab [correct]
    Reserved: 0 (Should always be zero)
    Target: 2001:db8:aaaa:1::200  ! Solicited IPv6 address,
                                  ! needing MAC address
    ICMPv6 Option (Source link-layer address)
        Type: Source link-layer address (1)
        Length: 8
        Link-layer address: 00:21:9b:d9:c6:44  ! MAC address of the
                                               ! sender PC1
```

Looking at the IPv6 header in Example 5-11, notice that the Next Header value is 58 decimal (3A hexadecimal). This means that an ICMPv6 header will immediately follow this IPv6 header. The source IPv6 address is the global unicast address of PC1. The destination address might be a little harder to recognize; it is the solicited-node multicast address for PC2. Within the ICMPv6 message, the Type field indicates that this is a Neighbor Solicitation message. The target address is the IPv6 address PC1 is trying to resolve, looking for its MAC address. The link layer address is PC1's MAC address, so the receiver, PC2, will have what it needs to encapsulate the Neighbor Advertisement in an Ethernet frame.

Example 5-12 shows PC2's Neighbor Advertisement message to PC1.

Example 5-12 *ND Neighbor Advertisement from PC2*

```
! Unicast MAC address of PC2
Ethernet II, Src: 00:1b:24:04:a2:1e, Dst: 00:21:9b:d9:c6:44

Internet Protocol Version 6
    0110 .... = Version: 6
    .... 0000 0000 .... .... .... .... .... = Traffic class: 0x00000000
    .... .... .... 0000 0000 0000 0000 0000 = Flowlabel: 0x00000000
    Payload length: 32
    Next header: ICMPv6 (0x3a)     ! Next header is and ICMPv6 header
    Hop limit: 255
    Source: 2001:db8:aaaa:1::200        ! Global unicast address
    Destination: 2001:db8:aaaa:1::100   ! Global unicast address

Internet Control Message Protocol v6
    Type: 136 (Neighbor advertisement) ! Neighbor advertisement
                                       ! message
    Code: 0
    Checksum: 0x1b4d [correct]
    Flags: 0x60000000  ! (110) Router Flag = 1,
                       ! Solicitation Flag = 1, Override Flag = 0
    Target: 2001:db8:aaaa:1::200  ! IPv6 address of the sender, PC2
    ICMPv6 Option (Target link-layer address)
        Type: Target link-layer address (2)
        Length: 8
        Link-layer address: 00:1b:24:04:a2:1e ! MAC address of the
                                              ! sender PC2
```

The IPv6 header in Example 5-12 shows the Next Header value of 58 decimal (3A hexadecimal), indicating that an ICMPv6 header will immediately follow this IPv6 header. The source IPv6 address is the global unicast address of PC2. The destination address is the global unicast address of PC1. Looking next at the ICMPv6 portion, we see that the Type field indicates that this is a Neighbor Advertisement message. The flags show that this message is coming from a router, and the Neighbor Advertisement is being sent in response to a Neighbor Solicitation. The target address is the IPv6 address of PC2—the source of the Neighbor Advertisement message. The link layer address is PC2's MAC address. This is the information that PC1 needs to encapsulate the IPv6 packet in an Ethernet frame.

Now that PC1 has the Ethernet MAC address of PC2, it can send the Echo Request, as shown in Example 5-13. Example 5-14 shows the corresponding Echo Reply from PC2.

Example 5-13 *Echo Request from PC1*

```
Ethernet II, Src: 00:21:9b:d9:c6:44, Dst: 00:1b:24:04:a2:1e

Internet Protocol Version 6
    0110 .... = Version: 6
    .... 0000 0000 .... .... .... .... .... = Traffic class: 0x00000000
    .... .... .... 0000 0000 0000 0000 0000 = Flowlabel: 0x00000000
    Payload length: 40
    Next header: ICMPv6 (0x3a)
    Hop limit: 128
    Source: 2001:db8:aaaa:1::100
    Destination: 2001:db8:aaaa:1::200

Internet Control Message Protocol v6
    Type: 128 (Echo (ping) request)
    Code: 0 (Should always be zero)
    Checksum: 0x7b37 [correct]
    ID: 0x0001
    Sequence: 13
    Data (32 bytes)
```

Example 5-14 *Echo Reply from PC2*

```
Ethernet II, Src: 00:1b:24:04:a2:1e, Dst: 00:21:9b:d9:c6:44

Internet Protocol Version 6
    0110 .... = Version: 6
    .... 0000 0000 .... .... .... .... .... = Traffic class: 0x00000000
    .... .... .... 0000 0000 0000 0000 0000 = Flowlabel: 0x00000000
    Payload length: 40
    Next header: ICMPv6 (0x3a)
    Hop limit: 64
    Source: 2001:db8:aaaa:1::200
    Destination: 2001:db8:aaaa:1::100
```

```
Internet Control Message Protocol v6
    Type: 129 (Echo (ping) reply)
    Code: 0 (Should always be zero)
    Checksum: 0x7a37 [correct]
    ID: 0x0001
    Sequence: 13
    Data (32 bytes)
```

A Closer Look at Solicited-Node Multicasts

Solicited-node multicast addresses were initially explained in Chapter 4. An IPv6 interface accepts packets for its unicast addresses as well as any multicast groups it belongs to. Besides common multicast addresses such as the all-nodes multicast address FF02::1, interfaces will also receive packets for their solicited-node multicast addresses.

A device automatically creates a solicited-node multicast address for each of its unicast addresses by using a special mapping technique. The solicited-node multicast is created by appending the prefix FF02:0:0:0:0:1:FF00::/104 to the last 24 bits of the unicast address. As shown in Figure 5-18, PC2's solicited-node multicast address has the prefix FF02:0:0:0:0:1:FF00::/104 plus the last 24 bits of its global unicast address 00:0200. The concatenation of the two results in a solicited-node multicast address of FF02::1:FF00:200. This address corresponds to its global unicast address 2001:DB8:AAAA:1::200. PC2 will also have a separate solicited-node multicast address for its link-local unicast address.

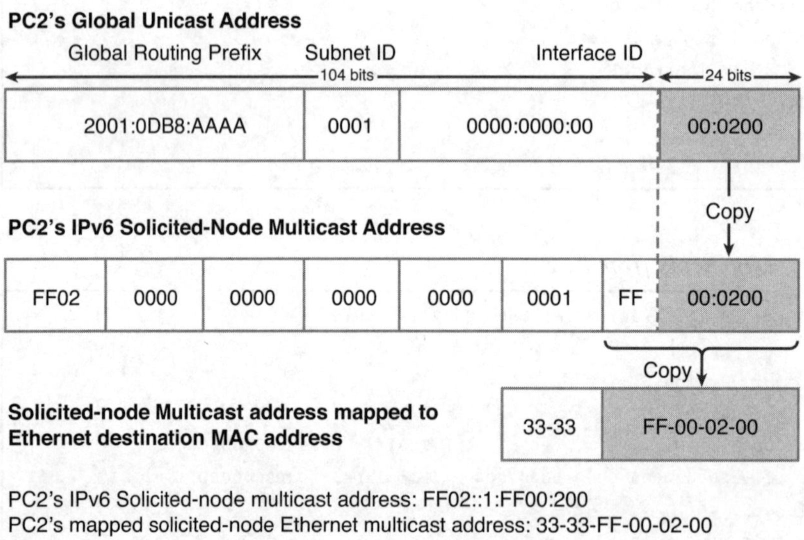

Figure 5-18 *Solicited-Node Multicast Address for PC2*

Looking again at the Neighbor Solicitation message in Example 5-11, notice that the destination IPv6 address is the solicited-node multicast address of PC2, FF02::1:FF00:200. When PC2 receives this packet, it recognizes the address as one of its solicited-node multicast addresses for that interface. PC2 processes the packet and recognizes that the ICMPv6 target address of 2001:db8:aaaa:1::200 matches its global unicast address. PC2 realizes that this Neighbor Solicitation is for itself and must respond with a Neighbor Advertisement.

Note Why is the destination IPv6 address the solicited-node multicast address and not the unicast address of PC2? Although PC1 recognizes PC2's IPv6 address, the 2001:db8:aaaa:1::200 entry in its Neighbor Cache is in the Incomplete state. RFC 2461 and RFC 4861 address this issue in more detail.

Although slight, there is a possibility that other devices might have the same last 24 bits for an Interface ID. This means that they will have the same solicited-node multicast address as PC2. It doesn't cause a problem as they process the packet and examine the ICMPv6 target address. In doing so, they determine that the target address does not match their own unicast address, and they do not respond with a Neighbor Advertisement.

Up until this point, Layer 3 IPv6 was examined. Let's talk about Layer 2, the Ethernet header. In IPv4, ARP Requests are typically sent as a Layer 2 broadcast with a destination MAC address of FF-FF-FF-FF-FF-FF. Although the ARP Request is only searching for one device, every device (Ethernet NIC) on the network must copy in the Ethernet frame and pass the contents on to their ARP process. It isn't until the ARP process examines the target address in the ARP Request that it can determine whether it is the target of the ARP Request. This process is accomplished more efficiently in IPv6.

RFC 2464, IPv6 Packets over Ethernet, specifies that the Ethernet multicast address 33-33-xx-xx-xx-xx should be used for this purpose. The last 4 bytes (xx) of the Ethernet multicast address are the last 4 bytes of the destination address (32 bits). In Example 5-11, notice that the destination MAC address PC1 is using to reach PC2 is 33-33-FF-00-02-00. This is 33-33 appended to the last 32 bits of the solicited-node multicast address, as illustrated in Figure 5-18.

PC2's Ethernet NIC will receive any frames with the destination MAC address 33-33-FF-00-02-00 because this is a MAC address corresponding to its solicited-node multicast address FF02::1:FF00:200. Instead of the Layer 2 broadcasts used in IPv4 ARP Requests, IPv6 Neighbor Solicitation messages use multicast addresses, which result in a very limited number of Ethernet NICs having to copy in the Ethernet frame.

> **Note** As mentioned earlier, it is possible that more than one device can have the same solicited-node multicast address; this means that their NICs will accept the same Ethernet multicast addresses. However, only the device that has an IPv6 address that matches the target address in the ICMPv6 message responds with a Neighbor Advertisement.

Duplicate Address Detection

A device uses Duplicate Address Detection (DAD) to determine whether an address it wants to use is already employed by another device. With some exceptions, RFC 4861 recommends that DAD be performed on every unicast address, link-local or global, before it is assigned to an interface. This is regardless of whether it was assigned using SLAAC, DHCPv6, or manual configuration.

If a duplicate address is discovered during the process, it cannot be used for the interface. The procedure for detecting duplicate addresses uses Neighbor Solicitation and Advertisement messages. Figure 5-19 illustrates this process using PC1 and its link-local unicast address, as shown in the following steps.

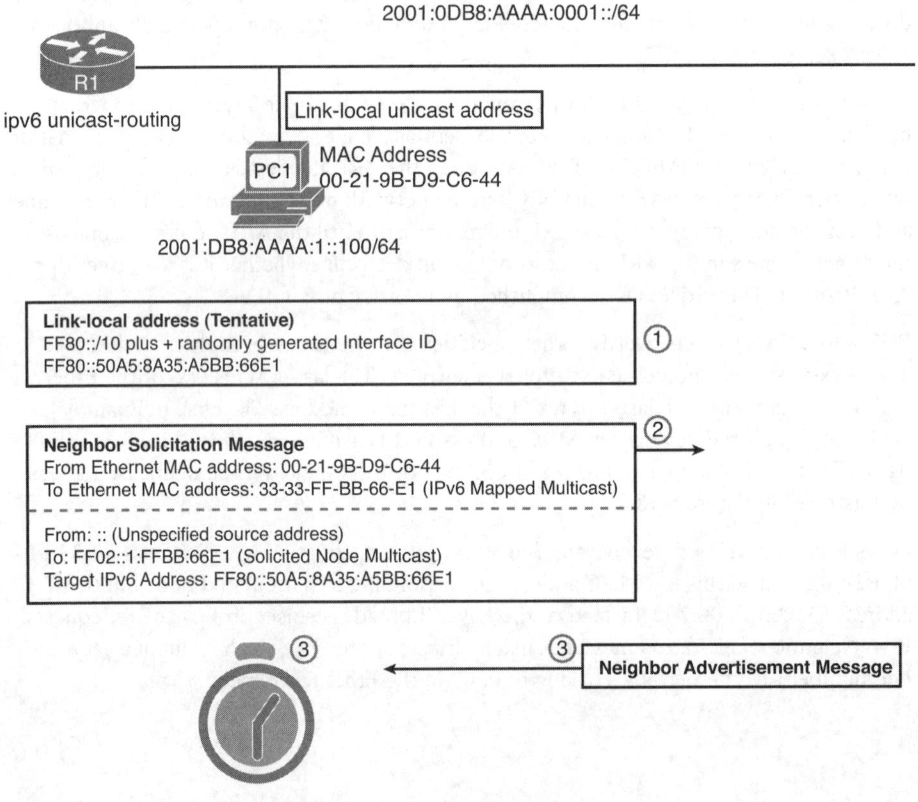

Figure 5-19 *Duplicate Address Detection (DAD)*

Step 1. PC1 automatically creates its own link-local unicast address for its Ethernet interface. The prefix FE80::/10 is appended to a random 64-bit Interface ID to create the link-local address FE80::50A5:8A35:A5BB:66E1. (Because PC1 is using a later version of Windows, it did not use EUI-64 to create the Interface ID.) Before using this link-local address, it must be tested to make sure that it is unique on the link. The link-local address is put into the tentative state until the DAD procedure is completed.

Step 2. PC1 sends out a Neighbor Solicitation message to see whether anyone else on the link is already using this link-local address. A closer examination of the Neighbor Solicitation message in Figure 5-19 reveals the following Ethernet header:

- **Source MAC address:** The source MAC address of PC1 is 00-21-9B-D9-C6-44.
- **Destination MAC address:** This is a multicast address of 33-33, with the last 32 bits mapped from 32 low-order bits of the IPv6 destination address, BB-66-E1. The destination MAC address results in 33-33-BB-66-E1.

The following IPv6 header:

- **Source IPv6 address:** The source IPv6 address is ::, an unspecified source address. The unspecified source address is used as PC1 does not have a valid IPv6 address. (The :: address will always be employed as the source address for DAD.)
- **Destination IPv6 address:** This is the solicited-node multicast address for PC1's link-local address FF02::1:FFBB:66E1.

The following ICMPv6 header (Neighbor Solicitation message):

- **Target IPv6 address:** This is PC1's own link-local address, FE80::50A5:8A35:A5BB:66E1. If another device is using this address, it needs to respond with a Neighbor Advertisement message.

Step 3. PC1 sets a timer to give the opportunity for another device using its tentative link-local address a chance to respond with a Neighbor Advertisement message. If no message is received within this time, the link-local address will transition from *tentative* to *assigned*. If another device on the link has the same link-local address, it must respond with a Neighbor Advertisement to let PC1 know that this address is already employed and cannot be used. The address will be suspended on PC1. The device that acquires the address first is the one that keeps it.

Neighbor Unreachability Detection

Neighbor Unreachability Detection (NUD) is defined in RFC 4861. Communications between any two IPv6 devices can fail for any number of reasons, such as the host lost power or a faulty cable. Devices actively track the reachability state for the neighbors to which they are sending packets.

The confirmation of reachability can be achieved in one of two ways:

- A Neighbor Advertisement message in response to a Neighbor Solicitation message.
- An upper-layer process indicates a successful connection, such as acknowledgments in an active TCP connection.

When a path to a neighbor appears to be failing, the specific recovery procedure depends on how the neighbor is being used. If the neighbor is the ultimate destination, address resolution should be performed again. This involves sending a Neighbor Solicitation message and awaiting a Neighbor Advertisement in response. If the neighbor is a router, it would be more appropriate for the device to use a different default gateway. Neighbor Unreachability Detection is only performed with neighbors where unicast packets are sent.

Previously in this chapter, Neighbor Cache states were discussed. Figure 5-16 illustrated the various states and events that transpire between them. Neighbor Unreachability Detection uses these same states and events to detect and resolve neighbor unreachability issues.

Stateless Address Autoconfiguration

Stateless Address Autoconfiguration (SLAAC) is a mechanism that allows a host to generate its own unicast addresses using a combination of locally available information and information advertised by routers. The autoconfiguration process includes generating a link-local address and global addresses through SLAAC, as well as the Duplicate Address Detection procedure, to verify the uniqueness of the addresses on a link.

Figure 5-20 illustrates the SLAAC process in four steps using the many processes and messages that have already been discussed.

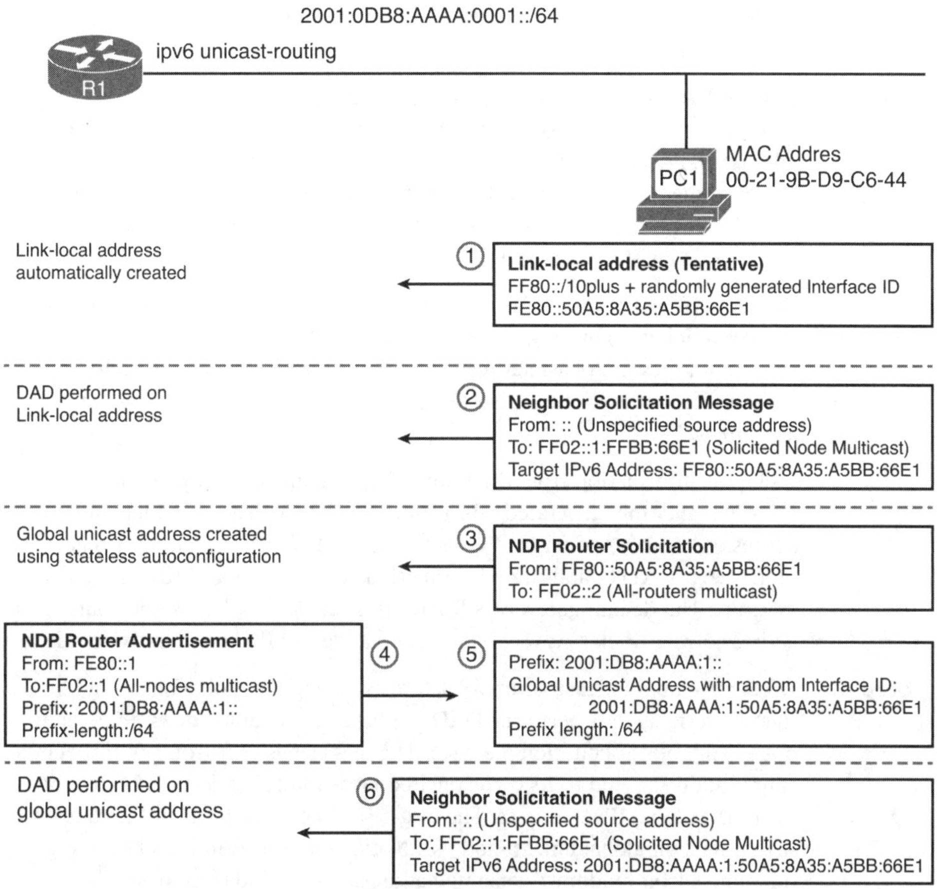

Figure 5-20 *Stateless Address Autoconfiguration*

Step 1. **Creation of link-local unicast address:** The host PC1 creates its own link-local unicast address, without the need for manual configuration or the assistance of a DHCPv6 server. The link-local address is FE80::/10, appended to a 64-bit Interface ID. The Interface ID can be created using the EUI-64 format or randomly generated, as is the case for PC1. The address is put into the tentative state, awaiting confirmation from DAD of its uniqueness.

Step 2. **DAD for link-local address:** Before using the link-local address, the host must perform DAD on the link-local address to make sure that it is unique. PC1 sends out a Neighbor Solicitation message. Notice that the message is sent from ::, an unspecified source address, and to its own solicited-node multicast address corresponding to its link-local address. The target IPv6 address in the ICMPv6 message is its own link-local address. If anyone is already using this address, it will respond with a Neighbor Advertisement. After waiting a certain time interval, if PC1 does not receive a Neighbor Advertisement message for this address, it will become an active link-local address. If the Neighbor

Advertisement is sent, it uses FF02::1, all-nodes multicast, as the destination address.

Step 3. **Router Advertisement address configuration information:** PC1 needs information contained in a Router Advertisement message for its global unicast address and other configuration information. If PC1 has not received a Router Advertisement message, it will prompt the router with a Router Solicitation. The Router Solicitation is sent from PC1's link-local address that was created in the previous steps, and sent to the all-routers multicast address FF02::2.

Router R1 sends a Router Advertisement periodically or if prompted by a Router Solicitation message. In either case, the Router Advertisement is sent to the all-nodes multicast address FF02::1 and from its link-local address. Information in the Router Advertisement includes the prefix, prefix length, and link MTU.

Using the information from the Router Advertisement, PC1 prepends the prefix to its randomly generated 64-bit Interface ID to create its global unicast address. (Another option for PC1 is to use the EUI-64 format.) It also gets the prefix length, MTU, and other information from the Router Advertisement message. The default gateway is Router R1's link-local address, the source address of the Router Advertisement, and added to PC1's default router list.

Step 4. **DAD for global unicast address:** Before assigning the global unicast address to the interface, PC1 performs DAD to guarantee its uniqueness. PC1 sends out a Neighbor Solicitation message. The message is sent from an unspecified source address :: and to its own solicited-node multicast address corresponding to the global IPv6 address. The target IPv6 address in the ICMPv6 message is its own global unicast address. Notice that the Windows host uses the same 64-bit randomly generated address for the Interface IDs of both the link-local address and the global unicast address.If anyone is already using this global address, it will respond with a Neighbor Advertisement. After waiting a certain time interval, if PC1 does not receive a Neighbor Advertisement message for this address, it will become an active global unicast address.

Redirect Messages

An ICMPv6 Redirect message is used to inform a device that there is a better first-hop router. It works the same as the Redirect message used in IPv4. Figure 5-21 shows the format of an ND ICMPv6 Redirect message.

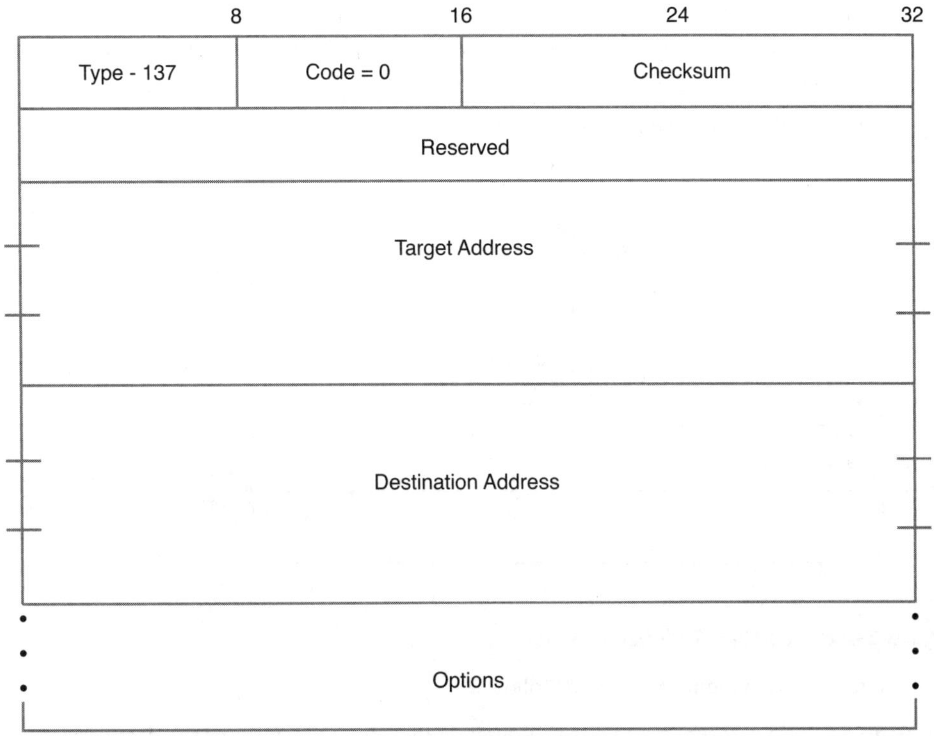

Figure 5-21 *ICMPv6 Redirect Message*

The description for the fields in the IPv6 and ICMPv6 headers are as follows:

- **IPv6 header:**
  - **Source address:** The link-local address assigned to the interface.
  - **Destination address:** The source address of the packet that triggered the redirect message.
  - **Hop limit:** The hop limit is always set to 255.
- **ICMPv6 fields:**
  - **Type:** Set to 137, indicating that this is a Redirect message.
  - **Code:** Set to 0 and ignored by the receiver.
  - **Checksum:** Validates the ICMPv6 header.
  - **Reserved:** This field is unused.
  - **Target Address:** The IPv6 address that is a better first hop to use.
  - **Destination Address:** The IP address of the destination that has been redirected to the target address.

- **Possible Option – Target Link Layer Address:** The link layer address of the target address, the recommended next-hop router. This prevents the host from having to resolve the link layer address of the other router.

Figure 5-22 illustrates the redirect process.

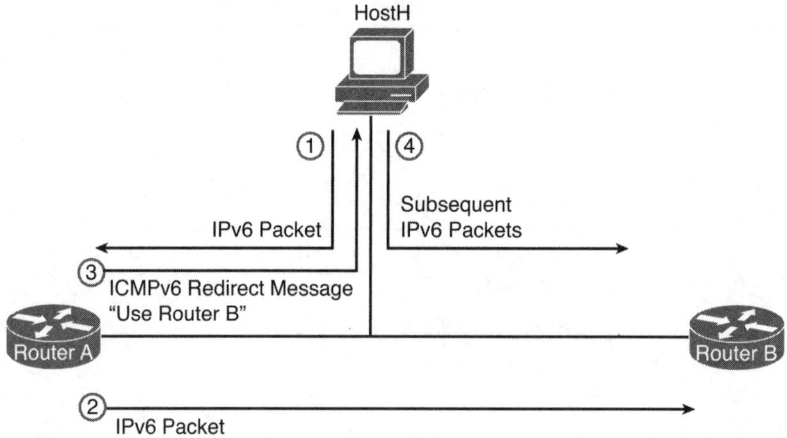

Figure 5-22 *ICMPv6 Redirect Message*

The four steps in Figure 5-22 are as follows:

Step 1. Host H sends a packet to Router A, its default gateway for the destination IPv6 address.

Step 2. Router A forwards this packet to Router B.

Step 3. Router A realizes that this is the same network it received the packet from and sends an ICMPv6 Redirect message to Host H, informing it of a better first-hop router.

Step 4. Host H receives the Redirect message and sends subsequent messages directly to Router B.

Summary

This chapter examined ICMPv6. ICMPv6 has many similarities to ICMPv4 but is a more robust protocol containing new functionality and many improvements.

Two types of ICMPv6 messages were discussed: error messages and informational messages.

The ICMPv6 error messages explored were

- **Destination Unreachable:** These messages are sent when a packet cannot be delivered to its destination for reasons other than congestion.

- **Packet Too Big:** An IPv6 router sends an ICMPv6 Packet Too Big message back to the source when it receives a packet larger than the MTU of the egress interface. The router drops the packet. This message is also used for Path MTU Discovery.
- **Time Exceeded:** Before a router forwards an IPv6 packet, it decrements the Hop Limit field by 1, similar to the TTL field in IPv4. If the Hop Limit results in a 0, the packet is dropped and an ICMPv6 Time Exceeded message is sent back to the source.
- **Parameter Problem:** This message is generated when a device processing a packet finds a problem with a field in the main IPv6 header or an extension header and must discard it.

The ICMPv6 informational messages were also covered. The first two are very common messages used by the **ping** command:

- **Echo Request:** A device sends an Echo Request to prompt the destination to return an Echo Reply to verify network layer connectivity.
- **Echo Reply:** An Echo Reply is sent in response to an Echo Request.

Multicast Listener Discovery allows hosts and routers to communicate so that hosts can join and leave multicast groups:

- **Multicast Listener Query:** The router periodically transmits host membership query messages to determine which multicast groups still have members on the router's directly attached networks.
- **Multicast Listener Report:** This message is sent by the listener to register for a multicast group.
- **Multicast Listener Done:** When a listener no longer wants to receive traffic for a particular multicast group, it will send a Multicast Listener Done message to inform the router it is leaving that multicast group.

Neighbor Discovery includes similar processes from IPv4, such as ARP, ICMP Router Discovery, and Redirect, but with significant differences. ND also includes new functionality such as Duplicate Address Detection (DAD) and Neighbor Unreachability Detection (NUD). The five ICMPv6 messages used by Neighbor Discovery are

- **Router Solicitation message:** A host sends a Router Solicitation message when it needs prefix, prefix length, default gateway, and other information for Stateless Address Autoconfiguration (SLAAC).
- **Router Advertisement message:** A Router Advertisement message is sent periodically or in response to a Router Solicitation message. It is used to provide hosts with addressing and other configuration information and is an important part of SLAAC.

- **Neighbor Solicitation message:** Neighbor Solicitation and Neighbor Advertisement messages are very similar to ARP Requests and ARP Replies in IPv4. Neighbor Solicitations are sent to request the Layer 2 address (typically an Ethernet MAC address) of a target device while also providing its own link layer address to the target.
- **Neighbor Advertisement message:** Neighbor Advertisements are sent in response to Neighbor Solicitations, providing the Layer 2 address (typically a MAC address) of an IPv6 address.
- **Redirect message:** An ICMPv6 Redirect message is used to inform a device that there is a better first-hop router. It works the same as the Redirect message used in IPv4.

These ND messages are used by various tables and processes:

- **Neighbor Cache:** This is equivalent to an ARP cache or table in IPv4. Neighbor Cache maintains a list of information to which traffic has been recently sent.
- **Destination Cache:** Like the Neighbor Cache, this maintains a list of destinations to which traffic has been recently sent, including those on other links or networks.
- **Address resolution:** Address resolution uses Neighbor Solicitation and Neighbor Advertisement messages to resolve Layer 3 addresses to a corresponding Layer 2 (MAC) address. This is similar to ARP in IPv4.
- **Duplicate Address Detection (DAD):** A device uses DAD to determine whether an address it wants to use is already in use by another device. DAD uses Neighbor Solicitation with the device's own address. If another device is already using that address, it will respond with a Neighbor Advertisement message.
- **Neighbor Unreachability Detection (NUD):** Devices will actively track the reachability state for the neighbors to which it is sending packets. Devices use Neighbor Solicitation and Neighbor Advertisement messages to make this determination.
- **Stateless Address Autoconfiguration (SLAAC):** SLAAC is a mechanism that allows a host to generate its own global unicast address using a combination of locally available information and information advertised by routers. The autoconfiguration process includes
  - Creating its own link-local address with an Interface ID that is randomly generated or uses the EUI-64 format.
  - Using Duplicate Address Detection (DAD) to ensure that the link-local address is unique.
  - Creating its own global unicast address using prefix and prefix length information from a local Router Advertisement. The Interface ID is randomly generated or created by using the EUI-64 format. Other information from the Router Advertisement includes the default gateway.
  - Using Duplicate Address Detection (DAD) to ensure that the global unicast address is unique.

References

RFCs:

RFC 1393, *Traceroute Using an IP Option*, G. Malkin, Xylogics, Inc., IETF, www.ietf.org/rfc/rfc1393.txt, January 1963

RFC 1981, *Path MTU Discovery for IP version 6*, J. McCann, DEC, IETF, www.ietf.org/rfc/rfc1918.txt, August 1996

RFC 2464, *Transmission of IPv6 Packets over Ethernet Networks*, M. Crawford, Fermilab, IETF, www.ietf.org/rfc/rfc2464.txt, December 1998

RFC 2710, *Multicast Listener Discovery (MLD) for IPv6*, S. Deering, IBM, IETF, www.ietf.org/rfc/rfc2710.txt, October 1999

RFC 2711, *IPv6 Router Alert Option*, C. Partridge, BBN, IETF, www.ietf.org/rfc/rfc2711.txt, October 1999

RFC 2894, *Router Renumbering for IPv6*, M. Crawford, Fermilab, IETF, www.ietf.org/rfc/rfc2894.txt, August 2000

RFC 3122, *Extensions to IPv6 Neighbor Discovery for Inverse Discovery Specification*, A. Conta, Transwitch Corp., IETF, www.ietf.org/rfc/rfc3122.txt, June 2001

RFC 3775, *Mobility Support in IPv6*, D. Johnson, Nokia, IETF, www.ietf.org/rfc/rfc3775.txt, June 2004

RFC 3810, *Multicast Listener Discovery Version 2 (MLDv2) for IPv6*, R. Vida, LIP6, IETF, www.ietf.org/rfc/rfc3810.txt, June 2004

RFC 4286, *Multicast Router Discovery*, B. Haberman, JHU APL, IETF, www.ietf.org/rfc/rfc4286.txt, December 2005

RFC 4443, *Internet Control Message Protocol (ICMPv6) for the Internet Protocol Version 6 (IPv6) Specification*, A. Conta, Transwitch, IETF, www.ietf.org/rfc/rfc4443.txt, March 2006

RFC 4861, *Neighbor Discovery for IP version 6 (IPv6)*, T. Narten, IBM, IETF, www.ietf.org/rfc/rfc4861.txt, September 2007

Chapter 6

IPv6 Configuration

The previous chapters covered the different types of IPv6 addresses such as global unicast and link-local addresses. Neighbor Discovery Protocol and the different types of messages associated with address resolution, Duplicate Address Detection (DAD), and Stateless Address Autoconfiguration (SLAAC) were explored. IPv6 is much more than just a longer IP address. The information that has been discussed in earlier chapters is important to understand the processes and protocols associated with implementing an IPv6 network. However, sometimes in the mist of all this new information, it's possible to lose sight of the basic commands necessary to configure IPv6. So, now it's time to accomplish just that.

This chapter will illustrate how to configure the IPv6 addresses for the topology that you will be using for the next two chapters, Introduction to Routing IPv6 and IPv6 IGP Routing Protocols. Most of these commands have already been discussed; some new ones will be introduced as well.

This chapter also examines IPv6 access control lists (ACL). Configuring IPv6 ACLs is similar to those in IPv4. If you are familiar with configuring IPv4 ACLs, the IPv6 ACL configurations are not all that different.

Figure 6-1 shows the topology that will be configured in this chapter. Assume that you are the network administrators of a local café and coffee roasting company, Rick's Café, and have obtained the IPv6 address 2001:0db8:cafe::/48 from the provider.

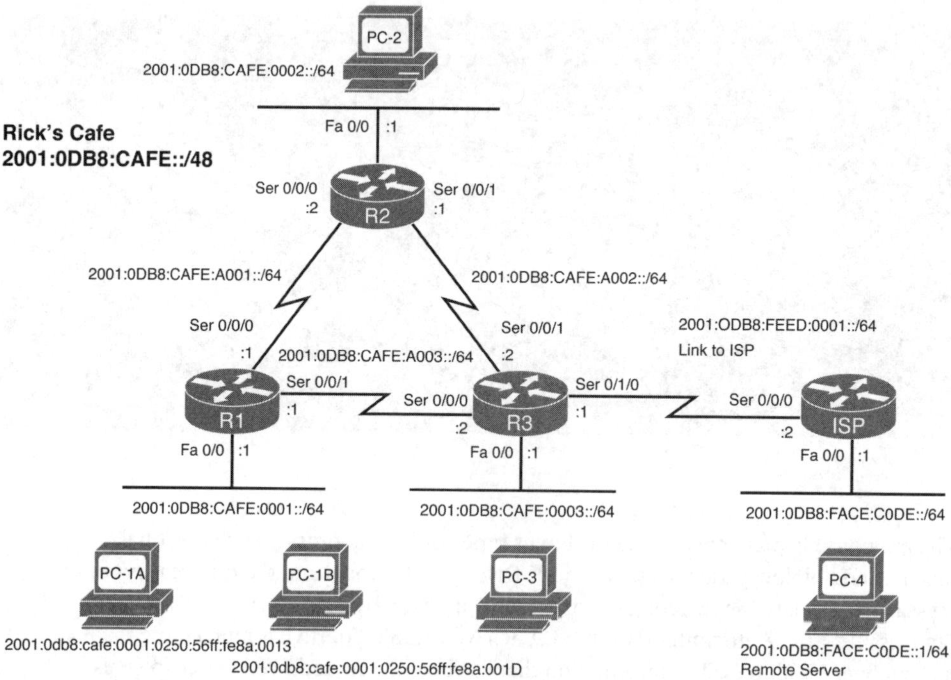

Figure 6-1 *Rick's Café Network Topology*

The network consists of three routers, R1, R2, and R3. Each router has a LAN attached to its Fast Ethernet 0/0 interface:

- R1: 2001:0db8:cafe:0001::/64
- R2: 2001:0db8:cafe:0002::/64
- R3: 2001:0db8:cafe:0003::/64

Note The use of hexadecimal digits for IPv6 addresses provides the opportunity to be a little bit descriptive. For example, Facebook uses the IPv6 address 2620:0:1cfe:**face:b00c**::3.

Internally, each of the routers is connected with a point-to-point serial link. To help better identify the serial connections, the Subnet ID begins with an *a*. The three internal serial networks are

- Between R1 and R2—2001:0db8:cafe:a001:/64
- Between R2 and R2—2001:0db8:cafe:a002:/64
- Between R1 and R3—2001:0db8:cafe:a003:/64

Rick's Café is connected to its ISP through the 2001:0db8:feed:0001:/64 network. As an example of a remote server, the ISP router has the host 2001:0db8:face:c0de::1/64 connected to its Fast Ethernet 0/0 interface. All the addresses shown in Figure 6-1 are global unicast addresses.

Note The addressing scheme used in this topology is designed to help make it easier to identify the networks in the diagram. It is not meant to demonstrate a proper addressing scheme. Best practices will depend upon the complexity of the network and the needs of the organization. SURFNET and RIPE provide some guidance in preparing an effective IPv6 addressing plan: https://labs.ripe.net/Members/steffann/preparing-an-ipv6-addressing-plan.

Configuring Global Unicast Addresses

This section begins by configuring the global unicast addresses on each router. Similar to addressing an IPv4 network, it is considered best practice to manually configure IPv6 addresses on routers, servers, and other network devices. This helps in implementing and troubleshooting network operations.

Example 6-1 shows the configuration of the global unicast addresses for R1 using the **ipv6 address** *ipv6-address/prefix-length* interface command.

Example 6-1 *Configuring R1's Global Unicast Addresses*

```
R1# conf t
R1(config)# interface fastethernet 0/0
R1(config-if)# ipv6 address 2001:0db8:cafe:0001::1/64
R1(config-if)# exit
R1(config)# interface serial 0/0/0
R1(config-if)# ipv6 address 2001:0db8:cafe:a001::1/64
R1(config-if)# exit
R1(config)# interface serial 0/0/1
R1(config-if)# ipv6 address 2001:0db8:cafe:a003::1/64
R1(config-if)# end
R1#

R1# show ipv6 interface brief
FastEthernet0/0            [up/up]
    FE80::21B:CFF:FEC2:82D8
    2001:DB8:CAFE:1::1
Serial0/0/0                [up/up]
    FE80::21B:CFF:FEC2:82D8
    2001:DB8:CAFE:A001::1
Serial0/0/1                [up/up]
    FE80::21B:CFF:FEC2:82D8
    2001:DB8:CAFE:A003::1
R1#
```

These addresses are verified with the **show ipv6 interface brief** command, also illustrated in Example 6-1. Both the link-local address and global unicast address of each interface are displayed. The link-local address is created automatically using EUI-64 whenever a global unicast address has been assigned.

Examples 6-2, 6-3, and 6-4 show the same configurations and verifications for Routers R2, R3, and ISP, respectively.

Example 6-2 *Configuring R2's Global Unicast Addresses*

```
R2(config)# interface fastethernet 0/0
R2(config-if)# ipv6 address 2001:0db8:cafe:0002::1/64
R2(config-if)# exit
R2(config)# interface serial 0/0/0
R2(config-if)# ipv6 address 2001:0db8:cafe:a001::2/64
R2(config-if)# exit
R2(config)# interface serial 0/0/1
R2(config-if)# ipv6 address 2001:0db8:cafe:a002::1/64
R2(config-if)# end
R2#

R2# show ipv6 interface brief
FastEthernet0/0            [up/up]
    FE80::21B:53FF:FE87:C050
    2001:DB8:CAFE:2::1
Serial0/0/0                [up/up]
    FE80::21B:53FF:FE87:C050
    2001:DB8:CAFE:A001::2
Serial0/0/1                [up/up]
    FE80::21B:53FF:FE87:C050
    2001:DB8:CAFE:A002::1
R2#
```

Example 6-3 *Configuring R3's Global Unicast Addresses*

```
R3(config)# interface fastethernet 0/0
R3(config-if)# ipv6 address 2001:0db8:cafe:0003::1/64
R3(config-if)# exit
R3(config)# interface serial 0/0/0
R3(config-if)# ipv6 address 2001:0db8:cafe:a003::2/64
R3(config-if)# exit
R3(config)# interface serial 0/0/1
R3(config-if)# ipv6 address 2001:0db8:cafe:a002::2/64
R3(config-if)# exit
R3(config)# interface serial 0/1/0
```

```
R3(config-if)# ipv6 address 2001:0db8:feed:0001::1/64
R3(config-if)# end

R3# show ipv6 interface brief
FastEthernet0/0            [up/up]
    FE80::226:99FF:FE89:88C8
    2001:DB8:CAFE:3::1
Serial0/0/0                [up/up]
    FE80::226:99FF:FE89:88C8
    2001:DB8:CAFE:A003::2
Serial0/0/1                [up/up]
    FE80::226:99FF:FE89:88C8
    2001:DB8:CAFE:A002::2
Serial0/1/0                [up/up]
    FE80::226:99FF:FE89:88C8
    2001:DB8:FEED:1::1
R3#
```

Example 6-4 *Configuring ISP's Global Unicast Addresses*

```
ISP(config)# interface fastethernet 0/0
ISP(config-if)# ipv6 address 2001:0db8:face:c0de::1/64
ISP(config-if)# exit
ISP(config)# interface serial 0/0/0
ISP(config-if)# ipv6 address 2001:0db8:feed:0001::2/64
ISP(config-if)# end

ISP# show ipv6 interface brief
FastEthernet0/0            [up/up]
    FE80::226:99FF:FED1:6E90
    2001:DB8:FACE:C0DE::1
Serial0/0/0                [up/up]
    FE80::226:99FF:FED1:6E90
    2001:DB8:FEED:1::2
ISP#
```

Configuring Link-local Addresses

Link-local addresses were automatically created when you assigned global unicast addresses to the interfaces. Unless configured manually, link-local addresses are created using an FE80::/10 prefix and an Interface ID using either EUI-64 or a randomly generated value. Cisco IOS uses the EUI-64 format. As previously noted, EUI-64 involves using the 48-bit Ethernet MAC address, inserting FFFE in the middle and flipping the seventh bit. For serial interfaces, Cisco uses the MAC address of a Fast Ethernet interface. Because the routers have a single Fast Ethernet interface, and at least one serial interface, this results in the multiple interfaces having the same link-local address. This is acceptable because link-local addresses only have to be unique on that link.

Link-local addresses play an important role in IPv6. As shown in Chapter 5, "ICMPv6 and Neighbor Discovery Protocol," link-local addresses are employed by Neighbor Discovery's Router Solicitation and Router Advertisement messages. When using SLAAC, the host will also implement the router's link-local address as its default gateway. Later chapters will cover how link-local addresses are used in IPv6 routing protocol messaging. Although a global unicast address is not mandatory for an IPv6 interface, it is for link-local addresses.

Using the EUI-64-formatted link-local addresses makes it difficult to identify the source or destination of these packets, or when verifying a neighbor adjacency with an IPv6 routing protocol. So, it is advantageous to manually configure the routers with link-local addresses that make these addresses more identifiable and easier to remember.

Example 6-5 shows the configuration of link-local addresses for R1's interfaces. The same address has been configured for each interface using this command:

```
Router(config-if)# ipv6 address ipv6-address link-local
```

Example 6-5 *Configuring R1's Link-local Addresses*

```
R1(config)# interface fastethernet 0/0
R1(config-if)# ipv6 address fe80::1 link-local
R1(config-if)# exit
R1(config)# interface serial 0/0/0
R1(config-if)# ipv6 address fe80::1 link-local
R1(config-if)# exit
R1(config)# interface serial 0/0/1
R1(config-if)# ipv6 address fe80::1 link-local
R1(config-if)# end
R1#
R1# show ipv6 interface brief
FastEthernet0/0            [up/up]
    FE80::1
    2001:DB8:CAFE:1::1
Serial0/0/0                [up/up]
    FE80::1
    2001:DB8:CAFE:A001::1
Serial0/0/1                [up/up]
    FE80::1
    2001:DB8:CAFE:A003::1
R1#
```

You can verify the addresses by using the **show ipv6 interface brief** command. Examples 6-6, 6-7, and 6-8 show the link-local address configurations and verifications for Routers R2, R3, and ISP, using an Interface ID to easily identify each router:

- **R1 (all interfaces)**—FE80::1
- **R2 (all interfaces)**—FE80::2
- **R3 (all interfaces)**—FE80::3
- **ISP (all interfaces)**—FE80::FEED

Example 6-6 *Configuring R2's Link-local Addresses*

```
R2(config)# interface fastethernet 0/0
R2(config-if)# ipv6 address fe80::2 link-local
R2(config-if)# exit
R2(config)# interface serial 0/0/0
R2(config-if)# ipv6 address fe80::2 link-local
R2(config-if)# exit
R2(config)# interface serial 0/0/1
R2(config-if)# ipv6 address fe80::2 link-local
R2(config-if)# end
R2#
R2# show ipv6 interface brief
FastEthernet0/0            [up/up]
    FE80::2
    2001:DB8:CAFE:2::1
Serial0/0/0                [up/up]
    FE80::2
    2001:DB8:CAFE:A001::2
Serial0/0/1                [up/up]
    FE80::2
    2001:DB8:CAFE:A002::1
R2#
```

Example 6-7 *Configuring R3's Link-local Addresses*

```
R3(config)# interface fastethernet 0/0
R3(config-if)# ipv6 address fe80::3 link-local
R3(config-if)# exit
R3(config)# interface serial 0/0/0
R3(config-if)# ipv6 address fe80::3 link-local
R3(config-if)# exit
R3(config)# interface serial 0/0/1
R3(config-if)# ipv6 address fe80::3 link-local
```

```
R3(config-if)# exit
R3(config)# interface serial 0/1/0
R3(config-if)# ipv6 address fe80::3 link-local
R3(config-if)# end
R3#
R3# show ipv6 interface brief
FastEthernet0/0            [up/up]
    FE80::3
    2001:DB8:CAFE:3::1
Serial0/0/0                [up/up]
    FE80::3
    2001:DB8:CAFE:A003::2
Serial0/0/1                [up/up]
    FE80::3
    2001:DB8:CAFE:A002::2
Serial0/1/0                [up/up]
    FE80::3
    2001:DB8:FEED:1::1
R3#
```

Example 6-8 *Configuring ISP's Link-local Addresses*

```
ISP(config)# interface fastethernet 0/0
ISP(config-if)# ipv6 address fe80::feed link-local
ISP(config-if)# exit
ISP(config)# interface serial 0/0/0
ISP(config-if)# ipv6 address fe80::feed link-local
ISP(config-if)# end
ISP#
ISP# show ipv6 interface brief
FastEthernet0/0            [up/up]
    FE80::FEED
    2001:DB8:FACE:C0DE::1
FastEthernet0/1            [administratively down/down]
Serial0/0/0                [up/up]
    FE80::FEED
    2001:DB8:FEED:1::2
Serial0/0/1                [administratively down/down]
ISP#
```

The ipv6 enable Command

When a global unicast address is assigned to an interface, a link-local address is automatically created. Link-local addresses are required on an IPv6 address while global unicast and unique-local addresses are not. There might be times when you want to enable IPv6 on an interface without specifying a global unicast or unique local unicast address. This can be accomplished by using the **ipv6 enable** interface command as shown here:

```
Router(config-if)# ipv6 enable
```

Example 6-9 demonstrates the use of this command on R1's Fast Ethernet 0/1 interface. The absence of output from the first **show ipv6 interface fastethernet 0/1** command indicates that IPv6 is not yet enabled on this interface; it has not been assigned any type of IPv6 address.

Example 6-9 *Configuring **ipv6 enable** on R1's Fast Ethernet 0/1 Interface*

```
R1# show ipv6 interface fastethernet 0/1

R1# conf t
R1(config)# interface fastethernet 0/1
R1(config-if)# ipv6 enable
R1(config-if)# end

R1# show ipv6 interface fastethernet 0/1
FastEthernet0/1 is up, line protocol is up
  IPv6 is enabled, link-local address is FE80::21B:CFF:FEC2:82D9
  No Virtual link-local address(es):
  No global unicast address is configured
  Joined group address(es):
    FF02::1
    FF02::2
    FF02::1:FFC2:82D9
  MTU is 1500 bytes
  ICMP error messages limited to one every 100 milliseconds
  ICMP redirects are enabled
  ICMP unreachables are sent
  ND DAD is enabled, number of DAD attempts: 1
  ND reachable time is 30000 milliseconds
  ND advertised reachable time is 0 milliseconds
  ND advertised retransmit interval is 0 milliseconds
  ND router advertisements are sent every 200 seconds
  ND router advertisements live for 1800 seconds
  ND advertised default router preference is Medium
  Hosts use stateless autoconfig for addresses.
R1#
```

Continuing with the output in Example 6-9, the **ipv6 enable** command automatically creates a link-local address. Once again, the **show ipv6 interface fastethernet 0/1** command is implemented, but this time, it verifies the presence of a link-local address while indicating the absence of a global unicast address. Using the **show ipv6 interface brief** command in Example 6-10 confirms that the Fast Ethernet 0/1 interface only has a link-local address and not a global unicast address.

Example 6-10 *Verifying Link-local Address on R1's Fast Ethernet 0/1 Interface*

```
R1# show ipv6 interface brief
FastEthernet0/0            [up/up]
    FE80::1
    2001:DB8:CAFE:1::1
FastEthernet0/1            [up/up]
    FE80::21B:CFF:FEC2:82D9
Serial0/0/0                [up/up]
    FE80::1
    2001:DB8:CAFE:A001::1
Serial0/0/1                [up/up]
    FE80::1
    2001:DB8:CAFE:A003::1
R1#
```

The **ipv6 enable** command does not prohibit the configuration of a global unicast or unique-local unicast address on the interface; it just means it isn't required. Also, a static link-local address can be configured manually; this will overwrite the one created using EUI-64.

Configuring a Global Unicast Address with the EUI-64 Option

In most cases, it is best practice to manually configure a global unicast address on an IPv6 interface. There might be times when it is advantageous for the Interface ID to be assigned using the EUI-64 technique. Example 6-11 uses Router R1's Fast Ethernet 0/1 interface.

The **show interface fastethernet 0/1** command in Example 6-11 displays a MAC address of 001b.0cc2.82d9, which is used for the Interface ID of the global unicast address.

Example 6-11 *Verifying MAC Address on R1's Fast Ethernet 0/1 Interface*

```
R1# show interface fastethernet 0/1
FastEthernet0/1 is up, line protocol is up
  Hardware is MV96340 Ethernet, address is 001b.0cc2.82d9 (bia 001b.0cc2.82d9)
  MTU 1500 bytes, BW 100000 Kbit, DLY 100 usec,
     reliability 255/255, txload 1/255, rxload 1/255
<rest of output omitted for brevity)
```

The interface command used to configure a global unicast address using the EUI-64 format is

```
Router(config-if)# ipv6 address ipv6-prefix/prefix-length eui-64
```

In Example 6-12, R1's Fast Ethernet 0/1 interface is configured with a global unicast address using the EUI-64 format.

Example 6-12 *Configuring R1's Fast Ethernet 0/1 Interface Using EUI-64*

```
R1(config)# interface fastethernet 0/1
R1(config-if)# ipv6 address 2001:0db8:cafe:1234::/64 ?
  anycast   Configure as an anycast
  eui-64    Use eui-64 interface identifier
  <cr>

R1(config-if)# ipv6 address 2001:0db8:cafe:1234::/64 eui-64
R1(config-if)# end

R1# show ipv6 interface fastethernet 0/1
FastEthernet0/1 is up, line protocol is up
  IPv6 is enabled, link-local address is FE80::21B:CFF:FEC2:82D9
  No Virtual link-local address(es):
  Global unicast address(es):
    2001:DB8:CAFE:1234:21B:CFF:FEC2:82D9, subnet is 2001:DB8:CAFE:1234::/64 [EUI]
  Joined group address(es):
    FF02::1
    FF02::2
    FF02::1:FFC2:82D9
<output omitted for brevity>
R1#
```

The **show interface fastethernet 0/1** command in Example 6-12 shows the global unicast address as 2001:0DB8:CAFE:1234:021B:0CFF:FEC2:82D9. This address was created using the following:

- **A prefix of 2001:DB8:CAFE:1234:** The prefix was assigned using the *ipv6-prefix* in the **ipv6 address** command.
- **An Interface ID of 021B:0CFF:FEC2:82D9 using the EUI process:**
  - The MAC address of the interface: 001b.0cc2.82d9
  - FFFE inserted in the middle
  - Seventh bit flipped, changing the hex value from 0 to 2

The **show running-config** command in Example 6-13 indicates that the global unicast address on R1's Fast Ethernet 0/1 interface was configured using EUI-64.

Example 6-13 *Examining R1's Interface Configuration Using **show running-config***

```
R1# show running-config
!
interface FastEthernet0/0
 no ip address
 duplex auto
 speed auto
 ipv6 address FE80::1 link-local
 ipv6 address 2001:DB8:CAFE:1::1/64
!
interface FastEthernet0/1
 no ip address
 duplex auto
 speed auto
 ipv6 address 2001:DB8:CAFE:1234::/64 eui-64
!
interface Serial0/0/0
 no ip address
 ipv6 address FE80::1 link-local
 ipv6 address 2001:DB8:CAFE:A001::1/64
 clock rate 64000
!
interface Serial0/0/1
 no ip address
 ipv6 address FE80::1 link-local
 ipv6 address 2001:DB8:CAFE:A003::1/64
```

Notice that the running config does not show the actual address like the manually configured addresses on the other interfaces. Also see that the only link-local addresses displayed in the running config are those that were manually configured. Link-local addresses that were automatically assigned to the interface using EUI-64 are shown in the configuration, as is the case with Fast Ethernet 0/1.

Removing an IPv6 Address

The **no ipv6 address** command is used to remove an IPv6 address from an interface. If this command is used without including a specific address, all IPv6 addresses are removed from the interface, including any global unicast addresses and the link-local addresses. The **no ipv6 address** command is shown here:

```
Router(config-if)# no ipv6 address [ipv6-address/prefix-length]
```

There is one exception to the **ipv6 enable** command. If an interface was previously configured with the **ipv6 enable** command, the **no ipv6 address** command will remove all IPv6 addresses except the link-local address. You must use the **no ipv6 enable** command to delete the link-local address.

In Example 6-14, all IPv6 addresses from R1's Fast Ethernet interface are removed. First, delete the global unicast address using the **no ipv6 address** command. (You can use this command without specifying the IPv6 address and prefix length.) Because the **ipv6 enable** command was previously used, you must enter **no ipv6 enable** to remove the link-local address. The **show ipv6 fastethernet 0/1** and **show ipv6 interface brief** commands verify that all IPv6 addresses have been deleted from this interface.

Example 6-14 *Removing All IPv6 Addresses from R1's Fast Ethernet 0/1 Interface*

```
R1(config)# interface fastethernet 0/1
R1(config-if)# no ipv6 address 2001:DB8:CAFE:1234:21B:CFF:FEC2:82D9/64
R1(config-if)# no ipv6 enable
R1(config-if)# end
R1#
R1# show ipv6 interface fastethernet 0/1

R1#

R1# show ipv6 interface fastethernet 0/1

R1#show ipv6 interface brief
FastEthernet0/0            [up/up]
    FE80::1
    2001:DB8:CAFE:1::1
FastEthernet0/1            [up/up]
    unassigned
Serial0/0/0                [up/up]
    FE80::1
    2001:DB8:CAFE:A001::1
Serial0/0/1                [up/up]
    FE80::1
    2001:DB8:CAFE:A003::1
R1#
```

Enabling IPv6 Packet Forwarding and ND Router Advertisements

IPv6 routers are used to forward IPv6 packets. IPv6 routers can also announce prefix, prefix length, default gateway, and other configuration information using ND Router

Advertisements. To enable the forwarding of IPv6 unicast packets, the global configuration command **ipv6 unicast-routing** is used:

```
Router(config)# ipv6 unicast-routing
```

If **ipv6 unicast-routing** has been disabled, a router can still be configured with IPv6 interfaces. Disabling **ipv6 unicast-routing** causes the following:

- Prohibits the forwarding of IPv6 unicast packets
- Prohibits the configuration of static IPv6 routing or dynamic IPv6 routing protocols
- Disables the sending of ICMPv6 Routing Advertisements used by Neighbor Discovery Protocol

As shown in Example 6-15, Router R1, along with all the other routers in the topology, have been enabled with the **ipv6 unicast-routing** command. The output from the **debug ipv6 nd** command confirms that ND Router Advertisement messages are being sent from R1's Fast Ethernet 0/0 interface.

Example 6-15 *Verifying Router Advertisements on R1*

```
R1(config)# ipv6 unicast-routing

R1# debug ipv6 nd
ICMP Neighbor Discovery events debugging is on
R1#
*Feb 11 18:03:23.439: ICMPv6-ND: Request to send RA for FE80::21B:CFF:FEC2:82D8
*Feb 11 18:03:23.439: ICMPv6-ND: Sending RA from FE80::21B:CFF:FEC2:82D8 to FF02::1
on FastEthernet0/0
*Feb 11 18:03:23.439: ICMPv6-ND:     MTU = 1500
*Feb 11 18:03:23.439: ICMPv6-ND:     prefix = 2001:DB8:CAFE:1::/64 onlink autoconfig
*Feb 11 18:03:23.439: ICMPv6-ND:             2592000/604800 (valid/preferred)
R1#
```

In the topology, both PC-1A and PC-1B are hosts on R1's LAN and are configured to obtain their IPv6 addresses automatically. Router R1 sends its ND Router Advertisement messages including the prefix, prefix length, and default gateway information out its Fast Ethernet 0/0 interface. Both of the hosts are using the Windows XP operating system, which uses the EUI-64 format for its Interface ID. Example 6-16 shows the output from their **ipconfig** commands. Notice that the Interface IDs of both their global unicast and link-local addresses were generated using their Ethernet MAC addresses and the EUI-64 technique.

Example 6-16 *IPv6 Addresses for PC-1A and PC-1B*

```
PC-1A> ipconfig

Windows XP IP Configuration

Ethernet adapter Local Area Connection:

   Connection-specific DNS Suffix  . :
   IPv6 Address. . . . . . . . . . . : 2001:0db8:cafe:0001:0250:56ff:fe8a:0013
   Link-local IPv6 Address . . . . . : FE80::0250:56ff:fe8a:0013
   Default Gateway . . . . . . . . . : FE80:021b:0cff:0fec2:82d8
```

```
PC-1B> ipconfig

Windows XP IP Configuration

Ethernet adapter Local Area Connection:

   Connection-specific DNS Suffix  . :
   IPv6 Address. . . . . . . . . . . : 2001:0db8:cafe:0001:0250:56ff:fe8a:001D
   Link-local IPv6 Address . . . . . : FE80::0250:56ff:fe8a:001D
   Default Gateway . . . . . . . . . : FE80:021b:0cff:0fec2:82d8
```

PC-1A's MAC address is 00-50-56-8A-00-13. PC-1B's MAC address is 00-50-56-8A-00-1D.

> **Note** In previous examples, our hosts used Windows Vista or a newer operating system, which generates a random 64-bit value for the Interface ID. Windows XP is used on these hosts to show an example of hosts using the EUI-64 technique.

Neighbor Cache

The IPv6 Neighbor Cache or Neighbor Discovery Cache is similar to the ARP Cache in IPv4. The Neighbor Cache is displayed using the **show ipv6 neighbors** command.

In Example 6-17, R1 pings the global unicast address of PC-1A. Similar to Address Resolution Protocol (ARP) in IPv4, R1 sends an ND Neighbor Solicitation message to obtain the Layer 2 MAC address of PC-1A. PC-1A responds with an ND Neighbor Advertisement containing its MAC address. R1 uses this PC-1A's MAC address to encapsulate its ICMPv6 Echo Requests to PC-1A. PC-1A sends ICMPv6 Echo Replies in return. The output from R1's **show ipv6 neighbors** command displays the Neighbor Cache on R1 with PC-1A's IPv6 address and corresponding MAC address.

Example 6-17 *Pinging PC-1A and Displaying the Neighbor Cache*

```
R1# ping 2001:db8:cafe:1:250:56ff:fe8a:13

Type escape sequence to abort.
Sending 5, 100-byte ICMP Echos to 2001:DB8:CAFE:1:250:56FF:FE8A:13, timeout is 2
seconds:
!!!!!
Success rate is 100 percent (5/5), round-trip min/avg/max = 0/0/4 ms
R1# show ipv6 neighbors
IPv6 Address                              Age Link-layer Addr State Interface
2001:DB8:CAFE:1:250:56FF:FE8A:13            0 0050.568a.0013  REACH Fa0/0

R1#
```

Shown in Example 6-18, R1 pings host PC-1B. R1's Neighbor Cache now includes the IPv6 addresses and MAC addresses of both PC-1A and PC-1B. The link-local addresses for both hosts are also in the Neighbor Cache as a result of Neighbor Solicitation messages originated by these two hosts.

Example 6-18 *Pinging PC-1B and Displaying the Neighbor Cache*

```
R1# ping 2001:db8:cafe:1:250:56ff:fe8a:1d

Type escape sequence to abort.
Sending 5, 100-byte ICMP Echos to 2001:DB8:CAFE:1:250:56FF:FE8A:1D, timeout is 2
seconds:
!!!!!
Success rate is 100 percent (5/5), round-trip min/avg/max = 0/1/4 ms
R1#

R1# show ipv6 neighbors
IPv6 Address                              Age Link-layer Addr State Interface
2001:DB8:CAFE:1:250:56FF:FE8A:13            0 0050.568a.0013  STALE Fa0/0
2001:DB8:CAFE:1:250:56FF:FE8A:1D            0 0050.568a.001d  REACH Fa0/0
FE80::250:56FF:FE8A:13                      0 0050.568a.0013  STALE Fa0/0
FE80::250:56FF:FE8A:1D                      0 0050.568a.001d  REACH Fa0/0

R1#
```

The Neighbor Cache is populated dynamically using Neighbor Solicitation and Neighbor Advertisement messages, similar to ARP Requests and ARP Replies in IPv4, as previously discussed in Chapter 5. Static entries can also be inserted into the Neighbor Cache. Example 6-19 demonstrates how to add a static entry to R1's Neighbor Cache using the following global configuration command:

```
Router(config)# ipv6 neighbor ipv6-address interface-type interface-number
hardware-address
```

The Neighbor Cache can be cleared using this command:

```
Router# clear ipv6 neighbors
```

Example 6-19 *Adding a Static Neighbor Entry to R1's Neighbor Cache*

```
R1(config)# ipv6 neighbor 2001:db8:cafe:1::1234 fastethernet 0/0 0050.568a.5555
R1(config)# end

R1# show ipv6 neighbors
IPv6 Address                                Age Link-layer Addr State Interface
2001:DB8:CAFE:1:250:56FF:FE8A:13            208 0050.568a.0013  STALE Fa0/0
2001:DB8:CAFE:1::1234                       -   0050.568a.5555  REACH Fa0/0
2001:DB8:CAFE:1:250:56FF:FE8A:1D            206 0050.568a.001d  STALE Fa0/0
FE80::250:56FF:FE8A:13                      207 0050.568a.0013  STALE Fa0/0
FE80::250:56FF:FE8A:1D                      205 0050.568a.001d  STALE Fa0/0

R1#
```

Tuning Neighbor Discovery Parameters

Chapter 5 discussed the Neighbor Discovery Protocol including Neighbor Advertisements in some detail. A Router Advertisement (RA) message is sent periodically or in response to a Router Solicitation (RS) message. It is used to provide hosts with addressing and other configuration information and is an important part of Stateless Address Autoconfiguration (SLAAC). By default, Cisco routers send Router Advertisement messages on Ethernet, Fast Ethernet, Gigabit Ethernet, and Ten Gigabit Ethernet interfaces.

Many of the Router Advertisement parameters are displayed in the output of the **show ipv6 interface** command, as shown in Example 6-20.

Example 6-20 *Default ND Router Advertisement Parameters*

```
R1# show ipv6 interface fastethernet 0/0
FastEthernet0/0 is up, line protocol is up
  IPv6 is enabled, link-local address is FE80::1
  No Virtual link-local address(es):
  Global unicast address(es):
    2001:DB8:CAFE:1::1, subnet is 2001:DB8:CAFE:1::/64
  Joined group address(es):
    FF02::1
    FF02::2
    FF02::1:FF00:1
  MTU is 1500 bytes
  ICMP error messages limited to one every 100 milliseconds
  ICMP redirects are enabled
  ICMP unreachables are sent
  ND DAD is enabled, number of DAD attempts: 1
  ND reachable time is 30000 milliseconds
  ND advertised reachable time is 0 milliseconds
  ND advertised retransmit interval is 0 milliseconds
! RA interval:
  ND router advertisements are sent every 200 seconds
! RA lifetime:
  ND router advertisements live for 1800 seconds
  ND advertised default router preference is Medium
! RA Managed-Config-Flag is 0. Hosts are to use stateless, not stateful
! configuration:
  Hosts use stateless autoconfig for addresses.
R1#
```

The parameters for Router Advertisement and other Neighbor Discovery messages can be configured using the **ipv6 nd** command. Example 6-21 shows some of the Neighbor Discovery configurations options, specifically when configuring ND Router Advertisements.

Example 6-21 *ipv6 nd Configuration Options*

```
R1(config)# interface fastethernet 0/0
R1(config-if)# ipv6 nd ?
  advertisement-interval  Send an advertisement interval option in RA's
  dad                     Duplicate Address Detection
  managed-config-flag     Hosts should use DHCP for address config
  ns-interval             Set advertised NS retransmission interval
  other-config-flag       Hosts should use DHCP for non-address config
  prefix                  Configure IPv6 Routing Prefix Advertisement
```

```
  ra                        Router Advertisement control
  reachable-time            Set advertised reachability time
  router-preference         Set default router preference value

R1(config-if)# ipv6 nd ra ?
  interval  Set IPv6 Router Advertisement Interval
  lifetime  Set IPv6 Router Advertisement Lifetime
  suppress  Suppress IPv6 Router Advertisements

R1(config-if)#
```

An IPv6 router does not have to participate in the sending of Router Advertisement messages. RA messages can be suppressed with this interface command:

```
Router(config-if)# ipv6 nd ra suppress
```

Note The **ipv6 nd suppress-ra** command will suppress periodic RA messages, but solicited RA messages (Router Advertisement messages in response to Router Solicitation messages) will still occur.

Note Effective with Cisco IOS Release 12.4(2)T, the **ipv6 nd suppress-ra** command is replaced by the **ipv6 nd ra suppress** command.

In Example 6-20, the **show ipv6 interface** command illustrates some of the default parameters associated with Router Advertisement messages. The RA interval is the amount of time in seconds between consecutive Router Advertisement messages. By default, the Router Advertisement interval is 200 seconds on Cisco routers. The **ipv6 nd ra-interval** command is used to modify this parameter:

```
Router(config-if)# ipv6 nd ra interval {maximum-secs [minimum-secs]
  | msec maximum-ms [minimum-ms]}
```

In Example 6-22, the RA interval is changed to 180 seconds.

Example 6-22 *Configuring Router Advertisement Parameters*

```
R1(config)# interface fastethernet 0/0
R1(config-if)# ipv6 nd ra interval 180
R1(config-if)# ipv6 nd ra lifetime 3600
R1(config-if)# ipv6 nd managed-config-flag
R1(config-if)# ipv6 nd other-config-flag
```

```
R1(config-if)# end
R1# show ipv6 interface fastethernet 0/0
*Feb 12 00:21:44.465: %SYS-5-CONFIG_I: Configured from console by console
R1# show ipv6 interface fastethernet 0/0
FastEthernet0/0 is up, line protocol is up
  IPv6 is enabled, link-local address is FE80::1
  No Virtual link-local address(es):
  Global unicast address(es):
    2001:DB8:CAFE:1::1, subnet is 2001:DB8:CAFE:1::/64
  Joined group address(es):
    FF02::1
    FF02::2
    FF02::1:FF00:1
  MTU is 1500 bytes
  ICMP error messages limited to one every 100 milliseconds
  ICMP redirects are enabled
  ICMP unreachables are sent
  ND DAD is enabled, number of DAD attempts: 1
  ND reachable time is 30000 milliseconds
  ND advertised reachable time is 0 milliseconds
  ND advertised retransmit interval is 0 milliseconds
  ND router advertisements are sent every 180 seconds    ! ipv6 nd ra interval 180
  ND router advertisements live for 3600 seconds         ! ipv6 nd ra lifetime 3600
  ND advertised default router preference is Medium
  Hosts use DHCP to obtain routable addresses.           ! ipv6 nd managed-config-flag
  Hosts use DHCP to obtain other configuration.          ! ipv6 nd other-config-flag
R1#
```

The RA lifetime defines how long a host should consider this router as a valid default gateway. It does not apply to the other configuration parameters contained in the Router Advertisement. The RA lifetime has a default of 1800 seconds (30 minutes) on Cisco routers. A lifetime of 0 indicates that this router is not a default gateway and should not be added to the host's default router list. The **ipv6 nd ra-lifetime** command is used to modify the RA lifetime:

```
Router(config-if)# ipv6 nd ra lifetime seconds
```

In Example 6-22, the RA lifetime is changed to 3600 seconds (60 minutes).

> **Note** In some documentation and in some IOSs, the commands to modify the RA interval and RA lifetime parameters include a hyphen following "ra": **ipv6 nd ra-interval** and **ipv6 nd ra-lifetime.**

The M Flag and the O Flag in the Router Advertisement message are associated with Stateless Address Autoconfiguration (SLAAC). The M Flag, or Managed Address Configuration Flag, tells a host that is configured to obtain its configuration information automatically whether to use SLAAC or stateful configuration (DHCPv6). The default, 0, notifies hosts on the network to use SLAAC. When set to 1, this tells the host to use stateful configuration (DHCPv6). To set the M Flag to 1 (DHCPv6), the **ipv6 nd managed-config-flag** command is used:

```
Router(config-if)# ipv6 managed-config-flag
```

In Example 6-22, the Router Advertisement Managed Address Configuration Flag is set to 1 (DHCPv6). The **no ipv6 nd managed-config-flag** command is used to set the flag back to its default of 0 (SLAAC).

The O Flag, or the Other Configuration Flag, informs a host whether additional configuration information can be obtained from a DHCPv6 server, such as DNS-related information. The default of 0 means that there is no additional information available from a DHCPv6 server. When set to 1, this tells the host that additional information is available from a DHCPv6 server. To set the O Flag to 1, the **ipv6 nd other-config-flag** command is used:

```
Router(config-if)# ipv6 other-config-flag
```

In Example 6-22, the Router Advertisement Other Configuration Flag is set to 1. The **no ipv6 nd other-config-flag** command is used to set the flag back to its default of 0. The default for both the M and O Flags is 0, which means that there is no information available from a DHCPv6 server.

The output from R1's **debug ipv6 nd** command in Example 6-23 verifies that that the M Flag and O Flag have both been set.

Example 6-23 *Verifying Connectivity of Serial Links*

```
R1# debug ipv6 nd
*Feb 12 00:22:59.205: ICMPv6-ND: Request to send RA for FE80::1
*Feb 12 00:22:59.205: ICMPv6-ND: Sending RA from FE80::1 to FF02::1 on
FastEthernet0/0
*Feb 12 00:22:59.205: ICMPv6-ND:     Managed address configuration
*Feb 12 00:22:59.205: ICMPv6-ND:     Other stateful configuration
*Feb 12 00:22:59.205: ICMPv6-ND:     MTU = 1500
*Feb 12 00:22:59.205: ICMPv6-ND:     prefix = 2001:DB8:CAFE:1::/64 onlink autoconfig
*Feb 12 00:22:59.205: ICMPv6-ND:      2592000/604800 (valid/preferred)
R1# undebug all
```

In Example 6-24, these ND Router Advertisement parameters are reset using the **no** option for each command and verify that these default parameters are using the **show ipv6 interface** command.

Example 6-24 *Configuring Router Advertisement Parameters Back to Default Values*

```
R1(config)# interface fastethernet 0/0
R1(config-if)# no ipv6 nd ra interval 180
R1(config-if)# no ipv6 nd ra lifetime 3600
R1(config-if)# no ipv6 nd managed-config-flag
R1(config-if)# no ipv6 nd other-config-flag
R1(config-if)# end
R1# show ipv6 interface fastethernet 0/0
FastEthernet0/0 is up, line protocol is up
  IPv6 is enabled, link-local address is FE80::1
  No Virtual link-local address(es):
  Global unicast address(es):
    2001:DB8:CAFE:1::1, subnet is 2001:DB8:CAFE:1::/64
  Joined group address(es):
    FF02::1
    FF02::2
    FF02::1:FF00:1
  MTU is 1500 bytes
  ICMP error messages limited to one every 100 milliseconds
  ICMP redirects are enabled
  ICMP unreachables are sent
  ND DAD is enabled, number of DAD attempts: 1
  ND reachable time is 30000 milliseconds
  ND advertised reachable time is 0 milliseconds
  ND advertised retransmit interval is 0 milliseconds
  ND router advertisements are sent every 200 seconds   ! no ipv6 nd ra interval 180
  ND router advertisements live for 1800 seconds        ! no ipv6 nd ra lifetime 3600
  ND advertised default router preference is Medium
  Hosts use stateless autoconfig for addresses.       ! no ipv6 nd managed-config-flag
                                                      ! no ipv6 nd other-config-flag
R1#
```

When there are multiple routers on the same Ethernet network, Router Advertisement messages are sent from all routers unless suppressed with the **ipv6 nd ra suppress** command. To display IPv6 Router Advertisement information received from other routers on the link, the following command is used:

```
Router# show ipv6 routers
```

Final Configurations

Examples 6-25 shows the final running config files for Routers R1, R2, R3, and ISP. Notice that on all four routers, **no ip address** is part of each interface configuration. This refers to the IPv4 address not being configured on the interface, not the IPv6 address.

Example 6-25 *Partial Running Config for Routers R1, R2, R3, and ISP*

```
R1# show running-config
!
hostname R1
!
ipv6 unicast-routing
!
interface FastEthernet0/0
 no ip address
 ipv6 address FE80::1 link-local
 ipv6 address 2001:DB8:CAFE:1::1/64
!
interface Serial0/0/0
 no ip address
 ipv6 address FE80::1 link-local
 ipv6 address 2001:DB8:CAFE:A001::1/64
!
interface Serial0/0/1
 no ip address
 ipv6 address FE80::1 link-local
 ipv6 address 2001:DB8:CAFE:A003::1/64
!
```

```
R2# show running-config
!
hostname R2
!
ipv6 unicast-routing
!
interface FastEthernet0/0
 no ip address
 ipv6 address FE80::2 link-local
 ipv6 address 2001:DB8:CAFE:2::1/64
!
interface Serial0/0/0
 no ip address
 ipv6 address FE80::2 link-local
 ipv6 address 2001:DB8:CAFE:A001::2/64
!
```

```
interface Serial0/0/1
 no ip address
 ipv6 address FE80::2 link-local
 ipv6 address 2001:DB8:CAFE:A002::1/64
```

```
R3# show running-config
!
hostname R3
!
ipv6 unicast-routing
!
interface FastEthernet0/0
 no ip address
 ipv6 address FE80::3 link-local
 ipv6 address 2001:DB8:CAFE:3::1/64
!
interface Serial0/0/0
 no ip address
 ipv6 address FE80::3 link-local
 ipv6 address 2001:DB8:CAFE:A003::2/64
!
interface Serial0/0/1
 no ip address
 ipv6 address FE80::3 link-local
 ipv6 address 2001:DB8:CAFE:A002::2/64
!
interface Serial0/1/0
 no ip address
 ipv6 address FE80::3 link-local
 ipv6 address 2001:DB8:FEED:1::1/64
!
```

```
ISP# show running-config
!
hostname ISP
!
ipv6 unicast-routing
!
interface FastEthernet0/0
 no ip address
 ipv6 address FE80::FEED link-local
 ipv6 address 2001:DB8:FACE:C0DE::1/64
!
interface Serial0/0/0
 no ip address
 ipv6 address FE80::FEED link-local
 ipv6 address 2001:DB8:FEED:1::2/64
```

In Example 6-26, verify the configurations by pinging the adjacent interfaces of neighboring routers. However, when you attempt to ping interfaces of remote networks, the pings fail, as shown in Example 6-27. This is because you haven't configured static or dynamic routing to make these remote networks reachable. This dilemma is solved in Chapter 7, "Introduction to Routing IPv6," and Chapter 8, "IPv6 IGP Routing Protocols." Chapter 7 demonstrates how to configure static IPv6 routes, and Chapter 8 illustrates how to configure dynamic IPv6 routing protocols.

Example 6-26 *Verifying Connectivity of Serial Links*

```
R1# ping 2001:db8:cafe:a001::2

Type escape sequence to abort.
Sending 5, 100-byte ICMP Echos to 2001:DB8:CAFE:A001::2, timeout is 2 seconds:
!!!!!
Success rate is 100 percent (5/5), round-trip min/avg/max = 28/28/28 ms
R1# ping 2001:db8:cafe:a003::2
Type escape sequence to abort.
Sending 5, 100-byte ICMP Echos to 2001:DB8:CAFE:A003::2, timeout is 2 seconds:
!!!!!
Success rate is 100 percent (5/5), round-trip min/avg/max = 28/28/32 ms
R1#

R3# ping 2001:db8:cafe:a002::1

Type escape sequence to abort.
Sending 5, 100-byte ICMP Echos to 2001:DB8:CAFE:A002::1, timeout is 2 seconds:
!!!!!
Success rate is 100 percent (5/5), round-trip min/avg/max = 28/28/32 ms
R3# ping 2001:db8:feed:0001::2

Type escape sequence to abort.
Sending 5, 100-byte ICMP Echos to 2001:DB8:FEED:1::2, timeout is 2 seconds:
!!!!!
Success rate is 100 percent (5/5), round-trip min/avg/max = 28/28/28 ms
R3#
```

Example 6-27 *No Communications to Remote Networks*

```
R1# ping 2001:db8:cafe:3::1

Type escape sequence to abort.
Sending 5, 100-byte ICMP Echos to 2001:DB8:CAFE:3::1, timeout is 2 seconds:
.....
Success rate is 0 percent (0/5)
```

```
R1# ping 2001:db8:feed::2

Type escape sequence to abort.
Sending 5, 100-byte ICMP Echos to 2001:DB8:FEED::2, timeout is 2 seconds:
.....
Success rate is 0 percent (0/5)
R1#
```

IPv6 Access Control Lists

Configuring IPv6 access control lists (ACL) is similar to configuring IPv4 ACLs. However, there are some notable differences. Let's assume that you are familiar with configuring IPv4 ACLs. In IPv4, there are two basic types of ACLs: standard and extended. Basically, a standard ACL can permit or deny traffic based only on the source address. An extended ACL provides greater control and can permit or deny traffic based both on the source and destination addresses, as well as protocols and services (TCP/UDP port numbers). Also, IPv6 only supports named (versus numbered) ACLs.

Note IPv6 also includes support for other types of ACLs, including reflective, time-based, and zone-based ACLs. These are beyond the scope of this book. For information on these and other types of IPv6 ACLs, refer to the *Cisco IOS IPv6 Configuration Guide, Implementing Traffic Filters and Firewalls for IPv6 Security*, www.cisco.com/en/US/docs/ios/ipv6/configuration/guide/ip6-sec_trfltr_fw.html.

Whether standard, extended, or both, these types of ACLs are available depending on the router's IOS. Quoting from the *Cisco IOS IPv6 Configuration Guide, Implementing Traffic Filters and Firewalls for IPv6 Security*:

> "Cisco IOS Release 12.2(2)T through Cisco IOS Release 12.2(13)T and Cisco IOS Release 12.0(22)S and later releases support only standard IPv6 access control list (ACL) functionality. In Cisco IOS Release 12.0(23)S and 12.2(13)T or later releases, the standard IPv6 ACL functionality is extended to support traffic filtering based on IPv6 option headers and optional, upper-layer protocol type information for finer granularity of control (functionality similar to extended ACLs in IPv4)."

In this section, extended IPv6 access control lists are used.

In IPv4, there is an implicit **deny any any** statement at the end of each access list. IPv6 access control lists have a similar **deny ipv6 any any** statement but also include two other statements by default:

- **permit icmp any any nd-na**
- **permit icmp any any nd-ns**

The IPv6 Neighbor Discovery (ND) process requires the use of the IPv6 network layer service. Therefore, by default, IPv6 ACLs need to implicitly allow IPv6 Neighbor Discovery packets to be sent and received on an interface. This means that both ND Neighbor Advertisement and ND Neighbor Solicitation messages must be permitted on the link. In IPv4, Address Resolution Protocol (ARP) messages, which are equivalent to the IPv6 Neighbor Discovery process, are not sent over IPv4. However, IPv6 Neighbor Discovery messages do use the services of IPv6 and must be implicitly included in the IPv6 ACLs.

Another notable difference between IPv4 and IPv6 ACLs is the use of numbered access lists. IPv6 ACLs can only be defined by a unique name and do not support the use of numbered lists. An IPv4 ACL and an IPv6 ACL cannot share the same name.

Denying Access from FACE:C0DE to CAFE

Configuring an IPv6 ACL is very similar to configuring IPv4 ACLs. Using the topology in Figure 6-2, filter out traffic from the 2001:db8:face:c0de::/48 network, which includes R4's LAN, from entering the 2001:db8:cafe::/48 network. Configure an IPv6 extended ACL on Router R3 to deny this traffic coming in from the ISP router.

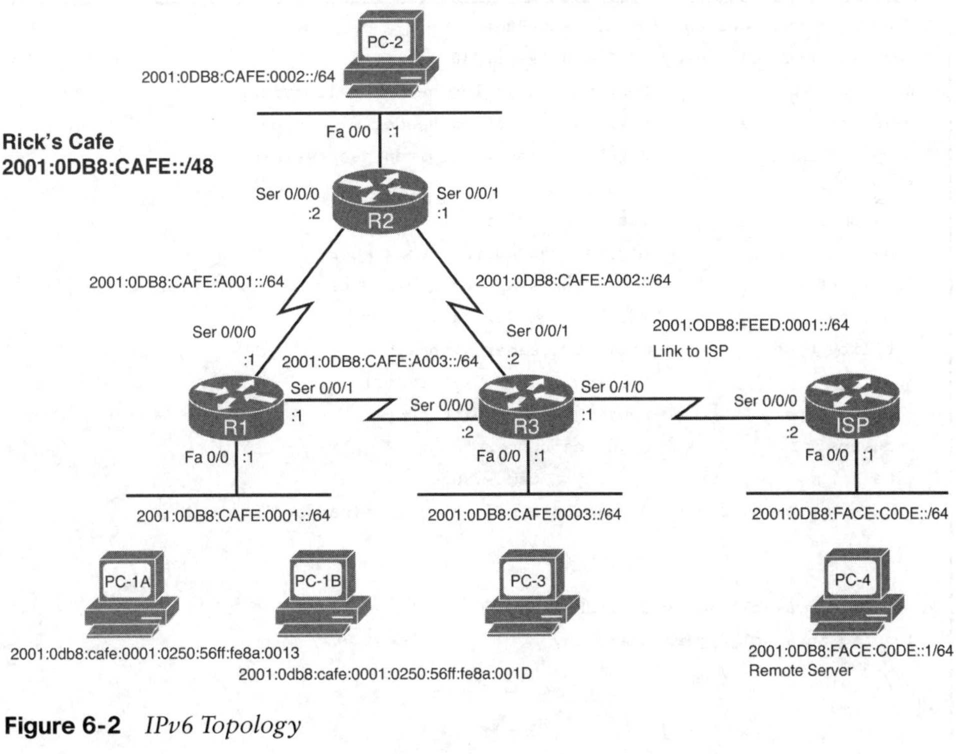

Figure 6-2 *IPv6 Topology*

> **Note** For the purposes of this section on IPv6 ACLs, assume that there is complete reachability within the network topology. Routing IPv6 is discussed in Chapters 7 and 8.

Begin by using the **ipv6 access-list** command on R3, which is similar to the **ip access-list** command, except that it is IPv6 specific. The syntax for this command is

```
Router(config)# ipv6 access-list access-list-name
```

In Example 6-28, an ACL on R3 is configured with the access list name no-face-c0de. In ACL configuration mode, configure the permit and deny statements. Again, these commands are similar to those in IPv4 but with IPv6-specific options. Using the ACL command **deny 2001:db8:face:c0de::/48 any**, R3 will deny any packets with the source IPv6 address containing the 2001:db8:face:c0de::/48 prefix. The next statement is **permit any any**, allowing all other IPv6 packets. Example 6-28 also includes an alternative method for configuring an extended IPv6 ACL.

Example 6-28 *Configuring an IPv6 Extended ACL on R3*

```
R3(config)# ipv6 access-list no-face-c0de
R3(config-ipv6-acl)# deny 2001:db8:feed::/48 any ?
  dest-option              Destination Option header (all types)
  dest-option-type         Destination Option header with type
  dscp                     Match packets with given dscp value
  flow-label               Flow label
  fragments                Check non-initial fragments
  log                      Log matches against this entry
  log-input                Log matches against this entry, including input
  mobility                 Mobility header (all types)
  mobility-type            Mobility header with type
  routing                  Routing header (all types)
  routing-type             Routing header with type
  sequence                 Sequence number for this entry
  time-range               Specify a time-range
  undetermined-transport   Transport cannot be determined or is missing
  <cr>

R3(config-ipv6-acl)# deny 2001:db8:face:c0de::/48 any
R3(config-ipv6-acl)# permit any any

OR

R3(config)# ipv6 access-list no-face-c0de deny 2001:db8:face:c0de::/48 any
R3(config)# ipv6 access-list no-face-c0de permit any any
```

> **Note** As with IPv4 ACLs, IPv6 allows you to filter on information in the IPv6 header and extension headers. This is platform dependent and beyond the scope of this book, which focuses only on the basics of configuring an IPv6 ACL.

Instead of the **ip access-group** command used in IPv4 for applying an ACL to an interface, IPv6 uses the **ipv6 traffic-filter** command. The **ipv6 traffic-filter** command filters traffic that is forwarded, not originated, by the router. To filter incoming or outgoing IPv6 traffic on an interface, use the **ipv6 traffic-filter** command in interface configuration mode:

```
Router(config-if)# ipv6 traffic-filter access-list-name {in | out}
```

To filter the packets with the IPv6 prefix of 2001:db8:face:c0de::/48, the **ipv6 traffic-filter no-face-c0de** command is configured on R3's serial 0/0/0 interface facing the ISP router, as shown in Example 6-29.

Example 6-29 *Applying the ACL to an Interface*

```
R3(config)# interface serial 0/1/0
R3(config-if)# ipv6 traffic-filter no-face-c0de in
R3(config-if)# end
R3#
```

Example 6-30 verifies this ACL configuration using the **show ipv6 access-list** command. Notice the default sequence number associated with each statement. The **show running-config** command is also used to verify the configuration of the no-face-c0de ACL.

Example 6-30 *Verifying R3's ACL*

```
R3# show ipv6 access-list
IPv6 access list no-face-c0de
    deny ipv6 2001:DB8:FACE::/48 any sequence 10
    permit ipv6 any any sequence 20
R3#

R3# show running-config
<output omitted for brevity)
!
interface Serial0/1/0
 no ip address
 ipv6 address FE80::3 link-local
 ipv6 address 2001:DB8:FEED:1::1/64
 ipv6 traffic-filter no-face-c0de in
 clock rate 64000
```

```
!
ipv6 access-list no-face-c0de
 deny ipv6 2001:DB8:FACE::/48 any
 permit ipv6 any any
!
<output omitted for brevity)
```

You can test the ACL configuration using the **ping** command on ISP and sourcing the ICMPv6 Echo Request from its Fast Ethernet 0/0 interface, a member of the 2001:db8:face:c0de:1::/64 network. As shown in the output in Example 6-31, pings with a source IPv6 address containing a lower-order prefix of 2001:db8:face:c0de::/48 are not successful.

Example 6-31 *Testing Our No-Face-c0de ACL*

```
ISP# ping 2001:db8:cafe:1::1 source fastethernet 0/0

Type escape sequence to abort.
Sending 5, 100-byte ICMP Echos to 2001:DB8:CAFE:1::1, timeout is 2 seconds:
Packet sent with a source address of 2001:DB8:FACE:C0DE::1
AAAAA
Success rate is 0 percent (0/5)
ISP#

ISP# ping 2001:db8:cafe:1::1
Type escape sequence to abort.
Sending 5, 100-byte ICMP Echos to 2001:DB8:CAFE:1::1, timeout is 2 seconds:
!!!!!
Success rate is 100 percent (5/5), round-trip min/avg/max = 68/70/72 ms
ISP#
```

The IPv6 test character on R3 shows all A's, indicating that these packets were administratively unreachable, usually the result of being blocked by an access list. Table 6-1 shows a listing of the IPv6 ping test characters.

Table 6-1 *IPv6 ping Test Characters*

Character	Description
!	Each exclamation point indicates receipt of a reply.
.	Each period indicates that the network server timed out while waiting for a reply.
?	Unknown error.

Character	Description
@	Unreachable for unknown reason.
A	Administratively unreachable. Usually, this output indicates that an access list is blocking traffic.
B	Packet too big.
H	Host unreachable.
N	Network unreachable (beyond scope).
P	Port unreachable.
R	Parameter problem.
S	Source address failed ingress/egress policy.
T	Time exceeded.
U	No route to host.
X	Reject route to destination.

Before moving on to the next example, remove the no-face-c0de ACL on R3 so there aren't any unintended effects. Example 6-32 shows the removal of the no-face-c0de ACL and the verification of its removal.

Example 6-32 *Removing the no-face-c0de ACL*

```
R3(config)# no ipv6 access-list no-face-c0de
R3(config)# end
R3# show ipv6 access-list

R3#
R3(config)# interface serial 0/1/0
R3(config-if)# no ipv6 traffic-filter no-face-c0de in
R3(config-if)# end
R3#
```

Permitting Local Telnet Access

Example 6-33 displays the configuration of an access list that permits only local Telnet access to Router R3. To filter incoming and outgoing connections to and from the router based on an IPv6 access list, the line configuration command **ipv6 access-class** is used:

```
Router(config-line) ipv6 access-class ipv6-access-list-name {in | out}
```

In Example 6-33, the access list no-outside-vty is configured. The **permit**

2001:db8:cafe::/48 any statement allows access from packets sourced from the 2001:db8:cafe::/48 network. An implicit **deny any any** statement at the end of the ACL will reject any packets with source addresses outside this network.

Example 6-33 *Configuring an ACL to Only Permit Local Telnet Access to R3*

```
R3(config)# ipv6 access-list no-outside-vty
R3(config-ipv6-acl)# permit 2001:db8:cafe::/48 any
R3(config-ipv6-acl)# end
R3#

R3(config)# line vty 0 4
R3(config-line)# password luigi
R3(config-line)# login
R3(config-line)# ipv6 access-class no-outside-vty in
R3(config-line)# end
R3#
```

Telnet access is configured on Router R3 as shown in Example 6-33. The **ipv6 access-class no-outside-vty in** command is used to filter the Telnet connections using the no-outside-vty ACL.

Example 6-34 verifies that Telnet access from outside the 2001:db8:cafe::/48 network is not permitted. A Telnet connection is attempted using two of R3's interfaces.

Example 6-34 *Verifying That There Is No Outside Telnet Access to R3*

```
ISP# telnet 2001:db8:feed:1::1
Trying 2001:DB8:FEED:1::1 ...
% Connection refused by remote host

ISP# telnet 2001:db8:cafe:a003::2
Trying 2001:DB8:CAFE:A003::2 ...
% Connection refused by remote host
```

Example 6-35 shows a different result when using Telnet from within the 2001:db8:cafe::/48 network. Because the source IPv6 address of R1 is permitted by the **permit 2001:db8:cafe::/48 any** statement, this Telnet connection is accepted by R3.

Example 6-35 *Verifying That There Is Inside Telnet Access to R3*

```
R1# telnet 2001:db8:cafe:a003::2
Trying 2001:DB8:CAFE:A003::2 ... Open


User Access Verification

Password:
R3>
```

Summary

This chapter demonstrated how to configure the addressing for the topology that you will be using in the following chapters. New commands were introduced, as well as some that were learned in previous chapters.

Addressing Commands

- **Configuring global unicast addresses:** The interface command for configuring a global unicast or unique-local unicast address is

  `Router(config-if)# ipv6 address ipv6-address/prefix-length`

- **Configuring link-local addresses:** The interface command for manually configuring a link-local address is

  `Router(config-if)# ipv6 address ipv6-address link-local`

- **Enabling an IPv6 interface:** To enable an IPv6 interface without specifying a global unicast or unique-local unicast address, use the following command:

  `Router(config-if)# ipv6 enable`

- **Configuring a global unicast address with the EUI-64 option:** The command to configure a global unicast address using the EUI-64 format is

  `Router(config-if)# ipv6 address ipv6-prefix/prefix-length eui-64`

- **Removing IPv6 addresses:** The command to delete all IPv6 addresses from an interface, including the global unicast and the link-local addresses (unless the **ipv6 enable** command has been configured), is

  `Router(config-if)# no ipv6 address [ipv6-address/prefix-length]`

Forwarding IPv6 Unicast Packets

To enable the forwarding of IPv6 unicast packets and the sending of ND Router Advertisement messages, use the following command:

```
Router(config)# ipv6 unicast-routing
```

Neighbor Cache

- **Neighbor Cache:** The Neighbor Cache, similar to an IPv4 ARP Cache, is displayed by using the following command:

```
Router# show ipv6 neighbors
```

- **Configuring a static Neighbor Cache entry:** A static entry to the Neighbor Cache is configured by using the following command:

```
Router(config)# ipv6 neighbor ipv6-address interface-type interface-number
hardware-address
```

- **Clearing the Neighbor Cache:** The Neighbor Cache can be cleared by using the following command:

```
Router# clear ipv6 neighbors
```

Tuning Neighbor Discovery Parameters

- **Suppressing Router Advertisement messages:** Router Advertisement messages can be suppressed with the following interface command:

```
Router(config-if)# ipv6 nd ra suppress
```

- **Modifying the RA interval:** To change the default Router Advertisement interval of 200 seconds on Cisco routers, the following command is used:

```
Router(config-if)# ipv6 nd ra interval {maximum-secs [minimum-secs] | msec
maximum-ms [minimum-ms]}
```

- **Modifying the RA lifetime:** To change the amount of time that a host considers this router a valid default gateway, the following command is used:

```
Router(config-if)# ipv6 nd ra lifetime seconds
```

- **Setting the Managed Address Configuration Flag (M Flag):** To set the M Flag to 1, telling hosts to use stateful DHCPv6 instead of SLAAC for addressing information, the following command is used:

```
Router(config-if)# ipv6 managed-config-flag
```

- **Setting the Other Configuration Flag (O Flag):** To set the O Flag to 1, telling hosts that additional information is available from a DHCPv6 server such as DNS-related information, the following command is used:

```
Router(config-if)# ipv6 other-config-flag
```

- **Displaying Router Advertisements received from other routers:** To display IPv6 Router Advertisement information received from other routers on the Ethernet, Token Ring, or FDDI link, the following command is used:

```
Router# show ipv6 routers
```

IPv6 ACLs

As shown in the examples, configuring IPv6 ACLs is very similar to configuring IPv4 ACLs. Like IPv4, IPv6 access control lists have an implicit **deny ipv6 any any** statement at the end of each sequence of statements. Because the IPv6 Neighbor Discovery process requires the use of the IPv6 network layer, two other access list statements are also implicitly added to the end of each ACL:

- **permit icmp any any nd-na**
- **permit icmp any any nd-ns**

The **ipv6 access-list** command is used to configure IPv6-specific ACLs. IPv6 ACLs cannot be numbered; they can only be configured as named access lists. The **ipv6 traffic-filter** interface command is used to apply an IPv6 ACL to an interface. If the ACL is being applied to a virtual interface such as a vty line, the line configuration command **ipv6 access-class** is used.

References

Cisco IOS IPv6 Command Reference: www.cisco.com/en/US/docs/ios/ipv6/command/reference/ipv6_book.html

Cisco IOS IPv6 Configuration Guide, Release 12.4: www.cisco.com/en/US/docs/ios/ipv6/configuration/guide/12_4/ipv6_12_4_book.html

Implementing Traffic Filters and Firewalls for IPv6 Security, www.cisco.com/en/US/docs/ios/ipv6/configuration/guide/ip6-sec_trfltr_fw.html

Chapter 7

Introduction to Routing IPv6

The previous chapters examined IPv6 in some detail—the IPv6 protocol and related protocols such as ICMPv6 and Neighbor Discovery Protocol, the heart of IPv6. As you learned, IPv6 is much more than just a 128-bit address. The configuration of IPv6 is really not all that different than that of IPv4. As explained in Chapter 6, "IPv6 Configuration," the address configuration of IPv6 interfaces is fairly straightforward.

This chapter explores two topics associated with routing IPv6:

- IPv6 routing table
- IPv6 static routes

Configuring IPv6 addresses on interfaces and configuring IPv6 static routes are similar to those in IPv4. The IPv6 routing table has similarities to the IPv4 routing table as well. If you are comfortable with configuring IPv4 static routes, the IPv6 configurations are not all that different. So, rest assured; the more challenging work has already been accomplished by becoming knowledgeable in the protocols and processes of IPv6. This chapter focuses on some of the configurations of IPv6 that are noticeably similar to the same operations in IPv4.

This chapter uses the topology that was previously configured in Chapter 6 and is shown in Figure 7-1. At the conclusion of Chapter 6, you configured all the global unicast and link-local addresses for each of the routers. (The link-local addresses are not shown in Figure 7-1.) Although you can ping the interfaces of adjacent routers, you have not yet configured any static routes or dynamic routing protocols; therefore, any remote networks are unreachable.

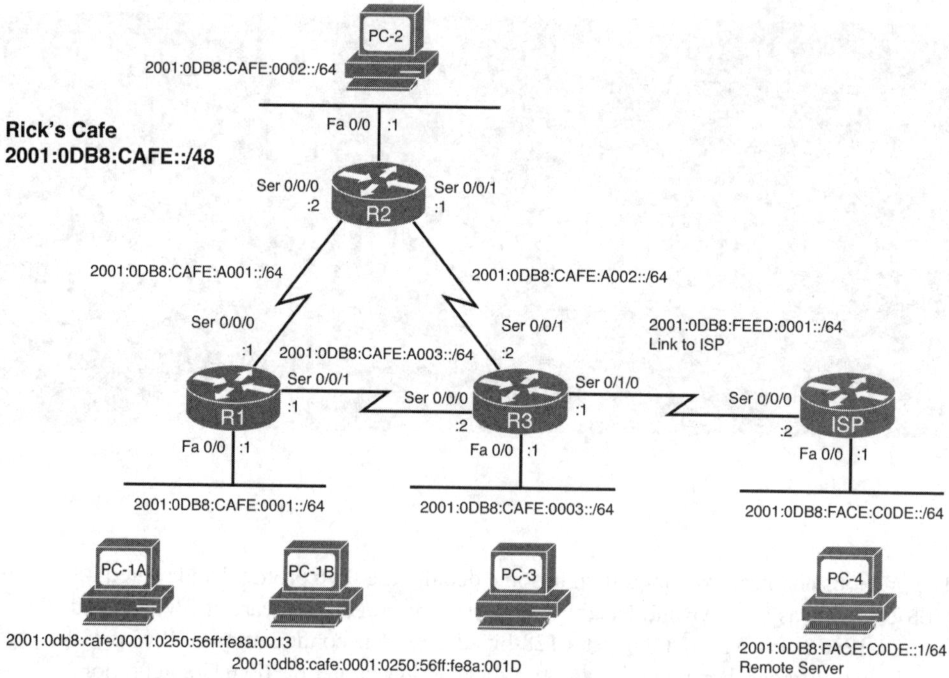

Figure 7-1 *Rick's Café Network Topology*

IPv6 Routing Table

Let's begin by examining the IPv6 routing table. Cisco IOS maintains a separate routing table for IPv6 and IPv4. To display the contents of the IPv6 routing table, the **show ipv6 route** command is used:

```
Router# show ipv6 route
```

There are several options to use with the **show ipv6 route** command, and some of these are discussed in this section. The full command syntax is

```
Router# show ipv6 route [ipv6-address | ipv6-prefix/prefix-length
[longer-prefixes] | [protocol] [updated [boot-up] [day month]
[time]] | interface interface-type interface-number | nsf | table
table-id | watch]
```

The following syntax options are described in Cisco IOS IPv6 Command Reference and included here for reference:

- *ipv6-address* (Optional): Displays routing information for a specific IPv6 address. This argument must be in the form documented in RFC 4291, where the address is specified in hexadecimal format using 16-bit values between colons.
- *ipv6-prefix* (Optional): Displays routing information for a specific IPv6 network. This argument must be in the form documented in RFC 4291, where the address is specified in hexadecimal format using 16-bit values between colons.
- */prefix-length* (Optional): The length of the IPv6 prefix. A decimal value that indicates how many of the high-order contiguous bits of the address comprise the prefix (the network portion of the address). A slash mark must precede the decimal value.
- **longer-prefixes** (Optional): Displays output for longer-prefix entries.
- *protocol* (Optional): Displays routes for the specified routing protocol using the keyword **bgp**, **isis**, **eigrp**, **ospf**, or **rip** or displays routes for the specified type of route using the keyword **connected**, **local**, **mobile**, or **static**.
- **updated** (Optional): Displays routes with timestamps.
- **boot-up** (Optional): Displays routing information since the bootup.
- *day month* (Optional): Displays routes since the day and month specified.
- *time* (Optional): Displays routes since the time specified. The time is specified in *hh:mm* format.
- **interface** *interface-type* (Optional): Interface type. For more information about supported interface types, use the question mark (?) online help function.
- *interface-number* (Optional): Interface number. For more information about the numbering syntax for supported interface types, use the question mark (?) online help function.
- **nsf** (Optional): Displays routes in the nonstop forwarding state.
- **table** *table-id* (Optional): Displays IPv6 Routing Information Base (RIB) table information for the specified table ID. The table must be in a hexadecimal format. The range for the table ID is 0 to 0-0xFFFFFFFF.
- **watch** (Optional): Displays information on route watchers.

The IPv4 **show ip route** command includes a timestamp with each route—the last time the route was updated, in hours:minutes:seconds. By default, the timestamp is not displayed in the IPv6 routing table. The updated option must be included—**show ipv6 route updated**—which displays the last time the route was updated in hours:minutes:seconds, day, month, and year.

> **Note** Most of these options are beyond the scope of this book and will not be discussed. For further information, refer to the Cisco IOS IPv6 Command Reference, at www.cisco.com/en/US/docs/ios/ipv6/command/reference/ipv6_16.html#wp2669925.

Let's begin by examining the routing tables of Router R1. Yes, routing tables—plural. In Example 7-1, the **show ip route** command is used to display the contents of the IPv4 routing table. Because any IPv4 interfaces are not configured, the IPv4 routing table is empty. Next, display the IPv6 routing table using the **show ipv6 route** command and notice that it is populated with IPv6 routes. Take a moment and examine this routing table a little more closely.

Example 7-1 *Displaying R1's IPv6 Routing Table*

```
R1# show ip route
Codes: C - connected, S - static, R - RIP, M - mobile, B - BGP
       D - EIGRP, EX - EIGRP external, O - OSPF, IA - OSPF inter area
       N1 - OSPF NSSA external type 1, N2 - OSPF NSSA external type 2
       E1 - OSPF external type 1, E2 - OSPF external type 2
       i - IS-IS, su - IS-IS summary, L1 - IS-IS level-1, L2 - IS-IS level-2
       ia - IS-IS inter area, * - candidate default, U - per-user static route
       o - ODR, P - periodic downloaded static route

Gateway of last resort is not set

R1# show ipv6 route
IPv6 Routing Table - 8 entries
Codes: C - Connected, L - Local, S - Static, R - RIP, B - BGP
       U - Per-user Static route
       I1 - ISIS L1, I2 - ISIS L2, IA - ISIS interarea, IS - ISIS summary
       O - OSPF intra, OI - OSPF inter, OE1 - OSPF ext 1, OE2 - OSPF ext 2
       ON1 - OSPF NSSA ext 1, ON2 - OSPF NSSA ext 2
       D - EIGRP, EX - EIGRP external
C   2001:DB8:CAFE:1::/64 [0/0]
     via ::, FastEthernet0/0
L   2001:DB8:CAFE:1::1/128 [0/0]
     via ::, FastEthernet0/0
C   2001:DB8:CAFE:A001::/64 [0/0]
     via ::, Serial0/0/0
L   2001:DB8:CAFE:A001::1/128 [0/0]
     via ::, Serial0/0/0
C   2001:DB8:CAFE:A003::/64 [0/0]
     via ::, Serial0/0/1
L   2001:DB8:CAFE:A003::1/128 [0/0]
     via ::, Serial0/0/1
```

```
L    FE80::/10 [0/0]
      via ::, Null0
L    FF00::/8 [0/0]
      via ::, Null0
R1#
```

Immediately following the **show ipv6 route** command, the first line of output displays the number of entries in the routing table:

```
IPv6 Routing Table - 8 entries
```

Eight entries might seem a little strange because you only have three interfaces and no static or dynamic routes, but that is explained shortly. These are followed by the codes that indicate the protocol that derived the route. After the codes, the eight entries or routes that make up the contents of R1's IPv6 routing table are displayed.

Code: Connected

The Code field C indicates that this is a directly connected network, similar to an IPv4 route of the same code. When an IPv6 interface with a global unicast or unique local unicast address is in the up state, the status and the line protocol, the IPv6 prefix, and the prefix length of that interface are added to the routing table as a connected route. An interface with only a link-local address will not be displayed in the routing table. Link-local addresses and the routing table are discussed shortly. In Example 7-1, the first entry in the IPv6 routing table is the directly connected network of R1's Fast Ethernet 0/0 interface:

```
C    2001:DB8:CAFE:1::/64 [0/0]
      via ::, FastEthernet0/0
```

This entry includes the prefix and prefix length 2001:DB8:CAFE:1::/64 of the Fast Ethernet 0/0 interface. [0/0] indicates the administrative distance and metric of the route. A directly connected network can only have an administrative distance of 0 and a metric of 0. The second line of the routing table entry displays the next-hop address, which in this case is an unspecified address. A directly connected network does not have a next-hop address, so an IPv6 unspecified address is used. The second line also includes the exit interface of Fast Ethernet 0/0.

Note The administrative distance is a measure of the *trustworthiness* or *preference* of the source of the routing information. If a router learns about a network from more than one routing source, it will choose the source with the lower administrative distance. Administrative distance only has local significance and is not advertised in routing updates.

Note There is some misinformation regarding the administrative distance of 0. Only a directly connected network in IPv4, or in IPv6 a directly connected network or local interface, can have an administrative distance of 0. A static route configured with an exit interface does not have an administrative distance of 0. Static routes and dynamically learned routes can never have an administrative distance of 0. Even though an IPv4 static route configured with an exit interface displays the phrase "directly connected" in the routing table, the administrative distance of that static route is still 1 by default.

There are three connected routes in R1's routing table, one for each interface configured routable IPv6 address. Using the **connected** option in the **show ipv6 route** command, you can filter the routing table output to display only the directly connected networks, as shown in Example 7-2.

Example 7-2 *Displaying R1's Connected Routes*

```
R1# show ipv6 route ?
     Hostname or X:X:X:X::X  IPv6 name or address
     X:X:X:X::X/<0-128>      IPv6 prefix
     bgp                     BGP routes
     connected               Connected routes
     eigrp                   EIGRP routes
     interface               interface specific routes
     isis                    IS-IS routes
     local                   Local routes
     ospf                    OSPFv3 routes
     rip                     RIPng routes
     static                  Static routes
     summary                 Summary display
     |                       Output modifiers
     <cr>

   R1# show ipv6 route connected
   IPv6 Routing Table - 11 entries
   Codes: C - Connected, L - Local, S - Static, R - RIP, B - BGP
          U - Per-user Static route
          I1 - ISIS L1, I2 - ISIS L2, IA - ISIS interarea, IS - ISIS summary
          O - OSPF intra, OI - OSPF inter, OE1 - OSPF ext 1, OE2 - OSPF ext 2
          ON1 - OSPF NSSA ext 1, ON2 - OSPF NSSA ext 2
          D - EIGRP, EX - EIGRP external
   C    2001:DB8:CAFE:1::/64 [0/0]
         via ::, FastEthernet0/0
   C    2001:DB8:CAFE:A001::/64 [0/0]
         via ::, Serial0/0/0
   C    2001:DB8:CAFE:A003::/64 [0/0]
         via ::, Serial0/0/1
   R1#
```

Code: Local

Besides the three connected routes in R1's routing table, notice that there are five other networks with the code of L, indicating a local route. Your first inclination might be to think that these are link-local networks, but they are not. Local routes are /128 routes and are essentially host routes for the router's IPv6 unicast address. These local routes allow the router to more efficiently process packets directed to the router itself rather than for packets directed toward connected subnets.

In Example 7-1, look again at the five local routes. Immediately following each connected network is its local network. This is the host route or the IPv6 unicast address of that interface. For example, in the previous section, R1's Fast Ethernet 0/0 connected network was discussed. This interface has been manually configured with an IPv6 global unicast address of 2001:DB8:CAFE:1::1 and is displayed as a local /128 host route:

```
L    2001:DB8:CAFE:1::1/128 [0/0]
      via ::, FastEthernet0/0
```

Similar to a connected network, a local route has an administrative distance of 0 and a metric of 0. Because R1 has three interfaces with routable addresses, this accounts for three of the five local routes in its IPv6 routing table.

What about the link-local addresses on IPv6 interfaces? These addresses are not included in the IPv6 routing table because packets with link-local addresses are not routable off the link. The IPv6 routing table explicitly lists the link-local prefix FE80::/10 with a null0 exit interface. This ensures that the router will discard any packets destined for a link-local address, other than its own:

```
L    FE80::/10 [0/0]
      via ::, Null0
```

The final local route in R1's IPv6 routing table is a null0 route to the multicast address FF00::/8:

```
L    FF00::/8 [0/0]
      via ::, Null0
```

This route pertains to the routing of multicast packets. The router will discard any multicast packets that are destined for a multicast group that is not explicitly listed in the IPv6 routing table. Using the **local** option in the **show ipv6 route** command, you can filter the routing table output to display only local networks, as shown in Example 7-3.

Example 7-3 *Displaying R1's Local Routes*

```
R1# show ipv6 route local
IPv6 Routing Table - 11 entries
Codes: C - Connected, L - Local, S - Static, R - RIP, B - BGP
       U - Per-user Static route
       I1 - ISIS L1, I2 - ISIS L2, IA - ISIS interarea, IS - ISIS summary
       O - OSPF intra, OI - OSPF inter, OE1 - OSPF ext 1, OE2 - OSPF ext 2
       ON1 - OSPF NSSA ext 1, ON2 - OSPF NSSA ext 2
       D - EIGRP, EX - EIGRP external
L   2001:DB8:CAFE:1::1/128 [0/0]
     via ::, FastEthernet0/0
L   2001:DB8:CAFE:A001::1/128 [0/0]
     via ::, Serial0/0/0
L   2001:DB8:CAFE:A003::1/128 [0/0]
     via ::, Serial0/0/1
L   FE80::/10 [0/0]
     via ::, Null0
L   FF00::/8 [0/0]
     via ::, Null0
R1#
```

Comparing IPv6 and IPv4 Routing Tables

In many ways, an IPv6 routing table is easier to understand than an IPv4 routing table. An IPv4 routing table is constructed in a classful manner, as shown in Example 7-4. With IPv6, there is no longer a concern with classful networks or VLSM (variable-length subnet masking). An IPv4 routing table is organized by its classful network address, with any subnets listed below the classful entry. An IPv6 routing table is much more straightforward. Because classful and classless addressing is nonexistent in IPv6, IPv6 routes are simply displayed as individual networks.

Example 7-4 *Sample IPv4 Routing Table*

```
Router# show ip route
Codes: I - IGRP derived, R - RIP derived, O - OSPF derived,
       C - connected, S - static, E - EGP derived, B - BGP derived,
       * - candidate default route, IA - OSPF inter area route,
       i - IS-IS derived, ia - IS-IS, U - per-user static route,
       o - on-demand routing, M - mobile, P - periodic downloaded static route,
       D - EIGRP, EX - EIGRP external, E1 - OSPF external type 1 route,
       E2 - OSPF external type 2 route, N1 - OSPF NSSA external type 1 route,
       N2 - OSPF NSSA external type 2 route

    192.168.10.0/30 is subnetted, 3 subnets
```

```
C       192.168.10.0 is directly connected, Serial0/0/0
C       192.168.10.4 is directly connected, Serial0/0/1
O       192.168.10.8 [110/128] via 192.168.10.2, 14:27:57, Serial0/0/0
    172.16.0.0/16 is variably subnetted, 2 subnets, 2 masks
O       172.16.1.32/29 [110/65] via 192.168.10.6, 14:27:57, Serial0/0/1
C       172.16.1.16/28 is directly connected, FastEthernet0/0
    10.0.0.0/8 is variably subnetted, 2 subnets, 2 masks
O       10.10.10.0/24 [110/65] via 192.168.10.2, 14:27:57, Serial0/0/0
C       10.1.1.1/32 is directly connected, Loopback0
```

Note You can find more information on the IPv4 routing table, its structure, and the lookup process in *Routing Protocols and Concepts*, by Rick Graziani and Allan Johnson.

Dynamically learned routes and summary routes are discussed in Chapter 8, "IPv6 IGP Routing Protocols." For completeness, the current routing tables for Routers R2, R3, and ISP are included in Examples 7-5 through 7-7.

Example 7-5 *Displaying R2's IPv6 Routing Table*

```
R2# show ipv6 route
IPv6 Routing Table - 8 entries
Codes: C - Connected, L - Local, S - Static, R - RIP, B - BGP
       U - Per-user Static route
       I1 - ISIS L1, I2 - ISIS L2, IA - ISIS interarea, IS - ISIS summary
       O - OSPF intra, OI - OSPF inter, OE1 - OSPF ext 1, OE2 - OSPF ext 2
       ON1 - OSPF NSSA ext 1, ON2 - OSPF NSSA ext 2
       D - EIGRP, EX - EIGRP external
C   2001:DB8:CAFE:2::/64 [0/0]
     via ::, FastEthernet0/0
L   2001:DB8:CAFE:2::1/128 [0/0]
     via ::, FastEthernet0/0
C   2001:DB8:CAFE:A001::/64 [0/0]
     via ::, Serial0/0/0
L   2001:DB8:CAFE:A001::2/128 [0/0]
     via ::, Serial0/0/0
C   2001:DB8:CAFE:A002::/64 [0/0]
     via ::, Serial0/0/1
L   2001:DB8:CAFE:A002::1/128 [0/0]
     via ::, Serial0/0/1
L   FE80::/10 [0/0]
     via ::, Null0
L   FF00::/8 [0/0]
     via ::, Null0
R2#
```

Example 7-6 *Displaying R3's IPv6 Routing Table*

```
R3# show ipv6 route
IPv6 Routing Table - 10 entries
Codes: C - Connected, L - Local, S - Static, R - RIP, B - BGP
       U - Per-user Static route
       I1 - ISIS L1, I2 - ISIS L2, IA - ISIS interarea, IS - ISIS summary
       O - OSPF intra, OI - OSPF inter, OE1 - OSPF ext 1, OE2 - OSPF ext 2
       ON1 - OSPF NSSA ext 1, ON2 - OSPF NSSA ext 2
       D - EIGRP, EX - EIGRP external
C   2001:DB8:CAFE:3::/64 [0/0]
     via ::, FastEthernet0/0
L   2001:DB8:CAFE:3::1/128 [0/0]
     via ::, FastEthernet0/0
C   2001:DB8:CAFE:A002::/64 [0/0]
     via ::, Serial0/0/1
L   2001:DB8:CAFE:A002::2/128 [0/0]
     via ::, Serial0/0/1
C   2001:DB8:CAFE:A003::/64 [0/0]
     via ::, Serial0/0/0
L   2001:DB8:CAFE:A003::2/128 [0/0]
     via ::, Serial0/0/0
C   2001:DB8:FEED:1::/64 [0/0]
     via ::, Serial0/1/0
L   2001:DB8:FEED:1::1/128 [0/0]
     via ::, Serial0/1/0
L   FE80::/10 [0/0]
     via ::, Null0
L   FF00::/8 [0/0]
     via ::, Null0
R3#
```

Example 7-7 *Displaying ISP's IPv6 Routing Table*

```
ISP# show ipv6 route
IPv6 Routing Table - 6 entries
Codes: C - Connected, L - Local, S - Static, R - RIP, B - BGP
       U - Per-user Static route
       I1 - ISIS L1, I2 - ISIS L2, IA - ISIS interarea, IS - ISIS summary
       O - OSPF intra, OI - OSPF inter, OE1 - OSPF ext 1, OE2 - OSPF ext 2
       ON1 - OSPF NSSA ext 1, ON2 - OSPF NSSA ext 2
       D - EIGRP, EX - EIGRP external
C   2001:DB8:FACE:C0DE::/64 [0/0]
     via ::, FastEthernet0/0
L   2001:DB8:FACE:C0DE::1/128 [0/0]
```

```
     via ::, FastEthernet0/0
C   2001:DB8:FEED:1::/64 [0/0]
     via ::, Serial0/0/0
L   2001:DB8:FEED:1::2/128 [0/0]
     via ::, Serial0/0/0
L   FE80::/10 [0/0]
     via ::, Null0
L   FF00::/8 [0/0]
     via ::, Null0
ISP#
```

Configuring IPv6 Static Routes

This section demonstrates the configuration process of the routers in the topology with static IPv6 routes to enable reachability between all the networks. To route IPv6 packets, a Cisco router must be configured with the **ipv6 unicast-routing** command in global configuration mode. This is disabled by default in Cisco IOS and must be enabled for the router to route IPv6 packets and to configure an IPv6 routing protocol. There is a similar command for IPv4, **ip routing**, which is enabled by default. Although IPv6 routing was enabled on all the routers in the topology in Chapter 6, the commands are once again shown in Example 7-8.

Example 7-8 *Enabling IPv6 Routing with the **ipv6 unicast-routing** Command*

```
R1(config)# ipv6 unicast-routing
________________________________________
R2(config)# ipv6 unicast-routing
________________________________________
R3(config)# ipv6 unicast-routing
________________________________________
ISP(config)# ipv6 unicast-routing
```

> **Note** The **ipv6 unicast-routing** command is also necessary for a router to send Neighbor Discovery Router Advertisement messages.

Configuring IPv6 static routes is similar to configuring static routes in IPv4. For the purposes of this section, assume that you are familiar with configuring IPv4 static routes. The basic syntax that is used in this chapter is

```
Router(config)# ipv6 route ipv6-prefix/prefix-length {ipv6-address
| interface-type interface-number [administrative-distance]
```

The complete syntax for configuring an IPv6 static route is

```
Router(config)# ipv6 route [vrf vrf-name] ipv6-prefix/prefix-length
{ipv6-address | interface-type interface-number [ipv6-address]}
[nexthop-vrf [vrf-name1 | default]] [administrative-distance]
[administrative-multicast-distance | unicast | multicast]
[next-hop-address] [tag tag] [name name]
```

Following are the descriptions for the **ipv6 route** syntax from the Cisco IOS IPv6 Command Reference:

- *ipv6-prefix*: The IPv6 network that is the destination of the static route. Can also be a host name when static host routes are configured.
- */prefix-length*: The length of the IPv6 prefix. A decimal value that indicates how many of the high-order contiguous bits of the address comprise the prefix (the network portion of the address). A slash mark must precede the decimal value.
- **vrf** (Optional): Specifies all Virtual Private Network (VPN) routing/forwarding instance (VRF) tables or a specific VRF table for an IPv4 or IPv6 address.
- *vrf-name* (Optional): Names a specific VRF table for an IPv4 or IPv6 address.
- *ipv6-address*: The IPv6 address of the next hop that can be used to reach the specified network. The IPv6 address of the next hop need not be directly connected; recursion is done to find the IPv6 address of the directly connected next hop. When an interface type and interface number are specified, you can optionally specify the IPv6 address of the next hop to which packets are output. Note that you must specify an interface type and an interface number when using a link-local address as the next hop (the link-local next hop must also be an adjacent router). This argument must be in the form documented in RFC 4291, where the address is specified in hexadecimal using 16-bit values between colons.
- *interface-type*: Interface type. For more information about supported interface types, use the question mark (?) online help function. You can use the *interface-type* argument to direct static routes out point-to-point interfaces (such as serial or tunnel interfaces) and broadcast interfaces (such as Ethernet interfaces). When using the *interface-type* argument with point-to-point interfaces, there is no need to specify the IPv6 address of the next hop. When using the *interface-type* argument with broadcast interfaces, you should always specify the IPv6 address of the next hop or ensure that the specified prefix is assigned to the link. A link-local address should be specified as the next hop for broadcast interfaces. The next-hop address is used only to determine the proper link layer (MAC) address of the next-hop router. This prevents any need for a recursive lookup of the next-hop address in the routing table. Link-local addresses are usually associated with the egress interface.
- *interface-number*: Interface number. For more information about the numbering syntax for supported interface types, use the question mark (?) online help function.

- **nexthop-vrf** (Optional): Indicator that the next hop is a VRF.
- *vrf-name1* (Optional): Name of the next-hop VRF.
- **default** (Optional): Indicator that the next hop is the default.
- *administrative-distance* (Optional): An administrative distance. The default value is 1, which gives static routes precedence over any other type of route except connected routes.
- *administrative-multicast-distance* (Optional): The distance used when selecting this route for multicast Reverse Path Forwarding (RPF).
- **unicast** (Optional): Specifies a route that must not be used in multicast RPF selection.
- **multicast** (Optional): Specifies a route that must not be populated in the unicast Routing Information Base (RIB).
- *next-hop-address* (Optional): Address of the next hop that can be used to reach the specified network.
- **tag** *tag* (Optional): Tag value that can be used as a "match" value for controlling redistribution through route maps.
- **name** *route-name* (Optional): Specifies a name for the route.

> **Note** Most of these **show ipv6 route** options are beyond the scope of this book and will not be discussed. Further information can be found in the Cisco IOS IPv6 Command Reference, at www.cisco.com/en/US/docs/ios/ipv6/command/reference/ipv6_08.html#wp2233116.

Let's begin the static IPv6 route configurations with Router R1. Example 7-9 shows the first static route on R1 to the serial network between R2 and R3, 2001:db8:cafe:a003::/64. In this example, the static route was configured with R3's next-hop address, specifically R3's serial 0/0/0 global unicast address 2001:db8:cafe:a003::2.

Example 7-9 *Configuring a Static Route with a Next-Hop Interface*

```
R1(config)# ipv6 route ?
  X:X:X:X::X/<0-128>  IPv6 prefix x:x::y/<z>

R1(config)# ipv6 route 2001:db8:cafe:a002::/64 ?
  Async               Async interface
  BVI                 Bridge-Group Virtual Interface
  CDMA-Ix             CDMA Ix interface
  CTunnel             CTunnel interface
  Dialer              Dialer interface
```

```
  FastEthernet        FastEthernet IEEE 802.3
  Lex                 Lex interface
  Loopback            Loopback interface
  MFR                 Multilink Frame Relay bundle interface
  Multilink           Multilink-group interface
  Null                Null interface
  Port-channel        Ethernet Channel of interfaces
  Serial              Serial
  Tunnel              Tunnel interface
  Vif                 PGM Multicast Host interface
  Virtual-Dot11Radio  Virtual dot11 interface
  Virtual-PPP         Virtual PPP interface
  Virtual-Template    Virtual Template interface
  Virtual-TokenRing   Virtual TokenRing
  X:X:X:X::X          IPv6 address of next-hop
  XTagATM             Extended Tag ATM interface

R1(config)# ipv6 route 2001:db8:cafe:a002::/64 2001:db8:cafe:a003::2 ?
  <1-254>    Administrative distance
  multicast  Route only usable by multicast
  tag        Tag value
  unicast    Route only usable by unicast
  <cr>

R1(config)# ipv6 route 2001:db8:cafe:a002::/64 2001:db8:cafe:a003::2
```

Note In Example 7-9, R3's serial 0/0/0 link-local address could have been used as the next-hop address, but it would have been necessary to add R1's exit interface as well. This is because link-local addresses are not included in the routing table and are not necessarily unique to any one link.

In Example 7-10, a second static route to the same 2001:db8:cafe:a002::/64 network was configured, this time using R1's exit interface serial 0/0/0. Unlike the previous static route, which forwards packets to R3, this route will forward packets destined for 2001:db8:cafe:a002::/64 to Router R2.

Example 7-10 *Configuring a Static Route with an Exit Interface*

```
R1(config)# ipv6 route 2001:db8:cafe:a002::/64 serial 0/0/0
```

Example 7-11 shows R1's routing table after configuring the two static routes. Depending upon the switching method—process switching, fast switching, or Cisco Express

Forwarding (CEF)—R2 will load-balance packets for this destination network between R2 and R3. Both static routes are included in the routing table because they both have the same administrative distance of 1.

Example 7-11 *R1's Routing Table After Configuring the Two Static Routes*

```
R1# show ipv6 route
IPv6 Routing Table - 11 entries
Codes: C - Connected, L - Local, S - Static, R - RIP, B - BGP
       U - Per-user Static route
       I1 - ISIS L1, I2 - ISIS L2, IA - ISIS interarea, IS - ISIS summary
       O - OSPF intra, OI - OSPF inter, OE1 - OSPF ext 1, OE2 - OSPF ext 2
       ON1 - OSPF NSSA ext 1, ON2 - OSPF NSSA ext 2
       D - EIGRP, EX - EIGRP external
C   2001:DB8:CAFE:1::/64 [0/0]
     via ::, FastEthernet0/0
L   2001:DB8:CAFE:1::1/128 [0/0]
     via ::, FastEthernet0/0
C   2001:DB8:CAFE:A001::/64 [0/0]
     via ::, Serial0/0/0
L   2001:DB8:CAFE:A001::1/128 [0/0]
     via ::, Serial0/0/0
S    2001:DB8:CAFE:A002::/64 [1/0]
     via 2001:DB8:CAFE:A003::2
     via ::, Serial0/0/0
C   2001:DB8:CAFE:A003::/64 [0/0]
     via ::, Serial0/0/1
L   2001:DB8:CAFE:A003::1/128 [0/0]
     via ::, Serial0/0/1
L   FE80::/10 [0/0]
     via ::, Null0
L   FF00::/8 [0/0]
     via ::, Null0
R1#
```

Note As previously mentioned, a static route configured with an exit interface will have a default administrative distance of 1, the same as a static route configured with a next-hop address. Static routes cannot have an administrative distance of 0.

Cisco Express Forwarding is introduced in Chapter 8. Process switching is available on every version of Cisco IOS and on every platform. The forwarding decision is made on a per-packet basis. For every packet that enters the router, the routing process must examine the destination IPv6 (or IPv4) address, determine the best path in its routing table, encapsulate the packet in a Layer 2 frame, and forward it out the specific egress interface. This requires the CPU to be involved with every forwarding decision. Using **debug ipv6 packet** on R1 and pinging R2's address 2001:db8:cafe:a002::1, Example 7-12 shows that R1 is process switching its IPv6 packets. Notice that with process switching, the source interface alternates between the different paths. In Example 7-12, the packets are process switched between the serial 0/0/0 and serial 0/0/1 interfaces. Process switching is not an option on some of the higher-end Cisco platforms.

Example 7-12 *Packets Processed Switched*

```
R1# debug ipv6 packet
IPv6 unicast packet debugging is on
R1# ping 2001:db8:cafe:a002::1

Type escape sequence to abort.
Sending 5, 100-byte ICMP Echos to 2001:DB8:CAFE:A002::1, timeout is 2 seconds:
!!!!!
Success rate is 100 percent (5/5), round-trip min/avg/max = 28/40/60 ms
R1#
*Feb 18 02:37:28.610: IPv6: SAS picked source 2001:DB8:CAFE:A001::1 for
2001:DB8:CAFE:A002::1 (Serial0/0/0)
*Feb 18 02:37:28.610: IPV6: source 2001:DB8:CAFE:A001::1 (local)
*Feb 18 02:37:28.610:       dest 2001:DB8:CAFE:A002::1 (Serial0/0/0)
*Feb 18 02:37:28.610:       traffic class 0, flow 0x0, len 100+0, prot 58, hops
64, originating
<output omitted>
*Feb 18 02:37:28.642: IPv6: SAS picked source 2001:DB8:CAFE:A003::1 for
2001:DB8:CAFE:A002::1 (Serial0/0/1)
*Feb 18 02:37:28.642: IPv6: nexthop 2001:DB8:CAFE:A003::2,
*Feb 18 02:37:28.642: IPV6: source 2001:DB8:CAFE:A003::1 (local)
*Feb 18 02:37:28.642:       dest 2001:DB8:CAFE:A002::1 (Serial0/0/1)
*Feb 18 02:37:28.642:       traffic class 0, flow 0x0, len 100+0, prot 58, hops
64, originating
<output omitted>
```

An interface that is configured for fast switching will still use the CPU, but only for the first packet in the flow. After the first packet has been forwarded using process switching, information about how to reach the destination is stored in a fast-switching cache. Subsequent packets for the same destination use the next-hop information in the fast-switching cache so that the CPU doesn't have to get involved. This results in the faster forwarding of packets.

Note Fast switching is being phased out in favor of CEF.

So far, you have only configured two static routes on R1, both for the same network 2001:db8:cafe:a002::/64. Example 7-13 shows the configuration of static routes to reach the rest of the networks in the topology.

Example 7-13 *Rest of R1's Static Route Configurations and Verification*

```
R1(config)# ipv6 route 2001:db8:cafe:2::/64 serial 0/0/0
R1(config)# ipv6 route 2001:db8:cafe:3::/64 serial 0/0/1
R1(config)# ipv6 route 2001:db8:feed::/48 serial 0/0/1
R1(config)# ipv6 route 2001:db8:face::/48 serial 0/0/1
R1(config)# end
R1#
R1# show running-config | include ipv6 route
ipv6 route 2001:DB8:CAFE:2::/64 Serial0/0/0
ipv6 route 2001:DB8:CAFE:3::/64 Serial0/0/1
ipv6 route 2001:DB8:CAFE:A002::/64 Serial0/0/0
ipv6 route 2001:DB8:CAFE:A002::/64 2001:DB8:CAFE:A003::2 5
ipv6 route 2001:DB8:FACE::/48 Serial0/0/1
ipv6 route 2001:DB8:FEED::/48 Serial0/0/1
R1#
```

Included in the configuration are two static routes, one for R2's LAN and one for R3's LAN. There are also two /48 summary routes, one for the 2001:db8:feed::/48 network and one for the 2001:db8:face::/48 network. The **show running-config | include ipv6 route** command in Example 7-13 filters the output with only lines beginning with "ipv6 route." Using the **show ipv6 route static** command, we further verify the configuration, as shown in Example 7-14.

Example 7-14 *Verifying Static Routes with the **show ipv6 route static** Command*

```
R1# show ipv6 route ?
    Hostname or X:X:X:X::X  IPv6 name or address
    X:X:X:X::X/<0-128>      IPv6 prefix
    bgp                     BGP routes
    connected               Connected routes
    eigrp                   EIGRP routes
    interface               interface specific routes
    isis                    IS-IS routes
    local                   Local routes
    ospf                    OSPFv3 routes
    rip                     RIPng routes
    static                  Static routes
    summary                 Summary display
    |                       Output modifiers
    <cr>
```

```
R1# show ipv6 route static
IPv6 Routing Table - 13 entries
Codes: C - Connected, L - Local, S - Static, R - RIP, B - BGP
       U - Per-user Static route
       I1 - ISIS L1, I2 - ISIS L2, IA - ISIS interarea, IS - ISIS summary
       O - OSPF intra, OI - OSPF inter, OE1 - OSPF ext 1, OE2 - OSPF ext 2
       ON1 - OSPF NSSA ext 1, ON2 - OSPF NSSA ext 2
       D - EIGRP, EX - EIGRP external
S   2001:DB8:CAFE:2::/64 [1/0]
     via ::, Serial0/0/0
S   2001:DB8:CAFE:3::/64 [1/0]
     via ::, Serial0/0/1
S   2001:DB8:CAFE:A002::/64 [1/0]
     via ::, Serial0/0/0
S   2001:DB8:FACE::/48 [1/0]
     via ::, Serial0/0/1
S   2001:DB8:FEED::/48 [1/0]
     via ::, Serial0/0/1
R1#
```

Note The static routes that were used to configure the routers in this topology help demonstrate the **ipv6 route** command and are not necessarily the most effective method in configuring a network using only static routes.

Example 7-15 displays the static route configurations and verification for Router R2. Notice that the **show running-config | section ipv6 route** command used the ***section*** option instead of **include**. The **section** option filters the output to a specific section of the running-config output.

Example 7-15 *R2's Static Route Configurations and Verification*

```
R2(config)# ipv6 route 2001:db8:cafe:0001::/64 serial 0/0/0
R2(config)# ipv6 route 2001:db8:cafe:a003::/64 serial 0/0/1
R2(config)# ipv6 route 2001:db8:cafe:0003::/64 serial 0/0/1
R2(config)# ipv6 route 2001:db8:feed::/48 serial 0/0/1
R2(config)# ipv6 route 2001:db8:face::/48 serial 0/0/1
R2(config)# end

R2# show running-config | section ipv6 route
ipv6 route 2001:DB8:CAFE:1::/64 Serial0/0/0
ipv6 route 2001:DB8:CAFE:3::/64 Serial0/0/1
ipv6 route 2001:DB8:CAFE:A003::/64 Serial0/0/1
```

```
ipv6 route 2001:DB8:FACE::/48 Serial0/0/1
ipv6 route 2001:DB8:FEED::/48 Serial0/0/1
R2#

R2# show ipv6 route static
IPv6 Routing Table - 13 entries
Codes: C - Connected, L - Local, S - Static, R - RIP, B - BGP
       U - Per-user Static route
       I1 - ISIS L1, I2 - ISIS L2, IA - ISIS interarea, IS - ISIS summary
       O - OSPF intra, OI - OSPF inter, OE1 - OSPF ext 1, OE2 - OSPF ext 2
       ON1 - OSPF NSSA ext 1, ON2 - OSPF NSSA ext 2
       D - EIGRP, EX - EIGRP external
S   2001:DB8:CAFE:1::/64 [1/0]
     via ::, Serial0/0/0
S   2001:DB8:CAFE:3::/64 [1/0]
     via ::, Serial0/0/1
S   2001:DB8:CAFE:A003::/64 [1/0]
     via ::, Serial0/0/1
S   2001:DB8:FACE::/48 [1/0]
     via ::, Serial0/0/1
S   2001:DB8:FEED::/48 [1/0]
     via ::, Serial0/0/1
R2#
```

The static route configurations and verifications for the topology are completed in Example 7-16 for Router R3 and in Example 7-17 for the ISP router. Notice in Example 7-17 that the configuration for R3 includes a static default route using this command:

```
R3(config)# ipv6 route ::/0 ser 0/1/0
```

Example 7-16 *R3's Static Route Configurations and Verification*

```
R3(config)# ipv6 route 2001:db8:cafe:a001::/64 serial 0/0/0
R3(config)# ipv6 route 2001:db8:cafe:0001::/64 serial 0/0/0
R3(config)# ipv6 route 2001:db8:cafe:0002::/64 serial 0/0/1
R3(config)# ipv6 route ::/0 ser 0/1/0
R3(config)# end

R3# show running-config | include ipv6 route
ipv6 route 2001:DB8:CAFE:1::/64 Serial0/0/0
ipv6 route 2001:DB8:CAFE:2::/64 Serial0/0/1
ipv6 route 2001:DB8:CAFE:A001::/64 Serial0/0/0
ipv6 route ::/0 Serial0/1/0
```

```
R3# show ipv6 route static
IPv6 Routing Table - 14 entries
Codes: C - Connected, L - Local, S - Static, R - RIP, B - BGP
       U - Per-user Static route
       I1 - ISIS L1, I2 - ISIS L2, IA - ISIS interarea, IS - ISIS summary
       O - OSPF intra, OI - OSPF inter, OE1 - OSPF ext 1, OE2 - OSPF ext 2
       ON1 - OSPF NSSA ext 1, ON2 - OSPF NSSA ext 2
       D - EIGRP, EX - EIGRP external
S   ::/0 [1/0]
     via ::, Serial0/1/0
S   2001:DB8:CAFE:1::/64 [1/0]
     via ::, Serial0/0/0
S   2001:DB8:CAFE:2::/64 [1/0]
     via ::, Serial0/0/1
S   2001:DB8:CAFE:A001::/64 [1/0]
     via ::, Serial0/0/0
R3#
```

Example 7-17 *ISP's Static Route Configurations and Verification*

```
ISP(config)# ipv6 route 2001:db8:cafe::/48 serial 0/0/0
ISP(config)# end

ISP# show running-config | include ipv6 route
ipv6 route 2001:DB8:CAFE::/48 Serial0/0/0

ISP# show ipv6 route static
IPv6 Routing Table - 7 entries
Codes: C - Connected, L - Local, S - Static, R - RIP, B - BGP
       U - Per-user Static route
       I1 - ISIS L1, I2 - ISIS L2, IA - ISIS interarea, IS - ISIS summary
       O - OSPF intra, OI - OSPF inter, OE1 - OSPF ext 1, OE2 - OSPF ext 2
       ON1 - OSPF NSSA ext 1, ON2 - OSPF NSSA ext 2
       D - EIGRP, EX - EIGRP external
S   2001:DB8:CAFE::/48 [1/0]
     via ::, Serial0/0/0
ISP#
```

As you might remember from Chapter 3, "IPv6 Addressing," ::/0 is used to indicate a default route similar to a 0.0.0.0/0 in IPv4. This should make sense; after all, in IPv6, :: indicates an all-0s address just like 0.0.0.0 in IPv4.

Changing the Administrative Distance

Looking back at R1's routing table in Example 7-11, two static routes were configured on R1 for the serial network between R2 and R3, 2001:db8:cafe:a003::/64. One static route used the global unicast next-hop address of R3, and the other one applied an exit interface forwarding packets to R2. In Example 7-18, the administrative distance of the static route is modified by using the next-hop interface using this command:

```
R1(config)# ipv6 route 2001:db8:cafe:a002::/64 2001:db8:cafe:a003::2 5
```

The 5 at the end of the command changes the administrative distance from its default of 1 to 5. Because there is another static route in the routing table pointing to the same network with a lower administrative distance of 1, this static route with administrative distance of 5 will not be included in the routing table. This is confirmed using the **show ipv6 route static** command in Example 7-18. Only the route using the exit interface and an administrative distance of 1 is included in the routing table. The **show running-config | include ipv6 route** command shows that the second route is still in the running-config. This route will only be installed in the routing table if the current route with the lower administrative distance is unreachable.

Example 7-18 *Modifying a Static Route's Administrative Distance*

```
R1(config)# ipv6 route 2001:db8:cafe:a002::/64 2001:db8:cafe:a003::2 5
R1(config)# end

R1# show ipv6 route static
IPv6 Routing Table - 13 entries
Codes: C - Connected, L - Local, S - Static, R - RIP, B - BGP
       U - Per-user Static route
       I1 - ISIS L1, I2 - ISIS L2, IA - ISIS interarea, IS - ISIS summary
       O - OSPF intra, OI - OSPF inter, OE1 - OSPF ext 1, OE2 - OSPF ext 2
       ON1 - OSPF NSSA ext 1, ON2 - OSPF NSSA ext 2
       D - EIGRP, EX - EIGRP external
S   2001:DB8:CAFE:2::/64 [1/0]
     via ::, Serial0/0/0
S   2001:DB8:CAFE:3::/64 [1/0]
     via ::, Serial0/0/1
S   2001:DB8:CAFE:A002::/64 [1/0]
     via ::, Serial0/0/0
S   2001:DB8:FACE::/48 [1/0]
     via ::, Serial0/0/1
S   2001:DB8:FEED::/48 [1/0]
     via ::, Serial0/0/1
R1#
R1# show running-config | include ipv6 route
ipv6 route 2001:DB8:CAFE:2::/64 Serial0/0/0
```

```
ipv6 route 2001:DB8:CAFE:3::/64 Serial0/0/1
ipv6 route 2001:DB8:CAFE:A002::/64 Serial0/0/0
ipv6 route 2001:DB8:CAFE:A002::/64 2001:DB8:CAFE:A003::2 5
ipv6 route 2001:DB8:FACE::/48 Serial0/0/1
ipv6 route 2001:DB8:FEED::/48 Serial0/0/1
R1#
```

In Example 7-19, this is verified further by using the **show ipv6 static** and **show ipv6 static detail** commands. In both commands, the static route to 2001:db8:cafe:a002::/64 with an administrative distance of 5 is included in the output but without the *, indicating that this route is not installed in the RIB (Routing Information Base) or routing table. Notice that the **show ipv6 static detail** command will also include the resolved exit interface for any static route that uses only a next-hop interface.

Example 7-19 *Using the show ipv6 static Command*

```
R1# show ipv6 static
IPv6 Static routes
Code: * - installed in RIB
* 2001:DB8:CAFE:2::/64 via interface Serial0/0/0, distance 1
* 2001:DB8:CAFE:3::/64 via interface Serial0/0/1, distance 1
* 2001:DB8:CAFE:A002::/64 via interface Serial0/0/0, distance 1
  2001:DB8:CAFE:A002::/64 via nexthop 2001:DB8:CAFE:A003::2, distance 5
* 2001:DB8:FACE::/48 via interface Serial0/0/1, distance 1
* 2001:DB8:FEED::/48 via interface Serial0/0/1, distance 1
R1#

R1# show ipv6 static detail
IPv6 Static routes
Code: * - installed in RIB
* 2001:DB8:CAFE:2::/64 via interface Serial0/0/0, distance 1
* 2001:DB8:CAFE:3::/64 via interface Serial0/0/1, distance 1
* 2001:DB8:CAFE:A002::/64 via interface Serial0/0/0, distance 1
  2001:DB8:CAFE:A002::/64 via nexthop 2001:DB8:CAFE:A003::2, distance 5
     Resolves to 1 paths (max depth 1)
     via Serial0/0/1
* 2001:DB8:FACE::/48 via interface Serial0/0/1, distance 1
* 2001:DB8:FEED::/48 via interface Serial0/0/1, distance 1
R1#
```

Once again, ping 2001:db8:cafe:a002::1 from R1. This time, there is only one route in the routing table. Comparing the output in Example 7-20 with that of Example 7-12, you can verify that these packets are only being sent using the current route in R2's routing table.

Example 7-20 *Verifying a Single Route to 2001:db8:cafe:a002::/64*

```
R1# debug ipv6 packet
IPv6 unicast packet debugging is on
R1# ping 2001:db8:cafe:a002::1

Type escape sequence to abort.
Sending 5, 100-byte ICMP Echos to 2001:DB8:CAFE:A002::1, timeout is 2 seconds:
!!!!!
Success rate is 100 percent (5/5), round-trip min/avg/max = 28/28/32 ms
R1#
*Feb 18 02:42:44.494: IPv6: SAS picked source 2001:DB8:CAFE:A001::1 for
2001:DB8:CAFE:A002::1 (Serial0/0/0)
*Feb 18 02:42:44.494: IPV6: source 2001:DB8:CAFE:A001::1 (local)
*Feb 18 02:42:44.494:       dest 2001:DB8:CAFE:A002::1 (Serial0/0/0)
*Feb 18 02:42:44.494:       traffic class 0, flow 0x0, len 100+0, prot 58, hops
64, originating
<output omitted>
*Feb 18 02:42:44.522: IPv6: SAS picked source 2001:DB8:CAFE:A001::1 for
2001:DB8:CAFE:A002::1 (Serial0/0/0)
*Feb 18 02:42:44.526: IPV6: source 2001:DB8:CAFE:A001::1 (local)
*Feb 18 02:42:44.526:       dest 2001:DB8:CAFE:A002::1 (Serial0/0/0)
*Feb 18 02:42:44.526:       traffic class 0, flow 0x0, len 100+0, prot 58, hops
64, originating
<output omitted>
```

Final Configurations and Verification

Using the **ping** command on the R1 and ISP routers verifies reachability across the topology, as shown in Example 7-21. Of course it would be advantageous to confirm reachability throughout the entire topology with a series of **ping** commands on each router to each of the networks.

Example 7-21 *Verifying Reachability*

```
R1# ping 2001:db8:feed:1::2

Type escape sequence to abort.
Sending 5, 100-byte ICMP Echos to 2001:DB8:FEED:1::2, timeout is 2 seconds:
!!!!!
Success rate is 100 percent (5/5), round-trip min/avg/max = 56/56/56 ms
R1# ping 2001:db8:face:c0de::1

Type escape sequence to abort.
Sending 5, 100-byte ICMP Echos to 2001:DB8:FACE:C0DE::1, timeout is 2 seconds:
!!!!!
```

```
Success rate is 100 percent (5/5), round-trip min/avg/max = 56/56/56 ms
R1#
```

```
ISP# ping 2001:db8:cafe:1::1

Type escape sequence to abort.
Sending 5, 100-byte ICMP Echos to 2001:DB8:CAFE:1::1, timeout is 2 seconds:
!!!!!
Success rate is 100 percent (5/5), round-trip min/avg/max = 68/70/72 ms
ISP#
```

Verify the connectivity by examining each router's routing table. Example 7-22 shows the final routing table for Router R1. The **show ipv6 route summary** command displays the number of prefixes in R1's routing table.

Example 7-22 *Verifying Static Routes by Examining R1's Routing Table*

```
R1# show ipv6 route
IPv6 Routing Table - 13 entries
Codes: C - Connected, L - Local, S - Static, R - RIP, B - BGP
       U - Per-user Static route
       I1 - ISIS L1, I2 - ISIS L2, IA - ISIS interarea, IS - ISIS summary
       O - OSPF intra, OI - OSPF inter, OE1 - OSPF ext 1, OE2 - OSPF ext 2
       ON1 - OSPF NSSA ext 1, ON2 - OSPF NSSA ext 2
       D - EIGRP, EX - EIGRP external
C   2001:DB8:CAFE:1::/64 [0/0]
     via ::, FastEthernet0/0
L   2001:DB8:CAFE:1::1/128 [0/0]
     via ::, FastEthernet0/0
S   2001:DB8:CAFE:2::/64 [1/0]
     via ::, Serial0/0/0
S   2001:DB8:CAFE:3::/64 [1/0]
     via ::, Serial0/0/1
C   2001:DB8:CAFE:A001::/64 [0/0]
     via ::, Serial0/0/0
L   2001:DB8:CAFE:A001::1/128 [0/0]
     via ::, Serial0/0/0
S   2001:DB8:CAFE:A002::/64 [1/0]
     via ::, Serial0/0/0
C   2001:DB8:CAFE:A003::/64 [0/0]
     via ::, Serial0/0/1
L   2001:DB8:CAFE:A003::1/128 [0/0]
     via ::, Serial0/0/1
S   2001:DB8:FACE::/48 [1/0]
```

```
     via ::, Serial0/0/1
S   2001:DB8:FEED::/48 [1/0]
     via ::, Serial0/0/1
L   FE80::/10 [0/0]
     via ::, Null0
L   FF00::/8 [0/0]
     via ::, Null0
R1#

R1# show ipv6 route summary
IPv6 Routing Table Summary - 13 entries
  5 local, 3 connected, 5 static, 0 RIP, 0 BGP, 0 IS-IS, 0 OSPF, 0 EIGRP
  Number of prefixes:
    /8: 1, /10: 1, /48: 2, /64: 6, /128: 3
R1#
```

CEF for IPv6

Earlier in this chapter, process switching and fast switching were discussed, as well as a third type of switching method—CEF, or Cisco Express Forwarding. Although the details of CEF are beyond the scope of this book, let's take a moment and introduce the concept for those who might not be familiar with it.

CEF is a Layer 3 switching technology designed for Cisco routers and multilayer switches for IPv4 and is also available for IPv6 as CEFv6. CEF uses a switching method that optimizes route lookups to achieve very fast packet forwarding.

> **Note** CEFv6 is referred to as just *CEF* because the behavior for CEFv6 is the same as CEF for IPv4.

CEF uses two tables to accomplish this:

- **Forwarding Information Base (FIB):** The FIB is similar to an IP routing table. It is an ordered list, with the most specific route first, for each IPv6 prefix/prefix length in the routing table or, in the case of IPv4, each IPv4 network/subnet. The FIB is a mirror image of the forwarding information contained in the IP routing table. When routing or topology changes occur in the network, the IP routing table is updated, and those changes are reflected in the FIB. The FIB maintains next-hop address information based on the information in the IP routing table.
- **Adjacency table:** The FIB contains Layer 3 network and next-hop information. To streamline packet forwarding, the FIB's corresponding Layer 2 information for every next-hop entry is maintained in a table called the adjacency table. The adjacency table

is built from the IPv6 Neighbor Cache (or ARP Cache for IPv4) and contains the Layer 3–to–Layer 2 address mappings. The adjacency table contains the MAC addresses of next-hop nodes such as routers and hosts. Whenever the router updates its IPv6 Neighbor Cache (or ARP Cache for IPv4), the adjacency table is also updated.

The process of how CEF operates is beyond the scope of this book, but further information can be found in *Implementing Cisco Switched Networks (SWITCH)*, published by Cisco Press.

CEFv6 is available on Cisco IOS Release 12.2(13)T and later and 12.2(9)S and later. CEFv6 is disabled by default. Before engaging CEF for IPv6, you must first enable CEF for IPv4. CEF for IPv4 is enabled by default on most platforms, but if it isn't, it is implemented using the **ip cef** global configuration command. After engaging CEF for IPv4, you can then enable CEF for IPv6 using the **ipv6 cef** command in global configuration mode:

```
Router(config) ip cef
Router(config) ipv6 cef
```

Summary

This chapter examined two topics associated with routing IPv6:

- IPv6 routing table
- IPv6 static routes

Cisco IOS maintains a separate routing table for IPv6 and IPv4. The contents of the IPv6 routing table are displayed using the **show ipv6 route** command. The Code field C indicates that this is a directly connected network. An IPv6 interface with a global unicast or unique local unicast address that is the up state will have its prefix and prefix length added to the routing table. Link-local addresses are not included in the IPv6 routing table. This interface's unicast address is also added to the IPv6 routing table as a local /128 host route using the Code field L.

A Cisco router must be enabled for routing IPv6 unicast packets using the **ipv6 unicast-routing** command in global configuration mode. This is disabled by default. Configuring IPv6 static routes is very similar to configuring static routes in IPv4. The basic syntax for configuring an IPv6 static route is

```
Router(config)# ipv6 route ipv6-prefix/prefix-length {ipv6-address | interface-
type interface-number [administrative-distance]
```

IPv6 static default routes are configured using ::/0 as the *ipv6-prefix/prefix-length*. Using the **show ipv6 route static** and **show running-config | include ipv6 route** commands, you can verify the configuration of the static routes.

CEF is a Layer 3 switching technology designed for Cisco routers and multilayer switches for IPv4 and is also available for IPv6 (CEFv6). CEF uses a switching method that optimizes route lookups to achieve very fast packet forwarding. CEF for IPv4 must be enabled before enabling CEFv6 using this command:

```
Router(config) ipv6 cef
```

References

Cisco IOS IPv6 Command Reference, www.cisco.com/en/US/docs/ios/ipv6/command/reference/ipv6_16.html

Cisco IOS IPv6 Configuration Guide, www.cisco.com/en/US/docs/ios/ipv6/configuration/guide/12_4/ipv6_12_4_book.html

Implementing Static Routes for IPv6, www.cisco.com/en/US/docs/ios/ipv6/configuration/guide/ip6-stat_routes.html

Implementing Traffic Filters and Firewalls for IPv6 Security, www.cisco.com/en/US/docs/ios/ipv6/configuration/guide/ip6-sec_trfltr_fw.html

Chapter 8

IPv6 IGP Routing Protocols

In Chapter 6, "IPv6 Configuration," you configured the addressing for Rick's Café network topology. Using this same topology in Chapter 7, "Introduction to Routing IPv6," you configured reachability throughout the topology using static routes. Static routes are excellent for routing to and from a stub network, or are used as a default route. But there are definite disadvantages in solely using static routes where the network is more than just a few routers and can also include redundant links. Some of the disadvantages in using static routes include

- Configuration and maintenance are time-consuming
- Configuration is error-prone, especially in large networks
- Does not adapt dynamically to changes in the network
- Does not scale well

Dynamic routing protocols help provide the solution to the issues associated with static routes. Dynamic routing protocols are more scalable, easier to manage, determine the best path to remote networks, and automatically adapt to changes in the network topology. This chapter covers three IPv6 IGP (Interior Gateway Protocol) routing protocols:

- Routing Information Protocol next generation (RIPng) for IPv6
- Enhanced Interior Gateway Routing Protocol (EIGRP) for IPv6
- Open Shortest Path First version 3 (OSPFv3)

Note IS-IS (Intermediate System–to–Intermediate System) is another IGP routing protocol available for both IPv4 and IPv6. Cisco IOS supports IS-IS for both protocols; however, IS-IS is beyond the scope of this book. For more information about IS-IS for IPv6, refer to the *Cisco IOS IPv6 Configuration Guide, Implementing IS-IS for IPv6*, www.cisco.com/en/US/docs/ios/ipv6/configuration/guide/ip6-is-is.html.

Note IGP routing protocols are used for routing within an autonomous system compared to an Exterior Gateway Protocol (EGP), which is used to route packets between autonomous systems. BGP (Border Gateway Protocol) is the current EGP used between autonomous systems on the Internet. The current version of BGP is BGP version 4 for IPv4 and is defined in RFC 4271, A Border Gateway Protocol 4 (BGP-4).

An enhanced version of BGP called BGP+ or multiprotocol BGP extends the BGP-4 specifications to include other address families such as BGP for IPv6. Multiprotocol BGP is defined in RFC 4760, Multiprotocol Extensions for BGP-4, and RFC 2545, Use of BGP-4 Multiprotocol Extensions for IPv6 Inter-Domain Routing. BGP is beyond the scope of this book.

RIPng, EIGRP for IPv6, and OSPFv3 are separate processes from their IPv4 counterparts. These routing protocols run as "ships in the night"—with separate tables, databases, and processes. IS-IS supports one process for both address families. In the future, OSPFv3 will also support both address families under one process.

These IPv6 routing protocols are not much different than their IPv4 counterparts. The processes and operations of the IPv6 routing protocols are basically the same as in IPv4. For example, EIGRP for IPv6 continues to use Diffusing Update Algorithm (DUAL), and OSPFv3 is still a multiarea link-state routing protocol. Even the IPv6 configuration and verification commands are all very similar to those used in their equivalent IPv4 protocols.

Note As mentioned in the introduction, this book assumes prior knowledge of IPv4 and IPv4 routing protocols. You should already have a general understanding of routing protocols for IPv4 such as RIPv2, EIGRP, and OSPFv2. If you need more information on these routing protocols, read *Routing Protocols and Concepts* or *Routing TCP/IP*, both published by Cisco Press. This book limits discussions to only the fundamental concepts and configurations of these IPv6 routing protocols—at a CCNA level of understanding. If you want to learn more, read *Implementing Cisco IP Routing (ROUTE)* and *Cisco Self Study: Implementing Cisco IPv6 Networks*, also both published by Cisco Press.

All three IPv6 routing protocols—RIPng, EIGRP for IPv6, and OSPFv3—use the same topology that was used in Chapters 6 and 7. The following will be discussed in this chapter:

- The similarities and differences between the IPv6 routing protocol and its equivalent in IPv4
- The commands necessary to configure the IPv6 routing protocol and distribute a default route
- The commands used to verify the implementation, confirm network convergence, and test reachability

RIPng for IPv6

RIP (Routing Information Protocol) is the oldest of the distance vector routing protocols still in use. Although RIP lacks the sophistication of more advanced routing protocols, its simplicity and continued use are a testament to its longevity. Many might think that RIP is a protocol "on the way out," but regardless, there is an IPv6 form of RIP called RIPng (next generation).

Charles Hedrick wrote the original specifications for RIP in 1988: RFC 1058, Routing Information Protocol. Since then, RIP has been updated, including RIPv2 in 1994 and RIPng in 1997. Routing Information Protocol next generation (RIPng), or RIP for IPv6, functions the same and offers the same benefits as RIPv2 in IPv4. RIP enhancements for IPv6 are detailed in RFC 2080, RIPng for IPv6. RIPv2 is defined in RFC 2453, RIP Version 2. Prior knowledge of RIPv2 is assumed and beyond the scope of this book.

Comparing RIPng for IPv6 and RIPv2

RIPng is the IPv6 counterpart to RIPv2 for IPv4. RIPng is very similar to RIPv2 in both its operations and configuration. There are some significant differences, however. The following is a comparison of the main features of RIPv2 and RIPng:

- **Advertised routes:** RIPv2 advertises IPv4 routes, whereas RIPng advertises routes to populate the IPv6 routing table.
- **Distance vector:** RIPv2 and RIPng are both distance vector protocols that apply the Bellman-Ford algorithm, compared to link-state routing protocols where each router has a topology map of the network. In a link-state environment, routers don't only have a view of their directly connected neighbors but all other routers and networks in the routing domain.
- **Metric:** RIPv2 and RIPng both use a metric between 1 and 16, representing hop count. The maximum hop count is 15. A route with a hop count of 16 (infinity) is considered unreachable.

- **IPv6 routing table metric:** In RIPv2 (and RIPv1), the metric received in the routing update is the metric the receiving router uses in its routing table for that network. For example, if Router-X sends an update for its directly connected network to Router Y, Router-X advertises that route with a hop count of 1. The next-hop router Router-Y receives the RIPv2 update and enters the route and its metric of 1 to its IPv4 routing table without incrementing it. In RIPv2, the metric or hop count displayed in the IPv4 routing table is the number of hops required to reach the remote network with the next-hop router as the first hop.

  In the Cisco implementation of RIPng, the same metric is sent but it is incremented by the router receiving the update. This is a big difference to IPv4 versions of RIP. Using the previous example, Router-X sends an update to Router-Y containing its directly connected network, advertising the route with a hop count of 1. Router-Y, the adjacent router receiving the update, increments the hop count by 1, resulting in a metric value of 2 before entering it into its IPv6 routing table. The end result is in the Cisco implementation of the RIPng hop count (metric): The router where the **show ipv6 route** command is entered includes itself as the first hop. This adds a hop count of 1 to what would normally be seen in RIPv2. This is demonstrated later in this section.

- **UDP-based protocol:** Both RIPv2 and RIPng messages are encapsulated in User Datagram Protocol (UDP) segments. RIPv2 uses port 520, while RIPng messages are sent using port 521.
- **Updates:** RIPv2 and RIPng both send periodic updates every 30 seconds. Triggered updates are also sent by both routing protocols.
- **Timers:** RIPv2 and RIPng both use holddown and other timers to help prevent routing loops.
- **Split horizon:** Split horizon or split horizon with poison reverse are used with both RIPv2 and RIPng to also help prevent routing loops.
- **Automatic summarization:** RIPv2 automatically summarizes networks at classful boundaries. The concept of classful addressing does not exist in IPv6, so this is not applicable in RIPng. IPv6 addresses are considered classless.
- **Source and destination addresses:** RIPv2 sends messages to the IPv4 multicast address 224.0.0.9, RIPv2's multicast group address. These messages use the source IPv4 address of the exit interface. RIPng sends RIP messages to the IPv6 multicast address FF02::9, the all-RIP-routers multicast address with link-local scope. RIPng messages are sourced using the link-local address of the exit interface.
- **Authentication:** RIPv2 can use either plain text authentication or Message Digest 5 (MD5) authentication. RIPng does not include its own authentication mechanism. Authentication and/or encryption are provided by the standard IPsec features defined for IPv6.

Configuring RIPng on Cisco Routers

Using the topology from Chapter 6 enables RIPng for the 2001:0DB8:CAFE::/48 network, as shown in Figure 8-1. We will configure Routers R1, R2, and R3 to share routing information using RIPng. Because the network is a stub network, R3 is configured with a default route through the ISP router. RIPng is applied to distribute R3's default route within the RIPng domain. The ISP router is configured with a static route to reach 2001:0DB8:CAFE::/48.

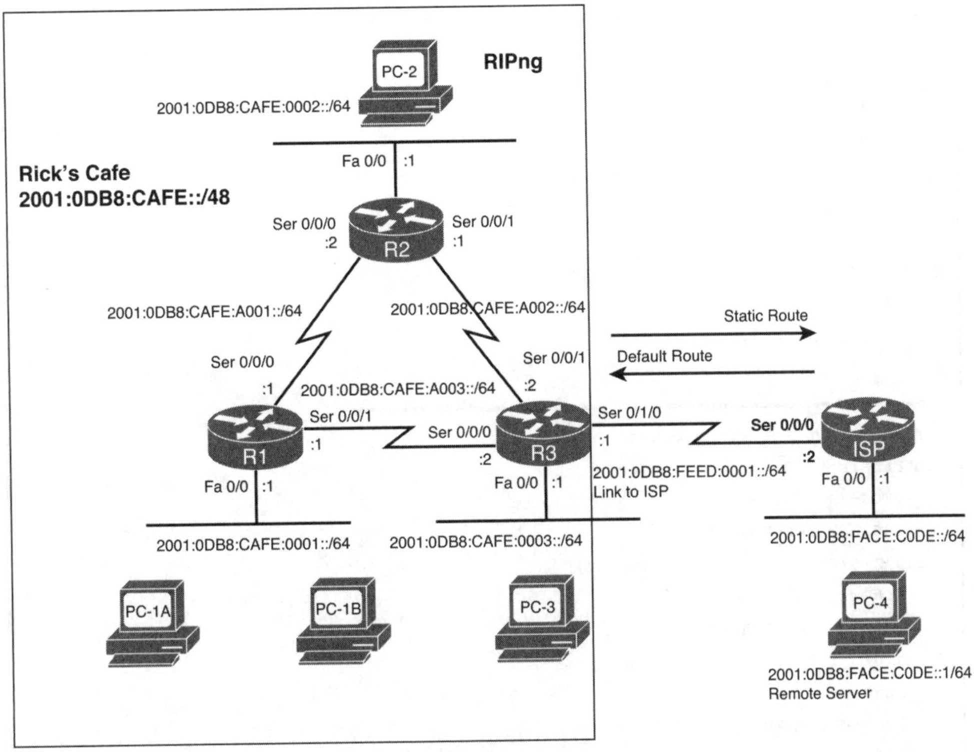

Figure 8-1 *Rick's Café Network RIPng Topology*

RIPng and the other IPv6 routing protocols use the routers' link-local addresses to source their messages. Begin by examining the interface configurations on all four routers in Example 8-1 that were previously configured in Chapter 6. Each router has the same link-local address on each of its interfaces, which were manually configured in Chapter 6 to help identify the router more easily. Remember, the link-local addresses only have to be unique on the link.

Example 8-1 *Global Unicast and Link-local Interface Addresses*

```
R1# show ipv6 interface brief
FastEthernet0/0            [up/up]
    FE80::1
```

```
    2001:DB8:CAFE:1::1
Serial0/0/0                  [up/up]
    FE80::1
    2001:DB8:CAFE:A001::1
Serial0/0/1                  [up/up]
    FE80::1
    2001:DB8:CAFE:A003::1
R1#
```

```
R2# show ipv6 interface brief
FastEthernet0/0              [up/up]
    FE80::2
    2001:DB8:CAFE:2::1
Serial0/0/0                  [up/up]
    FE80::2
    2001:DB8:CAFE:A001::2
Serial0/0/1                  [up/up]
    FE80::2
    2001:DB8:CAFE:A002::1
R2#
```

```
R3# show ipv6 interface brief
FastEthernet0/0              [up/up]
    FE80::3
    2001:DB8:CAFE:3::1
Serial0/0/0                  [up/up]
    FE80::3
    2001:DB8:CAFE:A003::2
Serial0/0/1                  [up/up]
    FE80::3
    2001:DB8:CAFE:A002::2
Serial0/1/0                  [up/up]
    FE80::3
    2001:DB8:FEED:1::1
R3#
```

```
ISP# show ipv6 interface brief
FastEthernet0/0              [up/up]
    FE80::FEED
    2001:DB8:FACE:C0DE::1
Serial0/0/0                  [up/up]
    FE80::FEED
    2001:DB8:FEED:1::2
ISP#
```

To configure a RIPng routing process, begin by using the **ipv6 router rip** command in global configuration mode. The **ipv6 router rip** command is similar to the **router rip** command, except that it is IPv6 specific. The syntax for this command is as follows:

```
Router(config)# ipv6 router rip name
```

This command enables the RIPng routing process for IPv6. The *name* identifies the specific routing process.

In Example 8-2, you attempt to enable RIPng on Router R1 with the **ipv6 router rip RIPNG-R1** command. However, the following error message is received:

```
% IPv6 routing not enabled
```

This is because IPv6 routing has not yet been enabled. Using the **ipv6 unicast-routing** global configuration command, enter IPv6 routing on R1 and reenter the **ipv6 router rip RIPNG-R1** command.

Example 8-2 *Enabling RIPng*

```
R1(config)# ipv6 router rip RIPNG-R1
% IPv6 routing not enabled
R1(config)#
R1(config)# ipv6 unicast-routing
R1(config)# ipv6 router rip RIPNG-R1
R1(config-rtr)#
```

The name is used to uniquely identify the RIPng process on the local router. It is case sensitive and locally significant. The name does not have to be the same on all routers in the RIPng routing domain. However, for operational purposes, the name is typically the same on all routers in the implementation so that dissimilar names don't confuse Network Operations Center (NOC) personnel.

Example 8-3 shows the IPv6 router subcommands for tuning the RIPng process.

Example 8-3 *ipv6 rip Subcommands*

```
R1(config)# ipv6 router rip RIPNG-R1
R1(config-rtr)# ?
  default          Set a command to its defaults
  distance         Administrative distance
  distribute-list  Filter networks in routing updates
  exit             Exit from IPv6 routing protocol configuration mode
  maximum-paths    Forward packets over multiple paths
  no               Negate a command or set its defaults
  poison-reverse   Poison reverse updates
```

```
  port              Port and multicast address
  redistribute      Redistribute IPv6 prefixes from another routing protocol
  shutdown          Shutdown protocol
  split-horizon     Split horizon updates
  timers            Adjust routing timers

R1(config-rtr)#
```

To configure the RIPng routing process on an interface, the **ipv6 rip** *name* **enable** interface command is used on each interface to enable RIPng, where *name* identifies the specific routing process. Example 8-4 shows the RIPng interface configuration commands for R1. Notice that the name used with the interface commands must be the same as the name used to enable the RIPng process in global configuration mode. The name is case sensitive and must match exactly.

Example 8-4 *Enabling RIPng on R1*

```
R1(config)# interface fastethernet 0/0
R1(config-if)# ipv6 rip RIPNG-R1 enable
R1(config-if)# exit
R1(config)# interface serial 0/0/0
R1(config-if)# ipv6 rip RIPNG-R1 enable
R1(config-if)# exit
R1(config)# interface serial 0/0/1
R1(config-if)# ipv6 rip RIPNG-R1 enable
R1(config-if)# end
R1#
```

Note With RIPng and other IPv6 routing protocols, Cisco IOS does not use the **network** command in router configuration mode used when configuring IPv4 routing protocols. IPv6 routing protocols are enabled directly on the interface.

Example 8-5 shows the commands used to complete the RIPng configurations for the topology for Routers R2 and R3. R3's serial 0/1/0 interface was not included in the RIPng process because this is the interface that will be used for the default route to the ISP router. Although this command was used in Chapter 7 to ensure that IPv6 routing is enabled, the **ipv6 unicast-routing** command is configured first. Notice that each router has a unique name, but the same name applied to enable RIPng in global configuration mode is used to enable RIPng on the interfaces. Routers R1, R2, and R3 are configured with different names to illustrate this point. Typically, the name should be the same on all routers in the routing domain.

Example 8-5 *Enabling RIPng on R2 and R3*

```
R2(config)# ipv6 unicast-routing
R2(config)# ipv6 router rip RIPNG-R2
R2(config-rtr)# exit
R2(config)# interface fastethernet 0/0
R2(config-if)# ipv6 rip RIPNG-R2 enable
R2(config-if)# exit
R2(config)# interface serial 0/0/0
R2(config-if)# ipv6 rip RIPNG-R2 enable
R2(config-if)# exit
R2(config)# interface serial 0/0/1
R2(config-if)# ipv6 rip RIPNG-R2 enable
R2(config-if)#
```

```
R3(config)# ipv6 unicast-routing
R3(config)# ipv6 router rip RIPNG-R3
R3(config-rtr)# exit
R3(config)# interface fastethernet 0/0
R3(config-if)# ipv6 rip RIPNG-R3 enable
R3(config-if)# exit
R3(config)# interface serial 0/0/0
R3(config-if)# ipv6 rip RIPNG-R3 enable
R3(config-if)# exit
R3(config)# interface serial 0/0/1
R3(config-if)# ipv6 rip RIPNG-R3 enable
R3(config-if)#
```

Now that RIPng is enabled for the three routers in the 2001:db8:cafe::/48 network, configure the static routes between R3 and ISP routers. Begin by configuring the default route on R3, as shown in Example 8-6.

Example 8-6 *Configuring a Default Route on R3 and Propagating It Through RIPng*

```
! This is the default route
R3(config)# ipv6 route ::/0 serial 0/1/0
R3(config)# interface serial 0/0/0
R3(config-if)# ipv6 rip RIPNG-R3 default-information originate
R3(config-if)# exit
R3(config)# interface serial 0/0/1
R3(config-if)# ipv6 rip RIPNG-R3 default-information originate
R3(config-if)#
```

To originate a default IPv6 route into the RIPng domain, the interface command **ipv6 rip default-information** is used. As shown in Example 8-6, this command is configured on both of R3's interfaces used to advertise the default route to adjacent RIPng routers. The complete syntax for the **ipv6 rip default-information** command is as follows:

```
Router(config-if)# ipv6 rip name default-information {only | originate} [metric
metric-value]
```

The terms in this syntax are as follows:

- *name*: Indicates the name of the IPv6 RIP routing process.
- **only:** Advertises the IPv6 default route (::/0) only. Suppresses the advertisement of all other routes.
- **originate:** Advertises the IPv6 default route (::/0). The advertisement of other routes is unaffected.
- **metric** *metric-value* (Optional): Associates a metric with the default route. The metric value range is from 1 through 15.

> **Note** The **ipv6 rip default-information** interface command in RIPng is similar to the **default-information originate** global configuration command used in RIPv2. The difference is that the RIPng command is configured on the interface, whereas the RIPv2 command is configured in global configuration mode.

Example 8-7 shows the configuration of ISP's static route to 2001:0DB8:CAFE::/48.

Example 8-7 *Configuring an IPv6 on ISP to Reach 2001:db8:cafe::/48*

```
ISP(config)# ipv6 route 2001:db8:cafe::/48 serial 0/0/0
```

Verifying RIPng

This section confirms the configuration with similar commands applied when verifying RIPv2. In Example 8-8, the **show ipv6 protocols** command is used to display the parameters and current state of all active IPv6 routing protocol processes. By default, connected and static IPv6 routing is active when **ipv6 unicast-routing** is enabled. The output on R1 also shows that the RIPng process RIPNG-R1 is active for three of its interfaces.

Example 8-8 *show ipv6 protocols Command*

```
R1# show ipv6 protocols
IPv6 Routing Protocol is "connected"
IPv6 Routing Protocol is "static"
IPv6 Routing Protocol is "rip RIPNG-R1"
```

```
  Interfaces:
    Serial0/0/1
    Serial0/0/0
    FastEthernet0/0
  Redistribution:
    None
R1#
R1# show ipv6 interface fastethernet 0/0
FastEthernet0/0 is up, line protocol is up
  IPv6 is enabled, link-local address is FE80::1
  No Virtual link-local address(es):
  Global unicast address(es):
    2001:DB8:CAFE:1::1, subnet is 2001:DB8:CAFE:1::/64
  Joined group address(es):
    FF02::1
    FF02::2
    FF02::9
    FF02::1:FF00:1
  MTU is 1500 bytes
<output omitted>
```

In Example 8-8, **show ipv6 interface fastethernet 0/0** verifies that R1's Fast Ethernet 0/0 interface is now a member of RIPng multicast group FF02::9. RIPng uses FF02::9 as the destination address for RIP update messages.

The **show ipv6 route rip** command in Example 8-9 illustrates the RIPng routes in R1's routing table. Notice that the default route (::/0) that you configured on R3 has been distributed to R1 through RIPng. Using the following route, you can examine the second route more closely:

```
R   2001:DB8:CAFE:2::/64 [120/2]
  via FE80::2, Serial0/0/0
```

This code uses the following terms:

- **R:** Indicates RIPng as the protocol that derived the route.
- **2001:DB8:CAFE:2::/64:** This is the prefix and prefix length of the remote network.
- **[120/2]:** The first number in the brackets is the administrative distance of the information source, 120. This is the same as with RIPv1 and RIPv2. The second number is the metric for the route. Notice that the number of hops is one more than what you would see for RIPv1 and RIPv2. Unlike RIP for IPv4, in the Cisco implementation of RIPng, the router increments the metric by 1 when receiving the routing update from a neighbor. In effect, the router includes itself in the number of hops to a destination network.

- **via FE80::2:** This is the link-local address of the next-hop router.
- **Serial0/0/0:** This is the exit interface of the next-hop router.

Example 8-9 *R1's IPv6 Routing Table*

```
R1# show ipv6 route rip
IPv6 Routing Table - 12 entries
Codes: C - Connected, L - Local, S - Static, R - RIP, B - BGP
       U - Per-user Static route
       I1 - ISIS L1, I2 - ISIS L2, IA - ISIS interarea, IS - ISIS summary
       O - OSPF intra, OI - OSPF inter, OE1 - OSPF ext 1, OE2 - OSPF ext 2
       ON1 - OSPF NSSA ext 1, ON2 - OSPF NSSA ext 2
       D - EIGRP, EX - EIGRP external
R   ::/0 [120/2]
    via FE80::3, Serial0/0/1
R   2001:DB8:CAFE:2::/64 [120/2]
     via FE80::2, Serial0/0/0
R   2001:DB8:CAFE:3::/64 [120/2]
     via FE80::3, Serial0/0/1
R   2001:DB8:CAFE:A002::/64 [120/2]
     via FE80::2, Serial0/0/0
     via FE80::3, Serial0/0/1
R1#
```

In Example 8-10, the **ping** command is used to verify reachability. The pings to the Fast Ethernet interfaces of the R2, R3, and ISP routers are all successful.

Example 8-10 *Using ping to Verify Reachability*

```
R1# ping 2001:db8:cafe:2::1

Type escape sequence to abort.
Sending 5, 100-byte ICMP Echos to 2001:DB8:CAFE:2::1, timeout is 2 seconds:
!!!!!
Success rate is 100 percent (5/5), round-trip min/avg/max = 28/28/32 ms
R1# ping 2001:db8:cafe:3::1

Type escape sequence to abort.
Sending 5, 100-byte ICMP Echos to 2001:DB8:CAFE:3::1, timeout is 2 seconds:
!!!!!
Success rate is 100 percent (5/5), round-trip min/avg/max = 28/28/28 ms
R1# ping 2001:db8:face:c0de::1

Type escape sequence to abort.
```

```
Sending 5, 100-byte ICMP Echos to 2001:DB8:FACE:C0DE::1, timeout is 2 seconds:
!!!!!
Success rate is 100 percent (5/5), round-trip min/avg/max = 56/56/60 ms
R1#
```

The **show ipv6 rip** command in Example 8-11 displays information regarding current RIPng processes. Except for the addition of a process name, UDP port number, multicast group, and process ID (pid), most of the other information is similar to that in RIPv2. (RIPv2 uses UDP port 520, whereas RIPng uses UDP port 521.)

Example 8-11 *show ipv6 rip on R1*

```
R1# show ipv6 rip
RIP process "RIPNG-R1", port 521, multicast-group FF02::9, pid 179
     Administrative distance is 120. Maximum paths is 16
     Updates every 30 seconds, expire after 180
     Holddown lasts 0 seconds, garbage collect after 120
     Split horizon is on; poison reverse is off
     Default routes are not generated
     Periodic updates 12, trigger updates 6
  Interfaces:
    Serial0/0/1
    Serial0/0/0
    FastEthernet0/0
  Redistribution:
    None
R1#
```

In the Cisco IOS Software implementation of RIPng, each IPv6 RIP process maintains a local routing table called the Routing Information Base (RIB). RIPng tries to insert every nonexpired route from its local database into the master IPv6 Routing Information Base, also known as the IPv6 routing table. If a router learns of multiple routes to the same network, RIPng stores only the lowest-cost route in the local RIPng RIB. If the same route has been learned from a routing source with a better administrative distance than RIPng, the RIP route will not be added to the IPv6 routing table but will still exist in the RIPng RIB. The **show ipv6 rip database** command is used to display the RIPng RIB, as shown in Example 8-12.

Example 8-12 *R1's RIPng Routing Information Base*

```
R1# show ipv6 rip database
RIP process "RIPNG-R1", local RIB
 2001:DB8:CAFE:2::/64, metric 2, installed
     Serial0/0/0/FE80::2, expires in 173 secs
 2001:DB8:CAFE:3::/64, metric 2, installed
```

```
      Serial0/0/1/FE80::3, expires in 176 secs
  2001:DB8:CAFE:A001::/64, metric 2
      Serial0/0/0/FE80::2, expires in 173 secs
  2001:DB8:CAFE:A002::/64, metric 2, installed
      Serial0/0/1/FE80::3, expires in 176 secs
      Serial0/0/0/FE80::2, expires in 173 secs
  2001:DB8:CAFE:A003::/64, metric 2
      Serial0/0/1/FE80::3, expires in 176 secs
  ::/0, metric 2, installed
      Serial0/0/1/FE80::3, expires in 176 secs
R1#
```

The **show ipv6 rip next-hops** command displays the next-hop addresses and the number of RIPng routes that use that next-hop address, whether or not that route is in the IPv6 routing table. This information is derived from the RIPng RIB, not the IPv6 routing table. Example 8-13 displays the output from the **show ipv6 rip next-hops** command on R1.

Example 8-13 *show ipv6 next-hops on R1*

```
R1# show ipv6 rip next-hops
 RIP process "RIPNG-R1", Next Hops
  FE80::2/Serial0/0/0 [3 paths]
  FE80::3/Serial0/0/1 [4 paths]
R1#
```

The **debug ipv6 rip** command in Example 8-14 displays the RIPng routing messages sent and received by Router R1. Notice that the source address of the routing update is the link-local address of the interface, and the destination address is FF02::9, the all-RIP-routers multicast address with link-local scope. The metric and prefix/prefix length of the route are also included. Unlike RIPv2, the receiving RIPng router will increment the metric by 1, which in effect makes itself the first-hop router.

Example 8-14 *debug ipv6 rip on R1*

```
R1# debug ipv6 rip
RIP Routing Protocol debugging is on
R1#
*Feb 20 18:01:18.511: RIPng: response received from FE80::3 on Serial0/0/1 for
RIPNG-R1
*Feb 20 18:01:18.515:         src=FE80::3 (Serial0/0/1)
*Feb 20 18:01:18.515:         dst=FF02::9
*Feb 20 18:01:18.515:         sport=521, dport=521, length=112
*Feb 20 18:01:18.515:         command=2, version=1, mbz=0, #rte=5
*Feb 20 18:01:18.515:         tag=0, metric=1, prefix=2001:DB8:CAFE:3::/64
*Feb 20 18:01:18.515:         tag=0, metric=1, prefix=2001:DB8:CAFE:A003::/64
```

```
*Feb 20 18:01:18.515:        tag=0, metric=1, prefix=2001:DB8:CAFE:A002::/64
*Feb 20 18:01:18.515:        tag=0, metric=2, prefix=2001:DB8:CAFE:2::/64
*Feb 20 18:01:18.515:        tag=0, metric=1, prefix=::/0
R1#
*Feb 20 18:01:25.071: RIPng: Sending multicast update on Serial0/0/1 for RIPNG-R1
*Feb 20 18:01:25.071:        src=FE80::1
*Feb 20 18:01:25.071:        dst=FF02::9 (Serial0/0/1)
*Feb 20 18:01:25.071:        sport=521, dport=521, length=92
*Feb 20 18:01:25.071:        command=2, version=1, mbz=0, #rte=4
*Feb 20 18:01:25.071:        tag=0, metric=1, prefix=2001:DB8:CAFE:1::/64
*Feb 20 18:01:25.071:        tag=0, metric=1, prefix=2001:DB8:CAFE:A001::/64
*Feb 20 18:01:25.071:        tag=0, metric=1, prefix=2001:DB8:CAFE:A003::/64
*Feb 20 18:01:25.071:        tag=0, metric=2, prefix=2001:DB8:CAFE:2::/64
```

For each of the four routers, Example 8-15 shows select output from the final running configs relevant to RIPng.

Example 8-15 *Selected Running Config Outputs Relevant to RIPng*

```
R1# show running-config
!
ipv6 unicast-routing
!
ipv6 router rip RIPNG-R1
!
interface FastEthernet0/0
 no ip address
 ipv6 address FE80::1 link-local
 ipv6 address 2001:DB8:CAFE:1::1/64
 ipv6 rip RIPNG-R1 enable
!
interface Serial0/0/0
 ipv6 address FE80::1 link-local
 ipv6 address 2001:DB8:CAFE:A001::1/64
 ipv6 rip RIPNG-R1 enable
!
interface Serial0/0/1
 no ip address
 ipv6 address FE80::1 link-local
 ipv6 address 2001:DB8:CAFE:A003::1/64
 ipv6 rip RIPNG-R1 enable
!
R1#

R2# show running-config
```

```
!
ipv6 router rip RIPNG-R2
!
ipv6 unicast-routing
!
interface FastEthernet0/0
 no ip address
 ipv6 address FE80::2 link-local
 ipv6 address 2001:DB8:CAFE:2::1/64
 ipv6 rip RIPNG-R2 enable
!
interface Serial0/0/0
 no ip address
 ipv6 address FE80::2 link-local
 ipv6 address 2001:DB8:CAFE:A001::2/64
 ipv6 rip RIPNG-R2 enable
!
interface Serial0/0/1
 no ip address
 ipv6 address FE80::2 link-local
 ipv6 address 2001:DB8:CAFE:A002::1/64
 ipv6 rip RIPNG-R2 enable
!
R2#
```

```
R3# show running-config
!
ipv6 unicast-routing
!
ipv6 router rip RIPNG-R3
!
interface FastEthernet0/0
 no ip address
 ipv6 address FE80::3 link-local
 ipv6 address 2001:DB8:CAFE:3::1/64
 ipv6 rip RIPNG-R3 enable
!
interface Serial0/0/0
 no ip address
 ipv6 address FE80::3 link-local
 ipv6 address 2001:DB8:CAFE:A003::2/64
 ipv6 rip RIPNG-R3 enable
 ipv6 rip RIPNG-R3 default-information originate
!
interface Serial0/0/1
```

```
 no ip address
 ipv6 address FE80::3 link-local
 ipv6 address 2001:DB8:CAFE:A002::2/64
 ipv6 rip RIPNG-R3 enable
 ipv6 rip RIPNG-R3 default-information originate
!
interface Serial0/1/0
 no ip address
 ipv6 address FE80::3 link-local
 ipv6 address 2001:DB8:FEED:1::1/64
!
ipv6 route ::/0 Serial0/1/0
!
R3#

ISP# show running-config
!
ipv6 unicast-routing
!
interface FastEthernet0/0
 no ip address
 ipv6 address FE80::FEED link-local
 ipv6 address 2001:DB8:FACE:C0DE::1/64
!
interface Serial0/0/0
 no ip address
 ipv6 address FE80::FEED link-local
 ipv6 address 2001:DB8:FEED:1::2/64
!
ipv6 route 2001:DB8:CAFE::/48 Serial0/0/0
!
ISP#
```

Before moving on to EIGRP for IPv6, Example 8-16 shows the command for removing a RIPng process. The **no ipv6 router rip** *name* global configuration command removes the RIPng process, including any interface configuration commands used by that process.

Example 8-16 *Removing the RIPng Process*

```
R1(config)# no ipv6 router rip RIPNG-R1
---
R2(config)# no ipv6 router rip RIPNG-R2
---
R3(config)# no ipv6 router rip RIPNG-R3
```

EIGRP for IPv6

Enhanced Interior Gateway Routing Protocol (EIGRP) is a distance vector, classless routing protocol that was released in 1992 with IOS 9.21. As its name suggests, EIGRP is an enhancement of Cisco IGRP (Interior Gateway Routing Protocol). Both are Cisco-proprietary protocols and only operate on Cisco routers. The main purpose in the Cisco development of EIGRP was to create a classless version of IGRP. EIGRP includes several features that are not commonly found in other distance vector routing protocols like RIP (RIPv1 and RIPv2).

Note The term *hybrid routing protocol* is sometimes used to define EIGRP. However, this term is misleading because EIGRP is not a hybrid between distance vector and link-state routing protocols; it is solely a distance vector routing protocol. Therefore, Cisco is no longer using this term to refer to EIGRP.

Unique to EIGRP is its Reliable Transport Protocol (RTP), which provides reliable and unreliable delivery of EIGRP packets. In addition, EIGRP establishes relationships with directly connected routers that are also enabled for EIGRP. Neighbor relationships are used to track the status of these neighbors. RTP and the tracking of neighbor adjacencies set the stage for the EIGRP workhorse, the Diffusing Update Algorithm (DUAL).

As the computational engine that drives EIGRP, DUAL resides at the center of the routing protocol, guaranteeing loop-free paths and backup paths throughout the routing domain. DUAL selects a primary route to install in the routing table, known as the successor, and also maintains a list of guaranteed loop-free backup routes, known as feasible successors. Both successors and feasible successors are maintained in EIGRP's topology table.

EIGRP for IPv6 is the EIGRP IPv4 equivalent for routing IPv6 prefixes. EIGRP IPv4 runs over an IPv4 network layer, communicating with other EIGRP IPv4 peers, and advertises only IPv4 routes. EIGRP for IPv6 has the same functionality as EIGRP for IPv4 but uses IPv6 as the network layer transport, communicating with EIGRP for IPv6 peers and advertising IPv6 routes. Prior knowledge of EIGRP is assumed and beyond the scope of this book.

Comparing EIGRP for IPv4 and EIGRP for IPv6

EIGRP for IPv6 is available in Cisco IOS Release 12.4(6)T and later. EIGRP for IPv4 and EIGRP for IPv6 are configured and managed separately. However, the configuration of EIGRP for IPv4 and EIGRP for IPv6 is similar. Many of the same processes and operational functionality are the same in both protocols.

The following is a comparison of the main features of EIGRP for IPv4 and EIGRP for IPv6:

- **Advertised routes:** EIGRP for IPv4 advertises IPv4 routes, whereas EIGRP for IPv6 advertises routes to populate the IPv6 routing table.

- **Distance vector:** Both EIGRP for IPv4 and IPv6 are distance vector routing protocols.
- **Convergence technology:** EIGRP for IPv4 and for IPv6 both use the DUAL algorithm. This embodies the same techniques and processes including successor, feasible successor, feasible distance, and reported distance.
- **Metric:** Both EIGRP for IPv4 and EIGRP for IPv6 use bandwidth, delay, reliability, and load for their composite metric. Only bandwidth and delay are used by default.
- **Transport protocol:** Reliable Transport Protocol (RTP) is responsible for guaranteed, ordered delivery of EIGRP packets to all neighbors for both protocols, EIGRP for IPv4 and for IPv6.
- **Partial updates:** EIGRP for IPv4 and IPv6 both send incremental updates when the state of a destination changes, instead of sending periodic updates of the entire contents of the routing table.
- **Neighbor discovery mechanism:** EIGRP for IPv4 and EIGRP for IPv6 use a simple hello mechanism to learn about neighboring routers and form adjacencies. EIGRP for IPv6 uses a link-local address for neighbor discovery and to form neighbor adjacencies.
- **Automatic summarization:** EIGRP for IPv4 automatically summarizes on classful boundaries. The concept of classful addressing does not exist in IPv6, so this is not applicable in EIGRP for IPv6.
- **Source and destination addresses:** EIGRP for IPv4 sends messages to the IPv4 multicast address 224.0.0.10, EIGRP multicast group address. These messages use the source IPv4 address of the exit interface. EIGRP for IPv6 sends its messages to the IPv6 multicast address FF02::10, the all-EIGRP-routers multicast address with link-local scope. EIGRP for IPv6 messages are sourced using the link-local address of the exit interface.
- **Authentication:** EIGRP for IPv4 can use either plain text authentication or Message Digest 5 (MD5) authentication. EIGRP for IPv6 also uses MD5.
- **Router ID:** Both EIGRP for IPv4 and EIGRP for IPv6 use a 32-bit number for the Router ID. The 32-bit Router ID is represented in dotted-decimal notation and is commonly an IPv4 address. If the router has not been configured with an IPv4 address, the EIGRP **router-id** command must be used to configure a Router ID using an IPv4 address. The process in determining the 32-bit Router ID is the same in both protocols.

Configuring EIGRP for IPv6

Once again, using the topology from Chapter 6, you will enable EIGRP for IPv6 for the 2001:0DB8:CAFE::/48 network, as shown in Figure 8-2.

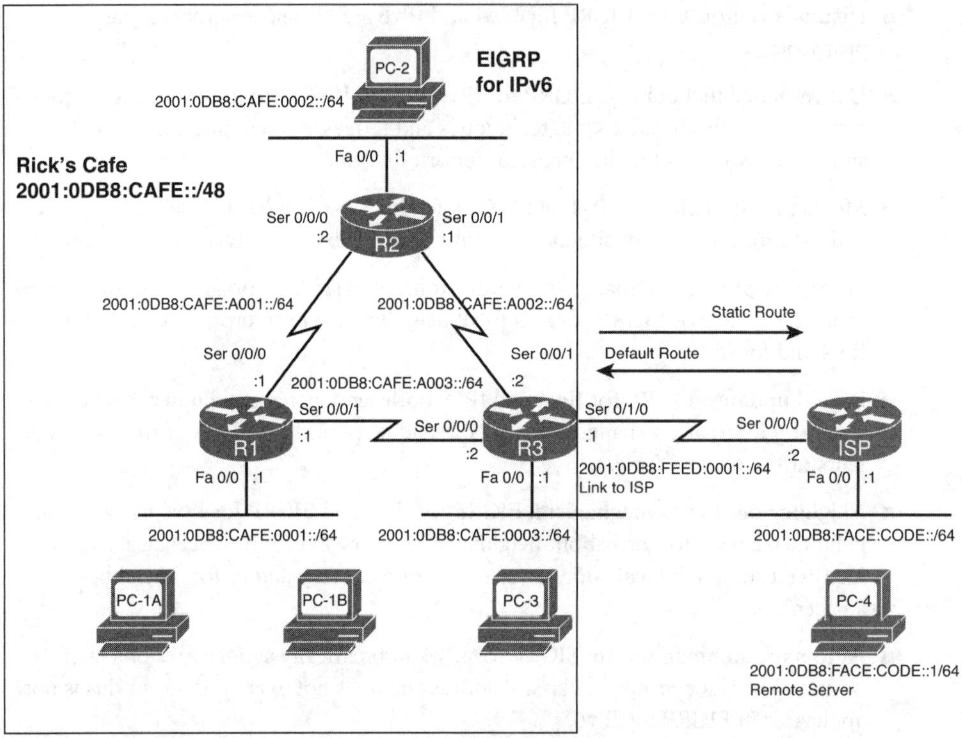

Figure 8-2 *Rick's Café Network EIGRP for IPv6 Topology*

Configure Routers R1, R2, and R3 to share routing information within the EIGRP for IPv6 routing domain. R3 is still configured with a default route through the ISP router. Configure R3 to propagate this default route to the other EIGRP routers. The ISP router is still configured with a static route to reach 2001:0DB8:CAFE::/48. Both of these static routes are shown in Example 8-17.

Example 8-17 *Static Routes on R3 and ISP Routers*

```
R3(config)# ipv6 route ::/0 serial 0/1/0

ISP(config)# ipv6 route 2001:db8:cafe::/48 serial 0/0/0
```

Example 8-18 illustrates Router R1's configuration of EIGRP for IPv6. First, enable IPv6 routing with the **ipv6 unicast-routing** command. Configuration of EIGRP begins with the **ipv6 router eigrp 100** command in global configuration mode to create an EIGRP for IPv6 routing process using the as-number 100. This command is similar to the **router eigrp** *as-number* command used in EIGRP for IPv4. Just as with EIGRP for IPv4, the as-number must be the same on all routers in the EIGRP for IPv6 routing domain. Continuing with the output in Example 8-18, the **router-id** mode is entered to configure the EIGRP Router ID. The Router ID is a 32-bit IPv4 number represented in dotted-decimal notation.

This command is necessary on all the EIGRP routers in the topology because none of them have been configured with an IPv4 address. The last router configuration command in Example 8-18 is **no shutdown**.

Example 8-18 *Enabling EIGRP for IPv6 on R1*

```
R1(config)# ipv6 unicast-routing

R1(config)# ipv6 router eigrp 100
R1(config-rtr)# router-id ?
  A.B.C.D  EIGRP Router-ID in IP address format

R1(config-rtr)# router-id 10.1.1.1
R1(config-rtr)# no shutdown
R1(config-rtr)# end
R1#
```

The **no shutdown** command is required to activate the EIGRP for IPv6 routing process. The default is **shutdown**. Table 8-1 shows the syntax for these commands.

Table 8-1 *Commands for Creating the Routing Process for EIGRP for IPv6*

Command	Description
Router(config)# **ipv6 router eigrp** *as-number*	Enables the EIGRP routing process for IPv6. The as-number identifies the specific routing process and must be the same on all routers in the EIGRP domain.
Router(config-rtr)# **router-id** *router-id*	The router uses the 32-bit IPv4 address to select the Router ID for an EIGRP for IPv6 process.
Router(config-rtr)# **no shutdown**	This command is required for the EIGRP process to begin running.

In Example 8-18, R1's interfaces for EIGRP for IPv6 were enabled using the **ipv6 eigrp** *as-number* command. The as-number in the interface command must be the same as the as-number used to enable the EIGRP routing process. The syntax to enable EIGRP for IPv6 on a specified interface is as follows:

```
Router(config-if)# ipv6 eigrp as-number
```

The as-number (autonomous system) identifies the specific routing process and must be the same as the as-number used to create the routing process in the **ipv6 router eigrp** *as-number* command.

In Example 8-19, the interfaces on R1 are enabled for the EIGRP for IPv6 routing process.

Example 8-19 *Enabling EIGRP for IPv6 on R1's Interfaces*

```
R1(config)# interface fastethernet 0/0
R1(config-if)# ipv6 eigrp 100
R1(config-if)# exit
R1(config)# interface serial 0/0/0
R1(config-if)# ipv6 eigrp 100
R1(config-if)# exit
R1(config)# interface serial 0/0/1
R1(config-if)# ipv6 eigrp 100
R1(config-if)# end
R1#
```

Examples 8-20 and 8-21 illustrate the IOS notification messages received when using the **show ipv6 neighbors** command if the EIGRP routing process has not been configured properly. If the EIGRP routing process is in shutdown, Example 8-20 shows that the IOS notification message "% EIGRP 100 is in SHUTDOWN" will be displayed. If you configure the EIGRP process and the Router ID cannot be automatically configured because there is not an active IPv4 address, Example 8-21 shows that the IOS will inform you of the issue with the message "% No router ID for EIGRP 100."

Example 8-20 *EIGRP for IPv6 Still in Shutdown*

```
R1# show ipv6 eigrp neighbors
IPv6-EIGRP neighbors for process 100
% EIGRP 100 is in SHUTDOWN
R1#
```

Example 8-21 *EIGRP for IPv6 Without a Valid Router ID*

```
R1# show ipv6 eigrp neighbors
IPv6-EIGRP neighbors for process 100
% No router ID for EIGRP 100
R1#
```

In Example 8-22, Routers R2 and R3 for EIGRP were configured for IPv6 using the same as-number that was used for R1.

Example 8-22 *Enabling EIGRP for IPv6 on R1's Interfaces*

```
R2(config)# ipv6 unicast-routing
R2(config)# ipv6 router eigrp 100
R2(config-rtr)# router-id 10.2.2.2
```

```
R2(config-rtr)# no shutdown
R2(config-rtr)# exit
R2(config)#
R2(config)# interface fastethernet 0/0
R2(config-if)# ipv6 eigrp 100
R2(config-if)# exit
R2(config)# interface serial 0/0/0
R2(config-if)# ipv6 eigrp 100
R2(config-if)# exit
R2(config)# interface serial 0/0/1
R2(config-if)# ipv6 eigrp 100
R2(config-if)# end
R2#
```

```
R3(config)# ipv6 unicast-routing
R3(config)# ipv6 router eigrp 100
R3(config-rtr)# router-id 10.3.3.3
R3(config-rtr)# no shutdown
R3(config-rtr)# exit
R3(config)#
R3(config)# interface fastethernet 0/0
R3(config-if)# ipv6 eigrp 100
R3(config-if)# exit
R3(config)# interface serial 0/0/0
R3(config-if)# ipv6 eigrp 100
R3(config-if)# exit
R3(config)# interface serial 0/0/1
R3(config-if)# ipv6 eigrp 100
R3(config-if)# end
R3#
```

As mentioned previously, both EIGRP for IPv4 and EIGRP for IPv6 use bandwidth and delay by default for their composite metric. Modifying interface bandwidth and delay parameters influences both the IPv4 and IPv6 EIGRP routing processes.

Example 8-17 showed the earlier configuration of a default route on R3 with the ISP router as the next hop. In Example 8-23, the default route is distributed as a summary route to Routers R1 and R2 using the **ipv6 summary-address eigrp** interface command, the syntax for which is as follows:

```
Router(config-if)# ipv6 summary-address eigrp as-number ipv6-address
[admin-distance]
```

This command configures a summary aggregate address for a specified interface. By default, an administrative distance of 5 is applied to EIGRP for IPv6 summary routes.

Because R3 has two EIGRP neighbors, you need to configure the command on both interfaces. An administrative distance of 5 is applied to EIGRP for IPv6 summary routes. The **ipv6 summary-address eigrp** command is used to configure interface-level address summarization. The administrative distance of 5 is used to advertise a summary address without installing it in the routing table of the router where the route is summarized.

Note The summary route will be installed in the routing table and EIGRP topology table with a next hop of null0. This is done so that those packets that don't have a more specific route will be properly dropped and not be routed throughout network until the hop limit expires.

You verify the propagation of the default route to R1 and R2 in the next section.

Example 8-23 *Propagating a Default Route as a Summary Route*

```
R3(config)# interface serial 0/0/0
R3(config-if)# ipv6 summary-address eigrp 100  ::/0
R3(config-if)# exit
R3(config)# interface serial 0/0/1
R3(config-if)# ipv6 summary-address eigrp 100  ::/0
R3(config-if)# end
R3#
```

Verifying EIGRP for IPv6

The **show ipv6 protocols** command in Example 8-24 displays the parameters and current state of all active IPv6 routing protocol processes, including EIGRP for IPv6. The highlighted portion is the default route (::/0) that was distributed to R1 and R2 as a summary route in Example 8-23. The summary route, which is the default route, has an administrative distance of 5 and will not be included in the routing table of R3. The static default route configured previously with a default administrative distance of 1 will be in R3's routing table, as shown in Example 8-25. Notice that the EIGRP for IPv6 routes have an administrative distance of 90, and all routes are sourced from the link-local address of the interface.

Example 8-24 *show ipv6 protocols on R3*

```
R3# show ipv6 protocols
IPv6 Routing Protocol is "connected"
IPv6 Routing Protocol is "static"
IPv6 Routing Protocol is "eigrp 100"
  EIGRP metric weight K1=1, K2=0, K3=1, K4=0, K5=0
  EIGRP maximum hopcount 100
```

```
  EIGRP maximum metric variance 1
  Interfaces:
    FastEthernet0/0
    Serial0/0/0
    Serial0/0/1
  Redistribution:
    None
! Summary-address command configured on
! Serial 0/0/0 and Serial 0/0/1 in Example 8-23:
! ipv6 summary-address eigrp 100 ::/0
  Address Summarization:
    ::/0 for Serial0/0/0, Serial0/0/1
      Summarizing with metric 28160
  Maximum path: 16
  Distance: internal 90 external 170

R3#
R3# show ipv6 interface fastethernet 0/0
FastEthernet0/0 is up, line protocol is up
  IPv6 is enabled, link-local address is FE80::3
  No Virtual link-local address(es):
  Global unicast address(es):
    2001:DB8:CAFE:3::1, subnet is 2001:DB8:CAFE:3::/64
  Joined group address(es):
    FF02::1
    FF02::2
    FF02::A
    FF02::1:FF00:3
  MTU is 1500 bytes
<output omitted>
```

In Example 8-24, **show ipv6 interface fastethernet 0/0** verifies that R3's Fast Ethernet 0/0 interface is now a member of EIGRP for IPv6 multicast group FF02::A. EIGRP for IPv6 uses FF02::A as the destination address for EIGRP update messages.

Example 8-25 *R3's Routing Table*

```
R3# show ipv6 route
IPv6 Routing Table - 14 entries
Codes: C - Connected, L - Local, S - Static, R - RIP, B - BGP
       U - Per-user Static route
       I1 - ISIS L1, I2 - ISIS L2, IA - ISIS interarea, IS - ISIS summary
       O - OSPF intra, OI - OSPF inter, OE1 - OSPF ext 1, OE2 - OSPF ext 2
       ON1 - OSPF NSSA ext 1, ON2 - OSPF NSSA ext 2
       D - EIGRP, EX - EIGRP external
```

```
S    ::/0 [1/0]
      via ::, Serial0/1/0
D    2001:DB8:CAFE:1::/64 [90/20514560]
      via FE80::1, Serial0/0/0
D    2001:DB8:CAFE:2::/64 [90/20514560]
      via FE80::1, Serial0/0/0
      via FE80::2, Serial0/0/1
D    2001:DB8:CAFE:A001::/64 [90/21024000]
      via FE80::1, Serial0/0/0
      via FE80::2, Serial0/0/1
<output omitted for brevity?
R3#
```

The **show ipv6 route eigrp** command in Example 8-26 displays the EIGRP for IPv6 routes in R1's routing table, including the default route distributed by R3. The administrative distance of 90 for internal EIGRP routes is the same as EIGRP for IPv4.

Example 8-26 *R1's EIGRP for IPv6 Routing Table Entries*

```
R1# show ipv6 route eigrp
IPv6 Routing Table - 11 entries
Codes: C - Connected, L - Local, S - Static, R - RIP, B - BGP
       U - Per-user Static route
       I1 - ISIS L1, I2 - ISIS L2, IA - ISIS interarea, IS - ISIS summary
       O - OSPF intra, OI - OSPF inter, OE1 - OSPF ext 1, OE2 - OSPF ext 2
       ON1 - OSPF NSSA ext 1, ON2 - OSPF NSSA ext 2
       D - EIGRP, EX - EIGRP external
! Default route
D    ::/0 [90/2172416]
      via FE80::3, Serial0/0/1
D    2001:DB8:CAFE:2::/64 [90/2172416]
      via FE80::2, Serial0/0/0
D    2001:DB8:CAFE:A002::/64 [90/2681856]
      via FE80::2, Serial0/0/0
R1#
```

In Example 8-27, R1's neighbor adjacencies are verified using the **show ipv6 eigrp neighbors** command. The only difference with the equivalent IPv4 command is that the IPv6 link-local address is applied to indicate the EIGRP peer. EIGRP for IPv6 messages are sourced using the router's link-local address. This is why it is beneficial to manually configure the router's link-local addresses so that you can more easily recognize the source or destination router. It is obvious from the output in Example 8-27 that in the Address column, the FE80::3 address is the link-local address of R3, whereas the FE80::2 address is the link-local address of R2.

Example 8-27 *Verifying Neighbor Adjacencies in EIGRP for IPv6*

```
R1# show ipv6 eigrp neighbors
IPv6-EIGRP neighbors for process 100
H   Address                 Interface       Hold Uptime   SRTT   RTO  Q  Seq
                                            (sec)         (ms)       Cnt Num
1   Link-local address:     Se0/0/1           14 00:02:34   49   294  0  8
    FE80::3
0   Link-local address:     Se0/0/0           13 00:13:08   28   200  0  9
    FE80::2
R1#
```

The topology table of EIGRP for IPv6 is displayed in Example 8-28 with the **show ipv6 eigrp topology** command. All of R3's routes are in the passive state, with some routes including both a successor and a feasible successor. Except for link-local addresses as the next-hop addresses, the remaining information is the same as EIGRP for IPv4. The first entry in the topology table is the summary route created when using the **ipv6 summary-address eigrp** interface command in Example 8-23.

Example 8-28 *Verifying the EIGRP for IPv6 Topology Table*

```
R3# show ipv6 eigrp topology
IPv6-EIGRP Topology Table for AS(100)/ID(10.3.3.3)

Codes: P - Passive, A - Active, U - Update, Q - Query, R - Reply,
       r - reply Status, s - sia Status

P ::/0, 1 successors, FD is 28160
        via Summary (28160/0), Null0
P 2001:DB8:CAFE:A003::/64, 1 successors, FD is 20512000
        via Connected, Serial0/0/0
        via FE80::2 (21536000/2681856), Serial0/0/1
        via FE80::1 (21024000/2169856), Serial0/0/0
P 2001:DB8:CAFE:3::/64, 1 successors, FD is 28160
        via Connected, FastEthernet0/0
P 2001:DB8:CAFE:A002::/64, 1 successors, FD is 20512000
        via Connected, Serial0/0/1
        via FE80::2 (21024000/2169856), Serial0/0/1
        via FE80::1 (21536000/2681856), Serial0/0/0
P 2001:DB8:CAFE:2::/64, 1 successors, FD is 20514560
        via FE80::2 (20514560/28160), Serial0/0/1
        via FE80::1 (21026560/2172416), Serial0/0/0
P 2001:DB8:CAFE:A001::/64, 2 successors, FD is 21024000
        via FE80::2 (21024000/2169856), Serial0/0/1
        via FE80::1 (21024000/2169856), Serial0/0/0
```

```
P 2001:DB8:CAFE:1::/64, 1 successors, FD is 20514560
        via FE80::1 (20514560/28160), Serial0/0/0
        via FE80::2 (21026560/2172416), Serial0/0/1
R3#
```

Note If you need more information on DUAL or the output from the **show ipv6 topology** command, read *Routing Protocols and Concepts* or *Implementing Cisco IP Routing (ROUTE)*, both by Cisco Press.

In Example 8-29, the **ping** command is used to verify reachability. The pings to the Fast Ethernet interfaces of the R2, R3, and ISP routers are all successful.

Example 8-29 *Verifying Reachability with the* **ping** *Command*

```
R1# ping 2001:db8:cafe:1::1

Type escape sequence to abort.
Sending 5, 100-byte ICMP Echos to 2001:DB8:CAFE:1::1, timeout is 2 seconds:
!!!!!
Success rate is 100 percent (5/5), round-trip min/avg/max = 0/0/0 ms
R1# ping 2001:db8:cafe:2::1

Type escape sequence to abort.
Sending 5, 100-byte ICMP Echos to 2001:DB8:CAFE:2::1, timeout is 2 seconds:
!!!!!
Success rate is 100 percent (5/5), round-trip min/avg/max = 28/28/28 ms
R1# ping 2001:db8:face:c0de::1
Type escape sequence to abort.
Sending 5, 100-byte ICMP Echos to 2001:DB8:FACE:C0DE::1, timeout is 2 seconds:
!!!!!
Success rate is 100 percent (5/5), round-trip min/avg/max = 56/56/60 ms
R1#
```

The **show ipv6 eigrp traffic** command in Example 8-30 shows the number of EIGRP packets sent and received. These are the same types of EIGRP packets used in EIGRP for IPv4:

- Hello
- Update
- Query
- Reply
- Acknowledgment

Example 8-30 *Verifying EIGRP for IPv6 Messages*

```
R3# show ipv6 eigrp traffic
IPv6-EIGRP Traffic Statistics for AS 100
  Hellos sent/received: 2689/1789
  Updates sent/received: 50/37
  Queries sent/received: 1/3
  Replies sent/received: 3/1
  Acks sent/received: 23/35
  Input queue high water mark 2, 0 drops
  SIA-Queries sent/received: 0/0
  SIA-Replies sent/received: 0/0
  Hello Process ID: 190
  PDM Process ID: 179

R3#
```

The **show ipv6 eigrp interfaces** command lists the interfaces configured for EIGRP for IPv6 and is shown in Example 8-31.

Example 8-31 *Verifying EIGRP for IPv6 Interfaces*

```
R3# show ipv6 eigrp interfaces
IPv6-EIGRP interfaces for process 100

                        Xmit Queue   Mean   Pacing Time   Multicast    Pending
Interface        Peers  Un/Reliable  SRTT   Un/Reliable   Flow Timer   Routes
Fa0/0              0        0/0         0       0/10           0           0
Se0/0/0            1        0/0        25       7/190        290           0
Se0/0/1            1        0/0        44       7/190        382           0
R3#
```

For each of the four routers, Example 8-32 illustrates the selected output from the final running configs relevant to EIGRP for IPv6.

Example 8-32 *Selected Running Config Outputs Relevant to EIGRP for IPv6*

```
R1# show running-config
!
ipv6 unicast-routing
!
interface FastEthernet0/0
 no ip address
 ipv6 address FE80::1 link-local
 ipv6 address 2001:DB8:CAFE:1::1/64
```

```
 ipv6 eigrp 100
!
interface Serial0/0/0
 no ip address
 ipv6 address FE80::1 link-local
 ipv6 address 2001:DB8:CAFE:A001::1/64
 ipv6 eigrp 100
!
interface Serial0/0/1
 no ip address
 ipv6 address FE80::1 link-local
 ipv6 address 2001:DB8:CAFE:A003::1/64
 ipv6 eigrp 100
!
ipv6 router eigrp 100
 router-id 10.1.1.1
 no shutdown
!
R1#
```

```
R2# show running-config
!
ipv6 unicast-routing
!
interface FastEthernet0/0
 no ip address
 ipv6 address FE80::2 link-local
 ipv6 address 2001:DB8:CAFE:2::1/64
 ipv6 eigrp 100
!
interface Serial0/0/0
 no ip address
 ipv6 address FE80::2 link-local
 ipv6 address 2001:DB8:CAFE:A001::2/64
 ipv6 eigrp 100
!
interface Serial0/0/1
 no ip address
 ipv6 address FE80::2 link-local
 ipv6 address 2001:DB8:CAFE:A002::1/64
 ipv6 eigrp 100
!
ipv6 router eigrp 100
 router-id 10.2.2.2
 no shutdown
```

```
!
R2#
```

```
R3# show running-config
!
hostname R3
!
ipv6 unicast-routing
!
interface FastEthernet0/0
 no ip address
 ipv6 address FE80::3 link-local
 ipv6 address 2001:DB8:CAFE:3::1/64
 ipv6 eigrp 100
!
interface Serial0/0/0
 no ip address
 ipv6 address FE80::3 link-local
 ipv6 address 2001:DB8:CAFE:A003::2/64
 ipv6 eigrp 100
 ipv6 summary-address eigrp 100 ::/0 5
!
interface Serial0/0/1
 no ip address
 ipv6 address FE80::3 link-local
 ipv6 address 2001:DB8:CAFE:A002::2/64
 ipv6 eigrp 100
 ipv6 summary-address eigrp 100 ::/0 5
!
interface Serial0/1/0
 no ip address
 ipv6 address FE80::3 link-local
 ipv6 address 2001:DB8:FEED:1::1/64
!
ipv6 route ::/0 Serial0/1/0
!
ipv6 router eigrp 100
 router-id 10.3.3.3
 no shutdown
!
R3#
```

```
ISP# show running-config
!
hostname ISP
```

```
!
ipv6 unicast-routing
!
interface FastEthernet0/0
 no ip address
 ipv6 address FE80::FEED link-local
 ipv6 address 2001:DB8:FACE:C0DE::1/64
!
interface Serial0/0/0
 no ip address
 ipv6 address FE80::FEED link-local
 ipv6 address 2001:DB8:FEED:1::2/64
!
ipv6 route 2001:DB8:CAFE::/48 Serial0/0/0
!
!
ISP#
```

Before moving to OSPFv3, Example 8-33 shows the command for removing the EIGRP for IPv6 process. The **no ipv6 router eigrp** *as-number* global configuration command removes the EIGRP process, including any interface configuration commands used by that process.

Example 8-33 *Removing EIGRP for IPv6*

```
R1(config)# no ipv6 router eigrp 100
________________________________________
R2(config)# no ipv6 router eigrp 100
________________________________________
R3(config)# no ipv6 router eigrp 100
```

OSPFv3

Open Shortest Path First (OSPF) is a link-state routing protocol that was developed as a replacement for the distance vector routing protocol RIP. RIP was an acceptable routing protocol in the early days of networking, but its reliance on hop count as the only measure for choosing the best route quickly became unacceptable in larger networks that needed a more robust routing solution. OSPF is a classless routing protocol that uses the concept of areas for scalability.

In 1989, the specifications for OSPFv1 were published in RFC 1131, The OSPF Specification. In 1991, John Moy introduced OSPFv2 in RFC 1247, OSPF Version 2. OSPFv2 offered significant technical improvements over OSPFv1. In 1998, the OSPFv2 specification was updated in RFC 2328, OSPF Version 2, and is the current RFC for

OSPFv2. RFC 2328 defines the OSPF metric as an arbitrary value called *cost*. The Cisco IOS uses bandwidth as the OSPF cost metric.

In 1999, OSPFv3 for IPv6 was published in RFC 2740, OSPF for IPv6, written by John Moy, Rob Coltun, and Dennis Ferguson. OSPFv3 was later updated in RFC 5340, OSPF for IPv6. OSPFv3 is not only a new protocol implementation for IPv6 but also a major rewrite of the internals of the protocol. Prior knowledge of OSPFv2 is assumed and beyond the scope of this book.

Comparing OSPFv2 and OSPFv3

Like RIPng and EIGRP for IPv6, the processes and operations of OSPFv3 are similar to those used with OSPFv2. The following is a comparison of the main features of OSPFv2 and OSPFv3:

- **Advertised routes:** OSPFv2 advertises IPv4 routes, whereas OSPFv3 advertises routes for IPv6.

> **Note** Cisco IOS also maintains the OSPFv3 address families feature, which enables both IPv4 and IPv6 unicast traffic to be supported. RFC 5838, Support of Address Families in OSPFv3, defines support for both IPv4 and IPv6. The OSPFv3 address families feature is beyond the scope of this book. For further information, refer to *Cisco IOS IPv6 Configuration Guide, Implementing OSPF for IPv6*, www.cisco.com/en/US/docs/ios/ipv6/configuration/guide/ip6-ospf_ps6922_TSD_Products_Configuration_Guide_Chapter.html.

- **Link-state:** OSPFv2 and OSPFv3 are both link-state routing protocols.
- **Metric:** The RFCs for both OSPFv2 and OSPFv3 define the metric as the cost of sending packets out the interface. In the Cisco implementation, the metric is the cumulative bandwidths of the outgoing interfaces to the destination network (108/bandwidth in bps). The reference bandwidth (108) in both OSPFv2 and OSPFv3 can be modified using the **auto-cost reference-bandwidth** *ref-bw* command in router configuration mode. In both cases, the ref-bw (reference bandwidth) parameter is in megabits per second. Because **auto-cost reference-bandwidth** *ref-bw* is entered in router configuration mode, it only influences the OSPF metric where it was configured. For example, if this command was entered for OSPFv3, it does not affect the OSPFv2 routing metrics.
- **OSPF packet types:** OSPFv3 uses the same five basic packet types as OSPFv2:
  - Hello
  - Database Description (DBD)
  - Link-state Request (LSR)

- Link-state Update (LSU)
- Link-state Acknowledgment (LSAck)

Note If you are familiar with the OSPFv2 Link-state Updates and the different types of Link-state Advertisements (LSA), you might be interested to know that OSPFv3 added two new types of LSAs: Link-LSA (Type 8) and Intra-Area-Prefix-LSA (Type 9). Some of the existing LSA types were also renamed. LSA types are beyond the scope of this book. For further information refer to RFC 5340, OSPF for IPv6.

- **LSA flooding mechanisms:** The aging of the link-state database, as well as flushing LSAs from the routing domain through the premature aging process, remains unchanged. Cisco routers running OSPFv2 or OSPFv3 periodically flood their link states every 30 minutes and flush LSAs after 60 minutes.
- **Router ID:** Both OSPFv2 and OSPFv3 use a 32-bit number for the Router ID represented in dotted-decimal notation. Typically this is an IPv4 address. If the router has not been configured with an IPv4 address, the OSPF **router-id** command must be used to configure the Router ID. The process in determining the 32-bit Router ID is the same in both protocols.
- **DR/BDR election process:** The DR/BDR (designated router/backup designated router) election process remains unchanged in OSPFv3.
- **Neighbor discovery mechanism:** The neighbor state machine, including the list of OSPF neighbor states and events, remains unchanged. OSPFv2 and OSPFv3 use the hello mechanism to learn about neighboring routers and form adjacencies. However, in OSPFv3, there is no "same subnet" requirement to form neighbor adjacencies as there is with OSPFv2. This is because neighbor adjacencies are formed using link-local addresses, not global unicast addresses.
- **Source and destination addresses:** The two standard multicast addresses used by OSPFv3 are
  - **FF02::5:** All SPF routers on the link-local scope; equivalent to 224.0.0.5 in OSPFv2.
  - **FF02::6:** All designated routers (DR) on the link-local scope; equivalent to 224.0.0.6 in OSPFv2.

  OSPFv2 messages are sourced from the IPv4 address of the exit interface. In OSPFv3, OSPF messages are sourced using the link-local address of the exit interface.
- **Authentication:** OSPFv2 uses either plain text authentication or Message Digest 5 (MD5) authentication. OSPFv3 uses the authentication and/or encryption features provided by IPsec.

- **NBMA topologies:** Operations of OSPFv3 over NBMA (nonbroadcast multiaccess) and point-to-multipoint topologies such as Frame Relay are the same as OSPFv2. The RFC-compliant modes as well as Cisco modes are supported in OSPFv3.
- **Areas:** The concept of multiple areas in OSPFv3 is the same as in OSPFv2 to minimize link-state flooding and provide better stability with the OSPF domain. In addition, stub, totally stubby, and NSSA (not-so-stubby area) area types were designed to minimize link-state database and routing table sizes for the areas' internal routers. These same area types used in OSPFv2 are also available in OSPFv3.

> **Note** Multiarea OSPF is beyond the scope of this book. If you want to know more about multiarea OSPF, read *Implementing Cisco IP Routing (ROUTE)* and *Cisco Self Study: Implementing Cisco IPv6 Networks*, both published by Cisco Press.

Configuring OSPFv3

As with RIPng and EIGRP for IPv6, we will be using the familiar topology from Chapter 6 for configuration of OSPFv3. The topology is shown in Figure 8-3.

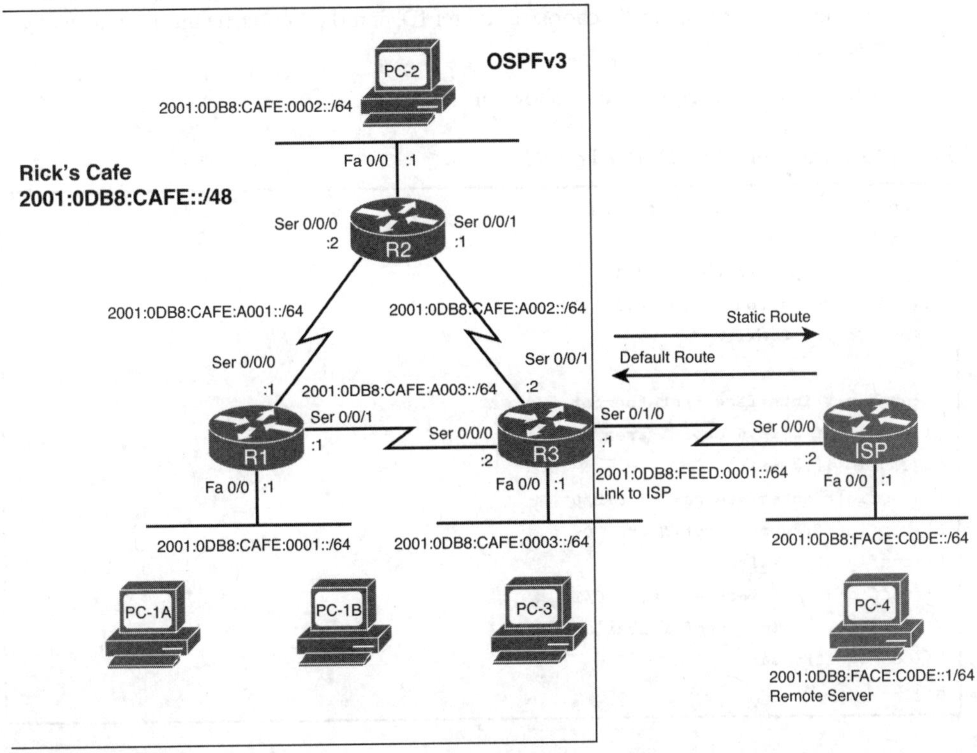

Figure 8-3 *Rick's Café Network OSPFv3 Topology*

Once again, configure Routers R1, R2, and R3 to share routing information, this time using OSPFv3 within the IGP routing domain. R3 is still configured with a default route through the ISP router. Using OSPFv3, configure R3 to distribute the default route to the other OSPFv3 routers. The ISP router is still configured with a static route to reach 2001:0DB8:CAFE::/48. Both the ISP and R3 static routes are shown in Example 8-34.

Example 8-34 *Static Routes on R3 and ISP Routers*

```
R3(config)# ipv6 route ::/0 serial 0/1/0
---------------------------------------------------------------------------
ISP(config)# ipv6 route 2001:db8:cafe::/48 serial 0/0/0
```

The **ipv6 unicast-routing** command is used to enable IPv6 routing on R1, as shown in Example 8-35. Next, begin the configuration process of OSPFv3 on Router R1 with the **ipv6 router ospf 1** global command. This command is similar to the **router ospf** *process-id* command used in OSPFv2. Like OPSFv2, the process-id in OSPFv3 is only locally significant and does not need to be the same on other routers in the OSPF domain. In router configuration mode, the **router-id** command is used to configure the OSPF Router ID. This OSPF **router-id** command must be configured on all the routers in the topology because it has not been configured as an IPv4 address on any of the interfaces. Therefore, the router cannot dynamically choose a Router ID, and the Router ID must be manually configured.

The syntax for these commands is shown in Table 8-2.

Example 8-35 *Enabling OSPFv3 on R1*

```
R1(config)# ipv6 unicast-routing

R1(config)# ipv6 router ospf 1
R1(config-rtr)# router-id 10.1.1.1
R1(config-rtr)# exit

R1(config)# interface fastethernet 0/0
R1(config-if)# ipv6 ospf 1 area 0
R1(config-if)# exit
R1(config)# interface serial 0/0/0
R1(config-if)# ipv6 ospf 1 area 0
R1(config-if)# exit
R1(config)# interface serial 0/0/1
R1(config-if)# ipv6 ospf 1 area 0
R1(config-if)# end
R1#
```

Table 8-2 *Commands for Creating the Routing Process for OSPFv3*

Command	Description
Router(config)# **ipv6 router ospf** *process-id*	Enables the OSPF routing process for IPv6. The process-id identifies the specific routing process and does not need to be the same on all routers in the OSPF routing domain.
Router(config-rtr)# **router-id** *router-id*	The router uses the 32-bit number, represented in dotted-decimal notation, to select the Router ID for OSPFv3.

Continuing with the configuration of R1 in Example 8-35, enable R1's interfaces for OSPFv3 using the **ipv6 ospf** *process-id* **area** *area-id* command. The process-id must be the same as the process-id used to create the routing process in the **ipv6 router ospf** *process-id* command. The syntax to enable OSPFv3 on a specified interface is as follows:

```
Router(config-if)# ipv6 ospf process-id area area-id
```

The process-id identifies the specific routing process and must be the same as the process-id used to create the routing process in the **ipv6 router ospf** *process-id* command. The *area-id* parameter is the area that is to be associated with the OSPFv3 interface. Although any value could have been configured for the area, 0 was chosen because area 0 is the backbone area that all other areas must attach to. This helps in the migration to multiple areas, multiarea OSPF, if the need arises.

In Example 8-36, notice the OSPFv3 configurations for Routers R2 and R3. Although it can be different, the same process-id number of 1 is used for consistency.

Example 8-36 *OSPFv3 Configurations for R2 and R3*

```
R2(config)# ipv6 unicast-routing
R2(config)# ipv6 router ospf 1
R2(config-rtr)# router-id 10.2.2.2
R2(config-rtr)# exit
R2(config)# interface fastethernet 0/0
R2(config-if)# ipv6 ospf 1 area 0
R2(config-if)# exit
R2(config)# interface serial 0/0/0
R2(config-if)# ipv6 ospf 1 area 0
R2(config-if)# exit
R2(config)# interface serial 0/0/1
R2(config-if)# ipv6 ospf 1 area 0
R2(config-if)# end
R2#
```

```
R3(config)# ipv6 unicast-routing
R3(config)# ipv6 router ospf 1
```

```
R3(config-rtr)# router-id 10.3.3.3
R3(config-rtr)# exit
R3(config)# interface fastethernet 0/0
R3(config-if)# ipv6 ospf 1 area 0
R3(config-if)# exit
R3(config)# interface serial 0/0/0
R3(config-if)# ipv6 ospf 1 area 0
R3(config-if)# exit
R3(config)# interface serial 0/0/1
R3(config-if)# ipv6 ospf 1 area 0
R3(config-if)# end
R3#
```

To complete the configuration of OSPFv3, distribute the default route on R3 to other routers in the OSPF domain. The router configuration command **default-information originate** is configured on R3, as shown in Example 8-37.

Example 8-37 *Distributing the Default Route on R3*

```
R3(config)# ipv6 router ospf 1
R3(config-rtr)# ?
  area                     OSPF area parameters
  auto-cost                Calculate OSPF interface cost according to bandwidth
  default                  Set a command to its defaults
  default-information      Distribution of default information
  default-metric           Set metric of redistributed routes
  discard-route            Enable or disable discard-route installation
  distance                 Administrative distance
  distribute-list          Filter networks in routing updates
  exit                     Exit from IPv6 routing protocol configuration mode
  ignore                   Do not complain about specific event
  interface-id             Source of the interface ID
  log-adjacency-changes    Log changes in adjacency state
  maximum-paths            Forward packets over multiple paths
  no                       Negate a command or set its defaults
  passive-interface        Suppress routing updates on an interface
  process-min-time         Percentage of quantum to be used before releasing CPU
  redistribute             Redistribute IPv6 prefixes from another routing
                           protocol
  router-id                router-id for this OSPF process
  shutdown                 Shutdown protocol
  summary-prefix           Configure IPv6 summary prefix
  timers                   Adjust routing timers

R3(config-rtr)# default-information originate
R3(config-rtr)# end
R3#
```

The complete syntax for the **default-information originate** command is as follows:

```
Router(config-rtr)# default-information originate [always | metric metric-value |
metric-type type-value | route-map map-name]
```

This command generates a default external route into the OSPFv3 routing domain. The parameters are as follows:

- **always** (Optional): Always advertises the default route regardless of whether the software has a default route.
- **metric** *metric-value* (Optional): Metric is used for generating the default route. If you omit a value and do not specify a value using the default metric router configuration command, the default metric value is 10. The default metric value range is from 0 to 16777214.
- **metric-type** *type-value* (Optional): External link type associated with the default route advertised into the OSPF for IPv6 routing domain. It can be one of the following values:
  - **1:** Type 1 external route
  - **2:** Type 2 external route
- **The default is type 2 external route.** The cost of a type 2 route is always the external cost, irrespective of the interior cost, the cost within the OSPF domain, to reach that route. A type 1 cost is the addition of the external cost and the internal cost used to reach that route.
- **route-map** *map-name* (Optional): Routing process will generate the default route if the route map is satisfied.

Verifying OSPFv3

To verify that the OSPFv3 domain is fully converged, begin by examining the routing table on R1. Using the **show ipv6 route** command, shown in Example 8-38, notice the remote networks in the OSPF domain along with the default route distributed by R3. The administrative distance of 110 for OSPFv3 routes is the same as for OSPFv2.

Example 8-38 *R1's Routing Table*

```
R1# show ipv6 route ospf
IPv6 Routing Table - 12 entries
Codes: C - Connected, L - Local, S - Static, R - RIP, B - BGP
       U - Per-user Static route
       I1 - ISIS L1, I2 - ISIS L2, IA - ISIS interarea, IS - ISIS summary
       O - OSPF intra, OI - OSPF inter, OE1 - OSPF ext 1, OE2 - OSPF ext 2
       ON1 - OSPF NSSA ext 1, ON2 - OSPF NSSA ext 2
       D - EIGRP, EX - EIGRP external
```

```
OE2  ::/0 [110/1], tag 1
      via FE80::3, Serial0/0/1
O   2001:DB8:CAFE:2::/64 [110/65]
      via FE80::2, Serial0/0/0
O   2001:DB8:CAFE:3::/64 [110/65]
      via FE80::3, Serial0/0/1
O   2001:DB8:CAFE:A002::/64 [110/128]
      via FE80::2, Serial0/0/0
R1#
```

In Example 8-39, using the **ping** command on R1, notice that all remote networks are reachable.

Example 8-39 *Verifying Reachability with the* **ping** *Command*

```
R1# ping 2001:db8:cafe:1::1

Type escape sequence to abort.
Sending 5, 100-byte ICMP Echos to 2001:DB8:CAFE:1::1, timeout is 2 seconds:
!!!!!
Success rate is 100 percent (5/5), round-trip min/avg/max = 0/0/4 ms
R1# ping 2001:db8:cafe:2::1

Type escape sequence to abort.
Sending 5, 100-byte ICMP Echos to 2001:DB8:CAFE:2::1, timeout is 2 seconds:
!!!!!
Success rate is 100 percent (5/5), round-trip min/avg/max = 28/28/28 ms
R1# ping 2001:db8:face:c0de::1

Type escape sequence to abort.
Sending 5, 100-byte ICMP Echos to 2001:DB8:FACE:C0DE::1, timeout is 2 seconds:
!!!!!
Success rate is 100 percent (5/5), round-trip min/avg/max = 56/56/60 ms
R1#
```

Example 8-40 shows the output from the **show ipv6 protocols** command. Similar to what was illustrated with the other IPv6 routing protocols in this chapter, this command displays the connected, static, and OSPF IPv6 processes running on the router.

Example 8-40 *show ipv6 protocols Command on R1*

```
R1# show ipv6 protocols
IPv6 Routing Protocol is "connected"
IPv6 Routing Protocol is "static"
IPv6 Routing Protocol is "ospf 1"
```

```
  Interfaces (Area 0):
    Serial0/0/1
    Serial0/0/0
    FastEthernet0/0
  Redistribution:
    None
R1#
R1# show ipv6 interface fastethernet 0/0
FastEthernet0/0 is up, line protocol is up
  IPv6 is enabled, link-local address is FE80::1
  No Virtual link-local address(es):
  Global unicast address(es):
    2001:DB8:CAFE:1::1, subnet is 2001:DB8:CAFE:1::/64
  Joined group address(es):
    FF02::1
    FF02::2
    FF02::5
    FF02::6
    FF02::1:FF00:1
  MTU is 1500 bytes
<output omitted>
```

In Example 8-40, **show ipv6 interface fastethernet 0/0** verifies that R1's Fast Ethernet 0/0 interface is now a member of OSPFv3 multicast group FF02::5, All-SPF Routers. R1 will process any OSPFv3 messages with the destination address FF02::5 such as OSPFv3 hello messages. R1's Fast Ethernet 0/0 interface is also the designated router for this segment and will listen for OSPFv3 All-DR Router, FF02::6 messages as well.

In Example 8-41, the **show ipv6 ospf neighbor** command lists the OSPFv3 neighbor adjacencies. Notice that the Router IDs of both neighbors are their 32-bit Router IDs used by OSPFv3.

Example 8-41 *show ipv6 ospf neighbor Command on R1*

```
R1# show ipv6 ospf neighbor

Neighbor ID     Pri   State           Dead Time   Interface ID    Interface
10.3.3.3          1   FULL/  -        00:00:32    6               Serial0/0/1
10.2.2.2          1   FULL/  -        00:00:31    6               Serial0/0/0
R1#
```

The output from the **show ipv6 ospf interface** command on R1 is similar to the equivalent command in OSPFv2, as shown in Example 8-42. The only difference is that OSPFv3 sources packets from the interface's link-local address, which is FE80::1 in the case of R1. In OSPFv2, these packets are sourced from the interface's IPv4 address.

Example 8-42 *show ipv6 ospf interface Command on R1*

```
R1# show ipv6 ospf interface serial 0/0/0
Serial0/0/0 is up, line protocol is up
  Link Local Address FE80::1, Interface ID 6
  Area 0, Process ID 1, Instance ID 0, Router ID 10.1.1.1
  Network Type POINT_TO_POINT, Cost: 64
  Transmit Delay is 1 sec, State POINT_TO_POINT,
  Timer intervals configured, Hello 10, Dead 40, Wait 40, Retransmit 5
    Hello due in 00:00:01
  Index 1/2/2, flood queue length 0
  Next 0x0(0)/0x0(0)/0x0(0)
  Last flood scan length is 1, maximum is 3
  Last flood scan time is 0 msec, maximum is 0 msec
  Neighbor Count is 1, Adjacent neighbor count is 1
    Adjacent with neighbor 10.2.2.2
  Suppress hello for 0 neighbor(s)
R1#
```

In Example 8-43, note the selected output for the final running configs for each router.

Example 8-43 *Selected Running Config Outputs Relevant to OSPFv3*

```
R1# show running-config
!
ipv6 unicast-routing
!
interface FastEthernet0/0
 no ip address
 ipv6 address FE80::1 link-local
 ipv6 address 2001:DB8:CAFE:1::1/64
 ipv6 ospf 1 area 0
!
interface Serial0/0/0
 no ip address
 ipv6 address FE80::1 link-local
 ipv6 address 2001:DB8:CAFE:A001::1/64
 ipv6 ospf 1 area 0
!
interface Serial0/0/1
 no ip address
 ipv6 address FE80::1 link-local
 ipv6 address 2001:DB8:CAFE:A003::1/64
 ipv6 ospf 1 area 0
!
```

```
ipv6 router ospf 1
 router-id 10.1.1.1
 log-adjacency-changes
!
R1#
```

```
R2# show running-config
!
ipv6 unicast-routing
!
interface FastEthernet0/0
 no ip address
 ipv6 address FE80::2 link-local
 ipv6 address 2001:DB8:CAFE:2::1/64
 ipv6 ospf 1 area 0
!
interface Serial0/0/0
 no ip address
 ipv6 address FE80::2 link-local
 ipv6 address 2001:DB8:CAFE:A001::2/64
 ipv6 ospf 1 area 0
!
interface Serial0/0/1
 no ip address
 ipv6 address FE80::2 link-local
 ipv6 address 2001:DB8:CAFE:A002::1/64
 ipv6 ospf 1 area 0
!
ipv6 router ospf 1
 router-id 10.2.2.2
 log-adjacency-changes
!
R2#
```

```
R3# show running-config
!
hostname R3
!
ipv6 unicast-routing
!
interface FastEthernet0/0
 no ip address
 ipv6 address FE80::3 link-local
 ipv6 address 2001:DB8:CAFE:3::1/64
 ipv6 ospf 1 area 0
```

```
!
interface Serial0/0/0
 no ip address
 ipv6 address FE80::3 link-local
 ipv6 address 2001:DB8:CAFE:A003::2/64
 ipv6 ospf 1 area 0
!
interface Serial0/0/1
 no ip address
 ipv6 address FE80::3 link-local
 ipv6 address 2001:DB8:CAFE:A002::2/64
 ipv6 ospf 1 area 0
!
interface Serial0/1/0
 no ip address
 ipv6 address FE80::3 link-local
 ipv6 address 2001:DB8:FEED:1::1/64
!
ipv6 route ::/0 Serial0/1/0
!
ipv6 router ospf 1
 router-id 10.3.3.3
 log-adjacency-changes
 default-information originate
!
R3#
```

```
ISP# show running-config
!
hostname ISP
!
ipv6 unicast-routing
!
interface FastEthernet0/0
 no ip address
 ipv6 address FE80::FEED link-local
 ipv6 address 2001:DB8:FACE:C0DE::1/64
!
interface Serial0/0/0
 no ip address
 ipv6 address FE80::FEED link-local
 ipv6 address 2001:DB8:FEED:1::2/64
!
ipv6 route 2001:DB8:CAFE::/48 Serial0/0/0
!
!
ISP#
```

To remove OSPFv3, the **no ipv6 router ospf** *process-id* global configuration command is used. This removes the OSPFv3 process, including any OSPFv3 interface configuration commands.

Summary

IPv6 routing protocols are not much different than their equivalents in IPv4. This chapter examined three IPv6 IGP routing protocols:

- RIPng for IPv6
- EIGRP for IPv6
- OSPFv3

Each of the three routing protocols was discussed:

- The similarities and differences between the IPv6 routing protocol and its equivalent in IPv4
- The commands necessary to configure the IPv6 routing protocol and distribute a default route
- The commands used to verify the implementation, confirm network convergence, and test reachability

Before an IPv6 routing protocol can be configured, IPv6 routing must be enabled on the router. The command to enable IPv6 routing is

```
Router(config)# ipv6 unicast-routing
```

RIPng

RIPng is the IPv6 counterpart of RIPv2 for IPv4 and has many of the same capabilities. The most notable difference is in the Cisco implementation of RIPng the router where the routing table is displayed and includes itself in the metric or hop count of the route. The router where the **show ipv6 route** command is entered includes itself as the first hop. This adds a hop count of 1 to what would normally be seen in RIPv2.

Configuration Commands

The following commands are used to enable and configure RIPng:

- Router(config)# **ipv6 router rip** *name*: Enables the RIPng routing process for IPv6. The name identifies the specific routing process.
- Router(config-if)# **ipv6 rip** *name* **enable:** Enables the RIPng routing process on an interface. The name identifies the specific routing process.

- Router(config-if)# **ipv6 rip** *name* **default-information:** Originates a default route into the RIPng routing domain.

Verification Commands

The following commands are used to verify RIPng:

- Router# **show ipv6 protocols:** Displays the parameters and current state of all active IPv6 routing protocol processes.
- Router# **show ipv6 route rip:** Displays RIPng routes in the IPv6 routing table.
- Router# **show ipv6 rip:** Displays information about current RIPng processes.
- Router# **show ipv6 rip database:** Displays the RIPng RIB (Routing Information Base).
- Router# **show ipv6 rip next-hops:** Displays the next-hop addresses and the number of RIPng routes that use those next-hop addresses, whether or not those routes are in the IPv6 routing table.
- Router# **debug ipv6 rip:** Displays the RIPng routing messages sent and received by a RIPng router.

EIGRP for IPv6

EIGRP for IPv6 for routing IPv6 prefixes is the equivalent of EIGRP for IPv4. Both use DUAL as their computational engine to guarantee loop-free paths.

Configuration Commands

The following commands are used to enable and configure EIGRP for IPv6:

- Router(config)# **ipv6 router eigrp** *as-number*: Enables the EIGRP routing process for IPv6. The as-number identifies the specific routing process and must be the same on all routers in the EIGRP domain.
- Router(config-rtr)# **router-id** *router-id*: The router uses the 32-bit value to select the Router ID for an EIGRP for IPv6 process.
- Router(config-if)# **ipv6 eigrp** *as-number*: Enables the EIGRP for IPv6 routing process on an interface. The as-number (autonomous system) identifies the specific routing process and must be the same as the as-number used to create the routing process in the **ipv6 router eigrp** *as-number* command.
- Router(config-if)# **ipv6 summary-address eigrp** *as-number ipv6-address* [*admin-distance*]: Configures a summary aggregate address for a specified interface. By default, an administrative distance of 5 is applied to EIGRP for IPv6 summary routes. Can be used to distribute a default route to EIGRP neighbors.

Verification Commands

The following commands are used to verify EIGRP for IPv6:

- Router# **show ipv6 protocols:** Displays the parameters and current state of all active IPv6 routing protocol processes.
- Router# **show ipv6 route eigrp:** Displays EIGRP routes in the IPv6 routing table.
- Router# **show ipv6 eigrp neighbors:** Displays EIGRP for IPv6 neighbor adjacencies.
- Router# **show ipv6 eigrp topology:** Displays the topology table for EIGRP for IPv6.
- Router# **show ipv6 eigrp traffic:** Displays the number of EIGRP for IPv6 packets sent and received.
- Router# **show ipv6 eigrp interfaces:** Displays the interfaces enabled for EIGRP for IPv6.

OSPFv3

OSPFv3 is the IPv6 equivalent of OSPFv2 for IPv4. The processes, packet types, and processes between the two protocols are still very similar; however, OSPFv3 was a major rewrite of the internals of the protocol.

Configuration Commands

The following commands are used to enable and configure OSPFv3:

- Router(config)# **ipv6 router ospf** *process-id*: Enables the OSPF routing process for IPv6. The process-id identifies the specific routing process and does not need to be the same on all routers in the OSPF routing domain.
- Router(config-rtr)# **router-id** *router-id*: The router uses the 32-bit value to select the Router ID for OSPFv3 represented in dotted decimal notation..
- Router(config-if)# **ipv6 ospf** *process-id* **area** *area-id*: Enables the OSPFv3 routing process on an interface. The process-id identifies the specific routing process and must be the same as the process-id used to create the routing process in the **ipv6 router ospf** *process-id* command. The area-id is the area that must be associated with the OSPFv3 interface.
- Router(config-rtr)# **default-information originate:** Generates a default external route into the OSPFv3 routing domain.

Verification Commands

The following commands are used to verify OSPFv3:

- Router# **show ipv6 protocols:** Displays the parameters and current state of all active IPv6 routing protocol processes.
- Router# **show ipv6 route ospf:** Displays OSPFv3 routes in the IPv6 routing table.
- Router# **show ipv6 ospf neighbors:** Displays OSPFv3 neighbor adjacencies.
- Router# **show ipv6 ospf interface:** Displays OSPF information on interfaces enabled for OSPFv3.

References

RIPng

RFC 1058, *Routing Information Protocol*, C. Hedrick, Rutgers University, IETF, www.ietf.org/rfc/rfc1058, June 1998

RFC 2453, *RIP Version 2*, G. Malkin, Bay Networks, IETF, www.ietf.org/rfc/rfc2453, November 1998

RFC 2080, *RIPng for IPv6*, G. Malkin, Xylogics, www.ietf.org/rfc/rfc2080, January 1997

Cisco IOS IPv6 Configuration Guide, Implementing RIP for IPv6, www.cisco.com/en/US/docs/ios/ipv6/configuration/guide/ip6-rip_ps6922_TSD_Products_Configuration_Guide_Chapter.html

EIGRP for IPv6

Cisco IOS IPv6 Configuration Guide, Implementing EIGRP for IPv6, www.cisco.com/en/US/docs/ios/ipv6/configuration/guide/ip6-eigrp.html

OSPFv3

RFC 2328, *OSPF Version 2*, J. Moy, Ascend Communications, www.ietf.org/rfc/rfc2328, April 1998

RFC 5340, *OSPF for IPv6*, R. Coltun, Acoustra Productions, www.ietf.org/rfc/rfc5340, July 2008

RFC 5838, *Support of Address Families in OSPFv3*, A. Lindem, Ericsson, http://tools.ietf.org/html/rfc5838, April 2010

"OSPFv3 Support for Address Families," www.cisco.com/en/US/prod/collateral/iosswrel/ps6537/ps6554/ps6599/ps6629/whitepaper_c11-668030.html

Cisco IOS IPv6 Configuration Guide, Implementing OSPF for IPv6, www.cisco.com/en/US/docs/ios/ipv6/configuration/guide/ip6-ospf_ps6922_TSD_Products_Configuration_Guide_Chapter.html

Chapter 9

DHCPv6 (Dynamic Host Configuration Protocol version 6)

IPv6 has a minimal impact on most upper-layer protocols. When changes are required, it is because of the protocol or application needing the extended 128-bit IPv6 address in the service that it provides. One of the upper-layer protocols where the IPv6 address changes are more evident is with DHCP for IPv6, known as DHCPv6. Besides accommodating the larger IPv6 address in the actual DHCP messages, there are other protocol changes as well.

Dynamic address assignment in IPv6 is more involved and provides more options than its IPv4 counterpart. Similar to IPv4, DHCPv6 provides stateful DHCP services, but as noted in Chapter 4, "IPv6 Address Types," IPv6 also provides Stateless Address Autoconfiguration, or SLAAC. SLAAC might or might not include the services of a DHCP server. Stateless Address Autoconfiguration might only involve the router and its Router Advertisement messages or entail both the RA message and other configuration parameters from a DHCP server.

It is important to understand the DHCPv6 process and the options available for dynamic address allocation.

In this chapter, we will discuss the following topics:

- DHCPv6 services
- DHCPv6 communications
- Other upper-layer protocols: DNS, TCP, and UDP

DHCPv6 Services

Much has been made about the stateless nature of IPv6 address assignment. As shown in previous chapters, a device can receive its IPv6 address and other configuration information without the services of a DHCPv6 server. Through the use of ICMPv6 Router Advertisements and the ability for a device to create its own Interface ID, SLAAC provides dynamic addressing without the services of DHCP. To some, this stateless form of address autoconfiguration is all that an IPv6 network should ever need for dynamic address assignment. However, for many others, stateful DHCP services are an important benefit to their network operations, even a requirement for managing address allocations.

For example, a company might like a specific IP addressing scheme. The company does not want to have hosts use their MAC addresses for their Interface IDs or to provide additional configuration parameters beyond the basic address/gateway information supported through SLAAC. Some do not see the need for stateful DHCPv6 services; many others disagree. Over the last several years, there has been much debate between the protagonists on both sides.

The fact is that both stateless (DHCPv6) and Stateful Address Autoconfiguration are a reality in IPv6. DHCPv6 is defined in RFC 3315, Dynamic Host Configuration Protocol for IPv6 (DHCPv6). There has been a lot of work done on this specification over the years. In 2001, Steve Deering from Cisco Systems stated at IETF 51 (Proceedings of the 51st Internet Engineering Task Force) that the DHCPv6 specification has the highest revision number of any Internet draft.

Note SLAAC is defined in RFC 4862, IPv6 Stateless Address Autoconfiguration, and discussed in detail in Chapter 5, "ICMPv6 and Neighbor Discovery Protocol."

There are two forms of DHCPv6:

- **Stateful DHCPv6 services:** RFC 3315, Dynamic Host Configuration Protocol for IPv6 (DHCPv6)
- **Stateless DHCPv6 services:** RFC 3736, Stateless Dynamic Host Configuration Protocol (DHCP) Service for IPv6

Note With service provider deployment of IPv6, several ISPs are beginning to offer IPv6 access to the public. In conjunction with widely deployed "always on" media such as DSL and cable Internet access, an efficient mechanism for delegating address prefixes to the customers' sites is needed. RFC 3769, Requirements for IPv6 Prefix Delegation, addresses the delegation mechanism intended to automate the process of informing the customer's networking equipment of the prefixes to be used at the customer's site. For more information on DHCPv6 prefix delegation, refer to RFC 3769.

Stateful DHCPv6 provides the same autoconfiguration services that DHCP performs for IPv4 (DHCPv4). Hosts receive all their addressing and other configuration information directly from a DHCPv6 server. The differences with stateless DHCPv6 are that hosts receive their addressing information from Router Advertisements and obtain other configuration parameters from a DHCPv6 server.

Although similar in what it provides, DHCPv6 is almost an entire rewrite of DHCPv4, and the two protocols are independent of each other. If you are currently running a dual-stack network that uses DHCP, you need two separate DHCP services running, one for each protocol.

The process and messaging used in DHCPv6 are not much different than with DHCPv4. However, in the DHCPv4 world, the client is configured to use DHCP simply by choosing an option such as "Obtain an IP address automatically" in Windows or "Using DHCP" on a Mac. In the world of IPv6, the client is configured the same way, but it does not know whether that information will come from a Router Advertisement (SLAAC), a DHCPv6 server (stateful DHCPv6), or a combination of both SLAAC and DHCPv6.

Note Before deploying hosts implementing dynamic IPv6 addressing techniques into the network, it is a good idea to first verify the behavior of the host operating system. It has been observed that not all operating systems honor the M and O bits (flags) in the Router Advertisement, and you can get unexpected results.

How an IPv6 client dynamically receives its configuration information is determined by the router in its Router Advertisement message and not by the client. The Router Advertisement configuration options are examined later in this chapter.

This chapter begins with a discussion of the fundamentals of DHCPv6, introducing the new but similar terminology, message types, and operations. It also examines how Router Advertisements are used to notify the client whether to apply SLAAC, stateful DHCPv6, or stateless DHCPv6. After the protocol and its operations are understood, you will configure the router's Router Advertisement to inform hosts on the link how they will dynamically receive their addressing and other configuration parameters, including stateless DHCPv6.

Note The discussion on DHCPv6 focuses specifically on the fundamental concepts and the router's role as a stateless DHCPv6 server. By no means is this meant to be the definitive guide on DHCPv6. For more information on DHCPv6 and implementing DCHPv6 on Cisco routers, read the following:

- RFC 3315, Dynamic Host Configuration Protocol for IPv6 (DHCPv6)
- *Cisco IOS IPv6 Configuration Guide, Implementing DHCP for IPv6*, www.cisco.com/en/US/docs/ios/ipv6/configuration/guide/ip6-dhcp.html

DHCPv6 Terminology, Multicast Addresses, and Message Types

DHCPv6 has its roots in DHCPv4 and there are many similarities. For the most part, it provides the same services as DHCPv4, but with some variations. The first three DHCPv6 terms are identical to their counterparts in DHCPv4:

- **DHCP client:** A DHCP client initiates the process by sending a request to obtain its configuration parameters from one or more DHCP servers.
- **DHCP server:** The DHCP server is configured to respond to the DHCP requests from DHCP clients. These clients might or might not be on the same link as the server.
- **DHCP relay agent:** Quite often the DHCP server and clients are on different networks or links. A relay agent is an intermediary device, typically a router, that receives the client's request and forwards it to one or more DHCP servers on another network. The DHCP relay agent operation is transparent to the client.

The next three terms—DUID, IA, and IAID—are specific to DHCPv6; however, the process of converting them to DHCPv4 is under development. Although not significant in these discussions, understanding these terms is important when configuring some of the various options provided by DHCPv6:

- **DUID (DHCP Unique Identifier):** Every DHCP participant, client, and server has a DUID that uniquely identifies the device. The DUID allows the clients and servers to identify each other. A DUID consists of a 2-byte type code followed by a variable number of bytes that make up the actual identifier. Not including the type code, a DUID can be no more than 128 bytes. RFC 3315 defines three types of DUIDs:
  - Link-layer address plus time
  - Vendor-assigned unique ID based on the Private Enterprise Number maintained by the Internet Assigned Numbers Authority (IANA)
  - Link-layer address

Note Selection of the DUID is device independent. DUIDs are treated as "opaque values" and have no significance other than to uniquely identify the DHCPv6 client or server. The difference between the three types of DUIDs and the selection process is beyond the scope of this book. Please refer to RFC 3315 for more information.

- **Identity Association (IA):** An IA is a collection of addresses assigned to a client. A client has at least one IA assigned for each interface using the services of DHCPv6. Each IA has an IAID (Identity Association Identifier) that is used to uniquely identify the ID and is assigned by the client.

- **Identity Association Identifier (IAID):** Each IA has an IAID, chosen by the client, and is unique among all IAIDs belonging to that client.

DHCPv6 clients and servers use the following multicast addresses:

- **All_DHCP_Relay_Agents_and_Servers (FF02::1:2):** All DHCPv6 servers and relay agents are members of this link-local scope multicast group. Clients use this multicast address to communicate with DHCPv6 servers and relay agents on their link.
- **All_DHCP_Servers (FF05::1:3):** All DHCPv6 servers are members of this site-local multicast group. Relay agents use this multicast address to send messages to all DHCPv6 servers within a site or when they do not know the unicast address of the server.

DHCPv6 uses the following User Datagram Protocol (UDP) ports:

- **UDP port 546:** DHCPv6 servers and relays send messages to clients using UDP destination port 546. Clients listen for DHCPv6 messages on UDP port 546.
- **UDP port 547:** DHCPv6 clients send messages to servers and relay agents using UDP destination port 547. Servers and relay agents listen for DHCPv6 messages on UDP port 547.

DHCPv6 defines various message types for client-server communications. The complete list of DHCPv6 message types is described in RFC 3315 and listed in Table 9-1. The next section on DHCPv6 communications explains how many of these messages are used. For a more comprehensive understanding, refer to the resources mentioned earlier in the chapter.

Four DHCPv6 message types are the primary messages used to communicate between a DHCPv6 client and server:

- **SOLICIT (1):** A SOLICIT message is used by DHCPv6 clients to locate servers.
- **ADVERTISE (2):** An ADVERTISE message is sent by a server in response to a client's SOLICIT message to indicate that it is available for DHCPv6 service.
- **REQUEST (3):** A REQUEST message is sent by a client to request configuration parameters, including IP addresses, from a specific DHCPv6 server.
- **REPLY (7):** A server sends a REPLY message containing assigned addresses and configuration parameters in response to a client's REQUEST message. A REPLY message will also be sent in response to a SOLICIT message when the Rapid Commit Option is used. The Rapid Commit Option is explained later in this section. A REPLY message can also be sent in response to an INFORMATION-REQUEST, CONFIRM, RELEASE, or DECLINE message.

Table 9-1 *Listing of DHCPv6 Message Types as Described in RFC 3315*

DHCPv6 Message Type	Description
SOLICIT (1)	A client sends a SOLICIT message to locate servers.
ADVERTISE (2)	A server sends an ADVERTISE message to indicate that it is available for DHCP service, in response to a SOLICIT message received from a client.
REQUEST (3)	A client sends a REQUEST message to request configuration parameters, including IP addresses, from a specific server.
CONFIRM (4)	A client sends a CONFIRM message to any available server to determine whether the addresses it was assigned are still appropriate to the link to which the client is connected.
RENEW (5)	A client sends a RENEW message to the server that originally provided the client's addresses and configuration parameters to extend the lifetimes on the addresses assigned to the client and to update other configuration parameters.
REBIND (6)	A client sends a REBIND message to any available server to extend the lifetimes on the addresses assigned to the client and to update other configuration parameters; this message is sent after a client receives no response to a RENEW message.
REPLY (7)	A server sends a REPLY message containing assigned addresses and configuration parameters in response to a SOLICIT, REQUEST, RENEW, or REBIND message received from a client. A server sends a REPLY message containing configuration parameters in response to an INFORMATION-REQUEST message. A server sends a REPLY message in response to a CONFIRM message, confirming or denying that the addresses assigned to the client are appropriate to the link to which the client is connected. A server sends a REPLY message to acknowledge receipt of a RELEASE or DECLINE message.
RELEASE (8)	A client sends a RELEASE message to the server that assigned addresses to the client to indicate that the client will no longer use one or more of the assigned addresses.
DECLINE (9)	A client sends a DECLINE message to a server to indicate that the client has determined that one or more addresses assigned by the server are already in use on the link to which the client is connected.

DHCPv6 Message Type	Description
RECONFIGURE (10)	A server sends a RECONFIGURE message to a client to inform the client that the server has new or updated configuration parameters, and that the client is to initiate a RENEW/REPLY or INFORMATION-REQUEST/REPLY transaction with the server to receive the updated information.
INFORMATION-REQUEST (11)	A client sends an INFORMATION-REQUEST message to a server to request configuration parameters without the assignment of any IP addresses to the client.
RELAY-FORW (12)	A relay agent sends a RELAY-FORWARD message to transfer messages to servers, either directly or through another relay agent. The received message, either a client message or a RELAY-FORWARD message from another relay agent, is encapsulated in an option in the RELAY-FORWARD message.
RELAY-REPL (13)	A server sends a REPLAY-REPLY message to a relay agent containing a message that the relay agent delivers to a client. The REPLAY-REPLY message can be passed on by other relay agents for delivery to the destination relay agent. The server encapsulates the client message as an option in the REPLAY-REPLY message, which the relay agent extracts and sends to the client.

DHCPv6 Communications

Figure 9-1 illustrates the steps of the DHCPv6 communication process, which involves the client, the server, and the router. Remember, the difference between DHCPv6 and DHCPv4 is that the router determines how the addresses will be allocated dynamically. A client configured to automatically obtain its addressing and other configuration information can use one of three methods:

- SLAAC (Stateless Address Autoconfiguration)
- Stateful DHCPv6
- Stateless DHCPv6

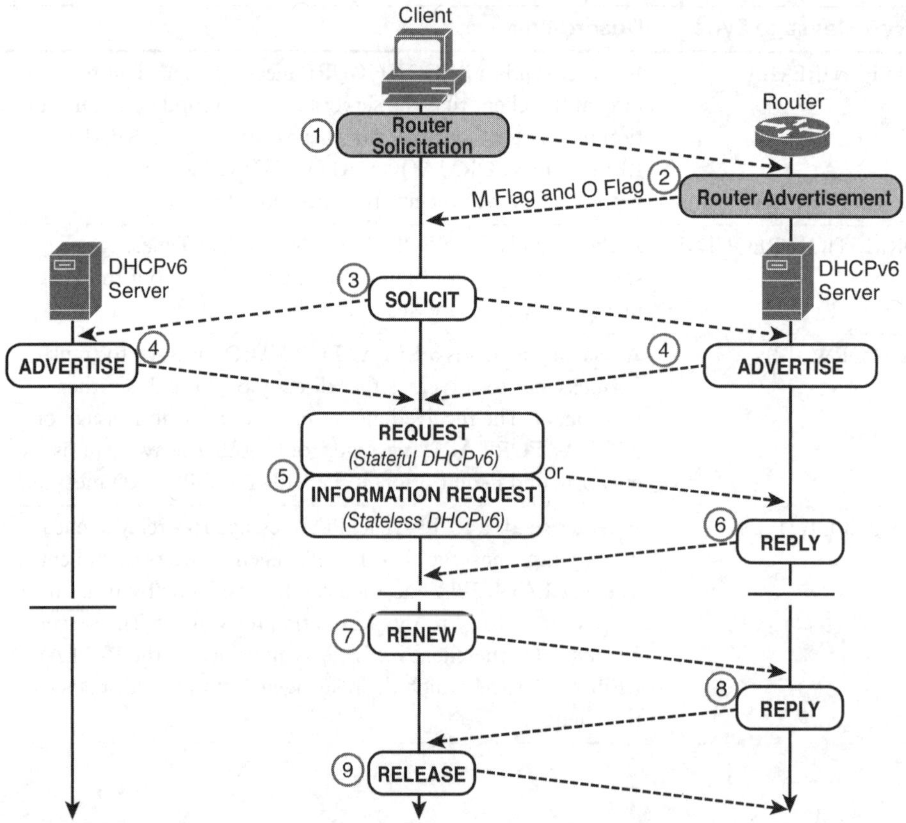

Figure 9-1 *DHCPv6*

The host does not necessarily determine the method it uses to dynamically obtain its addressing information. If the host is depending on the Router Advertisement, the router controls this decision using the information contained in its RA message, specifically the M flag (Managed Address Configuration flag) and the O flag (Other Configuration flag). Depending upon the operating system, a host can ignore the router's Router Advertisements and use stateful DHCPv6 to obtain its addressing information. As noted previously, it is a good idea to verify the behavior of the host operating system before deployment into the network.

Note Besides the M flag and O flag, the Router Advertisement also contains the Autonomous Address Configuration flag, or *A flag*. The A flag indicates whether the prefix in the RA can be used for SLAAC. By default, the A flag is set to 1, which enables the prefix to be used for SLAAC. The A flag provides additional options for address configurations and is beyond the scope of this book. For further information, refer to http://blogs.cisco.com/borderless/ipv6-automatic-addressing and RFC 4861, Neighbor Discovery for IP version 6 (IPv6).

Note ICMPv6 Router Solicitation and Router Advertisement messages are discussed in detail in Chapter 5.

Using Figure 9-1, the DHCPv6 communications process is as follows:

Router Solicitation and Router Advertisement Messages

Step 1. If the client has not already received a Router Advertisement, it sends a Router Solicitation message to the all-routers multicast group FF02::2. A host sends a Router Solicitation message when it has been configured to dynamically receive its prefix, prefix length, default gateway, and other information.

Step 2. A router periodically sends a Router Advertisement message or in response to a Router Solicitation from a host. There are two flags contained in the RA that decide which method a host will use to receive its addressing and other configuration information: the M flag, Managed Address Configuration flag, and the O flag, Other Configuration flag. In Cisco IOS there are three options:

- **SLAAC (Stateless Address Autoconfiguration):** On Cisco routers, both the M and O flags are set to 0 by default, meaning that there is no information available from a DHCPv6 server. A host requiring dynamic address assignment receives all its information from the data in the Router Advertisement.
- **Stateful DHCPv6:** When the M flag is set to 1, this tells the host to use stateful DHCPv6 services. All addressing and other configuration information must be obtained directly from a DHCPv6 server. It is important to note that DHCPv6 service for address configuration might still be available even if no routers are present.
- **Stateless DHCPv6:** When the M flag is set to 0 and the O flag is set to 1, this informs the host that the prefix, prefix length, default gateway, and other information (for example, maximum transmission unit [MTU]) is contained in the Router Advertisement. However, there is additional information to be obtained from a DHCPv6 server, such as addresses for Domain Name System (DNS) servers.

Note RFC 6101, IPv6 Router Advertisement Options for DNS Configuration, standardizes an option in the RA message that provides hosts with a list of recursive DNS servers with their associated lifetimes. Again, it is a good idea to first verify the behavior of the host operating systems before implementing this option. Not all operating systems support RFC 6106. If both the M flag and the O flag are set to 0, SLAAC is used and the DHCPv6 process ends.

If the M and/or O flag is set to 1, the DHCPv6 process continues, meaning that stateless or stateful DHCPv6 is being used. Step 5 illustrates how the client sends the appropriate request to the server depending on whether stateful or stateless DHCPv6 is being used.

DHCPv6 Messages

The M and/or O flag is set to 1 in the Router Advertisement message.

Step 3. The host, now a DHCPv6 client, sends a SOLICIT message to the destination All_DHCP_Relay_Agents_and_Servers address, FF02::1:2, to locate a DHCPv6 server. In some cases, the client can be configured to use a unicast address to reach a specific server.

Step 4. One or more DHCPv6 servers respond with an ADVERTISE message to let the client know that it is available for DHCPv6 service. If the client receives more than one ADVERTISE message, there is a decision process used to choose the appropriate server as defined in RFC 3315. These options are configured on both the client and the server.

> **Note** The criteria for selecting a DHCPv6 server when a client receives ADVERTISE messages from multiple servers is beyond the scope of this book and is discussed in RFC 3315, section 17.1.3, Receipt of Advertise Messages.

Step 5. The client sends a REQUEST or INFORMATION-REQUEST message to the server, depending on whether stateful or stateless DHCPv6 is being used. The type of message sent by the client is dependent upon the M flag contained in the router's Router Advertisement. The two possibilities are

- If stateful DHCPv6 is being used (the Router Advertisement M Flag was set to 1), the client sends a REQUEST to obtain IPv6 addresses and configuration parameters.
- If the client is using stateless DHCPv6 (the Router Advertisement M Flag is set to 0 and the O Flag is set to 1), the client sends an INFORMATION-REQUEST message requesting only the configuration parameters from the server, and no addressing information.

Step 6. If the server received a REQUEST from the client, it sends a REPLY containing assigned addresses and other configuration parameters. In response to an INFORMATION-REQUEST, the server sends a REPLY with only the configuration parameters.

Renew and Release

Step 7. When the DHCPv6 lease is about to expire, a client sends a RENEW message to the server that originally provided the client's addresses and configuration information to extend the lifetime of the lease.

Step 8. The server sends a REPLY message to acknowledge to the client that it is renewing the lease for its addresses and configuration parameters.

Step 9. When the client no longer needs one or more of its assigned addresses, it sends a RELEASE message to inform the DHCPv6 server.

Note A server also sends a REPLY message to acknowledge receipt of a RELEASE or DECLINE message.

Note If a client determines that an allocated address is already in use, typically through DAD (Duplicate Address Detection), it sends a DELCINE message to the server. The address will be suspended on the host. The server marks this address as used by an unknown host and assigns another address to a client.

Configuring Stateless DHCPv6

Configuring stateless DHCPv6 is simple and straightforward. Except for the configuration of the Router Advertisement, the basic configuration of DHCPv6 services is similar to configuring DHCP services for IPv4. Three basic steps are used to configure stateless DHCPv6 services:

Step 1. Configure a DHCPv6 server pool name with configuration parameters.

Step 2. Enable the DHCPv6 server pool on an interface.

Step 3. Modify any Router Advertisement parameters to let the hosts know that other configuration information is available from a DHCPv6 server.

Table 9-2 shows the commands used to create the DHCPv6 pool and specifies some of the configuration parameters available.

Note There is much more to configuring DHCPv6 than what is covered here. For all the DHCPv6 configuration options and commands, refer to the *Cisco IOS IPv6 Configuration Guide, Implementing DHCP for IPv6*, www.cisco.com/en/US/docs/ios/ipv6/configuration/guide/ip6-dhcp.html.

Table 9-2 *DHCPv6 Configuration Pool Commands*

Command	Description
Router(config)# **ipv6 dhcp pool** *poolname*	Creates a DHCPv6 pool and enters DHCPv6 pool configuration mode
Router(config-dhcp)# **dns-server** *ipv6-address*	Specifies the IPv6 DNS servers available to a DHCPv6 client
Router(config-dhcp)# **domain** *domain*	Configures a domain name for a DHCPv6 client

Command	Description
Router(config-dhcp)# **prefix-delegation** *ipv6-prefix/prefix-length client-duid* [**iaid** *iaid*] [**lifetime**]	Specifies a manually configured numeric prefix to be delegated to a specified client's IAID

To enable the DHCPv6 service on an interface, the **ipv6 dhcp server** command is used in interface configuration mode. Table 9-3 shows the commands used to associate a DHCPv6 pool with an interface. The Rapid Commit Option in the **ipv6 dhcp server** command is discussed in the next section.

Table 9-3 *Associating the DHCPv6 Pool to an Interface*

Command	Description
Router(config)# **interface** *type number*	Specifies an interface type and number, and places the router in interface configuration mode.
Router(config-dhcp)# **ipv6 dhcp server** *poolname* [**rapid-commit**]	Enables DHCPv6 service on an interface. *pool-name* (Optional) is a user-defined name for the local prefix pool. The pool name can be a symbolic string (such as Engineering) or an integer (such as 0). **rapid-commit** (Optional) allows the two-message exchange method for prefix delegation.

Table 9-4 shows the interface commands used to configure the router's Router Advertisement message to let the hosts know that other configuration information is available from a DHCPv6 server.

Table 9-4 *Setting the Router Advertisement's Other Configuration Flag to 1*

Command	Description
Router(config)# **interface** *type number*	Specifies an interface type and number, and places the router in interface configuration mode.
Router(config-if)# **ipv6 nd other-config-flag**	Sets the Other Configuration flag in the router advertisement to 1, meaning that there is additional information available from a DHCPv6 server. The **no** option of this command sets this flag to its default of 0.

Using the Rick's Café topology, configure R1's LAN for stateless DHCPv6. The hosts on the LAN will be using SLAAC for their address information (prefix, prefix length, and default gateway). However, not all the information that the hosts require is in the router's Router Advertisement. Other configuration data, such as the DNS server address, needs to be obtained by the host from a DHCPv6 server. To accomplish this

- Configure R1 to act as a stateless DHCPv6 server for its LAN and provide the DNS server address.
- Modify the O flag in Router R1's Router Advertisement message to let hosts know that other configuration information is available from a DHCPv6 server.

Figure 9-2 shows the stateless DHCPv6 process between R1 and host PC-1C. Steps 1 and 2 show PC-1C getting its prefix, prefix length, and default gateway information from the Router Advertisement. The O flag in the RA message is set to 1, which tells the PC-1C that there is additional configuration information that must be retrieved from a DHCPv6 server. Steps 3–8 show the DHCPv6 process between PC-1C and the stateless DHCPv6 server, Router R1.

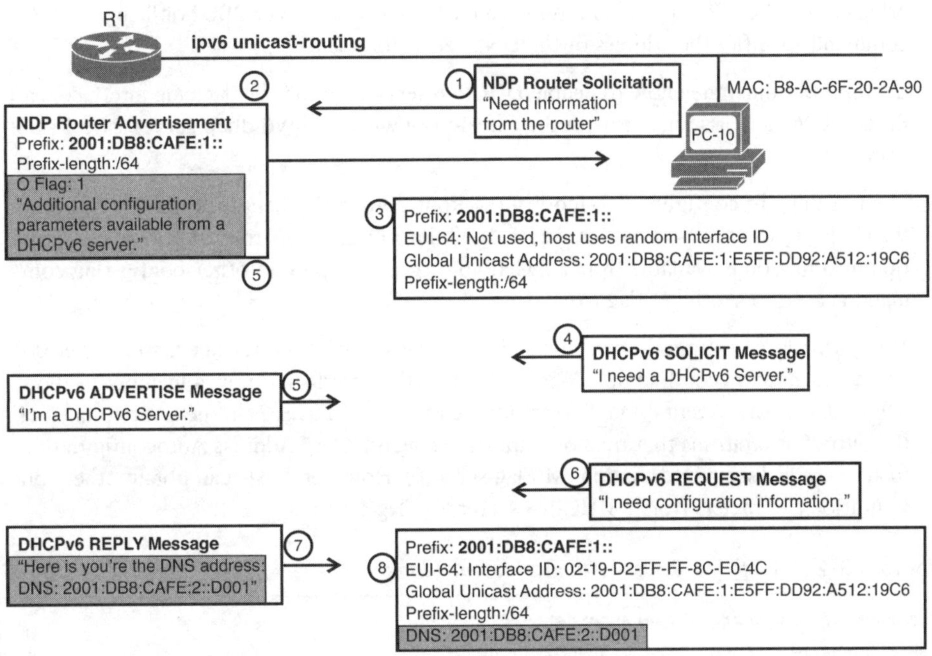

Figure 9-2 *Stateless DHCPv6*

The commands to configure Router R1 as a stateless DHCPv6 server are shown in Example 9-1.

Example 9-1 *Stateless DHCPv6 Configuration on R1*

```
! The first two commands are the DHCP configuration pool commands
R1(config)# ipv6 dhcp pool cafe-1-pool
R1(config-dhcp)# dns-server 2001:db8:cafe:2::d001
R1(config-dhcp)# exit

R1(config)# interface fa 0/0
! The next command enables DHCPv6 service on the interface
R1(config-if)# ipv6 dhcp server cafe-1-pool
! The next command sets the Router Advertisement O flag (Other Configuration flag)
! to 1
R1(config-if)# ipv6 nd other-config-flag
R1(config-if)# end
R1#
```

The **ipv6 dhcp pool cafe-1-pool** command creates the DHCPv6 pool cafe-1-pool and brings it into DHCPv6 pool configuration mode. The **dns-server 2001:db8:cafe:2::d001** command specifies the address of the DNS server for clients.

Example 9-1 illustrates how to enable DHCPv6 service on the client-facing interface, Fast Ethernet 0/0, and associate it with the cafe-1-pool with the **ipv6 dhcp server cafe-1-pool** command.

The last thing to configure is to modify the Router Advertisement message. By default, the O flag is set to 0. Setting this flag to 1 will inform the hosts that additional configuration information is available from a DCHPv6 server. The **ipv6 nd other-config-flag** command is used to set the O flag to 1.

Verify that R1's O flag has been changed using the **show ipv6 interface fastethernet 0/0** command, as shown in Example 9-2. Notice that this interface is now a member of the All_DHCP_Relay_Agents_and_Servers multicast group FF02::1:2. In the last two lines of the output, it confirms that the hosts are still using Stateless Address Autoconfiguration to access addressing information (M Flag set to 0). However, hosts can obtain other configuration parameters from a DHCPv6 server (O Flag set to 1).

Example 9-2 *Verifying Router Advertisement Flags*

```
R1# show ipv6 interface fastethernet 0/0
FastEthernet0/0 is up, line protocol is up
  IPv6 is enabled, link-local address is FE80::1
  No Virtual link-local address(es):
  Global unicast address(es):
    2001:DB8:CAFE:1::1, subnet is 2001:DB8:CAFE:1::/64
  Joined group address(es):
    FF02::1
    FF02::2
```

```
    FF02::5
    FF02::6
    FF02::1:2      ! All_DHCP_Relay_Agents_and_Servers multicast group
    FF02::1:FF00:1
  MTU is 1500 bytes
  ICMP error messages limited to one every 100 milliseconds
  ICMP redirects are enabled
  ICMP unreachables are sent
  ND DAD is enabled, number of DAD attempts: 1
  ND reachable time is 30000 milliseconds
  ND advertised reachable time is 0 milliseconds
  ND advertised retransmit interval is 0 milliseconds
  ND router advertisements are sent every 200 seconds
  ND router advertisements live for 1800 seconds
  ND advertised default router preference is Medium
  Hosts use stateless autoconfig for addresses.    ! RA's M Flag set to 0
  Hosts use DHCP to obtain other configuration.    ! RA's O Flag set to 1

R1#
```

Using the **ipconfig /all** command on PC-1C in Example 9-3, notice that the client has received all its necessary addressing and configuration information. The prefix, prefix length (not shown), and default gateway address were all received from R1's Router Advertisement. (Because this is a Windows host, the Interface IDs were randomly generated.) The address of the IPv6 DNS server was obtained from the DHCPv6 server, which in this case is also R1.

Example 9-3 *PC-1C*

```
PC-1C> ipconfig /all
Ethernet adapter Local Area Connection:

   Connection-specific DNS Suffix  . :
   Description . . . . . . . . . . . : Intel(R) 82567LM-3 Gigabit Network Connection
   Physical Address. . . . . . . . . : B8-AC-6F-20-2A-90
   DHCP Enabled. . . . . . . . . . . : Yes
   Autoconfiguration Enabled . . . . : Yes
   IPv6 Address. . . . . . . . . . . : 2001:db8:cafe:1:e5ff:dd92:a512:19c6(Preferred)
   Link-local IPv6 Address . . . . . : fe80::e5ff:dd92:a512:19c6
   Default Gateway . . . . . . . . . : fe80::1
   DHCPv6 IAID . . . . . . . . . . . : 250629538
   DHCPv6 Client DUID. . . . . . . . : 00-01-00-01-15-EF-49-66-B8-AC-6F-20-2A-90
   DNS Servers . . . . . . . . . . . : 2001:db8:cafe:2::d001
```

The **show ipv6 dhcp** and **show ipv6 dhcp interface** commands can be used to examine the DHCPv6 services on the router, as shown in Example 9-4. The **show ipv6 dhcp** command displays the DHCP Unique Identifier (DUID) of the router. Both DHCPv6 clients and servers have a DUID, which is used by DHCP to uniquely identify the device. The **show ipv6 dhcp interface** command is used to display DHCP information on an interface, including the associated DHCP pools and whether the Rapid Commit Option is being used.

Example 9-4 *Verifying DHCP Services on R1*

```
R1# show ipv6 dhcp
This device's DHCPv6 unique identifier(DUID): 00030001001B0CC282D8
R1#

R1# show ipv6 dhcp interface fastethernet 0/0
FastEthernet0/0 is in server mode
  Using pool: cafe-1-pool
  Preference value: 0
  Hint from client: ignored
  Rapid-Commit: disabled
R1#
```

Typically router interfaces are configured manually with an IPv6 address. There might be times when you will need a router to obtain its IPv6 address automatically using Stateless Address Autoconfiguration. The **ipv6 address autoconfig** interface command performs IPv6 Stateless Address Autoconfiguration using Router Advertisement messages to discover prefixes on the link and then to add the EUI-64-based addresses to the interface. The syntax for the **ipv6 address autoconfig** interface command is described in Table 9-5.

Table 9-5 *Configuring the Router Interface for Stateless Autoconfiguration*

Command	Description
Router(config)# **interface** *type number*	Specifies an interface type and number, and places the router in interface configuration mode
Router(config-if)# **ipv6 address autoconfig**	Enables automatic configuration of IPv6 addresses using Stateless Address Autoconfiguration on an interface and enables IPv6 processing on the interface

Rapid Commit Option

The DHCPv6 message exchange between the client and the server can take a shortcut by reducing the number of messages from four to two. This is done by including the Rapid Commit Option in the SOLICIT message from the client to the DHCPv6 server. This informs the server that it wants to shorten the exchange from four messages to two, as illustrated in Figure 9-3. If a server is enabled for the Rapid Commit Option, it responds with a REPLY message containing the Rapid Commit Option and commits the assigned addresses included in the REPLY. Therefore, only two messages are exchanged (SOLICIT and REPLY) instead of the normal four messages discussed previously (SOLICIT, ADVERTISE, REQUEST, and REPLY).

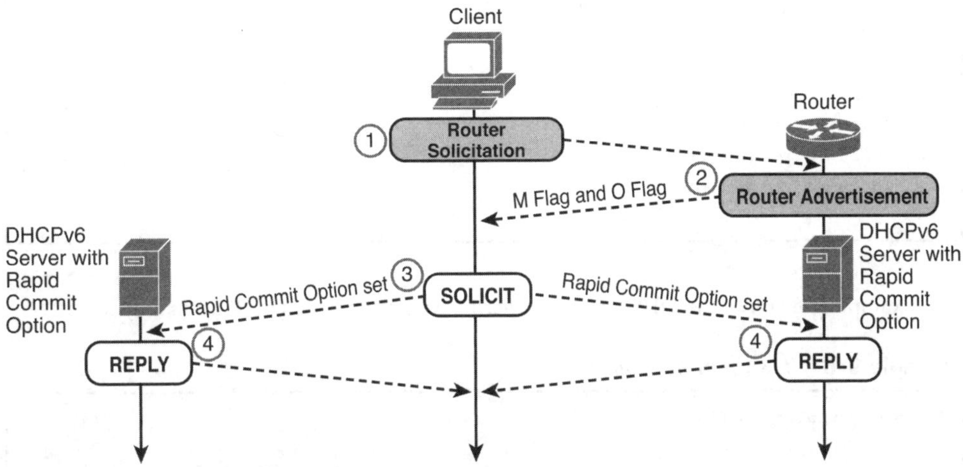

Figure 9-3 *DHCPv6 with Rapid Commit Option*

When the Rapid Commit Option is used, the server will not expect nor receive any confirmation from the client that it has received the REPLY message. Therefore, if more than one server responds to a SOLICIT message that includes the Rapid Commit Option, all but one server commit addresses that end up not being used by the client. Configuring only one DHCPv6 server with the Rapid Commit Option can minimize this issue of unused addresses. If a client sends a SOLICIT message with the Rapid Commit Option, it will prefer REPLY messages from servers with the Rapid Commit Option set over those that are not. If the client does not receive any REPLY messages with the Rapid Commit Option, it can accept the server's ADVERTISE message and proceed with the normal four-message exchange.

Configuring the Rapid Commit Option

Configuring a router with the Rapid Commit Option is done by including the **rapid-commit** parameter in the **ipv6 server dhcp interface** command. In Example 9-5, R1's previous DHCPv6 configuration is modified to include the Rapid Commit two-message exchange. The **show ipv6 dhcp interface** command is used to confirm that this option has been enabled.

Example 9-5 *Configuring and Verifying the Rapid Commit Option*

```
R1(config)# interface fastethernet 0/0
! Including the Rapid Commit Option:
R1(config-if)# ipv6 dhcp server cafe-1-pool rapid-commit
R1(config-if)# end

R1# show ipv6 dhcp interface fastethernet 0/0
FastEthernet0/0 is in server mode
  Using pool: cafe-1-pool
  Preference value: 0
  Hint from client: ignored
  Rapid-Commit: enabled
R1#
```

Example 9-6 shows the DHCPv6 and other relevant commands in R1's running config.

Example 9-6 *R1's Running Config*

```
R1# show running-config
!
ipv6 unicast-routing
!
ipv6 dhcp pool cafe-1-pool
 dns-server 2001:DB8:CAFE:2::D001
!
interface FastEthernet0/0
 ipv6 address FE80::1 link-local
 ipv6 address 2001:DB8:CAFE:1::1/64
 ipv6 nd other-config-flag
 ipv6 dhcp server cafe-1-pool
 ipv6 dhcp server cafe-1-pool rapid-commit
 ipv6 ospf 1 area 0
!
<output omitted for brevity>
```

Relay Agent Communications

At times, the DHCP server is on a different network than the client requesting the addressing and other configuration parameters. Routers or relay agents can be configured to forward DHCP messages between clients and servers on different networks. If you are familiar with DHCPv4 and Cisco routers, you are also most likely familiar with the **ip helper** command used with DHCPv4. However, routers or relay agents forward DHCPv6 messages slightly differently from DHCPv4.

Figure 9-4 illustrates the DHCPv6 process using a relay agent. From the perspective of the client, nothing changes. Although only one router is shown, more than one relay agent can be in the path between the client and the server, as shown in the following steps.

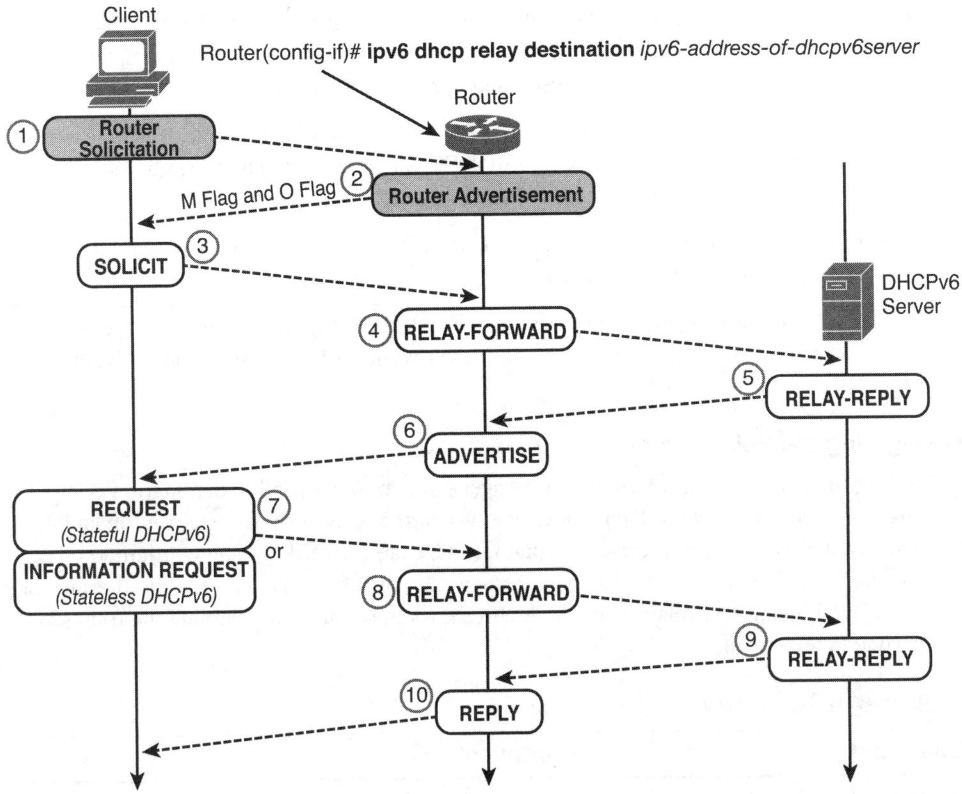

Figure 9-4 *DHCPv6 Relay Agent Communications*

Steps 1–3. These steps are the same as the normal DHCPv6 communication process described previously. The client's SOLICIT message is sent to the multicast address All_DHCP_Relay_Agents_and_Servers, FF02::1:2, which, as indicated by the name, includes both DHCPv6 servers and relay agents.

Step 4. The relay agent creates a RELAY-FORWARD message containing the original SOLICIT message from the client and forwards the message to a server using the All_DHCP_Servers multicast address FF05::1:3 with site-local scope. The relay agent can also be configured to use a unicast address for the DHCPv6 server.

Step 5. The server returns a RELAY-REPLY message to a relay agent containing (encapsulating) the ADVERTISE message that the final relay agent uses to deliver to the client. (If the Rapid Commit Option is being used, the RELAY-REPLY contains a REPLY message with the required addressing and/or other configuration parameters.)

Step 6. The client-facing relay agent (there can be more than one relay agent in the path) receives the RELAY-REPLY. After decapsulating the message, it forwards the ADVERTISE message on to the client.

Step 7. The client sends a REQUEST or INFORMATION-REQUEST message to the server, depending on whether stateful or stateless DHCPv6 is being used. This is the same process as discussed in the previous section.

Step 8. The relay agent creates another RELAY-FORWARD message, this time containing (encapsulating) the REQUEST or INFORMATION-REQUEST message from the client, and forwards this message on to the server.

Step 9. The server responds with a RELAY-REPLY message to a relay agent containing the REPLY message.

Step 10. The relay agent receives the RELAY-REPLY. The client-facing relay agent decapsulates the message and forwards the REPLY message on to the client.

Configuring the Relay Agent

To configure a router as a DHCPv6 relay agent, the **ipv6 dhcp relay destination** command is used on the client-facing interface. When the relay service is enabled on an interface, DHCPv6 messages received on that interface are forwarded to all configured relay destinations. The incoming DHCPv6 message can come from a client on that interface or be relayed by another relay agent. Table 9-6 shows the syntax for enabling the router as a DHCPv6 relay agent.

Table 9-6 *DHCPv6 Relay Agent Commands*

Command	Description
Router(config)# **interface** *type number*	Specifies an interface type and number, and places the router in interface configuration mode.
Router(config-if)# **ipv6 dhcp relay destination** *ipv6-address* [*interface-type interface-number*]	Specifies a destination address to which client packets are forwarded and enables DHCPv6 relay service on the interface. The *ipv6-address* parameter defines the relay destination address. There are two types of relay destination address: ■ Link-scoped unicast or multicast IPv6 address. A user must specify an output interface for this kind of address. ■ Global or site-scoped unicast or multicast IPv6 address.

If the **ipv6 dhcp relay destination** command does not include an output interface, the IPv6 routing table determines the exit interface.

Note There is much more to DHCPv6 that is beyond the scope of this book, including providing security considerations (DHCPv6 spoofing), delivering stateful DHCPv6 service, and configuring other client/server options. Like many things in IPv6, DHCPv6 seems to be a moving target. Throughout this chapter and in the chapter summary, several RFCs and other resources pertaining to DHCPv6 are listed. These will help if you are interested in learning more about configuring DHCPv6 or the intricacies of the protocol itself.

Other Upper-Layer Protocols

Because of the underlying larger IPv6 addresses, other upper-layer protocols might need to undergo some minor changes, many of which do not require reconfiguration of IPv6 devices. For example, the transport layer protocols TCP and UDP have undergone a minor modification for IPv6. Both TCP and UDP use the IP addresses as part of their checksums, so these checksum calculations must be modified for IPv6. There are other upper-layer protocols that require application changes, such as DNS.

DNS

DNS is used in both IPv4 and IPv6 to do name-to-address mappings. Like IPv4, IPv6 also supports the reverse mapping of IPv6 addresses to DNS names. In many ways, the need for DNS in the IPv6 world is much greater because of the longer IPv6 addresses.

A name server or DNS server is used to track information associated with domain names including a database of host name–to–address mappings. Each name can map to one or more IPv4 addresses, IPv6 addresses, or both address types. As in IPv4, each host name is represented in the DNS server by two DNS records, a resource record (or address record) and a reverse mapping pointer record.

In IPv4, a DNS A resource record maps a domain name to an IPv4 address. Similarly, in IPv6, the AAAA ("quad-A") resource record maps a domain name to an IPv6 address. The AAAA-type record is described in RFC 3596, DNS Extensions to Support IP Version 6. The four A's (AAAA) indicate that the IPv6 address is four times the size of the IPv4 address. The AAAA record is structured in very much the same way as the A record but is much larger. IPv4 or IPv6 can be used to transport both record types.

Both types of records are shown in Table 9-7 using the fully qualified domain name (FQDN). FQDN specifies the exact location in the DNS hierarchy, such as www.test.org or mail.example.com.

Table 9-7 *DNS Resource Records for IPv4 and IPv6*

Protocol	Resource Record	DNS Mapping
IPv4	A record	www.test.org A 209.165.200.225
IPv6	AAAA record	www.test.org AAAA 2001:DB8:CAFE:1234:0:0:0:A1

For reverse DNS lookups, IPv6 addresses use the special domain ip6.arpa. Equivalent to a pointer record (PTR) in IPv4, the IPv6 pointer record maps an IPv6 address to a host name. An IPv6 pointer record appears as a name in the domain with a sequence of nibbles (hexadecimal values), separated by a period (.), in reverse order. The IPv6 pointer records for www.test.org IPv4 and IPv6 addresses are shown in Table 9-8.

Table 9-8 *DNS Pointer Records for IPv4 and IPv6*

Protocol	Pointer Record Format
IPv4	225.200.165.209 www.test.org
IPv6	1.a.0.0.0.0.0.0.0.0.0.0.0.0.0.0.4.3.2.1.e.f.a.c.d..b.0.1.0.0.2 www.test.org

BIND (Berkeley Internet Name Domain) is the most widely used DNS software on the Internet. BIND is an open source software that implements the Domain Name System (DNS) protocols for the Internet. BIND has supported DNS for IPv6 since version 9.

DNS resolvers are the client side of DNS communications responsible for initiating queries to servers for the translation of domain names to IP addresses. A DNS server that supports IPv6 AAAA records does not necessarily have to be queried over IPv6. It can reply to these requests using IPv4.

As with IPv4, you can configure static host names for IPv6 addresses. The **ipv6 host** command is similar to the **ip host** command used with IPv4, except that it is IPv6 specific. The command syntax for the **ipv6 host** command, which defines a static host name–to–address mapping in the host name cache, is as follows:

```
Router(config)# ipv6 host name [port] ipv6-address1 [ipv6-address2...ipv6-
address4]
```

This command sequence features the following terms:

- *name*: Name of the IPv6 host. The first character can be either a letter or a number. If you use a number, the operations you can perform are limited.
- **port** (Optional): The default Telnet port number for the associated IPv6 addresses.
- *ipv6-address1*: The associated IPv6 address. This argument must be in the form documented in RFC 2373, where the address is specified in hexadecimal using 16-bit values between colons.
- *ipv6-address2...ipv6-address4* (Optional): Additional associated IPv6 addresses. You can bind up to four addresses to a host name.

In Example 9-7, the **ipv6 host** command is applied on R1 to map the IPv6 interface addresses of Routers R2 and R3. Mapping host names to addresses in IPv6 can be much more advantageous than with IPv4. The long IPv6 addresses make employing either a DNS server or static mapping using the **ipv6 host** command a more attractive option. A simple ping or telnet to an IPv6 address can be more cumbersome and prone to typing errors than with IPv4. As shown in Example 9-7, it is much easier to use a host name. Of course, it helps to have a naming scheme in your organization so that the names are easy to remember.

Example 9-7 *Static Host Name–to–IPv6 Mappings on R1*

```
R1(config)# ipv6 host R2-s0 2001:db8:cafe:a001::2
R1(config)# ipv6 host R3-any 2001:db8:cafe:a003::2 2001:db8:cafe:a002::2
R1(config)# end

R1# ping r2-s0

Type escape sequence to abort.
Sending 5, 100-byte ICMP Echos to 2001:DB8:CAFE:A001::2, timeout is 2 seconds:
!!!!!
Success rate is 100 percent (5/5), round-trip min/avg/max = 28/28/32 ms
R1#

R1# telnet r3-any
Trying R3-any (2001:DB8:CAFE:A003::2)... Open

User Access Verification

Password:
R3>
```

Confirm the configuration using the **show hosts** command, as shown in Example 9-8. The **show hosts** command is used to display the default domain name, the style of the name lookup service, a list of name server hosts, and the cached list of host names and addresses.

Example 9-8 *show hosts Command*

```
R1# show hosts
Name lookup view: Global
Default domain is not set
Name/address lookup uses static mappings

Codes: UN - unknown, EX - expired, OK - OK, ?? - revalidate
       temp - temporary, perm - permanent
       NA - Not Applicable None - Not defined
```

```
Host                      Port  Flags       Age Type   Address(es)
R2-s0                     None  (perm, OK)   0  IPv6   2001:DB8:CAFE:A001::2
R3-any                    None  (perm, OK)   0  IPv6   2001:DB8:CAFE:A003::2
2001:DB8:CAFE:A002::2
R1#
```

Using the **ipv6 host** command is convenient when there is a limited number of host name–to–IPv6 address mappings. But when the number of mappings is considerable, it might be more desirable to use the services of a DNS server. The DNS resolver in Cisco IOS accepts either an IPv4 address and/or an IPv6 address as a name server. The **ip name-server** command, which specifies the address of one or more DNS servers to use for name and address resolution, is the same command used in IPv4. The syntax for this command is as follows:

```
Router(config)# ip name-server server-address1 [server-address2...server-address6]
```

This command sequence features the following terms:

- *server-address1*: IPv4 or IPv6 addresses of a name server
- *server-address2...server-address6* (Optional): IP addresses of additional name servers (a maximum of six name servers)

> **Note** If multiple DNS servers are configured, the router will usually use the first server listed. However, dependent upon the network activity level, the router can query multiple DNS servers listed in the configuration.

In Example 9-9, the **ip name-server** command is configured on R1. Notice that both IPv6 and an IPv4 addresses are specified.

Example 9-9 *Specifying the Address of Name Servers*

```
R1(config)# ip name-server 2001:db8:cafe:2::77 192.168.2.77
R1(config)#
```

DNS Query and Response

Resolving domain names in the IPv6 world is really no different than it is in IPv4. For example, the user at an IPv6 client types **www.facebook.com** into his browser.

The web browser recognizes the request for a name and invokes the client's local resolver to unite the name with an address. Before querying its DNS server, the client's resolver will first check its name cache and local host table. If the name cannot be found in either, the resolver sends the request on to the address of the local DNS server statically or dynamically configured on the client.

It is now the local DNS server's responsibility to resolve this name for the client. This can require a process of several recursive queries and responses between the local DNS server and the root, TLD (Top Level Domain), and authoritative name servers. After the local DNS server has a response with the IPv6 address of the queried domain name, it sends that information back to the client that originated the request. The client now has the IPv6 address it needs as the destination IP address of the packet.

Using the www.facebook.com example, Example 9-10 shows the DNS query from the client to the DNS server for domain name. After the DNS server has the answer, it sends a response to the client with the IPv6 address, which is 2a03:2880:2110:3f01:face:b00c:: for www.facebook.com. The response from the DNS server is shown in Example 9-11.

Example 9-10 *DNS Query for www.facebook.com*

```
Domain Name System (query)
    [Response In: 7]
    Transaction ID: 0x01e1
    Flags: 0x0100 (Standard query)
        0... .... .... .... = Response: Message is a query
        .000 0... .... .... = Opcode: Standard query (0)
        .... ..0. .... .... = Truncated: Message is not truncated
        .... ...1 .... .... = Recursion desired: Do query recursively
        .... .... .0.. .... = Z: reserved (0)
        .... .... ...0 .... = Non-authenticated data: Unacceptable
    Questions: 1
    Answer RRs: 0
    Authority RRs: 0
    Additional RRs: 0
    Queries
        www.facebook.com: type AAAA, class IN
            Name: www.facebook.com
            Type: AAAA (IPv6 address)
            Class: IN (0x0001)
```

Example 9-11 *DNS Response for www.facebook.com*

```
Domain Name System (response)
    Transaction ID: 0x01e1
    Flags: 0x8180 (Standard query response, No error)
        1... .... .... .... = Response: Message is a response
        .000 0... .... .... = Opcode: Standard query (0)
        .... .0.. .... .... = Authoritative: Server is not an authority for domain
        .... ..0. .... .... = Truncated: Message is not truncated
        .... ...1 .... .... = Recursion desired: Do query recursively
        .... .... 1... .... = Recursion available: Server can do recursive queries
```

```
        .... .... .0.. .... = Z: reserved (0)
        .... .... ..0. .... = Answer authenticated: Answer/authority portion was not
authenticated by the server
        .... .... ...0 .... = Non-authenticated data: Unacceptable
        .... .... .... 0000 = Reply code: No error (0)
    Questions: 1
    Answer RRs: 1
    Authority RRs: 5
    Additional RRs: 5
    Queries
        www.facebook.com: type AAAA, class IN
            Name: www.facebook.com
            Type: AAAA (IPv6 address)
            Class: IN (0x0001)
    Answers
        www.facebook.com: type AAAA, class IN, addr 2a03:2880:2110:3f01:face:b00c::
            Name: www.facebook.com
            Type: AAAA (IPv6 address)
            Class: IN (0x0001)
            Time to live: 47 minutes, 40 seconds
            Data length: 16
            Addr: 2a03:2880:2110:3f01:face:b00c::
```

Verify the name-to-address mapping using the **nslookup** (name server lookup) command to query the DNS server. This command is shown in Example 9-12.

Example 9-12 *Resolving the Domain Name with the nslookup Command*

```
PC> nslookup
> set type=AAAA
> www.facebook.com
Non-authoritative answer:
www.facebook.com  AAAA IPv6 address = 2a03:2880:2110:3f01:face:b00c::

PC> nslookup
```

For more information on DNS for IPv6, refer to RFC 3596, DNS Extensions to Support IP Version 6, http://tools.ietf.org/html/rfc3596.

TCP and UDP

Checksums are used by various protocols and at different layers. Checksums are a fixed-size computation on a block of data for the purpose of detecting accidental errors that might have been introduced during transmission. Any transport layer or other upper-layer protocol that includes the IP addresses in its checksum computation must be modified for use over IPv6. This is necessary to include the larger 128-bit IPv6 addresses. TCP and UDP both include a 16-bit checksum in their headers, as shown in Figure 9-5.

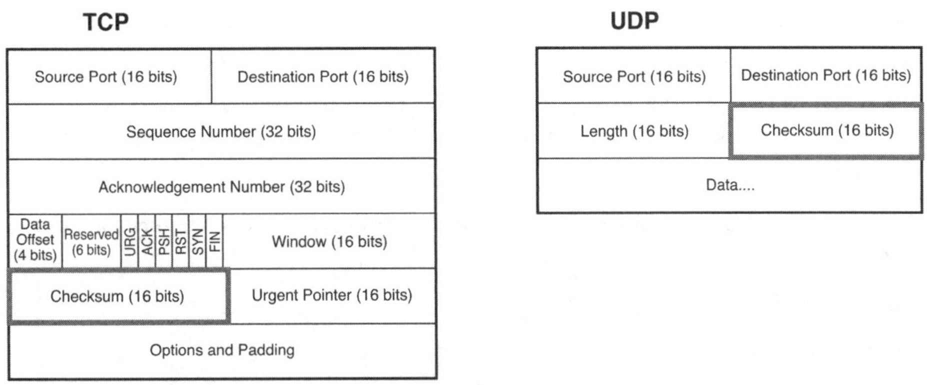

Figure 9-5 *TCP and UDP*

Both TCP and UDP generate a pseudoheader for checksum computational purposes only. The pseudoheader contains the fields from the network and transport layers that are used to compute the checksum. When TCP or UDP is transported over IPv6, this checksum includes

- Source IPv6 address
- Destination IPv6 address
- Upper-layer payload length (length of the TCP/UDP header and data)
- IPv6 next-header value (including any extension headers)

Modification to both TCP and UDP protocols is required for transport over IPv6. Because both of these checksums use the IPv6 addresses, the internals of the protocol had to be rewritten to accommodate the longer addresses. Although addresses are longer, the same algorithm is used to compute the checksum in IPv6 that is used in IPv4.

An IPv4 header includes a checksum, so the use of the checksum in UDP over IPv4 is optional. However, in the IPv6 header, the checksum was removed to improve processing speed. Besides the transport layer protocols, UDP and TCP already have a checksum. Because IPv6 does not include a checksum, it is no longer optional (now mandatory) when being carried over IPv6.

IP is a best-effort delivery protocol; it is the responsibility of the transport layer protocols to ensure the integrity of the data. The checksums for upper-layer protocols are described in RFC 2460, Internet Protocol, Version 6 (IPv6) Specification.

Summary

This chapter focused on DHCPv6. It explained that DHCPv6 is similar to its IPv6 counterpart but also has some significant differences. There are two forms of DHCPv6:

- **Stateful DHCP services:** Addressing and configuration information is obtained from a DHCPv6 server.
- **Stateless DHCP services:** Addressing information is received by the host in Router Advertisements, while other configuration information is obtained from a DHCPv6 server.

A client configured to automatically obtain its addressing and other configuration information can use one of three methods:

- SLAAC (Stateless Address Autoconfiguration)
- Stateful DHCPv6
- Stateless DHCPv6

The method used by the host is determined by the information contained in the router's Router Advertisement message, specifically the M flag, Managed Address Configuration flag, and the O flag, Other Configuration flag.

- **SLAAC (Stateless Address Autoconfiguration):** On Cisco routers, both flags are set to 0 by default, meaning that there is no information available from a DHCPv6 server. A host requiring dynamic address assignment receives all its information from the Router Advertisement.
- **Stateful DHCPv6:** When the M flag is set to 1, this informs the host to use stateful DHCPv6 services. All addressing and other configuration information will be obtained from a DHCPv6 server.
- **Stateless DHCPv6:** When the M flag is set to 0 and the O flag is set to 1, this tells the host that prefix, prefix length, default gateway, and other information are contained in the Router Advertisement. However, there is additional information that is obtained from a DHCPv6 server, such as DNS addresses.

There are three basic steps that you need to complete to configure stateless DHCPv6 services:

1. Configure a DHCPv6 server pool name with configuration parameters.
2. Enable the DHCPv6 server pool on an interface.
3. Modify any Router Advertisement parameters to let the hosts know that other configuration information is available from a DHCPv6 server.

The commands to configure the DHCPv6 server pool name and configuration parameters are as follows:

- Router(config)# **ipv6 dhcp pool** *poolname*: Creates a DHCPv6 pool and enters DHCPv6 pool configuration mode
- Router(config-dhcp)# **dns-server** *ipv6-address*: Specifies the IPv6 DNS servers available to a DHCPv6 client
- Router(config-dhcp)# **domain** *domain*: Configures a domain name for a DHCPv6 client

The commands used to enable the DHCPv6 server pool on an interface are as follows:

- Router(config)# **interface** *type number*: Specifies an interface type and number, and places the router in interface configuration mode.
- Router(config-dhcp)# **ipv6 dhcp server** *poolname* [**rapid-commit**]: Enables DHCPv6 service on an interface. The **rapid-commit** option allows the two-message exchange method for prefix delegation.

By default, the Router Advertisement O flag is set to 0. Setting this flag to 1 informs the hosts that additional configuration information is available from a DCHPv6 server. The command to modify the O flag in the Router Advertisement is as follows:

```
Router(config-if)# ipv6 nd other-config-flag
```

As with DHCPv4, DHCPv6 routers can act as relay agents to forward DHCPv6 messages between clients and servers on different networks. The interface command used to specify a destination address to which client packets are forwarded and to enable DHCPv6 relay service on the interface is as follows:

```
Router(config-if)# ipv6 dhcp relay destination ipv6-address [interface-type
interface-number]
```

Just as DNS in IPv4 is used to resolve domain names to IPv4 addresses, DNS in IPv6 is used to resolve domain names to IPv6 addresses. Cisco uses a similar command in IPv6 as in IPv4 to statically map addresses. The **ip host** command in IPv4 is the **ipv6 host** command in IPv6, which defines a static host name–to–address mapping in the host name cache:

```
Router(config)# ipv6 host name [port] ipv6-address1 [ipv6-address2...ipv6-
address4]
```

To specify the address of one or more DNS servers for address resolution, use the same command in IPv6 as in IPv4:

```
Router(config)# ip name-server server-address1 [server-address2...server-address6]
```

References

RFCs:

RFC 2460, *Internet Protocol, Version 6 (IPv6) Specification*, S. Deering, Cisco Systems, www.ietf.org/rfc/rfc2460, December 1988

RFC 3315, *Dynamic Host Configuration Protocol for IPv6 (DHCPv6)*, R. Droms, Cisco Systems, www.ietf.org/rfc/rfc3315, July 2003

RFC 3596, *DNS Extensions to Support IP Version 6*, Thompson, Cisco Systems, www.ietf.org/rfc/rfc3596, October 2003

RFC 3736, *Stateless Dynamic Host Configuration Protocol (DHCP) Service for IPv6*, R. Droms, Cisco Systems, www.ietf.org/rfc/rfc3736, April 2004

RFC 4862, *IPv6 Stateless Address Autoconfiguration*, S. Thompson, Cisco Systems, www.ietf.org/rfc/rfc4862, September 2007

Website:

Cisco IOS IPv6 Configuration Guide, Implementing DHCP for IPv6, www.cisco.com/en/US/docs/ios/ipv6/configuration/guide/ip6-dhcp.html

Chapter 10

Dual-Stack and Tunneling

The next two chapters deal with IPv4 and IPv6 coexistence and integration strategies. IPv4 isn't going away anytime soon, but as discussed in Chapter 1, "Introduction to IPv6," the migration to IPv6 needs to happen. For at least the foreseeable future, IPv4 and IPv6 will coexist. Unlike the Year 2000 (Y2K) "bug" that hardware and software developers had to deal with, there is no deadline or switchover date to go from IPv4 to IPv6. The transition is expected to take years. The Internet Engineering Task Force (IETF) has created various protocols, tools, and mechanisms to help network administrators migrate their networks to IPv6. These techniques can be divided into three categories:

- **Dual-stack:** Dual-stack allows IPv4 and IPv6 devices to coexist on the same network. A dual-stack device can be a host, a server, or a router configured to run both IPv4 and IPv6 stacks simultaneously.
- **Tunneling:** Tunneling is a method of transporting IPv6 packets over IPv4-only networks. Tunneling is accomplished by encapsulating the IPv6 packet inside IPv4.
- **Translation:** Network Address Translation 64 (NAT64) allows IPv6-only devices to communicate with IPv4-only devices using a translation technique similar to NAT used in IPv4. NAT64 is discussed in Chapter 11, "Network Address Translation IPv6 to IPv4 (NAT64)."

Note Network Address Translation – Protocol Translation (NAT-PT) is also discussed in Chapter 11. However, NAT-PT has been deemed deprecated by IETF because of its tight coupling with Domain Name System (DNS) and its general limitations in translation, all of which are documented in RFC 4966, Reasons to Move the Network Address Translator - Protocol Translator (NAT-PT) to Historic Status.

Dual-Stack

A dual-stack device has complete support for both IPv4 and IPv6. It can be a host, printer, server, router, or any device that can be configured to support both protocols. In the IPv4 world, this includes IPv4 addresses, Address Resolution Protocol (ARP), and Internet Control Message Protocol (ICMP) for IPv4. An IPv4 router supports IPv4 static routes and IPv4 routing protocols such as Enhanced Interior Gateway Routing Protocol (EIGRP) and Open Shortest Path First version 2 (OSPFv2). In the IPv6 realm, support means more than just a network header with longer addresses. IPv6 support includes IPv6 global unicast and link-local addresses, ICMPv6 operations including Stateless Address Autoconfiguration (SLAAC), and Duplicate Address Detection (DAD). An IPv6 router needs to route IPv6 packets using static routes and IPv6 routing protocols such as EIGRP for IPv6 and OSPFv3. An IPv6 router sends out ICMPv6 Router Advertisement messages and can perform tunneling or translation services.

As illustrated throughout this book, there is much more to IPv6 than just 128-bit source and destination addresses. Support for IPv6 includes implementing new protocols and processes such as SLAAC and DAD. IPv6 support for most host operating systems such as Windows, Mac OS, and Linux has been available for several years. Cisco introduced IPv6 support with Cisco IOS Release 12.2(2)T in 2000.

Dual-stack devices are nothing new with IPv6. Before IPv4 became the predominant network protocol, many organizations ran IPX, AppleTalk, DECnet, or SNA on their devices along with IPv4.

When communicating with an IPv4 device, it behaves like an IPv4-only device. When communicating with an IPv6 device, it acts like an IPv6-only device. Figure 10-1 illustrates an IPv4-only application. The application can be carried in a TCP or UDP segment identified by the transport layer's port number. The segment is then encapsulated in an IPv4 packet, with the data or payload identified by the value in the IPv4 protocol field. For transport over the link, the IPv4 packet is encapsulated in an Ethernet frame and identified by 0x800 in the Ethernet Type field.

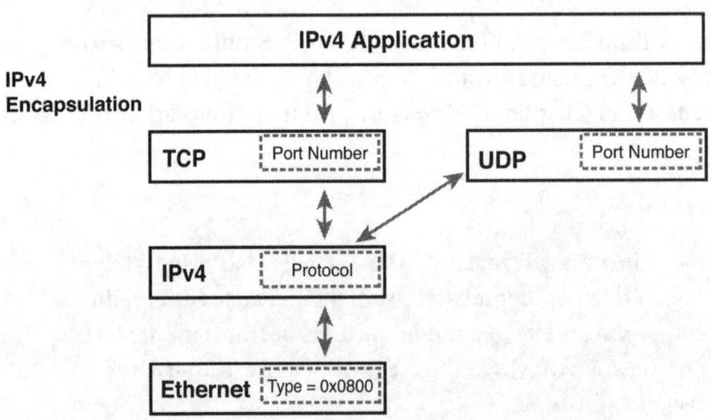

Figure 10-1 *IPv4 Application Using the IPv4 Stack*

On dual-stack devices with an application that supports both IPv4 and IPv6 protocols, the process is almost identical, as shown in Figure 10-2. TCP and UDP port numbers identify the application. When the IPv6 stack is selected, the next header field in the IPv6 header identifies the transport protocol. The IPv6 packet is encapsulated in an Ethernet frame, which is using the Ethernet Type field of 0x86DD. It is important to remember that Ethernet is at Layer 2. Although it has a different Type field when carrying an IPv6 packet, the Ethernet frame is not treated any differently by the switch. A typical Layer 2 access switch that does not support IPv6 only means that you will not be able to manage the switch using IPv6. The switch can still forward frames regardless of whether its payload is an IPv4 or IPv6 packet.

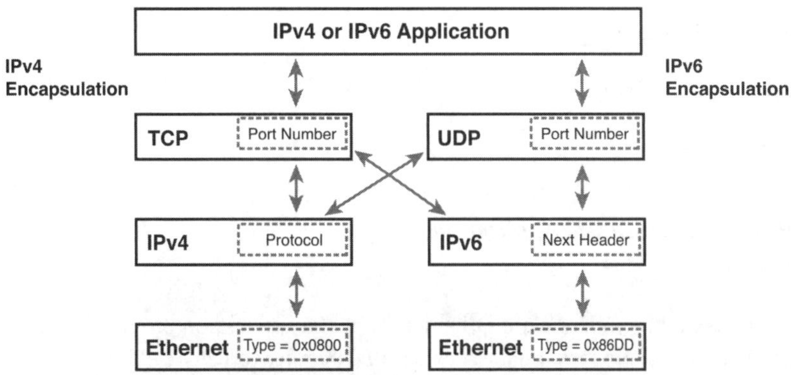

Figure 10-2 *Application Using Both IPv4 and IPv6 Stacks*

Although an application can support both IPv4 and IPv6, the device doesn't just randomly select which protocol to use. Figure 10-3 shows an example of a dual-stack host. If an application supports both IPv4 and IPv6 protocol stacks, it requests all available addresses for the fully qualified domain name (FQDN) from a Domain Name System (DNS) server. The DNS server replies with all available addresses. This can include both IPv4 and IPv6 addresses. If the DNS server sends both IPv4 and IPv6 addresses, the operating system chooses which one to use. In most cases, the application defaults to the IPv6 address, but this is dependent upon the operating system. The device then connects to the source using the selected IP protocol stack.

In Step 1 of Figure 10-3, dual-stack host A sends a DNS query for the quad-A (AAAA) record for www.example.com. In Step 2, the DNS server returns a DNS query response containing both the quad-A and A records for www.example.com. Host A uses the quad-A record to begin communications with the www.example.com server.

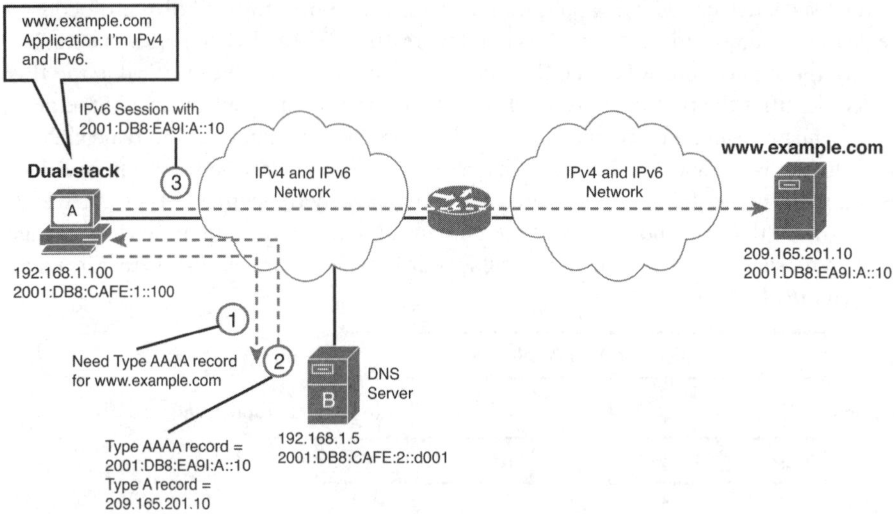

Figure 10-3 *IPv4- and IPv6-Aware Application*

Note If you are interested in understanding the details of the application programming interface (API) for IPv6 and the operational issues with DNS, refer to RFC 3493, Basic Socket Interface Extensions for IPv6, and RFC 4472, Operational Considerations and Issues with IPv6 DNS. Again, it is typically left to the underlying operating system to determine the transport.

IPv6 Address Format in URL Syntax

When an IP address is used instead of a domain name, the application uses the protocol stack associated with the particular IP address. If the user enters an IPv4 address, the application uses IPv4. If the user enters an IPv6 address, the application chooses IPv6. Most of the time when using a web browser, the address is entered by using the URL (Uniform Resource Locator) such as http://www.example.com. The IP address could be implemented instead, but the whole idea of using domain names is to avoid having to remember IP addresses. There are times when it is necessary to enter an IP address instead of the URL in the browser, such as when debugging or using the browser interface to configure a device. For example, using IPv4, you can enter **http://192.168.1.1** to connect and configure the Linksys home router.

So, how is this accomplished by using an IPv6 address? IPv6 addresses are not directly compatible with URLs because of that pesky colon (:) in the address. The colon used by IPv6 addresses is interpreted by the browser as a port number. For example, accessing the

Linksys router on port 5000 would mean entering the URL **http://192.168.1.1:5000.** RFC 3986, Uniform Resource Identifier (URI): Generic Syntax, defines the format for literal IPv6 addresses in URLs. The idea is to make it easy to cut and paste IPv6 addresses into a browser's address bar. The IPv6 address is contained in brackets followed by any additional URL syntax. Table 10-1 shows examples of literal IPv6 addresses using the URL syntax as described in RFC 3986.

Table 10-1 Literal IPv6 Address Format in URL Syntax

Literal IPv6 Address	URL
FEDC:BA98:7654:3210:FEDC:BA98:7654:3210	http://[FEDC:BA98:7654:3210:FEDC:BA98:7654:3210]:80/index.html
1080:0:0:0:8:800:200C:4171	http://[1080:0:0:0:8:800:200C:417A]/index.html
3ffe:2a00:100:7031::1	http://[3ffe:2a00:100:7031::1]
1080::8:800:200C:417A	http://[1080::8:800:200C:417A]/foo
::192.9.5.5	http://[::192.9.5.5]/ipng
::FFFF:129.144.52.38	http://[::FFFF:129.144.52.38]:80/index.html
2010:836B:4179::836B:4179	http://[2010:836B:4179::836B:4179]

Configuring a Dual-Stack Network

Configuring a dual-stack network means configuring devices for both IPv4 and IPv6. This can include hosts, routers, multilayer switches, printers, and any device with an IP address. As far as IP is concerned, these are two totally separate networks—just sharing the same "space." They are like roommates who don't really see or notice each other or pass each other like "ships in the night."

In Chapter 7, "Introduction to Routing IPv6," Rick's Café network was configured for IPv6 and OSPFv3. This section illustrates how to enable dual-stack support on the network by configuring the routers for IPv4 and OSPFv2. The dual-stack hosts now have the capability of sending both IPv4 and IPv6 packets over the Rick's Café network. Figure 10-4 shows the addressing scheme for both protocols. The routers have already been configured for IPv6 and OSPFv3. In Chapter 6, "IPv6 Configuration," IPv6 was configured on the interfaces, and in Chapter 8, "IPv6 IGP Routing Protocols," you configured OSPFv3. The previous IPv6 configurations are shown when the routers' running configs are examined.

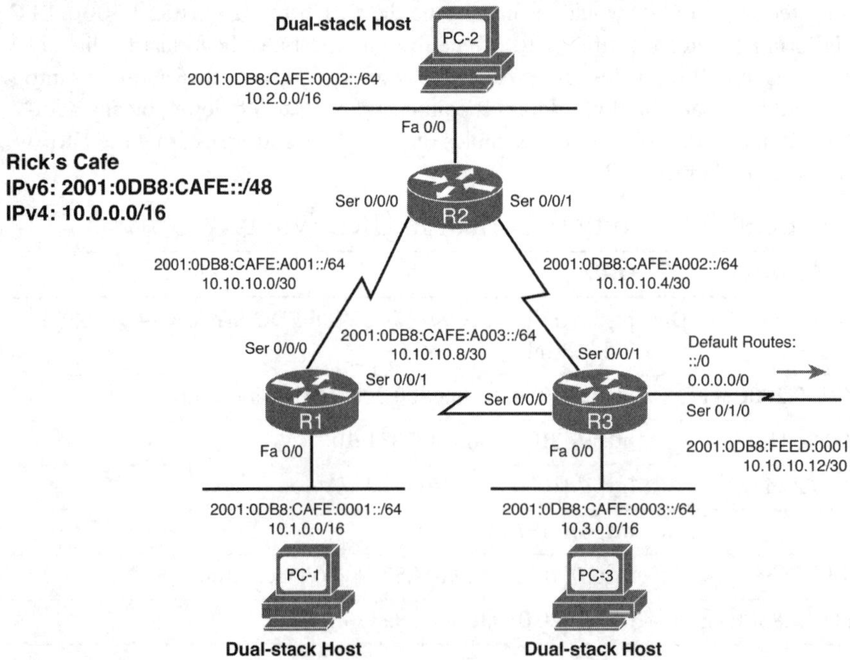

Figure 10-4 *Rick's Café Network OSPFv3 Topology*

Beginning with Router R1, configure the IPv4 addresses on its Fast Ethernet interface and both of its serial interfaces. After the interfaces have been configured, the next task is to configure OSPFv2. Example 10-1 shows the configuration of R1's interfaces for IPv4 and enabling OSPFv2 on all three interfaces. These are the same commands always used with IPv4. It is as if IPv6 didn't even exist on this router, but of course it does.

Example 10-1 *Configuration of IPv4 Addresses and OSPFv2 on R1*

```
R1(config)# interface FastEthernet0/0
R1(config-if)# ip address 10.1.0.1 255.255.0.0
R1(config-if)# exit
R1(config)# interface Serial0/0/0
R1(config-if)# ip address 10.10.10.1 255.255.255.252
R1(config-if)# exit
R1(config)# interface Serial0/0/1
R1(config-if)# ip address 10.10.10.9 255.255.255.252
R1(config-if)# exit

R1(config)# router ospf 2
R1(config-rtr)# network 10.1.0.0 0.0.255.255 area 0
R1(config-rtr)# network 10.10.10.0 0.0.0.3 area 0
R1(config-rtr)# network 10.10.10.8 0.0.0.3 area 0
```

Example 10-2 examines the current running config for Router R1. Notice that both IPv4 and IPv6 commands are included; commands for both protocols are coexisting on the same router. Each interface has an IPv4 and an IPv6 routable address. IPv6 interfaces also include a link-local address that was statically configured previously to identify the address more easily.

Example 10-2 *Selected Output from R1's Running Config*

```
interface FastEthernet0/0
 ip address 10.1.0.1 255.255.0.0          ! IPv4 address
 ipv6 address FE80::1 link-local          ! IPv6 address
 ipv6 address 2001:DB8:CAFE:1::1/64       ! IPv6 address
 ipv6 ospf 1 area 0                       ! IPv6 - OSPFv3 command
!
interface Serial0/0/0
 ip address 10.10.10.1 255.255.255.252    ! IPv4 address
 ipv6 address FE80::1 link-local          ! IPv6 address
 ipv6 address 2001:DB8:CAFE:A001::1/64    ! IPv6 address
 ipv6 ospf 1 area 0                       ! IPv6 - OSPFv3 command
!
interface Serial0/0/1
 ip address 10.10.10.9 255.255.255.252    ! IPv4 address
 ipv6 address FE80::1 link-local          ! IPv6 address
 ipv6 address 2001:DB8:CAFE:A003::1/64    ! IPv6 address
 ipv6 ospf 1 area 0                       ! IPv6 - OSPFv3 command
!
ipv6 router ospf 1                        ! IPv6 - OSPFv3 commands
 router-id 10.1.1.1
 log-adjacency-changes
!
router ospf 2                             ! IPv4 - OSPFv2 commands
 network 10.1.0.0 0.0.255.255 area 0
 network 10.10.10.0 0.0.0.3 area 0
 network 10.10.10.8 0.0.0.3 area 0
 log-adjacency-changes
```

Continuing the examination of R1's running config, remember that unlike OSPFv2, OSPFv3 does not use the **network** command to enable OSPF on the interface. With OSPFv3, the **ipv6 opsf** interface command is used to enable OSPF directly on the interface.

Router R1 is a dual-stack router, wearing "two hats," one for IPv4 and one for IPv6.

- **Interfaces:** Each interface is configured with the appropriate IPv4 and IPv6 addresses.
    - **IPv4:** IPv4 addresses are configured using the **ip address** command.
    - **IPv6:** Global unicast IPv6 addresses and link-local IPv6 addresses are configured using the **ipv6 address** command.

- **Routing tables:** The router maintains two routing tables, one for IPv4 and one for IPv6.
  - **IPv4:** The **show ip route** command is used to display the IPv4 routing table.
  - **IPv6:** The **show ipv6 route** command is used to display the IPv6 routing table.
- **Routing protocol:** Router R1 has been configured for dynamic routing of both protocols using OSPF. The router maintains separate databases, tables, and processes for each protocol.
  - **IPv4:** OSPFv2 is the routing protocol used for IPv4 on R1.
  - **IPv6:** OSPFv3 is the routing protocol used for IPv6 on R1.
- **IP processes:** Various protocols are used by IP for address resolution, messaging, and basic network operations.
  - **IPv4:** The router participates in ARP, ICMPv4, and other IPv4 protocols.
  - **IPv6:** An IPv6 router participates in various processes and protocols including ICMPv6 Neighbor Discovery and Duplicate Address Detection.

Next, let's configure Router R2 for IPv4 and OSPFv2 but do something a little differently. Notice in Example 10-3 that the OSPFv2 configuration is not the same on R1. Instead of using the OSPF **network** command as with R1, OSPFv2 was configured directly on the interface using the **ip ospf area** interface command to enable OSPF on the interface. This is similar to how OSPFv3 was configured on the interface using the **ipv6 ospf area** interface command. The **ip ospf area** interface command for OSPFv2 was integrated into Cisco IOS with Release 12.3(11)T.

Example 10-3 *Configuration of IPv4 Addresses and OSPFv2 on R2*

```
R2(config)# interface fastethernet 0/0
R2(config-if)# ip address 10.2.0.1 255.255.255.0
! Replaces the OSPFv2 network command:
R2(config-if)# ip ospf 2 area 0
R2(config-if)# exit
R2(config)# interface serial 0/0/0
R2(config-if)# ip address 10.10.10.2 255.255.255.252
! Replaces the OSPFv2 network command:
R2(config-if)# ip ospf 2 area 0
R2(config-if)# exit
R2(config)# interface serial 0/0/1
R2(config-if)# ip address 10.10.10.5 255.255.255.252
! Replaces the OSPFv2 network command:
R2(config-if)# ip ospf 2 area 0
R2(config-if)#
```

By looking at the running config for R2 in Example 10-4, notice all the interface and OSPF commands for both protocols. The configuration of both protocols is very similar. In many cases, it is the same command with the only difference being **ip** for IPv4 and **ipv6** for IPv6 in the command syntax where appropriate. Of course, there can be different command options for each protocol. Most likely, if you know the IPv4 commands, the configuration and verification of its IPv6 counterpart will be fairly straightforward.

Example 10-4 *Selected Output from R2's Running Config*

```
interface FastEthernet0/0
 ip address 10.2.0.1 255.255.0.0          ! IPv4 address
 ip ospf 2 area 0                         ! IPv4 - OSPFv2 command
 ipv6 address FE80::2 link-local          ! IPv6 address
 ipv6 address 2001:DB8:CAFE:2::1/64       ! IPv6 address
 ipv6 ospf 1 area 0                       ! IPv6 - OSPFv3 command
!
interface Serial0/0/0
 ip address 10.10.10.2 255.255.255.252    ! IPv4 address
 ip ospf 2 area 0                         ! IPv4 - OSPFv2 command
 ipv6 address FE80::2 link-local          ! IPv6 address
 ipv6 address 2001:DB8:CAFE:A001::2/64    ! IPv6 address
 ipv6 ospf 1 area 0                       ! IPv6 - OSPFv3 command
!
interface Serial0/0/1
 ip address 10.10.10.5 255.255.255.252    ! IPv4 address
 ip ospf 2 area 0                         ! IPv4 - OSPFv2 command
 ipv6 address FE80::2 link-local          ! IPv6 address
 ipv6 address 2001:DB8:CAFE:A002::1/64    ! IPv6 address
 ipv6 ospf 1 area 0                       ! IPv6 - OSPFv3 command
!
router ospf 2                             ! IPv4 - OSPFv2 commands
 log-adjacency-changes
!
ipv6 router ospf 1                        ! IPv6 - OSPFv3 commands
 router-id 10.2.2.2
 log-adjacency-changes
```

Example 10-5 shows the running config for Router R3 after it has been configured for IPv4. (The actual configuration commands for R3 are not included.)

Example 10-5 *Selected Output from R3's Running Config*

```
interface FastEthernet0/0
 ip address 10.3.0.1 255.255.0.0          ! IPv4 address
 ip ospf 2 area 0                         ! IPv4 - OSPFv2 command
 ipv6 address FE80::3 link-local          ! IPv6 address
 ipv6 address 2001:DB8:CAFE:3::1/64       ! IPv6 address
 ipv6 ospf 1 area 0                       ! IPv6 - OSPFv3 command
!
interface Serial0/0/0
 ip address 10.10.10.10 255.255.255.252   ! IPv4 address
 ip ospf 2 area 0                         ! IPv4 - OSPFv2 command
 ipv6 address FE80::3 link-local          ! IPv6 address
 ipv6 address 2001:DB8:CAFE:A003::2/64    ! IPv6 address
 ipv6 ospf 1 area 0                       ! IPv6 - OSPFv3 command
!
interface Serial0/0/1
 ip address 10.10.10.6 255.255.255.252    ! IPv4 address
 ip ospf 2 area 0                         ! IPv4 - OSPFv2 command
 ipv6 address FE80::3 link-local          ! IPv6 address
 ipv6 address 2001:DB8:CAFE:A002::2/64    ! IPv6 address
 ipv6 ospf 1 area 0                       ! IPv6 - OSPFv3 command
!
interface Serial0/1/0
 ip address 10.10.10.13 255.255.255.252   ! IPv4 address
 ipv6 address FE80::3 link-local          ! IPv6 address
 ipv6 address 2001:DB8:FEED:1::1/64       ! IPv6 address
!
!
ip route 0.0.0.0 0.0.0.0 Serial0/1/0 ! IPv4 static default route
!
ipv6 route ::/0 Serial0/1/0          ! IPv6 static default route
!
router ospf 2
 log-adjacency-changes
 default-information originate       ! Propagate IPv4 default route
                                     ! into OSPFv2 domain
!
ipv6 router ospf 1
 router-id 10.3.3.3
 log-adjacency-changes
 default-information originate      ! Propagate IPv6 default route
                                    ! into OSPFv3 domain
```

Similar to R2, OSPFv2 was configured using the **ip ospf area** interface command in lieu of the OSPF **network** command. An IPv4 static route was configured with the same exit interface as the IPv6 static route using this command:

```
R3(config)# ip route 0.0.0.0 0.0.0.0 serial 0/1/0
```

To distribute the default route in OSPFv2, the same **default-information originate** command is used in router configuration mode:

```
R3(config)# router ospf 2
R3(config-rtr)# default-information originate
```

Example 10-6 illustrates the routing tables for each protocol. The **show ip route** command is used to display all directly connected, static, and dynamically learned IPv4 routes, whereas the **show ipv6 route** command is used to do the same for IPv6 networks. Chapter 8 discussed the commands for configuring and verifying OSPFv3, along with an examination of the IPv6 routing table. Notice that the IPv6 routes do not include a timestamp as displayed with the IPv4 routes.

Example 10-6 *Verifying the IPv4 and IPv6 Routing Tables*

```
R1# show ip route
Codes: C - connected, S - static, R - RIP, M - mobile, B - BGP
       D - EIGRP, EX - EIGRP external, O - OSPF, IA - OSPF inter area
       N1 - OSPF NSSA external type 1, N2 - OSPF NSSA external type 2
       E1 - OSPF external type 1, E2 - OSPF external type 2
       i - IS-IS, su - IS-IS summary, L1 - IS-IS level-1, L2 - IS-IS level-2
       ia - IS-IS inter area, * - candidate default, U - per-user static route
       o - ODR, P - periodic downloaded static route

Gateway of last resort is 10.10.10.10 to network 0.0.0.0

     10.0.0.0/8 is variably subnetted, 6 subnets, 2 masks
C       10.10.10.8/30 is directly connected, Serial0/0/1
O       10.2.0.0/16 [110/65] via 10.10.10.2, 01:20:14, Serial0/0/0
O       10.3.0.0/16 [110/65] via 10.10.10.10, 01:20:14, Serial0/0/1
C       10.10.10.0/30 is directly connected, Serial0/0/0
C       10.1.0.0/16 is directly connected, FastEthernet0/0
O       10.10.10.4/30 [110/128] via 10.10.10.2, 01:20:14, Serial0/0/0
O*E2 0.0.0.0/0 [110/1] via 10.10.10.10, 01:15:51, Serial0/0/1
R1#

R1# show ipv6 route
IPv6 Routing Table - 12 entries
Codes: C - Connected, L - Local, S - Static, R - RIP, B - BGP
```

```
       U - Per-user Static route
       I1 - ISIS L1, I2 - ISIS L2, IA - ISIS interarea, IS - ISIS summary
       O - OSPF intra, OI - OSPF inter, OE1 - OSPF ext 1, OE2 - OSPF ext 2
       ON1 - OSPF NSSA ext 1, ON2 - OSPF NSSA ext 2
       D - EIGRP, EX - EIGRP external
OE2  ::/0 [110/1], tag 1
     via FE80::3, Serial0/0/1
C    2001:DB8:CAFE:1::/64 [0/0]
     via ::, FastEthernet0/0
L    2001:DB8:CAFE:1::1/128 [0/0]
     via ::, FastEthernet0/0
O    2001:DB8:CAFE:2::/64 [110/65]
     via FE80::2, Serial0/0/0
O    2001:DB8:CAFE:3::/64 [110/65]
     via FE80::3, Serial0/0/1
C    2001:DB8:CAFE:A001::/64 [0/0]
     via ::, Serial0/0/0
L    2001:DB8:CAFE:A001::1/128 [0/0]
     via ::, Serial0/0/0
O    2001:DB8:CAFE:A002::/64 [110/128]
     via FE80::2, Serial0/0/0
C    2001:DB8:CAFE:A003::/64 [0/0]
     via ::, Serial0/0/1
L    2001:DB8:CAFE:A003::1/128 [0/0]
     via ::, Serial0/0/1
L    FE80::/10 [0/0]
     via ::, Null0
L    FF00::/8 [0/0]
     via ::, Null0
R1#
```

Tunneling

Another type of IPv4-to-IPv6 transition mechanism is tunneling. Like other transition methods, tunneling should be considered a temporary solution until native IPv6 can be employed. A tunnel is nothing more than encapsulating one IP packet inside another. A tunnel can be an IPv4 packet encapsulated in another IPv4 packet or, for that matter, any network layer protocol over another network layer protocol. One of the challenges in integrating IPv6 into the current IPv4 networks is the ability to transport IPv6 packets over IPv4-only networks. One way to do this is to use a tunnel or, in IPv6, what is known as an *overlay* tunnel. Overlay tunnels encapsulate IPv6 packets in IPv4 packets for delivery across an IPv4 infrastructure.

Figure 10-5 shows an example of two IPv6-only networks or "IPv6 islands" separated by an IPv4-only network.

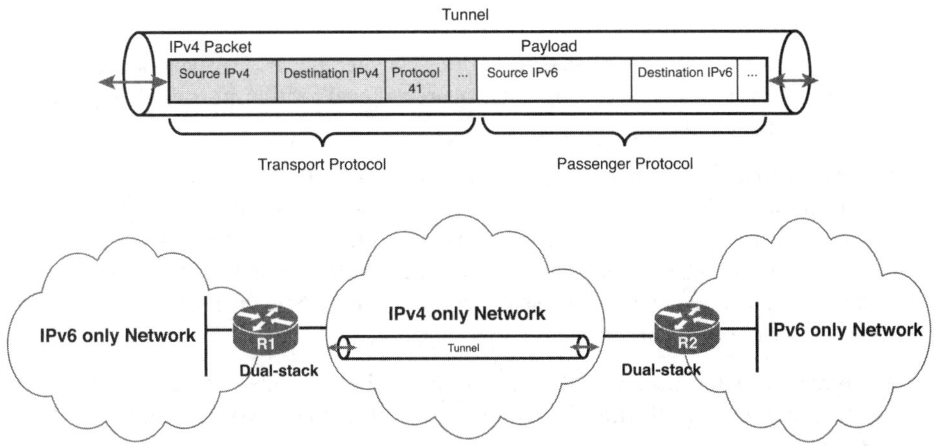

Figure 10-5 *Tunnel Connecting Islands of IPv6 Networks*

Tunneling is a technique that allows devices in isolated IPv6 networks to send IPv6 packets over the IPv4 network. A tunnel has two types of protocols, a transport protocol and a passenger protocol. Figure 10-5 illustrates these two protocols in an IPv6 overlay tunnel:

- **Transport protocol:** IPv4 is the transport protocol, in which the tunnel is created. Protocol 41 in the IPv4 header indicates that the encapsulated data portion is an IPv6 packet.
- **Passenger protocol:** IPv6 is the passenger protocol, encapsulated in the tunnel and carried through the tunnel.

Tunnels involve two devices, the endpoints of the tunnel, and a management protocol to manage the tunnel. The three components of a tunnel are

- **Tunnel entry point:** A tunnel entry point is where the encapsulation of the IPv6 packet (passenger protocol) inside an IPv4 packet (transport protocol) occurs. A tunnel entry point must be a dual-stack device that receives an IPv6 packet and encapsulates it inside an IPv4 packet for transport over the IPv4 network.
- **Tunnel exit point:** The tunnel exit point is another dual-stack device and is where the IPv4 packet is received. The IPv6 packet is then decapsulated for transport over the IPv6 network.
- **Tunnel management:** Tunnel management is done by the tunnel entry and exit points and deals with tunnel encapsulation/decapsulation, addressing, maximum transmission unit (MTU), fragmentation, and error processing.

Tunneling can involve any combination of routers and hosts depending upon the endpoints (entry and exit points) of the tunnel. Figure 10-6 illustrates the three scenarios that can exist:

- **Host-to-host:** Isolated dual-stack hosts are separated by an IPv4-only network. The hosts, acting as tunnel endpoints, create a tunnel for transporting IPv6 packets between the two hosts.
- **Host-to-router:** The tunnel endpoints are a host and a router connected by an IPv4-only network. At one end of the tunnel is a dual-stack host, and at the other end is a dual-stack router. The router sends and receives the IPv6 packets natively over its IPv6 network. When communicating with the host, the IPv6 packets are encapsulated within an IPv4 packet and sent over the tunnel, where the host receives and processes the IPv6 packet.
- **Router-to-router:** Both tunnel endpoints are dual-stack routers. A dual-stack router can establish a tunnel with another dual-stack router to interconnect islands of IPv6 hosts.

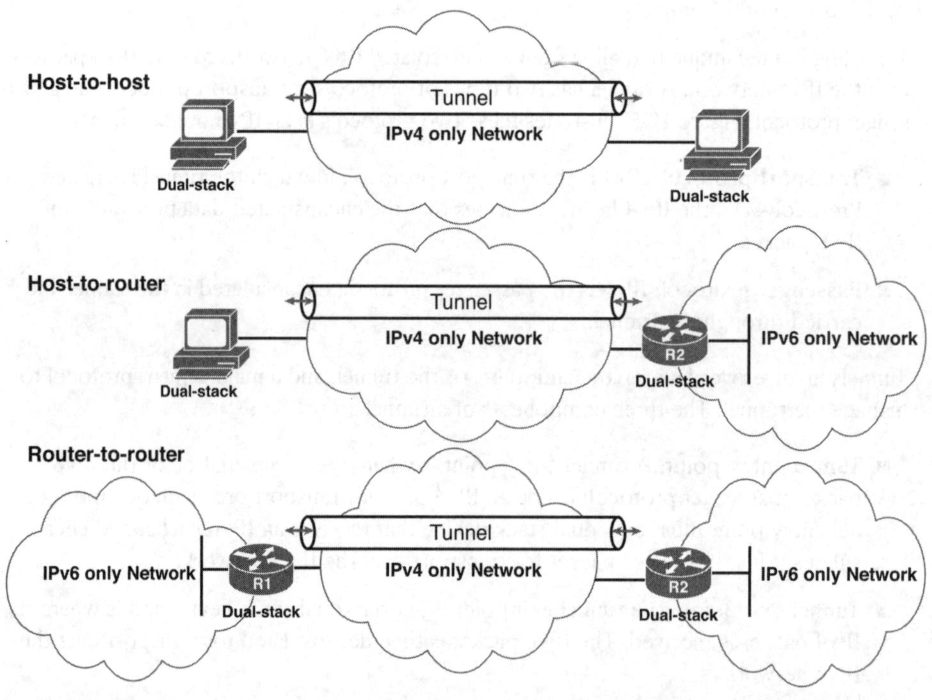

Figure 10-6 *IPv6 Tunnel Endpoints*

The IETF defined several protocols and techniques for establishing tunnels between dual-stack nodes. The number of tunneling options can be confusing and even a bit overwhelming. This chapter provides details for a better understanding of the similarities and differences with these different types of tunnels. Basically, all the tunnels do the same thing: transport an IPv6 packet inside an IPv4 packet between the two endpoints of the tunnel. After that, the choice comes down to

- How many tunnels need to be configured? If there are just a few, manual tunnels can be fine; otherwise, automatic tunnels might be the better option.
- Are there any specific requirements that would make one tunnel type more desirable over another—such as the need to tunnel non-IP packets?

Table 10-2 summarizes the following tunneling types for IPv6:

- **Manual:** A manual tunnel is equivalent to a point-to-point link. The primary use is for stable connections that require regular secure communication between two edge routers (or between an end system and an edge router), or for connection to remote IPv6 networks.
- **IPv4-compatible:** IPv4-compatible tunnels do not scale well for large networks. Cisco does not recommend this tunnel type, and it is not covered in this chapter.
- **6to4:** The key difference with 6to4 or automatic 6to4 tunnels is that the tunnel is not point-to-point, but a point-to-multipoint tunnel. The destination IPv4 address of the tunnel is determined from the destination IPv6 address of the packet. 6to4 tunnels require a relationship between the IPv6 prefix or network address and IPv4 tunnel addresses. The IPv6 address is reverse engineered from the IPv4 tunnel address using the format 2002:*tunnel-IPv4-address*::/48. This allows a single tunnel to be created that has multiple destinations—a point-to-multipoint tunnel. 6to4 tunnels are defined in RFC 3056, Connection of IPv6 Domains via IPv4 Clouds.
- **ISATAP (Intra-Site Automatic Tunnel Addressing Protocol):** ISATAP is designed for transporting IPv6 packets within a site where a native IPv6 infrastructure is not yet available, for example, when sparse IPv6 hosts are deployed for testing. ISATAP is defined in RFC 5214, Intra-Site Automatic Tunnel Addressing Protocol (ISATAP).

Table 10-2 *Types of IPv6 Tunnels*

<table>
<tr><th>Tunneling Type</th><th>Tunnel Mode Command</th><th>Tunnel Source</th><th>Tunnel Destination</th><th>Interface Prefix or Address</th><th>Notes</th></tr>
<tr><td>Manual</td><td>ipv6ip</td><td rowspan="5">An IPv4 address or a reference to an interface on which IPv4 is configured. This can be the IPv4 address of the physical interface or a loopback interface.</td><td>An IPv4 address</td><td>An IPv6 address</td><td>Can carry IPv6 packets only.</td></tr>
<tr><td>GRE</td><td>gre ip</td><td>An IPv4 address</td><td>An IPv6 address</td><td rowspan="2">Can carry IPv6, Connectionless Network Service (CLNS), and many other types of packets.
Note: IPv4-compatible uses the ::/96 prefix. Cisco recommends not to use this tunnel type.</td></tr>
<tr><td>IPv4-compatible</td><td>ipv6ip auto-tunnel</td><td>Not required. These are all point-to-multipoint tunneling types.</td><td>Not required. The interface address is generated as ::tunnel-source/96.</td></tr>
<tr><td>6to4</td><td>ipv6ip 6to4</td><td>The IPv4 destination address is calculated on a per-packet basis, using the IPv6 destination address.</td><td>An IPv6 address</td><td>Site uses the addresses from the 2002::/16 prefix. Point-to-multipoint tunnels that can be used to connect isolated IPv6 sites.</td></tr>
<tr><td>ISATAP</td><td>ipv6ip isatap</td><td>—</td><td>An IPv6 prefix in modified EUI-64 format. The IPv6 address is generated from the prefix and the tunnel source IPv4 address.</td><td>Point-to-multipoint tunnels that can be used to connect systems within a site.
Allows individual dual-stack hosts within a site to communicate.
Sites can use any IPv6 unicast addresses.</td></tr>
</table>

Note This chapter focuses on three of the more common types of tunnels used for transporting IPv6 packets over IPv4: manual, 6to4, and ISATAP. If you are interested in learning about other tunneling technologies, including some that are not included in Table 10-2, two Cisco Press books are suggested: *Cisco Self-Study: Implementing Cisco IPv6 Networks*, by Regis Desmeules, and *Implementing Cisco IP Routing (ROUTE)*, by Diane Teare. Another good reference is *Implementing Tunneling for IPv6*, www.cisco.com/en/US/docs/ios/ipv6/configuration/guide/ip6-tunnel.html.

Manual Tunnels

A manual tunnel is a bidirectional, point-to-point tunnel where the IPv4 endpoint addresses are determined in the configuration. In many ways, this is the easiest tunnel to implement. The advantage to manual tunnels is that configuration is very straightforward. The disadvantage is that manual tunnels don't scale well. Manual tunnels are point-to-point tunnels. If the environment requires multiple tunnels between several routers, a separate tunnel is required between every two endpoints or routers. This results in a full mesh of endpoints. The number of tunnels required would be as follows (n = number of endpoints):

Number of tunnels = n(n – 1) / 2

Although manual tunnels might work fine for a limited number of routers and interconnected tunnels, after only a few connections, the number of tunnels could become unwieldy. Figure 10-7 shows the topology for the manual tunnel to be created between two IPv6 islands, Rick's Café network of 2001:0DB8:CAFE::/48 and Ace's Surfboards' 2001:0DB8:ACE::/48 network. Between these two isolated IPv6 networks is an IPv4-only network. Routers R1 and R2 are dual-stack routers acting as the edge or border routers to tunnel the IPv6 packets over IPv4. Again, Protocol 41 in the IPv4 header indicates that the encapsulated data portion is an IPv6 packet.

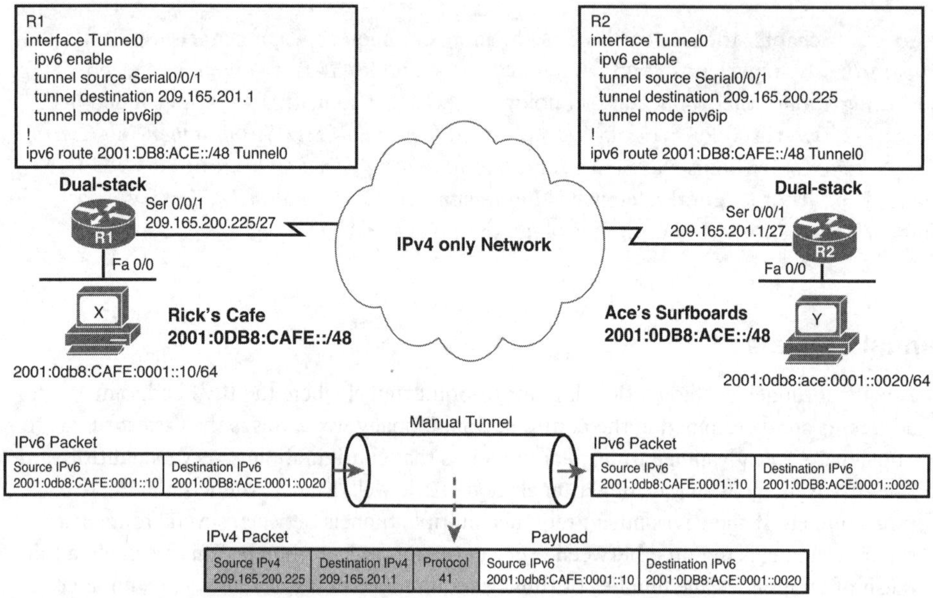

Figure 10-7 *Manual Tunnel*

Although the tunnel will be a point-to-point virtual link, the IPv4-only network between the two border routers does not have to be a point-to-point network. In other words, the IPv4 interfaces on Routers R1 and R2 do not have to be on the same subnet. Just as in any IP network, reachability between both routers is required. R1 must be able to reach the 209.165.201.0/27 network of R2's serial interface, and R2 must be able to reach the 209.165.200.224/24 network of R1's serial interface.

The commands used to configure a manual tunnel are shown in Table 10-3.

Table 10-3 *Configuration Commands for a Manual Tunnel*

Command	Description
Router(config)# **interface tunnel** *tunnel-number*	Specifies a tunnel interface and number, and enters interface configuration mode.
Router(config-if)# **ipv6-address** *ipv6-prefix/prefix-length* [**eui-64**]	Specifies the IPv6 network assigned to the interface and enables IPv6 processing on the interface. Instead of specifying an IPv6 address, the **ipv6 enable** command can be used to create a link-local address and enable IPv6 on the interface.

Command	Description
Router(config-if)# **tunnel source** {*ip-address* | *interface-type interface number*}	Specifies the source IPv4 address or the source interface type and number for the tunnel interface. The source IPv4 address must be reachable from the other side of the tunnel. If an interface is specified, the interface must be configured with an IPv4 address. The address can be a physical or loopback address, but must be reachable from the other end of the tunnel.
Router(config-if)# **tunnel destination** *ip-address*	Specifies the destination IPv4 address or host name for the tunnel interface.
Router(config-if)# **tunnel mode ipv6ip**	Specifies a manual IPv6 tunnel. **Note:** The **tunnel mode ipv6ip** command specifies IPv6 as the passenger protocol and IPv4 as both the encapsulation and transport protocol for the manual IPv6 tunnel.
Router(config)# **ipv6 route** *ipv6-prefix/ prefix-length* **tunnel** *tunnel-number*	Configures a static route for the IPv6 prefix using the tunnel number specified in the **interface tunnel** command.

In Example 10-7, notice how these configuration commands are used on R1 and R2 to create their manual tunnel.

Example 10-7 *Configuring a Manual Tunnel on R1 and R2*

```
R1(config)# interface Serial0/0/1
! The next command establishes the tunnel source for the tunnel from R1 to R2
R1(config-if)# ip address 209.165.200.225 255.255.255.224
R1(config-if)# exit

R1(config)# interface Tunnel 0
R1(config-if)# ipv6 enable
R1(config-if)# tunnel source Serial0/0/1
! The next command specifies the tunnel destination
R1(config-if)# tunnel destination 209.165.201.1
R1(config-if)# tunnel mode ipv6ip
R1(config-if)# exit

R1(config)# ipv6 route 2001:DB8:ACE::/48 Tunnel 0
_______________________________________________
R2(config)# interface Serial0/0/1
```

```
! The next command is the tunnel destination
R2(config-if)# ip address 209.165.201.1 255.255.255.224
R2(config-if)# exit

R2(config)# interface Tunnel 0
R2(config-if)# ipv6 enable
R2(config-if)# tunnel source Serial0/0/1
R2(config-if)# tunnel destination 209.165.200.225
R2(config-if)# tunnel mode ipv6ip
R2(config-if)# exit

R1(config)# ipv6 route 2001:DB8:CAFE::/48 Tunnel 0
```

Look at the configuration of R1:

```
R1(config)# interface Serial0/0/1
R1(config-if)# ip address 209.165.200.225 255.255.255.224
```

This command configures the IPv4 address for R1's serial interface.

```
R1(config)# interface Tunnel 0
```

This command specifies the tunnel interface/number and puts it into interface configuration mode.

```
R1(config-if)# ipv6 enable
```

Configuring an IPv6 address on the tunnel interface enables the interface for IPv6 processing. It is not meant for reachability. So, there are several options that can be used. Configure an address using the **ipv6 address** command, specify a loopback interface on the router that has an IPv6 address, or use the **ipv6 unnumbered** command using the IPv6 address of one of the router's physical interfaces. Again, the IPv6 address itself is not what is important. It is necessary to enable the tunnel interface for IPv6 processing.

```
R1(config-if)# tunnel source Serial0/0/1
```

The **tunnel source** command specifies the IPv4 address of the tunnel. This address must be reachable from the router at the other end of the tunnel. A specific IPv4 address can be used or an IPv4 address of a physical interface can be used, as was done by using serial 0/0/1. Regardless of how the tunnel's IPv4 address is determined, it must be reachable from the other endpoint of the tunnel. This is the IPv4 source address of the transport protocol.

```
R1(config-if)# tunnel destination 209.165.201.1
```

The **tunnel destination** command specifies the IPv4 address of the other end of the tunnel. In this case, the address must be reachable by R1. This is the IPv4 destination address of the transport protocol.

```
R1(config-if)# tunnel mode ipv6ip
```

This command specifies IPv6 as the passenger protocol (the "ipv6" part of "ipv6ip") and IPv4 ("ip" at the end of "ipv6ip") as the transport protocol for the manual IPv6 tunnel.

```
R1(config)# ipv6 route 2001:DB8:ACE::/48 Tunnel 0
```

R1's IPv6 routing process must be informed how to reach the 2001:0DB8:ACE::/48 network on R2. This is done with an IPv6 static route using the tunnel as the exit interface.

As shown in Example 10-7, the configuration of R2 is similar to that of R1. Example 10-8 verifies the configuration of R1's tunnel, including the tunnel source, tunnel destination, and type of tunnel.

Example 10-8 *Verifying Tunnel Configuration*

```
R1# show interface tunnel 0
Tunnel0 is up, line protocol is up
  Hardware is Tunnel
  MTU 1514 bytes, BW 9 Kbit, DLY 500000 usec,
     reliability 255/255, txload 1/255, rxload 1/255
  Encapsulation TUNNEL, loopback not set
  Keepalive not set
  Tunnel source 209.165.200.225 (Serial0/0/1), destination 209.165.201.1
  Tunnel protocol/transport IPv6/IP
<Rest of output omitted for brevity>
```

In Example 10-9, verify the status of Tunnel 0 using the commands **show ip interface brief** for IPv4 and **show ipv6 interface** for IPv6. Notice that the status and protocol are "up" for both protocols, but the Tunnel 0 interface only has an IPv6 address. The IPv6 address of Tunnel 0 is the link-local address FE80::D1A5:C8E1, which is automatically created when the **ipv6 enable** command was used on the tunnel interface. The actual source IPv4 address of the tunnel is the serial 0/0/1 interface of R1.

Example 10-9 *Verifying Tunnel 0 on R1*

```
R1# show ipv6 interface brief
FastEthernet0/0            [up/up]
    FE80::1
    2001:DB8:CAFE:1::1
Serial0/0/1                [up/up]
```

```
Tunnel0                    [up/up]
    FE80::D1A5:C8E1
R1#

R1# show ip interface brief
Interface                  IP-Address      OK? Method Status                Protocol
FastEthernet0/0            unassigned      YES manual up                    up
Serial0/0/1                209.165.200.225 YES manual up                    up
Tunnel0                    unassigned      YES unset  up                    up
R1#
```

Example 10-10 verifies R1's reachability to Ace's Surfboards' 2001:0DB8:ACE::/48 network by pinging the IPv6 address on R2. Use the **debug ip packet detail** command to view the IPv4 source and destination addresses of the transport protocol. Next, issue the **ping 2001:db8:ace:1::1 source fastethernet 0/0** command using R1's Fast Ethernet 0/0 interface as the source IPv6 address of the ping. The debug output confirms that the IPv4 source address is 209.165.200.225, the source address of the tunnel, and the IPv4 destination address is 209.165.201.1, the destination address of the tunnel.

Example 10-10 *Examining the Transport Protocol Header*

```
R1# debug ip packet detail
IP packet debugging is on (detailed)
R1# ping 2001:db8:ace:1::1 source fastethernet 0/0

Type escape sequence to abort.
Sending 5, 100-byte ICMP Echos to 2001:DB8:ACE:1::1, timeout is 2 seconds:
Packet sent with a source address of 2001:DB8:CAFE:1::1
!!!!!

02:08:40: IP: s=209.165.200.225 (Tunnel0), d=209.165.201.1
(Serial0/0/1), len 120, sending, proto=41
02:08:40: IP: s=209.165.201.1 (Serial0/0/1), d=209.165.200.225
(Serial0/0/1), len 120, rcvd 3, proto=41
```

By applying the same **ping** command, you can also verify the IPv6 source and destination addresses of the passenger protocol using the **debug ipv6 packet** command prior to issuing the ping, as shown in Example 10-11. The IPv6 source address is 2001:db8:cafe::1, the IPv6 address of R1's Fast Ethernet 0/0 interface specified in the **ping** command. The IPv6 destination address in the debug output matches that issued in the **ping** command, 2001:db8:ace:1::1.

Example 10-11 *Examining the Passenger Protocol Header*

```
R1# debug ipv6 packet
IPv6 unicast packet debugging is on

R1# ping 2001:db8:ace:1::1 source fastethernet 0/0

Type escape sequence to abort.
Sending 5, 100-byte ICMP Echos to 2001:DB8:ACE:1::1, timeout is 2 seconds:
Packet sent with a source address of 2001:DB8:CAFE:1::1
!!!!!
Success rate is 100 percent (5/5), round-trip min/avg/max = 64/67/68 ms
R1#

02:24:13: IPv6: SAS picked source 2001:DB8:CAFE:1::1 for 2001:DB8:ACE:1::1
(FastEthernet0/0)
02:24:13: IPV6: source 2001:DB8:CAFE:1::1 (local)
02:24:13:       dest 2001:DB8:ACE:1::1 (Tunnel0)
02:24:13:       traffic class 0, flow 0x0, len 100+0, prot 58, hops
64, originating
```

The process of configuring a tunnel and verifying its operation has been addressed. You might be wondering how the actual routing occurs. After all, you are routing an IPv6 packet over an IPv4 network. When the **ping** command was issued, as shown in Example 10-11, an IPv6 packet was created with the

- IPv6 source address: 2001:db8:cafe::1
- IPv6 destination address: 2001:db8:ace:1::1

Example 10-12 illustrates R1's routing process to forward the IPv6 packet over the tunnel, and is further described in the list that follows. The commented numbers to the right coincide with the descriptions that follow.

Example 10-12 *Routing Process*

```
R1# show ipv6 route
<Rest of output omitted for brevity>

S   2001:DB8:ACE::/48 [1/0]    ! (1)
     via ::, Tunnel0

R1# show ip route
<Rest of output omitted for brevity>

     209.165.200.0/27 is subnetted, 1 subnets
```

```
C        209.165.200.224 is directly connected, Serial0/0/1    ! (3)
     209.165.201.0/27 is subnetted, 1 subnets
S        209.165.201.0 is directly connected, Serial0/0/1   ! (4)
R1#


R1(config)# interface Tunnel 0
R1(config-if)# ipv6 enable
R1(config-if)# tunnel source Serial0/0/1  ! (3)
R1(config-if)# tunnel destination 209.165.201.1  ! (4)
R1(config-if)# tunnel mode ipv6ip          ! (2)
```

Passenger protocol:

1. R1's IPv6 routing table is searched to find the best match for the packet's IPv6 destination address of 2001:db8:ace:1::1. Using the entry created by the static route, the exit interface is determined to be Tunnel 0.

2. The tunneling mode of Tunnel 0 indicates that this IPv6 packet will be encapsulated in an IPv4 packet. The manual tunnel mode means that the IPv4 source and destination addresses (transport protocol) are specified within the tunnel interface commands.

Transport protocol:

3. The **tunnel source** command points to the IPv4 address of the serial 0/0/1 interface of 209.165.200.225. This will be IPv4 source address used by the IPv4 transport protocol. The source address must be in the "up" state and therefore must be in R1's routing table.

4. The **tunnel destination** command gives the IPv4 address of the other end of the tunnel 209.165.201.1, the IPv4 destination address of the transport protocol. This address must be reachable by R1; in other words, it can be located in its routing table. The tunnel destination address of 209.165.201.1 matches a static route in the IPv4 routing table with serial 0/0/1 as the exit interface.

The IPv4 packet with its IPv6 payload is now forwarded out the serial 0/0/1 interface. When R2 receives the packet, it decapsulates the IPv6 packet and uses its IPv6 routing table to forward the packet to its destination.

6to4 Tunnels

Manual tunnels are easy to configure, but as mentioned, they do not scale well when a large number of tunnels is necessary. A separate manual tunnel must be configured for every pair of routers. Any time another router is added to the mix, a new tunnel must be configured on all the existing routers. This is similar to the disadvantage of using only static routes for network reachability. For some organizations, managing a few statically configured manual tunnels is acceptable, while others might want a more scalable solution.

IETF has defined a mechanism called 6to4 to automatically connect to multiple IPv6 networks over one configured tunnel. 6to4 tunnels are defined in RFC 3056, Connection of IPv6 Domains via IPv4 Clouds. A 6to4 tunnel is a point-to-multipoint connection. A single 6to4 tunnel can be used to connect to any number of IPv6 networks—in other words, having any number of tunnel destinations, as shown in Figure 10-8. Router R1 can be configured with a single 6to4 tunnel capable of reaching the IPv6 networks through Routers R2 through R6.

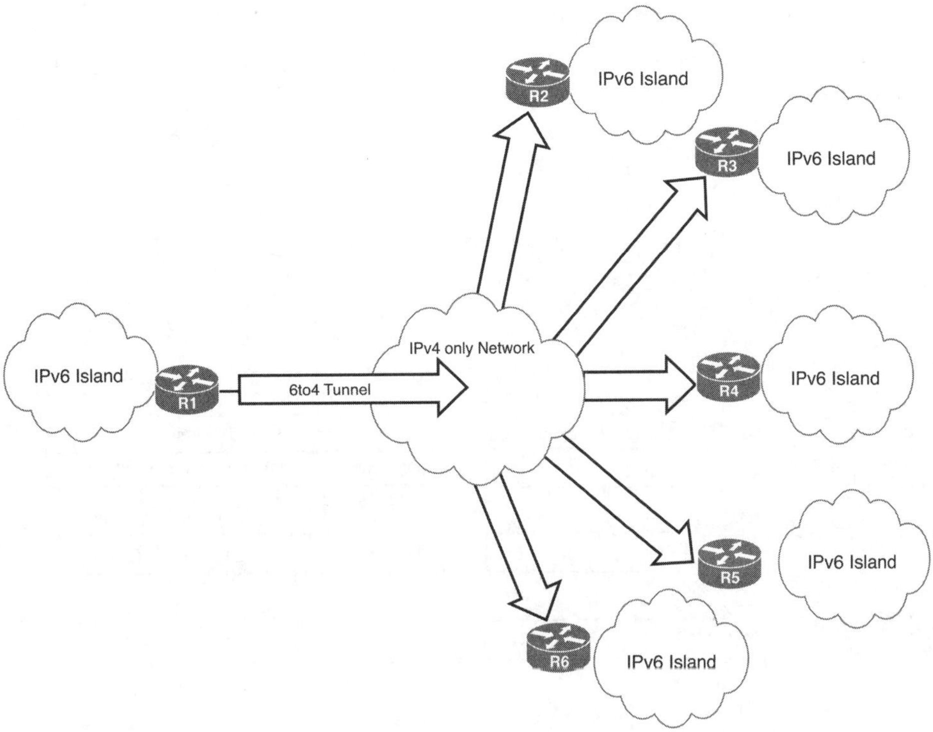

Figure 10-8 *6to4 Tunnels*

The difference between 6to4 tunnels (also known as automatic 6to4 tunnels) and manual tunnels is that manual tunnels must statically configure the other end of the tunnel, the tunnel IPv4 destination address. With a 6to4 tunnel, the tunnel IPv4 destination address is automatically derived from the IPv6 destination of the packet. This means that there must be some sort of correlation between the two addresses. The IPv6 network address is based on a reachable IPv4 address plus a special prefix reserved for this purpose as defined in RFC 3056. The Internet Assigned Numbers Authority (IANA) has permanently assigned the 2002::/16 prefix to be used for IPv6 networks automatically accessible using a 6to4 tunnel.

Note A limitation of 6to4 tunneling is the inability to send traffic outside your domain. Both routers at the end of the tunnel must be configured as a 6to4 tunneling router; otherwise, your traffic is black holed. Also, 6to4 tunneling only supports static routes; there is no dynamic routing support.

Using the 32 bits of the IPv4 address results in an IPv6 address of 2002:*ipv4-address*::/48. Let's see how this is done.

Figure 10-9 illustrates the process of reverse-engineering the IPv6 address from an IPv4 address illustrated in three simple steps that follow.

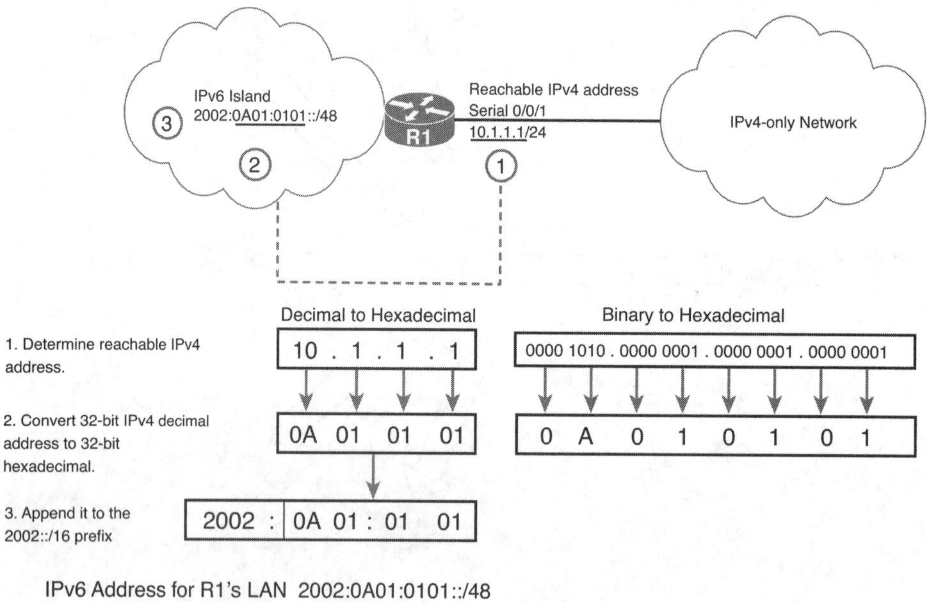

Figure 10-9 *6to4 Reverse Engineering of IPv4 Address to Form IPv6 Address*

Step 1. Determine the IPv4-reachable address you want to use for the IPv6 address. This example uses the reachable 10.1.1.1/24 IPv4 address, R1's serial 0/0/1 interface. This is a routable address that can be reached by other routers at the other end of the tunnel.

Note This address was chosen to make the conversion easier to see, but if this were an Internet-facing router, the address would have to be a public IPv4 address instead of the RFC 1918 address used in this example.

Note The IPv4 address can be any routable address reachable by the other routers at the other end of the tunnel. Later in this chapter, an example of using a loopback address instead of the address of the physical interface is examined.

Step 2. Convert the 32-bit IPv4 address 10.1.1.1 expressed in decimal to hexadecimal. This results in the 32-bit hexadecimal value 0A01:0101.

Step 3. Append the 32-bit hexadecimal value 0A01:0101 to the IANA-reserved 6to4 prefix 2002::/16, making the IPv6 prefix or network address 2002:0A01:0101::/48. The hosts on R1's IPv6 network will have an IPv6 address using this prefix. The prefix can be subnetted and routed within R1's IPv6 domain.

Extend this method to other routers in the previous diagram. Figure 10-10 shows the IPv6 addresses for each of the networks determined (reverse engineered) using the routable IPv4 address of their provider-facing interface. Although 10.0.0.0/8 addresses are not public addresses, they are used in this example to illustrate the conversion of an IPv4 address in decimal notation to the 32-bit hexadecimal notation used in the IPv6 address. Looking at Figure 10-10, notice that all the IPv6 addresses have the 2002::/16 prefix followed by the converted 32-bit IPv4 address of their routable interface.

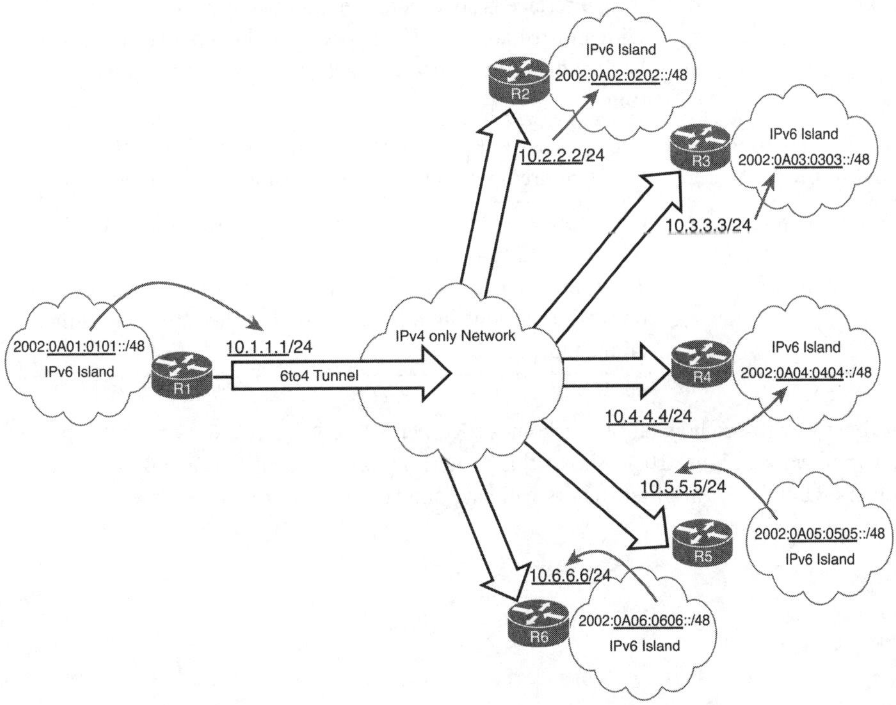

Figure 10-10 *Examples of 6to4 Reverse Engineering of IPv4 Address to Form IPv6 Address*

The commands used to configure a 6to4 tunnel are shown in Table 10-4. Note that these are very similar to the commands used to configure a manual tunnel. Example 10-13 highlights the differences and the operation of the 6to4 tunnel.

Table 10-4 Configuration Commands for a 6to4 Tunnel

Command	Description
Router(config)# **interface tunnel** *tunnel-number*	Specifies a tunnel interface and number, and enters interface configuration mode.
Router(config-if)# **ipv6-address** *ipv6-prefix/prefix-length* [**eui-64**]	Specifies the IPv6 network assigned to the interface and enables IPv6 processing on the interface. Instead of specifying an IPv6 address, the **ipv6 enable** command can be used to create a link-local address and enable IPv6 on the interface. If an IPv6 address is specified, the 32 bits following the initial 2002::/16 prefix must correspond to an IPv4 address assigned to the tunnel source.
Router(config-if)# **tunnel source** {*ip-address* | *interface-type interface number*}	Specifies the source IPv4 address or the source interface type and number for the tunnel interface. The source IPv4 address must be reachable from the other side of the tunnel. If an interface is specified, the interface must be configured with an IPv4 address. The address can be a physical or loopback address, but must be reachable from the other end of the tunnel.
Router(config-if)# **tunnel mode ipv6ip 6to4**	Specifies an IPv6 tunnel using a 6to4 address. The IPv4 destination address will be determined using the 6to4 technique.
Router(config)# **ipv6 route** *ipv6-prefix/prefix-length* **tunnel** *tunnel-number*	Configures a static route for the IPv6 6to4 prefix 2002::/16 to the specified tunnel interface. The tunnel number specified in the **ipv6 route** command must be the same tunnel number specified in the **interface tunnel** command.

The best way to see how all of this comes together is to configure a 6to4 tunnel and see how it all works. Figure 10-11 shows this scenario. Begin by configuring a 6to4 tunnel on Routers R1 and R2. All other routers will have similar configurations.

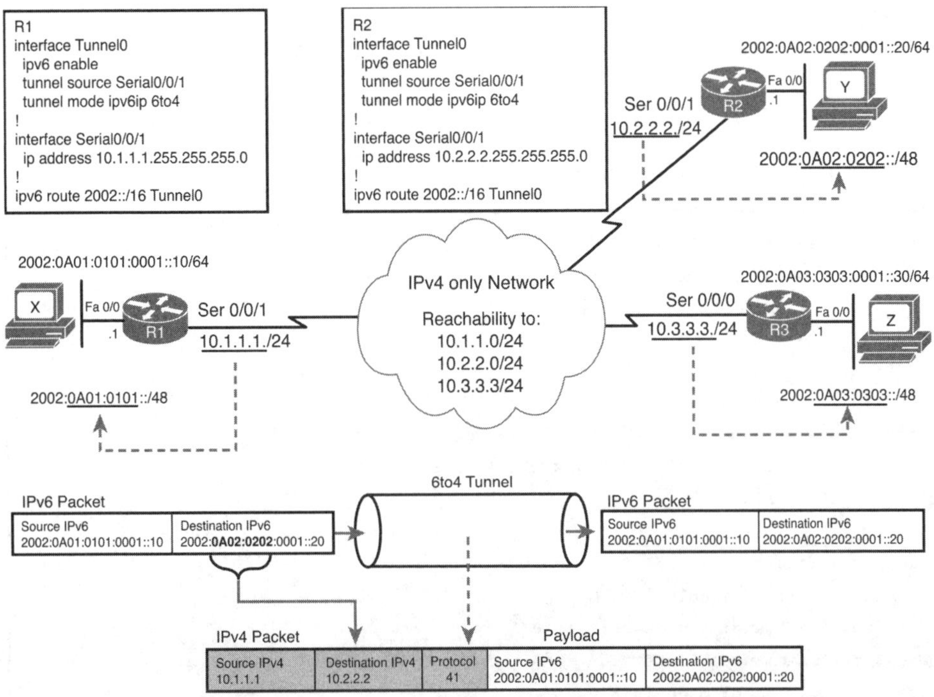

Figure 10-11 *6to4 Tunnel Using Serial Interfaces*

Example 10-13 shows the configurations for Routers R1 and R2. Most of this is similar to the configuration of the manual tunnel shown earlier. Notice that the IPv6 addresses on the Fast Ethernet 0/0 interfaces of R1 and R2 are their serial IPv4 addresses appended with the 2002::/16 prefix. Remember, the goal is the same as with a manual tunnel. As illustrated in Figure 10-5 you are encapsulating an IPv6 packet (passenger protocol) inside an IPv4 packet (transport protocol). This allows IPv6 packets to be sent between isolated IPv6 networks over an IPv4 network.

Example 10-13 *Configuring a 6to4 Tunnel on R1 and R2*

```
R1(config)# interface Serial0/0/1
! IPv4 address matches 32 bits of FastEthernet0/0 IPv6 address
R1(config-if)# ip address 10.1.1.1 255.255.255.0
R1(config-if)# exit

R1(config)# interface FastEthernet0/0
! 32 bits of IPv6 address matches Serial0/0/1 IPv4 address
R1(config-if)# ipv6 address 2002:A01:101:1::1/64
R1(config-if)# exit

R1(config)# interface Tunnel 0
R1(config-if)# ipv6 enable
```

```
R1(config-if)# tunnel source Serial0/0/1
! Use 6to4 technique to determine tunnel destination IPv4 address
R1(config-if)# tunnel mode ipv6ip 6to4
R1(config-if)# exit

R1(config)# ipv6 route 2002::/16 Tunnel 0
```

```
R2(config)# interface Serial0/0/1
! IPv4 address matches 32 bits of FastEthernet0/0 IPv6 address
R2(config-if)# ip address 10.2.2.2 255.255.255.0
R2(config-if)# exit

R2(config)# interface FastEthernet0/0
! 32 bits of IPv6 address matches Serial0/0/1 IPv4 address
R2(config-if)# ipv6 address 2002:A02:202:1::1/64
R2(config-if)# exit

R2(config)# interface Tunnel 0
R2(config-if)# ipv6 enable
R2(config-if)# tunnel source Serial0/0/1
! Use 6to4 technique to determine tunnel destination IPv4 address
R2(config-if)# tunnel mode ipv6ip 6to4
R2(config-if)# exit

R2(config)# ipv6 route 2002::/16 Tunnel 0
```

Continuing with the configuration in Example 10-13, notice that the tunnel interface commands are similar to what was used for the manual tunnel. However, there are two exceptions: the **tunnel mode ipv6ip 6to4** command and the lack of a **tunnel destination** command. The **tunnel mode ipv6ip 6to4** command tells the router to use the IPv6 destination address (passenger protocol) to determine the tunnel destination IPv4 address (transport protocol). Because the tunnel destination addresses are automatically ascertained from the IPv6 packet, there is no need for a **tunnel destination** command and a predetermined destination address. This is where the magic happens! Because the tunnel destination is automatically determined based on the destination of the IPv6 packet, any IPv6 network is now reachable as long as it adheres to the 2002:*ipv4-address*::/48 format.

The last part is the static route, **ipv6 route 2002::/16 Tunnel 0**. Any IPv6 packet with the 2002::/16 prefix is delivered to the Tunnel 0 interface for forwarding. As mentioned, the **tunnel mode ipv6ip 6to4** command determines the actual IPv4 destination address to be used when encapsulating the IPv6 packet into IPv4.

Example 10-14 shows successful pings from R1 to the IPv6 networks of R2 and R3.

Example 10-14 *Verifying Connectivity Using the ping Command*

```
R1# ping 2002:0a02:0202:1::1 source fastethernet 0/0

Type escape sequence to abort.
Sending 5, 100-byte ICMP Echos to 2002:A02:202:1::1, timeout is 2 seconds:
Packet sent with a source address of 2002:A01:101:1::1
!!!!!
Success rate is 100 percent (5/5), round-trip min/avg/max = 64/72/92 ms

R1# ping 2002:0a03:0303:1::1 source fastethernet 0/0

Type escape sequence to abort.
Sending 5, 100-byte ICMP Echos to 2002:A03:303:1::1, timeout is 2 seconds:
Packet sent with a source address of 2002:A01:101:1::1
!!!!!
Success rate is 100 percent (5/5), round-trip min/avg/max = 64/66/68 ms
R1#
```

Using the first **ping** command, notice how R1 determines the IPv4 destination address of the other end of the tunnel. The command issued on R1 is

```
R1# ping 2002:0a02:0202:1::1 source fastethernet 0/0
```

The best match in the IPv6 routing table for the destination address 2002:0a02:0202:1::1 is the entry from the configured static route:

```
R1(config)# ipv6 route 2002::/16 Tunnel 0
```

The resulting exit interface is Tunnel 0. Looking at R1's configuration in Example 10-13, notice how this tunnel is used to forward the IPv6 packet. An IPv6 packet, the passenger protocol, is encapsulated inside an IPv4 packet, the transport protocol. Similar to a manual tunnel, the **tunnel source** is defined—in this case, the IPv4 address of serial 0/0/1, 10.1.1.1.

Unlike manual tunnels, the **tunnel destination** is not defined. The **tunnel mode ipv6ip 6to4** command directs the router to use the IPv6 packet's destination address to determine the IPv4 address of the other end of the tunnel. The 32 bits following the 2002::/16 prefix, 0a02:0202, are used as the destination IPv4 address for the transport protocol, 10.2.2.2. This is illustrated at the bottom of Figure 10-11.

So, as long as the IPv6 addresses adhere to the 2002:*ipv4-address*::/48 format, any of our IPv6 islands are reachable using a single 6to4 tunnel.

6to4 Tunnels and Loopback Interfaces

An alternative to using the IPv4 address of a physical interface is to use a loopback address. A loopback address provides several advantages, including the fact that it never goes down as long as the router is still up. Just like the IPv4 address of a physical interface, the IPv4 address of a loopback interface must be reachable by the router at the other end of the tunnel. Figure 10-12 shows the same topology used previously; however, loopback interfaces are used instead of the physical provider-facing interfaces to determine the IPv6 address of the network. The loopback address is used as the **tunnel source** IPv4 address. Example 10-15 shows the configuration for R1 and R2 using loopback interfaces for the **tunnel source**.

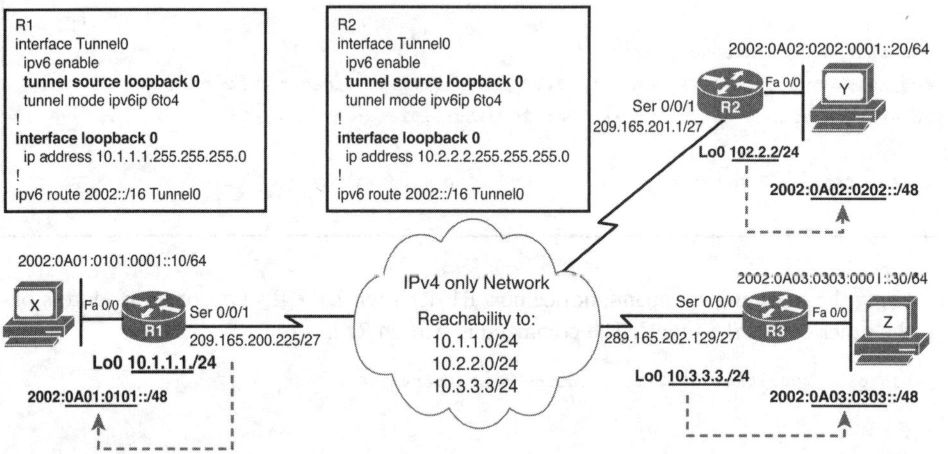

Figure 10-12 *6to4 Tunnel Using Loopback Interfaces*

Example 10-15 *Configuring a 6to4 Tunnel on R1 and R2 Using Loopback Interfaces*

```
R1(config)# interface Serial0/0/1
R1(config-if)# ip address 209.165.200.225 255.255.255.224
R1(config-if)# exit
R1(config)# interface loopback0
R1(config-if)# ip address 10.1.1.1 255.255.255.0
R1(config)# interface FastEthernet0/0
R1(config-if)# ipv6 address 2002:A01:101:1::1/64
R1(config-if)# exit

R1(config)# interface Tunnel 0
R1(config-if)# ipv6 enable
R1(config-if)# tunnel source loopback0
R1(config-if)# tunnel mode ipv6ip 6to4
R1(config-if)# exit

R1(config)# ipv6 route 2002::/16 Tunnel 0
```

```
R2(config)# interface Serial0/0/1
R2(config-if)# ip address 209.165.201.1 255.255.255.224
R2(config-if)# exit
R2(config)# interface loopback0
R2(config-if)# ip address 10.2.2.2 255.255.255.0
R2(config)# interface FastEthernet0/0
R2(config-if)# ipv6 address 2002:A02:202:1::1/64
R2(config-if)# exit

R2(config)# interface Tunnel 0
R2(config-if)# ipv6 enable
R2(config-if)# tunnel source loopback0
R2(config-if)# tunnel mode ipv6ip 6to4
R2(config-if)# exit

R2(config)# ipv6 route 2002::/16 Tunnel 0
```

ISATAP

ISATAP (Intra-Site Automatic Tunnel Addressing Protocol) tunnels are designed for transporting IPv6 packets within a site where a native IPv6 infrastructure is not yet available. Although the ISATAP tunneling mechanism is similar to other automatic tunneling mechanisms, such as IPv6 6to4, ISATAP is designed for transporting IPv6 packets within a site, but not between sites. ISATAP uses a well-defined IPv6 address format composed of any /64 unicast IPv6 prefix and a 64-bit Interface ID that includes the last 32 bits of the IPv6 address.

Like other tunneling methods, an ISATAP tunnel can exist between any two dual-stack devices: host-to-router, router-to-host, or host-to-host. However, the main feature of ISATAP tunnels is to provide dual-stack hosts with access to the IPv6 network over an IPv4-only network. ISATAP is an IPv6 transition technology that allows hosts on an IPv4 network to communicate with hosts on an IPv6-only network and will be the focus in this chapter.

Note ISATAP is considered a quick and temporary solution to give access to IPv6 resources. Imagine if there were ten developers in a building that needed access to IPv6 resources. Instead of enabling IPv6 everywhere, you could use ISATAP as a temporary solution to give IPv6 access only to those ten developers.

ISATAP is defined in RFC 5214, Intra-Site Automatic Tunnel Addressing Protocol (ISATAP). The topology in Figure 10-13 illustrates a dual-stack host connected to a dual-stack ISATAP router. In Figure 10-13, a lot of information is provided to give you a view of ISATAP at a glance.

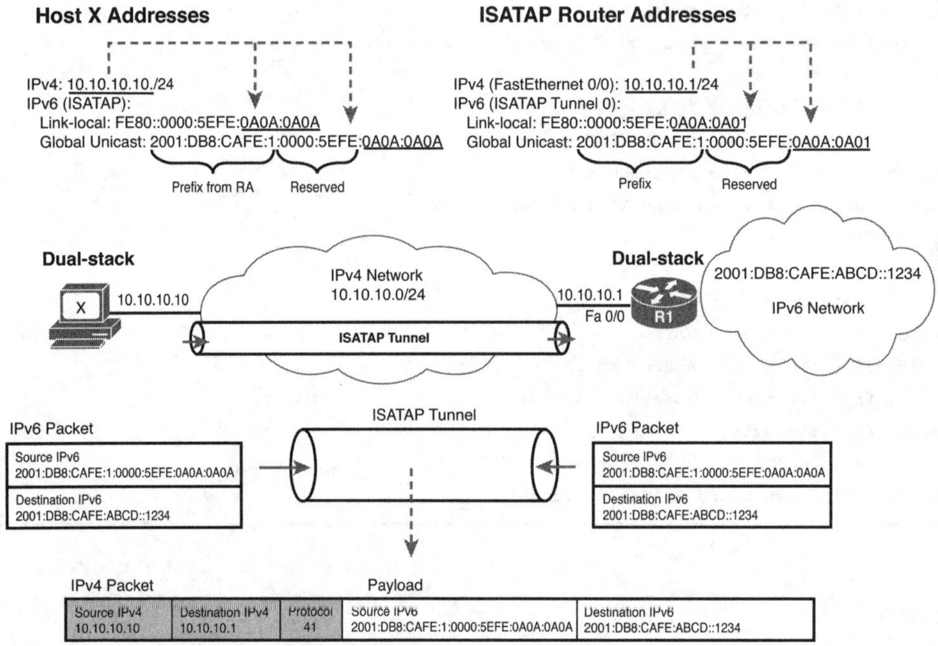

Figure 10-13 *ISATAP Tunnel*

Router R1 is an ISATAP router, and at the other end of the tunnel is a dual-stack device, host X. The ISATAP router provides host X with IPv6 access over the IPv4 network using an ISATAP tunnel. R1, the ISATAP router, provides network configuration support to hosts over the ISATAP tunnel using Router Advertisements. This is the same Stateless Address Autoconfiguration process that takes place when a host and router are connected by a native IPv6 network. Let's look more closely at the ISATAP address format, which is shown in Figure 10-14.

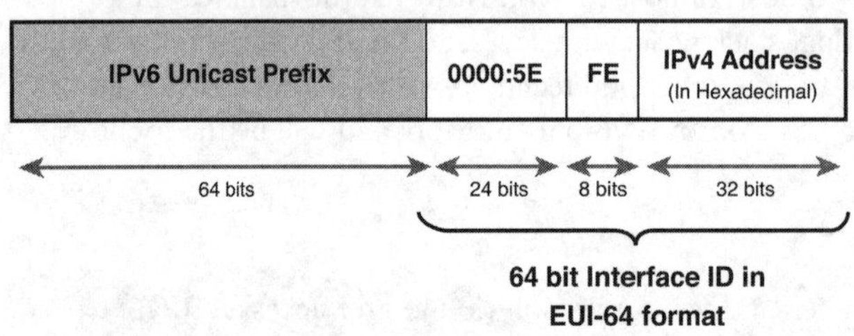

Figure 10-14 *ISATAP Address Format*

The ISATAP address includes the following:

- **Prefix: IPv6 unicast prefix (64 bits):** This can be any valid unicast prefix, including a global routable prefix, a unique-local prefix, a link-local prefix, and even a 6to4 prefix. The prefix should be selected as part of the address plan for the network.

- **Interface ID (EUI-64 format):**
  - **00-00-5E (24 bits):** This is an Ethernet OUI (Organizationally Unique Identifier) reserved by IANA. This OUI is used by several protocols including ISATAP. This OUI is used for dynamic mapping between IP addresses and IEEE 802 MAC addresses.
  - **FE (8 bits):** This indicates that this address contains an embedded IPv4 address.
  - **IPv4 address (32 bits):** The last 4 bytes contain the IPv4 address in hexadecimal.

Note The EUI-64 format used by ISATAP is different than the one discussed in Chapter 4, "IPv6 Address Types," which embeds FFFE in the middle of the Ethernet MAC address and flips the U/L bit to form the 64-bit Interface ID. In RFC 5342, IANA & IETF Use of IEEE 802 Parameters, IETF defines the EUI-64 format as any address constructed from an OUI owned by the IANA.

Table 10-5 shows the commands for configuring an ISATAP tunnel interface on a router.

Table 10-5 *Configuration Commands for an ISATAP Tunnel*

Command	Description
Router(config)# **interface tunnel** *tunnel-number*	Specifies a tunnel interface and number, and enters interface configuration mode.
Router(config-if)# **ipv6-address** *ipv6-prefix/prefix-length* [**eui-64**]	Specifies the IPv6 network assigned to the interface and enables IPv6 processing on the interface. Any IPv6 address will do. Using the **eui-64** option will create an IPv6 address using the ISATAP EUI-64 format.
Router(config-if)# **no ipv6 nd suppress-ra**	The sending of IPv6 Router Advertisements is disabled by default on tunnel interfaces. This command reenables the sending of IPv6 Router Advertisements to allow client autoconfiguration. This command can also be entered as **no ipv6 nd ra suppress.**

Command	Description
Router(config-if)# **tunnel source** {*ip-address* | *interface-type interface number*}	Specifies the source IPv4 address or the source interface type and number for the tunnel interface. The source IPv4 address must be reachable from the other side of the tunnel. If an interface is specified, the interface must be configured with an IPv4 address. The address can be a physical or loopback address, but must be reachable from the other end of the tunnel.
Router(config-if)# **tunnel mode ipv6ip isatap**	Specifies an IPv6 tunnel using an ISATAP address.

Using the topology shown in Figure 10-13, Example 10-16 shows the commands used to configure Router R1 as an ISATAP router.

Example 10-16 *ISATAP Router Configuration for R1*

```
R1(config)# interface fastethernet 0/0
R1(config-if)# ip address 10.10.10.1 255.255.255.0
R1(config-if)# exit

R1(config)# interface tunnel 0
R1(config-if)# ipv6 address 2001:db8:cafe:1::/64 eui-64
R1(config-if)# no ipv6 nd suppress-ra
R1(config-if)# tunnel source fastethernet 0/0
R1(config-if)# tunnel mode ipv6ip isatap
R1(config-if)# exit

R1(config)# interface loopback 1
R1(config-if)# ipv6 address 2001:db8:cafe:abcd::1234/64
R1(config-if)#
```

Following the configuration in Example 10-16:

```
R1(config)# interface fastethernet 0/0
R1(config-if)# ip address 10.10.10.1 255.255.255.0
```

This is the IPv4 address that the host X and other clients on the 10.10.10.0/24 LAN use as their default gateway address, usually from a DHCP server.

```
R1(config)# interface tunnel 0
```

This is the tunnel interface used to forward IPv6 packets over IPv4.

```
R1(config-if)# ipv6 address 2001:db8:cafe:1::/64 eui-64
```

This command enables IPv6 processing on the interface and also assigns an IPv6 address to the tunnel. Any IPv6 address will work. In this case, the **eui-64** option is used, which creates an IPv6 address using the ISATAP format.

```
R1(config-if)# no ipv6 nd suppress-ra
```

By default, Cisco IOS disables ICMPv6 Router Advertisement messages on tunnel interfaces. This command enables RA messages to be sent across the tunnel. These RA messages allow hosts to autoconfigure their IPv6 addresses and receive an IPv6 default gateway address.

```
R1(config-if)# tunnel source fastethernet 0/0
```

This command specifies Fast Ethernet 0/0 as the source interface for the tunnel. This interface must have an IPv4 address assigned. You previously configured R1's Fast Ethernet 0/0 interface as 10.10.10.1/24.

```
R1(config-if)# tunnel mode ipv6ip isatap
```

With this command, R1's Tunnel 0 is defined as an ISATAP tunnel. This allows transporting IPv6 packets over IPv4 and uses the ISATAP address format for the tunnel's IPv6 address.

```
R1(config)# interface loopback 1
R1(config-if)# ipv6 address 2001:db8:cafe:abcd::1234/64
```

This command creates a virtual address on R1 to demonstrate how the host reaches a remote IPv6 network. This command is not specific to the configuration of ISATAP.

Example 10-17 shows several commands used to verify R1's address configuration. The **show ip interface brief** command displays the statically configured IPv4 address of Fast Ethernet 0/0 as 10.10.10.1.

Example 10-17 *Verifying R1's Addresses*

```
R1# show ip interface brief
Interface                  IP-Address      OK? Method Status                Protocol
FastEthernet0/0            10.10.10.1      YES manual up                    up
Tunnel0                    unassigned      YES unset  up                    up
R1# show ipv6 interface brief
FastEthernet0/0            [up/up]
```

```
Tunnel0                    [up/up]
    FE80::5EFE:A0A:A01
    2001:DB8:CAFE:1:0:5EFE:A0A:A01
R1#

R1# show ipv6 interface tunnel 0
Tunnel0 is up, line protocol is up
  IPv6 is enabled, link-local address is FE80::5EFE:A0A:A01
  No Virtual link-local address(es):
  Global unicast address(es):
    2001:DB8:CAFE:1:0:5EFE:A0A:A01, subnet is 2001:DB8:CAFE:1::/64 [EUI]
  Joined group address(es):
    FF02::1
    FF02::2
    FF02::1:FF0A:A01
  MTU is 1480 bytes
  ICMP error messages limited to one every 100 milliseconds
  ICMP redirects are enabled
  ICMP unreachables are sent
  ND DAD is not supported
  ND reachable time is 30000 milliseconds
  ND advertised reachable time is 0 milliseconds
  ND advertised retransmit interval is 0 milliseconds
  ND router advertisements live for 1800 seconds
  ND advertised default router preference is Medium
  Hosts use stateless autoconfig for addresses.
R1#
```

The **show ipv6 interface brief** command in Example 10-17 shows the IPv6 addresses of R1's Tunnel 0 interface. The IPv6 address uses the ISATAP format. In Example 10-16, you configured the global unicast address of Tunnel 0 using the **ipv6 address 2001:db8:cafe:1::/64 eui-64** command. This command specifies the prefix as 2001:db8:cafe:1. The **eui-64** option uses ISATAP's EUI-64 format to determine the 64-bit Interface ID. The first 32 bits are the ISATAP-reserved OUI plus FE, 0000:5EFE. The low-order 32 bits are the IPv4 address converted to hexadecimal, 0A0A:0A01.

The same process occurred for the link-local address for Tunnel 0. The link-local address uses the reserved prefix FE80::/10 plus the same ISATAP EUI-64 Interface ID created for the global unicast address, 0000:5EFE: 0A0A:0A01. The global unicast and link-local address for Tunnel 0 are also displayed by the **show ipv6 interface tunnel 0** command in Example 10-17.

Using the **show interface tunnel 0** command in Example 10-18, verify that the tunneling type for the Tunnel 0 interface is ISATAP.

Example 10-18 *Verifying R1's Tunnel Protocol*

```
R1# show interface tunnel 0
Tunnel0 is up, line protocol is up
  Hardware is Tunnel
  MTU 1514 bytes, BW 9 Kbit, DLY 500000 usec,
     reliability 255/255, txload 1/255, rxload 1/255
  Encapsulation TUNNEL, loopback not set
  Keepalive not set
  Tunnel source 10.10.10.1 (FastEthernet0/0), destination UNKNOWN
  Tunnel protocol/transport IPv6 ISATAP
<Rest of output omitted for brevity>
```

Now that R1's configuration has been examined, see how host X uses the ISATAP tunnel to receive its IPv6 configuration information. Similar to 6to4 tunneling, ISATAP automatically creates its IPv6 address from an IPv4 address but, in addition, uses the services of Router Advertisements for Stateless Address Autoconfiguration.

Using Figure 10-15, you can see the process of how host X gets its IPv6 global unicast address, prefix length, and IPv6 default gateway address.

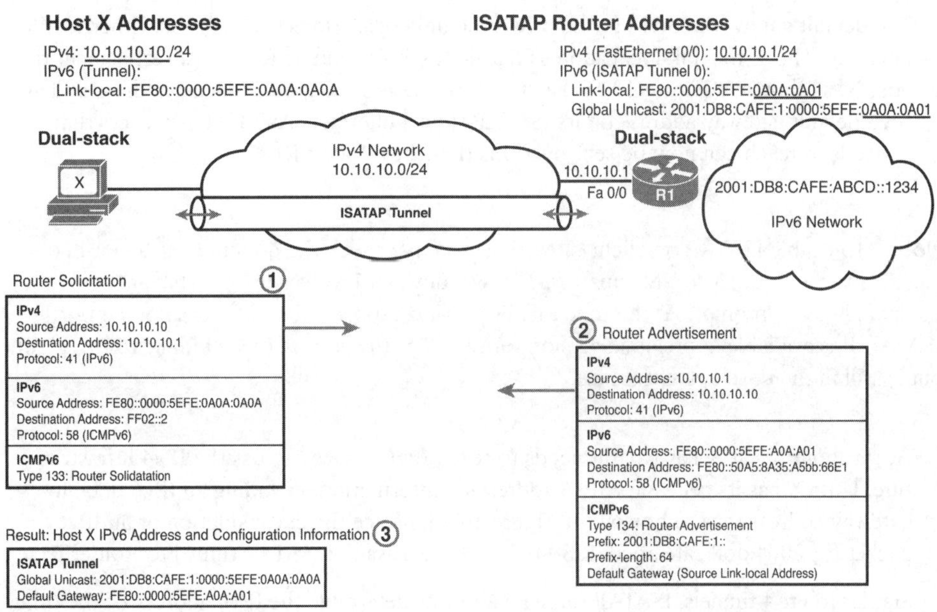

Figure 10-15 *Router Solicitations and Router Advertisements over ISATAP*

Host X has been configured, either statically or dynamically, with an IPv4 address of 10.10.10.10/24 and enabled for ISATAP. ISATAP is supported in most common operating systems including Windows XP, Windows Vista, Windows 7, and Linux. Part of host X's ISATAP tunnel configuration contains the IPv4 address of the other end of the tunnel. In this case, it is 10.10.10.1, the IPv4 address of Router R1. Host X's interface automatically creates itself an IPv6 link-local address using the ISATAP format, as shown in the following steps:

Step 1. Using this link-local address, host X sends a Router Solicitation message over the ISATAP tunnel to the all-routers multicast address FF02::2. The RS message is encapsulated in an IPv4 packet and sent over the ISATAP tunnel to Router R1.

Step 2. R1 responds with a Router Advertisement message including the IPv6 prefix, prefix length, and default gateway address. The ICMPv6 Router Advertisement is encapsulated in an IPv4 packet before being sent over the tunnel to host X.

Step 3. Host X now has what it needs to create a routable IPv6 address and to communicate with an IPv6 default gateway. The Router Advertisement from R1 includes the prefix and prefix length 2001:DB8:CAFE:1::/64. Using the ISATAP format, host X creates its 64-bit Interface ID by appending the prefix with 0000:5EFE and its IPv4 address in hexadecimal, 0A0A:0A0A. As a result, host X's global unicast address is 2001:DB8:CAFE:1:0000:5EFE:0A0A:0A 0A/64.

The default gateway address for host X is the link-local address of R1's Fast Ethernet 0/0 interface. This is the link-local address that R1 used to send its Router Advertisement to host X, as shown in Figure 10-15. Host X now has an IPv6 global unicast address and an IPv6 default gateway address on its ISATAP tunnel interface. Any IPv6 networks that host X needs to reach can now be sent over this tunnel to Router R1.

Note To enable ISATAP on client operating systems, check the documentation or, better yet, search the Internet for information. For Windows, it involves using **netsh** at the command (DOS) prompt. At the time of this writing, Apple's Mac OS does not support ISATAP. It is available in prealpha version for Mac OS 10.6.4 or later, including 10.7.x (Lion), but is still in the development stages.

At this point, host X has what it needs to reach IPv6 devices across the IPv4 infrastructure. Host X has its necessary IPv6 addressing information, including an IPv6 default gateway address. At the bottom of Figure 10-13, notice the encapsulation of an IPv6 packet for 2001:db8:cafe:abcd::1234 being sent across the ISATAP tunnel to Router R1.

Similar to 6to4 tunnels, ISATAP tunnel endpoints determine the IPv4 address of the other end of the tunnel, the destination IPv6 address of the packet. The IPv4 address is encoded in the last 32 bits of the IPv6 address, enabling automatic IPv6-in-IPv4 tunneling. The low-order 32 bits in the IPv6 address contain the necessary IPv4 addressing information; otherwise, the default gateway is used. The bottom part of Figure 10-13 shows the encapsulation for a packet from host X to 2001:DB8:CAFE:ABCD::1234.

Other Tunneling Technologies

This chapter focused on three tunneling types used to carry IPv6 packets over IPv4:

- Manual
- 6to4
- ISATAP

Table 10-2 gives an overview of several overlay tunneling methods, including the ones that were discussed. It is very easy to get lost in all the different types of tunneling and translation techniques. Having a good understanding of the tunnels covered in this chapter will prepare you for additional tunnels that might be needed in your environment, such as GRE, 6RD, and Teredo:

- **GRE (Generic Routing Encapsulation):** Similar to a manual tunnel, a GRE tunnel is a point-to-point tunnel for secure communication between two endpoints but can carry protocols other than IP. GRE tunnels allow other protocols besides IP to be the passenger protocol, such as IS-IS (Intermediate System–to–Intermediate System). The configuration of GRE tunnels is similar to configuring manual tunnels. GRE is defined in RFC 2784, Generic Routing Encapsulation (GRE). GRE adds an additional header in the tunneling process and is the default tunneling type for the Cisco IOS **tunnel mode** command.

  The Protocol field of the IPv4 header is 47, indicating that the data portion is a GRE packet.

- **IPv6 Rapid Deployment (6RD) Tunnels:** An IPv6 Rapid Deployment (6RD) tunnel is an extension of the 6to4 feature. The 6RD feature allows an ISP or service provider to offer IPv6 service to customers over its IPv4 network. The main differences between 6RD and 6to4 tunneling are as follows:

  - 6RD does not require addresses to have a 2002::/16 prefix; therefore, the prefix can be from the service provider's own address block.
  - Not all 32 bits of the IPv4 destination address need to be carried in the IPv6 payload header. The IPv4 destination address is obtained from a combination of bits in the payload header and information configured in the router.

  6RD is defined in RFC 5569, IPv6 Rapid Deployment on IPv4 Infrastructures (6rd).

- **Teredo (RFC 4380):** Teredo, also known as shipworm, allows two dual-stack devices to send IPv6 packets when one is located behind an IPv4 NAT. Teredo uses UDP port 3544 to communicate with Teredo servers, which are used as dispatchers between Teredo clients and Teredo relays. Although Teredo was proposed by Microsoft, there exists a version for Linux known as Miredo. Teredo is defined in RFC 4380, Teredo: Tunneling IPv6 over UDP through Network Address Translations (NATs).

GRE, 6RD, and Teredo are all beyond the scope of this book. For more information, read the following:

- *Cisco Self-Study: Implementing Cisco IPv6 Networks*, by Regis Desmeules
- Implementing Tunneling for IPv6: www.cisco.com/en/US/docs/ios/ipv6/configuration/guide/ip6-tunnel.html

Summary

This chapter looked at using dual-stack and three common tunneling techniques to transition from IPv4 to IPv6. As shown, a dual-stack device has complete support for both IPv4 and IPv6. Understanding the protocols and nuances of IPv6 can be daunting. A dual-stack network allows you to become more familiar with IPv6 while still maintaining a stable IPv4 infrastructure.

Tunnels or overlay tunnels were discussed. This is another way that IPv4 and IPv6 devices can coexist. Tunneling allows IPv6 devices to communicate over an IPv4-only network by encapsulating the IPv6 packets inside an IPv4 packet. Tunneling should be considered a temporary solution until native IPv6 can be employed.

The first type of tunnel examined was a manual tunnel. Manual tunnels are point-to-point tunnels where the IPv4 source and destination addresses are statically configured on the router. Although manual tunnels are easy to configure, they require a separate tunnel configuration between every two endpoints. Therefore, manual tunnels do not scale well in large environments.

The next type of tunnel discussed was a 6to4 tunnel. These are point-to-multipoint tunnels where the IPv4 address of the other end of the tunnel can be automatically determined from the destination address of the IPv6 packet. The IPv6 network address is based on a reachable IPv4 address plus a special 2002::/16 prefix reserved for this purpose. The 32 bits of the IPv4 address are used for the low-order bits of the IPv6 address, resulting in a network prefix of 2002:*ipv4-address*::/48. By using this addressing format, a single 6to4 tunnel can reach any 2002:*ipv4-address*::/48 network. Unlike a manual tunnel, the destination IPv4 address of the tunnel is not configured.

ISATAP tunnels, another automatic tunneling method, are used primarily for tunneling within a site. One of ISATAP's main features allows a host to use Stateless Address Autoconfiguration to obtain its IPv6 address configuration using Router Advertisement messages from an ISATAP router. The IPv6 prefix is derived from the prefix information contained in the RA message. The 64-bit Interface ID portion of the address is 0000:5EFE followed by the 32-bit IPv4 address in hexadecimal. Similar to a 6to4 tunnel, there is no need to configure the destination IPv4 address of the other end of the tunnel.

References

RFCs:

RFC 2784, *Generic Routing Encapsulation (GRE)*, D. Farinacci, Procet Networks, www.ietf.org/rfc/rfc2784, March 2000

RFC 3056, *Connection of IPv6 Domains via IPv4 Clouds (6to4)*, B. Carpenter, www.ietf.org/rfc/rfc3056, February 2001

RFC 3493, *Basic Socket Interface Extensions for IPv6*, R. Gilligan, Intransa, Inc., www.ietf.org/rfc/rfc3493, February 2003

RFC 3986, *Uniform Resource Identifier (URI): Generic Syntax*, T. Berners-Lee, W3C/MIT, www.ietf.org/rfc/rfc3986, January 2005

RFC 4380, *Teredo: Tunneling IPv6 over UDP through Network Address Translations (NATs)*, C. Huitema, Microsoft, www.ietf.org/rfc/rfc4380, February 2006

RFC 4966, *Reasons to Move the Network Address Translator - Protocol Translator (NAT-PT) to Historic Status*, C. Aoun, Energize Urnet, www.ietf.org/rfc/rfc4966, July 2007

RFC 4472, *Operational Considerations and Issues with IPv6 DNS*, A. Duran, Comcast, www.ietf.org/rfc/rfc4472, April 2006

RFC 5214, *Intra-Site Automatic Tunnel Addressing Protocol (ISATAP)*, F. Templin, Boeing Phantom Works, www.ietf.org/rfc/rfc5214.txt, March 2008

RFC 5342, *IANA & IETF Use of IEEE 802 Parameters*, D. Eastlake, Eastlake Enterprises, www.ietf.org/rfc/rfc5342.txt, September 2009

RFC 5569, *IPv6 Rapid Deployment on IPv4 Infrastructures (6rd)*, R. Despres, RD-IPtech, www.ietf.org/rfc/rfc5569, January 2010

Website:

Implementing Tunneling for IPv6, www.cisco.com/en/US/docs/ios/ipv6/configuration/guide/ip6-tunnel.html

Chapter 11

Network Address Translation IPv6 to IPv4 (NAT64)

As stated previously, the worlds of IPv4 and IPv6 will coexist for the foreseeable future. How and when an organization migrates to IPv6 will depend on its specific situation. Many service providers and larger enterprise networks were early adopters of IPv6. They began their planning, training, and transition strategy years ago. Because of the lack of IPv4 address space, many organizations, mostly in Asia and Europe, have already begun actively deploying IPv6. The Regional Internet Registry (RIR) Réseaux IP Européens Network Coordination Centre (RIPE NCC) maintains statistics for IPv6 deployment at www.ipv6actnow.org/statistics. Google also collects statistics about IPv6 adoption in the Internet on an ongoing basis at www.google.com/intl/en/ipv6/statistics.

Ideally, IPv6 should be run natively wherever possible, IPv6 devices communicating with each other over IPv6 networks. However, the move from IPv4 to IPv6 will happen in increments and over time. In the meantime, the Internet Engineering Task Force (IETF) has developed several transition techniques to accommodate a variety of IPv4-to-IPv6 scenarios, including dual-stack, tunneling, and translation. We discussed dual-stack and tunneling in the previous chapter.

This chapter explores two types of translation:

- NAT64: Network Address Translation IPv6 to IPv4
- NAT-PT: Network Address Translation – Protocol Translation

Network Address Translation (NAT) is a familiar method in IPv4, commonly used to translate between private (RFC 1918) addresses and public IPv4 address space. NAT64 transparently provides access between IPv6-only and IPv4-only networks. Address Family Translation (AFT) or simply translation, provides communications between IPv6-only and IPv4-only hosts and networks. AFT performs IP header and address translations between these two network layer protocols. Like other transition methods, translation is not a long-term strategy and the ultimate goal should be native IPv6. However translation offers two major advantages over tunneling:

- Translation provides a means for gradual and seamless migration to IPv6.
- Content providers can provide services transparently to IPv6 Internet users.

NAT64 is the replacement for NAT-PT, Network Address Translation – Protocol Translation, as documented in RFC 6144, Framework for IPv4/IPv6 Translation. Cisco recommends not using NAT-PT, supporting its replacement NAT64. NAT-PT has been included at the end of this chapter for reference and continuity. At the time of this writing, NAT-PT is still part of some Cisco curriculums, although it will eventually be phased out. At present, NAT-PT is more widely supported on Cisco platforms than NAT64. This will most likely change.

NAT-PT has been deemed deprecated by IETF because of its tight coupling with Domain Name System (DNS) and general limitation in translation. These reasons are documented in RFC 4966, Reasons to Move the Network Address Translator - Protocol Translator (NAT-PT) to Historic Status. IETF proposed NAT64 as the successor to NAT-PT.

NAT64

NAT64 is a mechanism for IPv4-to-IPv6 transition and IPv4-IPv6 coexistence. Together with DNS64, the primary purpose of NAT64 is to allow an IPv6-only client to initiate communications to an IPv4-only server, as shown in Figure 11-1. NAT64 can also be used for IPv4-only clients initiating communications with IPv6-only servers using static or manual bindings. Both scenarios are examined in this chapter.

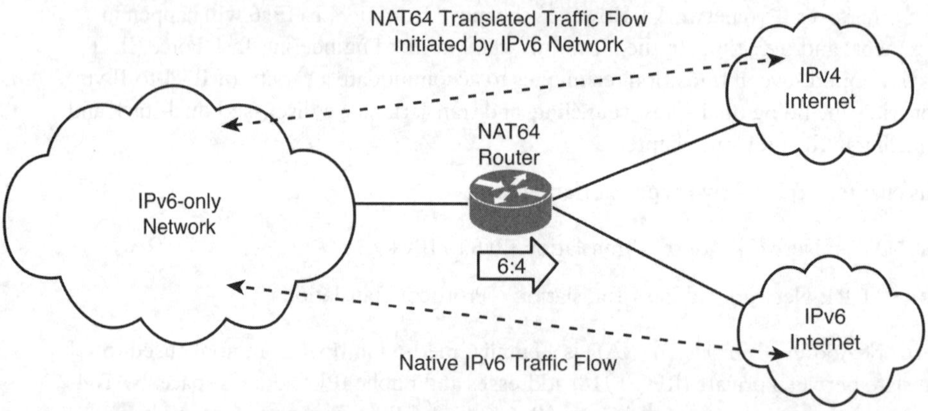

Figure 11-1 *IPv6-only Network Accessing IPv4 and IPv6 Internet*

NAT64 is described in RFC 6146, Stateful NAT64: Network Address and Protocol Translation from IPv6 Clients to IPv4 Servers. Similar to stateful NAT used for IPv4, stateful NAT64 creates or modifies bindings between IPv6 and IPv4 while performing translation. NAT64 performs translation between IPv6 and IPv4 by performing the following:

- IP header translation between the two protocols using an algorithm defined in RFC 6145, IP/ICMP Translation Algorithm
- IP address translation between the two protocols using an algorithm defined in RFC 6052, IPv6 Addressing of IPv4/IPv6 Translators

Note Stateless NAT64 is also an option. Unlike stateful NAT64, stateless NAT64 does not maintain any sort of bindings or session state while performing the translation. This chapter only covers stateful NAT64.

There are three components to NAT64:

- **NAT64 prefix:** Any /32, /40, /48, /56, /64, or /96 prefix used with a converted IPv4 address to transmit the packet over the IPv6-only network. The NAT64 prefix can be a network-specific prefix (NSP) or a well-known prefix (WKP). An NSP is assigned by an organization and is usually a subnet from the organization's IPv6 prefix. The WKP for NAT64 is 64:ff9b::/96. If an NSP is not specified or configured, NAT64 will use the WKP to prepend the converted IPv4 address. The NAT64 prefix is also referred to as Pref64::/n.
- **DNS64 server:** The DNS64 server functions as a normal DNS server for IPv6 AAAA records but will also attempt to locate an IPv4 A record when a AAAA record is not available. If an A record is located, DNS64 converts the IPv4 A record into an IPv6 AAAA record using the NAT64 prefix. This gives the impression to the IPv6-only host that it can communicate with a server using IPv6.
- **NAT64 router:** The NAT64 router advertises the NAT64 prefix into the IPv6-only network along with performing the translation between the IPv6-only and IPv4-only networks.

Traffic Initiated from IPv6-only Clients to IPv4-only Servers

Figure 11-2 shows a scenario where clients in an IPv6-only network, 2001:DB8:CAFE::/48, communicate with IPv4-only servers using NAT64. This is the most common scenario and use of NAT64. The following steps illustrate this process:

Step 1. Host A is an IPv6-only host that wants to communicate with the server www.example.com. This triggers a DNS query (AAAA: www.example.com) to the DNS64 server. The DNS64 is a key component to this process. A DNS64 server is both a DNS server for IPv6 and IPv4. It creates the illusion for the client that IPv4 servers can be reached using an IPv6 address.

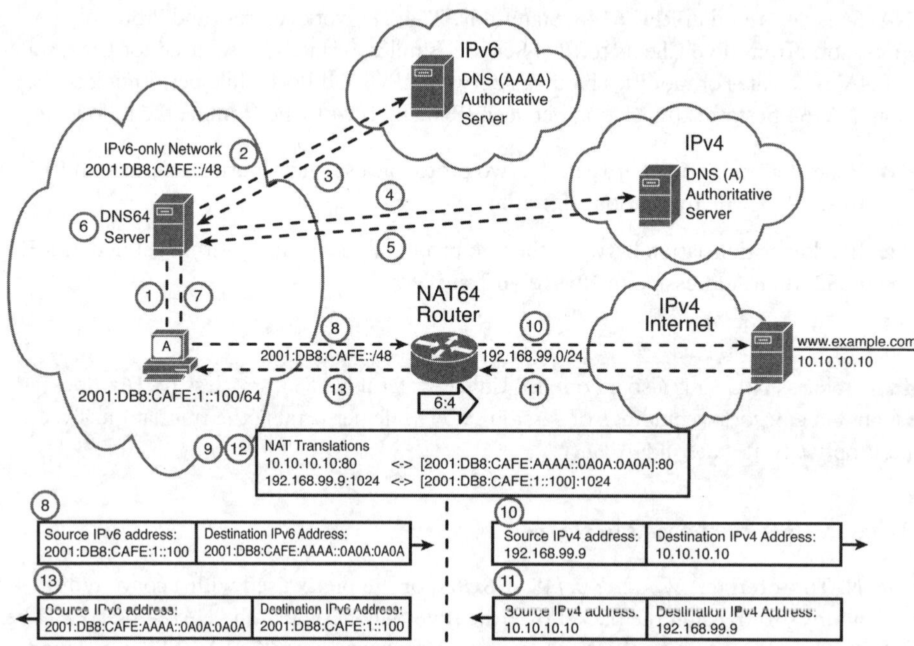

Figure 11-2 *NAT64 Router Translating IPv6 Traffic to IPv4 and Returning Traffic*

Figure 11-3 illustrates the DNS64 operation in Steps 1 through 7 more closely. The steps in Figure 11-3 are identical to the same steps in Figure 11-2. Both diagrams can be used to help you better understand the DNS64 process.

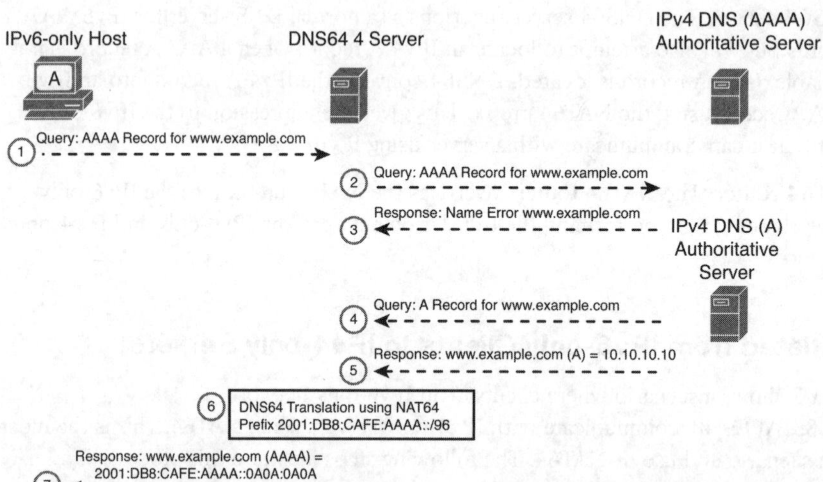

Figure 11-3 *DNS64 Operation*

Host A sends a DNS query (AAAA: www.example.com) to the DNS64 server. As far as host A is concerned, this is a normal DNS AAAA query for an IPv6 server.

Step 2. The DNS64 server receives the DNS AAAA query from host A. In an attempt to resolve the domain name, the DNS64 server sends a query to the DNS AAAA authoritative server for www.example.com.

Step 3. The IPv6 DNS AAAA authoritative server returns a response indicating that it does not have a AAAA resource record for www.example.com.

Step 4. On receiving an empty answer (name error) response to the AAAA query, this triggers the DNS64 server to send an A query (A: www.example.com) to the IPv4 DNS A authoritative server.

Step 5. The IPv4 DNS A authoritative server does have an A resource record for www.example.com and returns a response with the IPv4 address for the server (A: www.example.com 10.10.10.10).

Step 6. The DNS64 server receives the IPv4 address from the DNS A authoritative server and synthesizes a AAAA record by prefixing the address with its NAT64 prefix, 2001:DB8:CAFE:1234::/96, and converts the IPv4 address to hexadecimal, 0A0A:0A0A.

Figure 11-4 illustrates the DNS64 synthesis of the IPv4 A record into an IPv6 AAAA record. The DNS64 server receives the IPv4 A record 10.10.10.10 for www.example.com. The 32-bit IPv4 address is converted into its hexadecimal equivalent, 0A0A:0A0A. The DNS64 server prefaces the address with the prefix 2001:DB8:CAFE:AAAA::/96, resulting in a DNS64-synthesized AAAA resource record of 2001:DB8:CAFE:AAAA::0A0A:0A0A for www.example.com. This address will be used by host A as the destination IPv6 address for reaching the www.example.com server.

Note A DNS server does not perform DNS64 services automatically. The DNS server must support and be specifically configured for DNS64 operations.

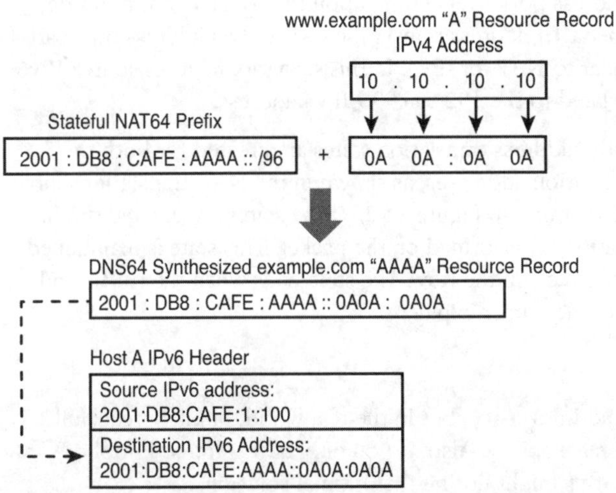

Figure 11-4 *DNS64 Synthesis of an A Record into a AAAA Record*

Note The NAT64 prefix can be a network-specific prefix (NSP) or a well-known prefix (WKP).

Step 7. The DNS64 server sends a AAAA response to host A with the address 2001:DB8:CAFE:AAAA::0A0A:0A0A for www.example.com.

Step 8. The synthesized AAAA record is completely transparent to host A. To host A, it appears as if www.example.com is reachable over the IPv6 network and Internet. Host A now has the addressing information necessary to transmit IPv6 packets to www.example.com with the following:

- IPv6 destination address: 2001:DB8:CAFE:AAAA::0A0A:0A0A
- IPv6 source address: 2001:DB8:CAFE:1::100

Step 9. The NAT64 router receives the IPv6 packet sent by host A on its NAT64-enabled interface. The NAT64 router is configured with the stateful NAT64 prefix of 2001:DB8:CAFE:AAAA::/96. The router attempts to forward this IPv6 packet. If the first 96 bits do not match the configured stateful NAT64 prefix, the packet is forwarded untranslated using normal IPv6 routing. If the packet's destination address does match the stateful NAT64 prefix, the packet undergoes the following translation:

- The IPv6 header is translated into an IPv4 header.
- The IPv6 destination address is translated into an IPv4 address by removing the IPv6 stateful NAT64 prefix 2001:DB8:CAFE:AAAA::/96. The lower 32 bits of the IPv6 address, 0A0A:0A0A, are represented as the dotted-decimal IPv4 address 10.10.10.10.
- The IPv6 source address is translated into an IPv4 address using the configured IPv4 address pool. Depending upon the NAT64 configuration, this can be either a 1:1 address translation or use IPv4 address overloading. This is similar to NAT for IPv4. In this scenario, host A's source IPv6 address is translated to the 192.168.99.9 IPv4 address.
- Stateful NAT64 IP address translation states are created for both the source and destination addresses, as shown in the NAT Translations table below the NAT64 router in Figure 11-2. These states are created the first time the translation is performed on the packet. This state is maintained for subsequent packets in the flow. The state ends when the traffic and the state maintenance timer expire.

Note This scenario uses private address space, but in the real world, publicly reachable addresses are necessary to ensure reachability. Also, if you only have a limited pool of publicly reachable IPv4 addresses, this might not be the optimal solution.

Step 10. After the NAT64 translation, the translated IPv4 packet is forwarded using the normal IPv4 route lookup process. In this scenario, the IPv4 destination address 10.10.10.10 is used to forward the packet.

Step 11. The www.example.com server at 10.10.10.10 replies, which is ultimately received by the NAT64 router.

Step 12. The NAT64 router receives the IPv4 packet from the www.example.com server on one of its NAT64-enabled interfaces. The router examines the IPv4 packet to determine whether a NAT64 translation state exists for the IPv4 destination address. If a translation state does not exist, the packet is discarded. If a translation state does exist for the IPv4 destination address, the NAT64 router performs the following tasks:

- The IPv4 header is translated into an IPv6 header.
- The IPv4 source address is translated into an IPv6 source address using the existing NAT64 translation state. In this scenario, the source address is translated from an IPv4 address of 10.10.10.10 to the IPv6 address 2001:DB8:CAFE:AAAA::0A0A:0A0A. The destination address is translated from an IPv4 address 192.168.99.9 to 2001:DB8:CAFE:1::100.

Step 13. After the translation, the IPv6 packet is forwarded using the normal IPv6 route lookup process.

The DNS64 server used with a NAT64 router creates a transparent environment for IPv6-only clients that need to communicate with IPv4 servers. The DNS64 server misleads the IPv6 hosts into thinking that the IPv4 destination is an IPv6 address. The DNS64 server has the capability of acting as a typical IPv6 DNS server or as a DNS64 translator using a NAT64 prefix.

Configuration

Table 11-1 shows the basic commands used to configure the router for NAT64 used in the previous scenario. There are various options and scenarios that can be used in the configuration of NAT64. For more information, read Stateful Network Address Translation 64, www.cisco.com/en/US/docs/ios-xml/ios/ipaddr_nat/configuration/xe-3s/iadnat-stateful-nat64.pdf. For stateless NAT64 configuration information, read Stateless Network Address Translation 64, www.cisco.com/en/US/docs/ios-xml/ios/ipaddr_nat/configuration/xe-3s/iadnat-stateless-nat64.pdf.

Table 11-1 *NAT64 Configuration Commands*

Command	Description
Router(config)# **interface** *type number*	Specifies an interface type and number, and places the router in interface configuration mode. This is the interface that faces the IPv6-only network and will be configured with an IPv6 address.
Router(config-if)# **ipv6 address** *ipv6-address/prefix-length*	Specifies the IPv6 address and prefix length to be assigned to the interface.
Router(config-if)# **nat64 enable**	Enables NAT64 translation on the interface.
Router(config)# **interface** *type number*	Specifies an interface type and number, and places the router in interface configuration mode. This is the interface that faces the IPv4-only network and will be configured with an IPv4 address.
Router(config-if)# **ip address** *ipv4-address subnet-mask*	Specifies the IPv4 address and subnet mask to be assigned to the interface.
Router(config-if)# **nat64 enable**	Enables NAT64 translation on the interface.
Router(config)# **nat64 prefix stateful** *ipv6-prefix/ prefix-length*	Defines the prefix and a prefix length for stateful NAT64: ■ *ipv6-prefix:* IPv6 network number to include in router advertisements. This argument must be in the form documented in RFC 2373, where the address is specified in hexadecimal using 16-bit values between colons. ■ */prefix-length:* Length of the IPv6 prefix. A decimal value that indicates how many of the high-order contiguous bits of the address comprise the prefix (the network portion of the address). A slash mark must precede the decimal value.
Router(config)# **nat64 v4 pool** *pool-name start-address-range end-address-range*	Enables NAT64 IPv4 configuration: ■ **pool:** Configures an IPv4 address pool. ■ *pool-name:* Name of the IPv4 address pool. ■ *start-address-range:* Starting address of the address pool range. ■ *end-address-range:* Ending address of the address pool range.

Command	Description
Router(config)# **nat64 v6v4 list** *list-name* **pool** *pool-name* [**overload**]	Translates an IPv6 source address to an IPv4 source address and an IPv4 destination address to an IPv6 destination address for NAT64: ■ **list:** Associates an IPv4 pool with the filtering mechanism that decides when to apply an IPv6 address mapping. ■ *list-name:* Name of the IPv6 access list. ■ **pool:** Specifies the NAT64 pool for dynamic mapping of addresses. ■ *pool-name:* Name of the NAT64 pool. ■ **overload:** (Optional) Enables NAT64 overload address translation.
Router(config)# **ipv6 access-list** *access-list-name*	■ Defines an IPv6 ACL, and enters IPv6 access list configuration mode.*access-list-name:* This argument specifies the name of the IPv6 ACL.
Router(config-ipv6-acl)# **ipv6 permit** *ipv6-address/ipv6-prefix-length*	Specifies the IPv6 address and prefix length to be translated.

Example 11-1 shows the configuration for the NAT64 router and the list that follows goes through the commands and steps of the configuration. Routing and any redistribution command options are not shown.

Example 11-1 *Sample NAT64 Configuration*

```
NAT64-Router(config)# interface GigabitEthernet 0/0/1
NAT64-Router(config-if)# description Connected to IPv6 Network
NAT64-Router(config-if)# ipv6 address 2001:DB8:CAFE:1::1/64
NAT64-Router(config-if)# nat64 enable
NAT64-Router(config-if)# exit
NAT64-Router(config)# interface GigabitEthernet 0/0/2
NAT64-Router(config-if)# description Connected to IPv4 Network
NAT64-Router(config-if)# ip address 192.168.99.1 255.255.255.0
NAT64-Router(config-if)# nat64 enable
NAT64-Router(config-if)# exit

NAT64-Router(config)# nat64 prefix stateful 2001:DB8:CAFE:AAAA::/96
NAT64-Router(config)# nat64 v4 pool pool1 192.168.99.9 192.168.99.10
NAT64-Router(config)# nat64 v6v4 list mylist pool1 overload
NAT64-Router(config)# ipv6 access-list mylist

NAT64-Router(config-ipv6-acl)# permit ipv6 2001:DB8:CAFE::/48 any
```

```
NAT64-Router(config)# interface GigabitEthernet 0/0/1
```

This is the interface connected to the IPv6-only network.

```
NAT64-Router(config-if)# ipv6 address 2001:DB8:CAFE:1::1/64
```

This command configures the IPv6 global unicast routing address of the interface.

```
NAT64-Router(config-if)# nat64 enable
```

This command enables stateless NAT64 translation on an IPv6 interface.

```
NAT64-Router(config)# interface GigabitEthernet 0/0/2
```

This is the interface connected to the IPv4-only network.

```
NAT64-Router(config-if)# ip address 192.168.99.1 255.255.255.0
```

This command configures the IPv4 address of the interface.

```
NAT64-Router(config-if)# nat64 enable
```

This command enables stateless NAT64 translation on an IPv6 interface.

```
NAT64-Router(config)# nat64 prefix stateful 2001:DB8:CAFE:AAAA::/96
```

This command enables NAT64 IPv6-to-IPv4 address mapping. The NAT64 prefix 2001:DB8:CAFE:AAAA::/96 will be used with an IPv4 addresses appended.

```
NAT64-Router(config)# nat64 v4 pool pool1 192.168.99.9 192.168.99.10
```

This command defines the stateful NAT64 IPv4 address pool. These are the IPv4 addresses that can be used for NAT64 translation.

```
NAT64-Router(config)# nat64 v6v4 list mylist pool1 overload
```

This command dynamically translates an IPv4 source address to an IPv6 source address and an IPv6 destination address to an IPv4 destination address for NAT64. The **overload** statement enables NAT64 overload address translation similar to NAT overloading for IPv4.

```
NAT64-Router(config)# ipv6 access-list mylist
```

This command defines an IPv6 access list and enters IPv6 access list configuration mode.

```
NAT64-Router(config-ipv6-acl)# permit ipv6 2001:DB8:CAFE::/48 any
```

This command specifies the IPv6 address and prefix length to be translated.

Traffic Initiated from IPv4-only Clients to IPv6-only Servers

Figure 11-5 shows a scenario where clients in an IPv4-only network communicate with an IPv6-only server using NAT64, which is further detailed in Steps 1 through 9. The goal is to provide access to IPv6 services transparent to the IPv4 clients. In this scenario, the DNS64 server is not required. Static mapping between the IPv6 and IPv4 address is configured on the NAT64 router.

> **Note** This scenario is unlikely for the foreseeable future. Most servers that are enabled for IPv6 will also be IPv4 capable. It is more likely that IPv6 servers will be running dual-stack for quite some time. IPv6-only servers will eventually become more common, but not anytime soon.

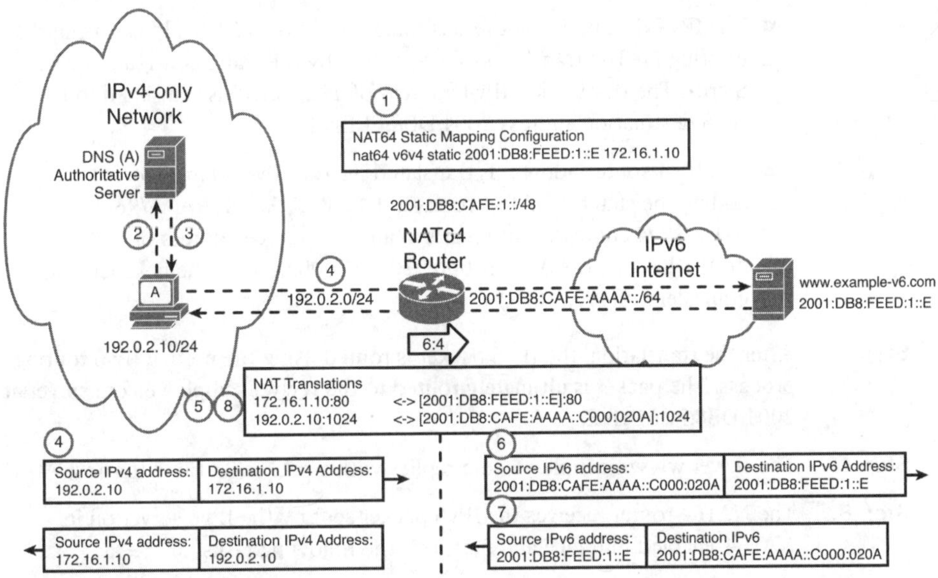

Figure 11-5 *NAT64 Router Translating IPv4 Traffic to IPv6 and Returning Traffic*

Step 1. The first step is to configure IPv6-to-IPv4 static mapping to provide access to the IPv6 server 2001:DB8:FEED:1::E from the IPv4 address 172.16.1.10. Also, the IPv4 address 172.16.1.10 needs to be registered as a DNS resource record for www.example-v6.com on the DNS server. The static NAT64 mapping is created using this command:

```
NAT64-Router(config)# nat64 v6v4 static 2001:DB8:FEED:1::E 172.16.10
```

Step 2. Host A is an IPv4-only host that wants to communicate with the server www.example-v6.com. This triggers a DNS query (A: www.example-v6.com) to its IPv4 DNS authoritative server.

Step 3. The DNS server responds with an A resource record for www.example-v6.com, 172.16.1.10.

Step 4. Host A now has the addressing information necessary to transmit IPv4 packets to www.example-v6.com with

- IPv4 destination address: 172.16.1.10
- IPv4 source address: 192.0.2.10

Step 5. The NAT64 router receives the IPv4 packet on its NAT64-enabled interface and performs the following tasks:

- The IPv4 header is translated into an IPv6 header.
- The IPv4 destination address is translated into an IPv6 address using the existing NAT64 translation state created by the static configuration in Step 1. The destination IPv4 address of 172.16.1,10 is translated to the IPv6 destination address 2001:DB8:FEED:1::E.
- The IPv4 source address is translated into an IPv6 address by adding the stateful NAT64 prefix 2001:DB8:CAFE:AAAA::/96 to the IPv4 address. This results in an IPv6 source address of 2001:DB8:CAFE:AAAA::C000:020A. (C000:020A is the hexadecimal equivalent of 192.0.2.10.)

Step 6. After the translation, the IPv6 packet is routed using the normal IPv6 routing process. The packet is ultimately routed to the www.example-v6.com server at 2001:DB8:FEED:1::E.

Step 7. The server www.example-v6.com replies with a packet destined for host A.

Step 8. The NAT64 router receives the IPv6 packet sent by the IPv6 server on its NAT64-enabled interface and performs the following tasks:

- The IPv6 header is translated into an IPv4 header.
- The IPv6 destination address is translated into an IPv4 address by removing the NAT64 2001:DB8:FEED:1::E.
- The IPv6 destination address is translated into an IPv4 address by removing the IPv6 stateful NAT64 prefix 2001:DB8:CAFE:AAAA::/96. The lower 32 bits of the IPv6 address, C000:020A, are represented as the dotted-decimal IPv4 address 192.0.2.10.

Step 9. After the translation, the NAT64 router forwards the packet to 192.0.2.10 using the normal IPv4 routing process.

Similar to the previous scenario, transparent communication is established between the IPv4-only client and the IPv6-only server using stateful NAT64. The configurations are similar except for the static mapping command discussed in Step 1. In the case where the IPv6-only client initiated communications with the IPv6 server, the DNS64 server played a significant role. This was not the case in this scenario, where static mapping of the IPv6-to-IPv4 address was required on the NAT64 router.

NAT-PT: Network Address Translation – Protocol Translation

This section explores translation or, more specifically, Network Address Translation – Protocol Translation (NAT-PT). NAT-PT is similar to the NAT mechanism utilized in IPv4 that is commonly used for translating private (RFC 1918) IPv4 addresses to public IPv4 addresses and vice versa. NAT-PT is used to translate IPv4 addresses to IPv6 addresses, and also IPv6 addresses to IPv4 addresses. The focus of this chapter will be on the configurations for static and dynamic NAT-PT.

> **Note** IPv4 NAT is also known as Network Address and Port Translation (NAPT), Port Address Translation (PAT), address overloading, or just plain Network Address Translation (NAT). Whatever the name, IPv4 NAT involves translating an IPv4 address to another IPv4 address. These days, IPv4 NAT is called NAT44 to differentiate it from other forms of NAT involving an IPv6 address such as NAT64 or NAT-PT.

NAT-PT is for situations where devices on IPv6-only networks need to communicate with devices on IPv4-only networks, as shown in Figure 11-6. NAT-PT is not a replacement for other transition methods such as dual-stack and tunneling. NAT-PT should be used only when there are no other methods to allow IPv6-only devices to communicate with IPv4-only devices.

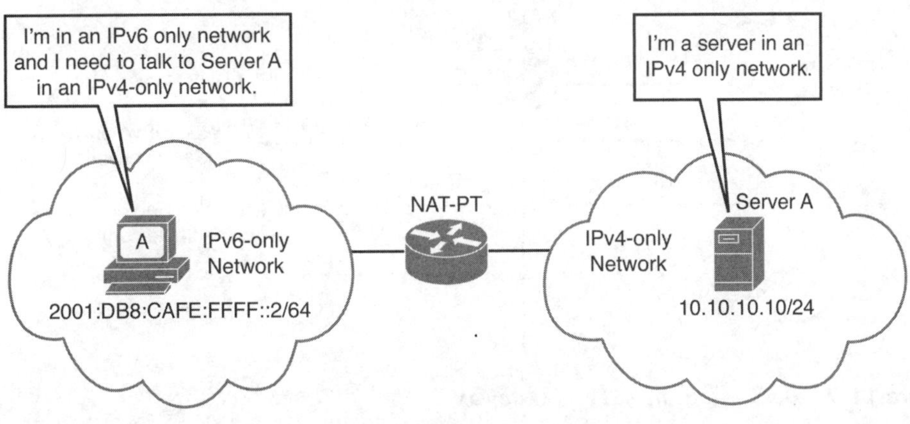

Figure 11-6 *Devices in IPv4-only and IPv6-only Networks Needing to Communicate*

NAT-PT is defined in RFC 2766, Network Address Translation - Protocol Translation (NAT-PT). The transition mechanism algorithm used by NAT-PT is defined in RFC 6145, IP/ICMP Translation Algorithm. The SIIT (Stateless IP/ICMP Translation) algorithm translates between the IPv4 and IPv6 packet headers, including ICMP headers. The NAT-PT router translates source addresses, destination addresses, and other Layer 3 fields in both directions. NAT-PT has several limitations including the ones it inherits from NAT for IPv4, as discussed in Chapter 1. Although NAT-PT is still being used as a translation method between the two protocols, RFC 2766 has been obsoleted by RFC 4966, Reasons to Move the Network Address Translator - Protocol Translator (NAT-PT) to Historic Status. NAT-PT is still supported by Cisco and other vendors, and is still considered a viable option. We will discuss the limitations of NAT-PT later in this chapter.

Application Level Gateway

During this transition period to IPv6, devices in IPv6-only networks might have to interact with devices in IPv4-only networks. NAT-PT is designed to allow the devices to communicate at the network layer—translating between IPv6 and IPv4 addresses. An Application Level Gateway (ALG), as the name suggests, operates at the application layer of the OSI model. NAT-PT is application unaware, because it does not snoop the payload. NAT-PT might require an ALG that allows the IPv6 application on the IPv6 device to communicate with an IPv4 application on the IPv4 device and vice versa. The ALG can work in conjunction with NAT-PT to provide support for such applications.

As we said, devices in IPv6-only and IPv4-only networks might need to interact. For example, an IPv6 client might need to connect using HTTP to an IPv4 web server, or an IPv6 client might need to send email messages using Simple Mail Transfer Protocol (SMTP) to its IPv4-only mail server.

DNS is an example of a protocol that requires the assistance of an ALG. The DNS ALG can be configured on the NAT-PT router, or it can be a separate server. Figure 11-7 illustrates what the DNS transaction looks like between an IPv6 client and the IPv4 servers using a DNS ALG and is further explained in Steps 1 through 5.

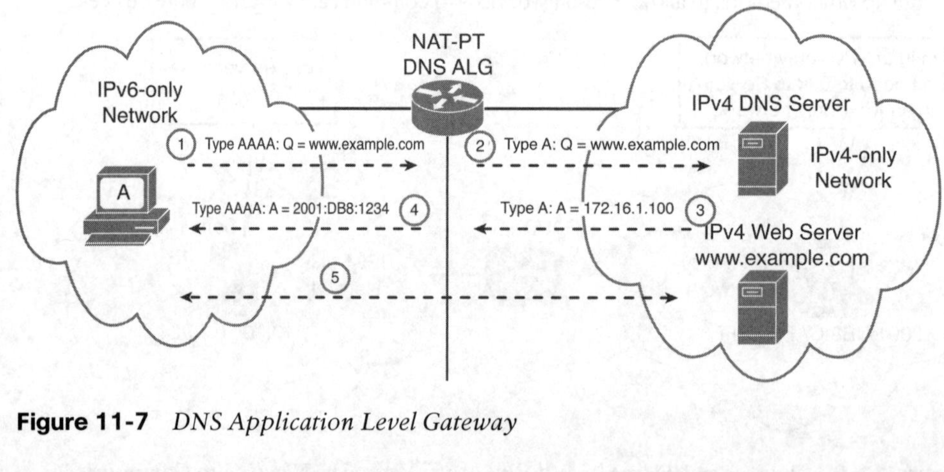

Figure 11-7 *DNS Application Level Gateway*

Step 1. Host A sends a DNS query AAAA record looking for the IPv6 address of www.example.com. The DNS query is forwarded to the NAT-PT router, which will translate and forward the packet to the IPv4 DNS server. NAT-PT operations are discussed in the next section.

Step 2. The NAT-PT/ALG router translates the AAAA record and forwards the DNS query to the IPv4 DNS server as an A record with the same query name www.example.com. The source and destination IPv6 addresses are translated to IPv4 addresses by the NAT-PT/ALG router.

Step 3. The IPv4 DNS server answers the www.example.com query with a corresponding answer—the IPv4 address (172.16.1.100)—and sends the DNS response back to the router.

Step 4. The NAT-PT/ALG router changes the DNS response from a type A record to a type AAAA record and modifies the IPv4 address in the DNS answer to an IPv6 address (2001:DB8:1234).

Step 5. Host A now has what it needs to communicate with www.example.com using an IPv6 address. The NAT-PT/ALG router will translate the IPv6 address to an IPv4 address and vice versa.

The details of Application Level Gateways and the implementation on Cisco routers are beyond the scope of this book. For more information, refer to the Cisco white paper Network Address Translator - Protocol Translator, www.cisco.com/en/US/prod/collateral/iosswrel/ps8802/ps6969/ps1835/prod_white_paper09186a008011ff51_ps6640_Products_White_Paper.html.

Using NAT-PT

NAT-PT involves network layer address translation and protocol translation. NAT-PT uses a configured 96-bit prefix for all IPv6 traffic needed to be translated by the NAT-PT router. All IPv6 traffic required to be translated to an IPv4 address by the NAT-PT router will use this /96 prefix for their destination address. Figure 11-8 shows an example using IPv6-only network 2001:DB8:CAFE::/48. All traffic is forwarded to Router R1, which is also a NAT-PT router. When R1 receives a packet containing an IPv6 destination address with the specific 2001:DB8:FEED::/96 prefix, it will translate the source and destination addresses to IPv4 addresses according to its mapping rules. All other IPv6 traffic is forwarded natively as IPv6 packets. The 2001:DB8:FEED::/96 prefix should be routed within the IPv6 domain so that all routers with the 2001:DB8:CAFE::/48 network can use the services of the NAT-PT router.

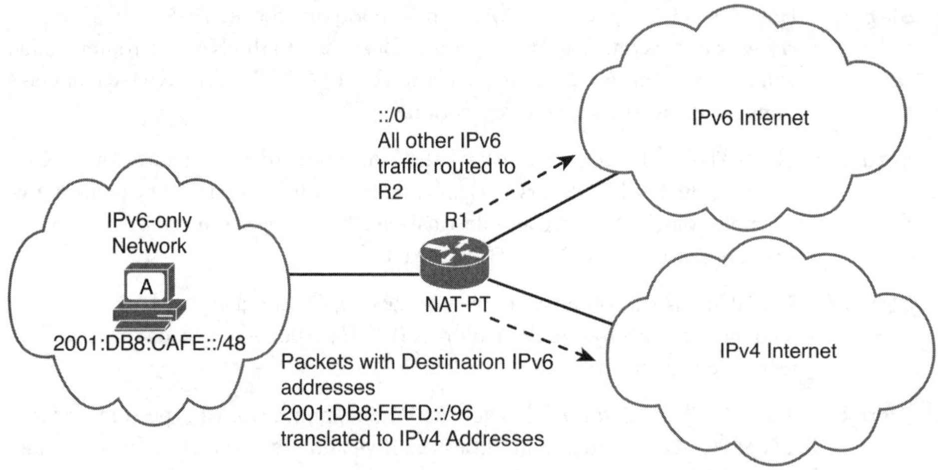

Figure 11-8 *Router R1 Performing NAT-PT Services*

Figure 11-9 shows another scenario in which the NAT-PT router can be separate from the native IPv6 forwarding router. IPv6 packets with a destination IPv6 address containing this prefix are sent to the NAT-PT Router R1 for translation to IPv4, while all other IPv6 packets are forwarded to Router R2 to be forwarded as native IPv6 packets.

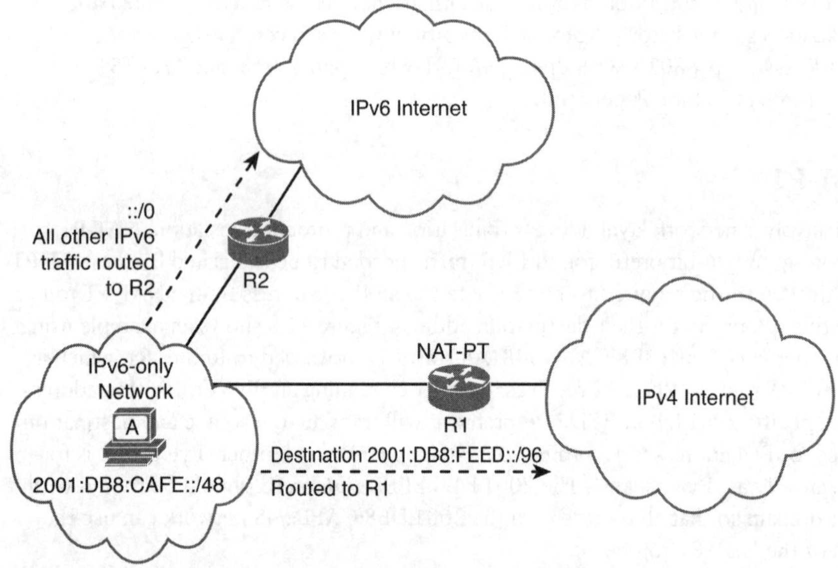

Figure 11-9 *Separate NAT-PT and Native IPv6 Routers*

The different types of NAT-PT are as follows:

- **Static NAT-PT:** Static NAT-PT uses static translation rules to map one IPv6 address to one IPv4 address. This one-to-one mapping of the IPv6 and IPv4 addresses is statically configured on the NAT-PT router. For every IPv6-only and IPv4-only host that needs to communicate, you will need to configure a static NAT-PT mapping for each. Static NAT-PT is useful when applications or servers require access to a stable IPv4 address, such as accessing an external IPv4 DNS server.

- **Dynamic NAT-PT:** Dynamic NAT-PT mapping also provides one-to-one mapping like static NAT-PT, but it uses a pool of IPv4 addresses. The number of source IPv4 addresses in the pool determines the number of simultaneous IPv6-to-IPv4 translations that can occur.

- **NAT-PT with Port Address Translation:** Also known as NAPT-PT (Network Address Port Translation – Protocol Translation), this provides a many-to-one dynamic mapping between multiple IPv6 addresses and one source IPv4 address. A single IPv4 address is used among multiple sessions by multiplexing on the port number to associate several IPv6 users with a single IPv4 address. Similar to NAT with Port Address Translation, NAPT-PT uses TCP/UDP port translation techniques. NAPT-PT can be accomplished through a specific interface or through a pool of addresses.

- **NAT-PT with IPv4 Mapped Operations:** Dynamic NAT-PT can be combined with the DNS ALG. With an IPv4-mapping configuration on the router, when the DNS ALG IPv4 address is converted to an IPv6 address, the IPv6 address is processed and the DNS packets from IPv4 network get their ALGs translated into the IPv6 network. The NAT-PT router translates the DNS AAAA-record queries to A-record queries and A-record responses to AAAA records.

Note This chapter discusses the configurations for static and dynamic NAT-PT.

NAT-PT has several limitations, including some that it inherits from IPv4 NAT. As we stated previously, NAT-PT should only be used when no other solution exists. RFC 4966, Reasons to Move the Network Address Translator - Protocol Translator (NAT-PT) to Historic Status, goes as far as to state, "These issues are sufficiently serious that recommending RFC 2766 as a general purpose transition mechanism is no longer desirable, and this document recommends that the IETF should reclassify RFC 2766 (NAT-PT) from Proposed Standard to Historic status." As a result, RFC 2766 has been "obsoleted." There are several limitations and restrictions when implementing NAT-PT, including the following:

- **Limited Application Layer Gateway (ALG) support:** NAT-PT provides limited ALG support. ALG support is limited to Internet Control Message Protocol (ICMP), File Transfer Protocol (FTP), and Domain Name System (DNS).

- **No end-to-end security:** NAT-PT has the same restrictions that apply to IPv4 NAT and does not provide end-to-end security. Transport and application layer security is not possible for applications that carry IP addresses to the application layer. Because NAT-PT modifies the packet headers during translation, the IP header's integrity check fails. This is an inherent limitation within NAT. End nodes that require the use of IPsec network-level security must support either IPv4 or IPv6, but not both.

- **Single point of failure:** A NAT-PT router can be a single point of failure in the network.
- **No multicast support:** NAT-PT does not handle multicast traffic.
- **No support for Path MTU Discovery (PMTUD):** Path MTU Discovery does not work with NAT-PT.
- **Does not support Cisco Express Forwarding (CEF):** NAT-PT is not supported in Cisco Express Forwarding. Both IPv4 and IPv6 CEF must be disabled when using NAT-PT.
- **Limited availability:** NAT-PT will only be available in lower-end platforms.

Static NAT-PT

Static NAT-PT mapping involves the one-to-one mapping of IPv6 and IPv4 addresses. Figure 11-10 shows our topology and the static mapping between the two protocols. The configuration is explained in a moment. The NAT-PT router has been configured with the NAT prefix 2001:DB8:FEED::/96. Any IPv6 packets that need to be sent to the IPv4-only network must use the 2001:DB8:FEED::/96 prefix in their destination IPv6 address. The NAT-PT router will translate packets containing this prefix in their destination IPv6 addresses to a corresponding IPv4 address according to its configured mapping.

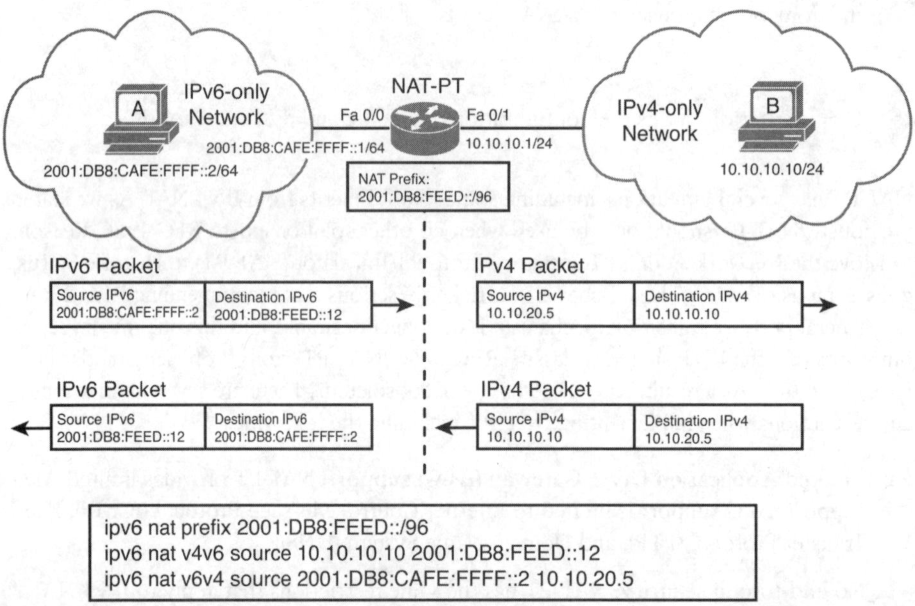

Figure 11-10 *Static NAT-PT Mapping*

Table 11-2 shows the commands used to configure the router for NAT-PT.

Table 11-2 *Static NAT-PT Configuration Commands*

Command	Description
Router(config)# **interface** *type number*	Specifies an interface type and number, and places the router in interface configuration mode. This is the interface that faces the IPv6-only network and will be configured with an IPv6 address.
Router(config-if)# **ipv6 address** *ipv6-address/prefix-length*	Specifies the IPv6 address and prefix length to be assigned to the interface.
Router(config-if)# **ipv6 nat**	Enables NAT-PT on the interface.
Router(config)# **interface** *type number*	Specifies an interface type and number, and places the router in interface configuration mode. This is the interface that faces the IPv4-only network and will be configured with an IPv4 address.
Router(config-if)# **ip address** *ipv4-address subnet-mask*	Specifies the IPv4 address and subnet mask to be assigned to the interface.
Router(config-if)# **ipv6 nat**	Enables NAT-PT on the interface.
Router(config)# **ipv6 nat prefix** *ipv6-prefix/prefix-length*	Defines the IPv6 prefix to be used as the NAT-PT prefix for the IPv6 domain. Packets destined for the IPv4-only network that need to be translated by NAT-PT must be sent to this prefix. The only prefix length supported is 96.
Router(config)# **ipv6 nat v4v6 source** *ipv4-address ipv6-address*	Packets with the source *ipv4-address* will be translated to the source *ipv6-address*. The *ipv6-address* is the destination IPv6 address used by the IPv6 host to reach the IPv4 host.
Router(config)# **ipv6 nat v6v4 source** *ipv6-address ipv4-address*	Packets with the source *ipv6-address* will be translated to the source *ipv4-address*. The *ipv4-address* is the destination IPv4 address used by the IPv4 host to reach the IPv6 host.

The best way to understand all of this is to examine the configuration used in Figure 11-10. Example 11-2 shows the complete configuration for our NAT-PT router and the list that follows goes through the commands and steps of the configuration.

Example 11-2 *Static NAT-PT configuration*

```
NAT-PT-Router(config)# no ip cef
NAT-PT-Router(config)# no ipv6 cef
NAT-PT-Router(config)# interface FastEthernet0/0
NAT-PT-Router(config-if)# ipv6 address 2001:DB8:CAFE:FFFF::1/64
NAT-PT-Router(config-if)# ipv6 nat
```

```
NAT-PT-Router(config-if)# exit
NAT-PT-Router(config)# interface FastEthernet0/1
NAT-PT-Router(config-if)# ip address 10.10.10.1 255.255.255.0
NAT-PT-Router(config-if)# ipv6 nat
NAT-PT-Router(config-if)# exit

NAT-PT-Router(config)# ipv6 nat prefix 2001:DB8:FEED::/96
NAT-PT-Router(config)# ipv6 nat v4v6 source 10.10.10.10 2001 :DB8 :FEED::12
NAT-PT-Router(config)# ipv6 nat v6v4 source 2001:DB8:CAFE:FFFF::2 10.10.20.5
```

```
NAT-PT-Router(config)# no ip cef
```

This command disables CEF for IPv4.

```
NAT-PT-Router(config)# no ipv6 cef
```

This command disables CEF for IPv6.

```
NAT-PT-Router(config)# interface FastEthernet0/0
```

This is the IPv6 interface of the router where NAT-PT will be enabled.

```
NAT-PT-Router(config-if)# ipv6 address 2001:DB8:CAFE:FFFF::1/64
```

This command configures the IPv6 global unicast routing address of the interface.

```
NAT-PT-Router(config-if)# ipv6 nat
```

This command enables the IPv6 interface for NAT-PT.

```
NAT-PT-Router(config)# interface FastEthernet0/1
```

This is the IPv4 interface of the router where NAT-PT will be enabled.

```
NAT-PT-Router(config-if)# ip address 10.10.10.1 255.255.255.0
```

This command configures the router's IPv4 address.

```
NAT-PT-Router(config-if)# ipv6 nat
```

This command enables the IPv4 interface for NAT-PT.

```
NAT-PT-Router(config)# ipv6 nat prefix 2001:DB8:FEED::/96
```

This command configures the NAT-PT prefix. Any packets with the destination IPv6 address of 2001:DB8:FEED::/96 will be translated to an IPv4 packet, including both the source and destination addresses. The actual addresses are statically configured using the **ipv6 nat v4v6 source** and **ipv6 nat v6v4 source** commands. Conversely, any IPv4 packets destined for the IPv6 network will be translated to a source IPv6 address.

```
NAT-PT-Router(config)# ipv6 nat v4v6 source 10.10.10.10 2001:DB8:FEED::12
```

When a router receives a packet with the source IPv4 address 10.10.10.10, it will translate it to the source IPv6 address of 2001:DB8:FEED:::12.

When a router receives a packet with the destination IPv6 address 2001:DB8:FEED::12, it will translate it to the destination IPv4 address of 10.10.10.10.

```
NAT-PT-Router(config)# ipv6 nat v6v4 source 2001:DB8:CAFE:FFFF::2 10.10.20.5
```

When a router receives a packet with the source IPv6 address 2001:DB8:CAFE:FFFF::2, it will translate it to the source IPv4 address of 10.10.20.5.

When a router receives a packet with the destination IPv4 address 10.10.20.5, it will translate it to the destination IPv6 address of 2001:DB8:CAFE:FFFF::2.

Let's test our configuration by having host A ping host B, as shown in Example 11-3. The **debug ipv6 nat** command verifies the address translation illustrated in Figure 11-10.

Example 11-3 *Verifying Static NAT-PT Translation*

```
PCA> ping 2001:DB8:FEED::12

Pinging 2001:DB8:FEED::12 from 2001:db8:ffff::2 with 32 bytes of data:

Reply from 2001:DB8:FEED::12: time=1ms
Reply from 2001:DB8:FEED::12: time=1ms
Reply from 2001:DB8:FEED::12: time=1ms
Reply from 2001:DB8:FEED::12: time=1ms

Ping statistics for 2001:DB8:FEED::12:
    Packets: Sent = 4, Received = 4, Lost = 0 (0% loss),
Approximate round trip times in milli-seconds:
    Minimum = 1ms, Maximum = 1ms, Average = 1ms

PCA>
```

```
NAT-PT-Router# debug ipv6 nat
IPv6 NAT-PT debugging is on
*Apr  1 21:36:28.631: IPv6 NAT: icmp src (2001:DB8:CAFE:FFFF::2) ->
(10.10.20.5), dst (2001:DB8:FEED::12) -> (10.10.10.10)
```

```
*Apr  1 21:36:28.631: IPv6 NAT: icmp src (10.10.10.10) ->
(2001:DB8:FEED::12), dst (10.10.20.5) -> (2001:DB8:CAFE:FFFF::2)
NAT-PT-Router#
```

Host A sends the ICMPv6 echo request with a source IPv6 address 2001:DB8:CAFE:FFFF::2 and a destination IPv6 address 2001:DB8:FEED::12. Packets with the destination prefix 2001:DB8:FEED::/96 are routed to the NAT-PT router. (In our topology, host A is on the same link as the router.) When the NAT-PT router receives the IPv6 packet, the 2001:DB8:FEED::12 destination address matches its configured NAT prefix of 2001:DB8:FEED::/96. Using its static **ipv6 nat v6v4 source** mapping entry, the NAT-PT router translates the source IPv6 address of 2001:DB8:CAFE:FFFF::2 to the source IPv4 address of 10.10.20.5. Using its static **ipv6 nat v4v6 source** mapping entry, the destination IPv6 address of 2001:DB8:FEED::12 is translated to the destination IPv4 address 10.10.10.10.

Host B receives the ICMPv4 echo request and responds with an ICMPv4 echo reply. Host B sends the IPv4 packet with its source IPv4 address 10.10.10.10 and the destination IPv4 address 10.10.20.5—the source IPv4 address of the echo request.

When the NAT-PT router receives the ICMPv4 echo reply from host B, it performs the NAT-PT translation for the opposite direction. The source IPv4 address of 10.10.10.10 is translated to a source IPv6 address 2001:DB8:FEED::12 using the static **ipv6 nat v4v6 source** command. The destination IPv4 address 10.10.20.5 is translated by the **ipv6 nat v6v4 source** command to 2001:DB8:CAFE:FFFF::2. The output from the **debug ipv6 nat** command in Example 11-3 confirms these translations.

You might be wondering why the 10.10.20.5 address is being used as the IPv4 address in the **ipv6 nat v4v6 source** command, which is on a different subnet than the NAT-PT router's IPv4 address of 10.10.10.1/24. If our mapping used an IPv4 address on the same subnet as the router's interface, host B would recognize that the two addresses are hosts on the same subnet when sending packets to host A. Before host B can respond with an echo reply, it will need the MAC address for the destination IPv4 address—which was the source IPv4 address of the echo request. If this address is on host B's subnet, it will send an Address Resolution Protocol (ARP) request, but the router will not return an ARP reply because it's not one of its interface addresses. This would be a problem. Instead, we used an IPv4 address 10.10.20.5, which is on a different subnet. When host B needs to encapsulate the echo request inside the Ethernet frame, it will require the MAC address of its default gateway 10.10.10.1 (the NAT-PT router) instead of the destination IPv4 address of the packet.

In Example 11-4, notice the output from the **show ipv6 nat translation** and **show ipv6 nat statistics** commands. The **show ipv6 nat translation** command is used to verify any active NAT-PT translations on the router, and the **show ipv6 nat statistics** command is used to display statistics regarding any translations.

Example 11-4 *show ipv6 nat translation Command*

```
NAT-PT-Router# show ipv6 nat translation
Prot  IPv4 source              IPv6 source
      IPv4 destination         IPv6 destination
---   ---                      ---
      10.10.10.10              2001:DB8:FEED::12

---   10.10.20.5               2001:DB8:CAFE:FFFF::2
      10.10.10.10              2001:DB8:FEED::12

---   10.10.20.5               2001:DB8:CAFE:FFFF::2
      ---                      ---

NAT-PT-Router# show ipv6 nat statistics

Total active translations: 2 (2 static, 0 dynamic; 0 extended)
NAT-PT interfaces:
  FastEthernet0/0, FastEthernet0/1, NVI0
Hits: 4  Misses: 0
Expired translations: 0

NAT-PT-Router#
```

When choosing the /96 prefix for NAT-PT, it is important to take into account the reachability of this prefix. This prefix will need to be reachable by other routers in the IPv6-only network. Typically, the NAT-PT router will use an interior gateway protocol (IGP) such as Open Shortest Path First version 3 (OSPFv3) or Enhanced Interior Gateway Routing Protocol (EIGRP) for IPv6 to advertise this prefix.

Dynamic NAT-PT

Static NAT-PT is useful when there are a limited number of IPv6-to-IPv4 mappings and when the addresses are stable—unchanging. With dynamic NAT-PT, IPv4 addresses are allocated from an address pool similar to what is done with dynamic IPv4 NAT.

With dynamic NAT-PT, when the NAT-PT router receives a packet with a destination IPv6 address using the assigned /96 NAT prefix, the same process occurs as did with static NAT-PT. However, instead of translating the IPv6 address from a statically configured IPv4 address, the NAT-PT router translates it from a pool of IPv4 addresses.

Configuring dynamic NAT-PT involves similar commands used to configure dynamic IPv4 NAT. Table 11-3 shows the commands used specifically for configuring dynamic NAT-PT.

Table 11-3 Static NAT-PT Configuration Commands

Command	**Description**
Router(config)# **ipv6 access-list** *ipv6-acl-name*	Defines the IPv6 access list and places the router in IPv6 access list configuration mode.
Router(config-ipv6-acl)# **permit** *source-ipv6-address/prefix-length destination-ipv6-address/prefix-length*	Defines the range of IPv6 addresses allowed to be translated. There is an implicit **deny any any** statement at the end of the ACL.
Router(config)# **ipv6 nat v6v4 source list** *ipv6-acl-name* **pool** *ipv4-pool-name*	Defines the dynamic mapping between the permitted IPv6 source addresses and the pool of IPv4 addresses. The *ipv6-acl-name* identifies the IPv6 ACL used to determine which IPv6 addresses will be translated. The *ipv4-pool-name* identifies the pool of IPv4 addresses to be used in the translation.
Router(config)# **ipv6 nat v6v4 pool** *ipv4-pool-name ipv6-acl-name start-ipv4-address end-ipv4-address*	Defines the pool of source IPv4 address used for translation.

Figure 11-11 shows our topology using dynamic NAT-PT.

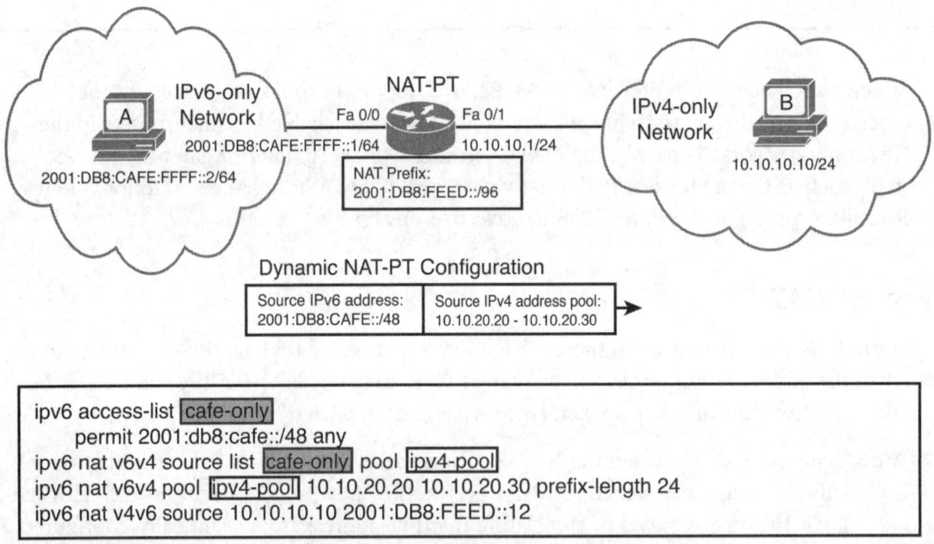

Figure 11-11 *Dynamic NAT-PT Mapping*

Example 11-5 shows the complete configuration for our dynamic NAT-PT router.

Example 11-5 *Dynamic NAT-PT Configuration*

```
NAT-PT-Router(config)# interface FastEthernet0/0
NAT-PT-Router(config-if)# ipv6 address 2001:DB8:CAFE:FFFF::1/64
NAT-PT-Router(config-if)# ipv6 nat
NAT-PT-Router(config-if)# exit
NAT-PT-Router(config)# interface FastEthernet0/1
NAT-PT-Router(config-if)# ip address 10.10.10.1 255.255.255.0
NAT-PT-Router(config-if)# ipv6 nat
NAT-PT-Router(config-if)# exit

NAT-PT-Router(config)# ipv6 nat prefix 2001:DB8:FEED::/96
NAT-PT-Router(config)# ipv6 nat v4v6 source 10.10.10.10 2001:DB8:FEED::12

NAT-PT-Router(config)# ipv6 access-list cafe-only
NAT-PT-Router(config-ipv6-acl)# permit 2001:db8:cafe::/48 any
NAT-PT-Router(config-ipv6-acl)# exit
NAT-PT-Router(config)# ipv6 nat v6v4 source list cafe-only pool ipv4-pool
NAT-PT-Router(config)# ipv6 nat v6v4 pool ipv4-pool 10.10.20.20 10.10.20.30 prefix-
length 24
NAT-PT-Router(config)# end
NAT-PT-Router#
```

The interface commands, the **ipv6 nat v4v6** command, and our **ipv6 nat prefix** 2001:DB8:FEED::/96 commands are the same as our previous static NAT-PT configuration. We have removed the **ipv6 nat v6v4** command used in our static configuration, and it will be replaced by the following commands used for dynamic NAT-PT.

```
NAT-PT-Router(config)# ipv6 access-list cafe-only
```

This command defines the IPv6 access-list **cafe-only**.

```
NAT-PT-Router(config-ipv6-acl)# permit 2001:db8:cafe::/48 any
```

Only source IPv6 addresses with the prefix 2001:db8:cafe::/48 are permitted to be translated by the NAT-PT router.

```
NAT-PT-Router(config)# ipv6 nat v6v4 source list cafe-only pool ipv4-pool
```

This command identifies the IPv6 access list **cafe-only**, which defines the source IPv6 addresses allowed to be mapped using the pool of IPv4 addresses defined by the **ipv4-pool**.

```
NAT-PT-Router(config)# ipv6 nat v6v4 pool ipv4-pool 10.10.20.20 10.10.20.30
prefix-length 24
```

This command lists the starting (10.10.20.20) and ending (10.10.20.30) pool of source IPv4 addresses to be used by NAT-PT.

The **ping** and **debug** commands in Example 11-6 verify reachability.

Example 11-6 *Verifying Dynamic NAT-PT Translation*

```
PCA> ping 2001:DB8:FEED::12

Pinging 2001:DB8:FEED::12 from 2001:db8:ffff::2 with 32 bytes of data:

Reply from 2001:DB8:FEED::12: time=1ms
Reply from 2001:DB8:FEED::12: time=1ms
Reply from 2001:DB8:FEED::12: time=1ms
Reply from 2001:DB8:FEED::12: time=1ms

Ping statistics for 2001:DB8:FEED::12:
    Packets: Sent = 4, Received = 4, Lost = 0 (0% loss),
Approximate round trip times in milli-seconds:
    Minimum = 1ms, Maximum = 1ms, Average = 1ms

PCA>
________________________________________________________
NAT-PT-Router# debug ipv6 nat
IPv6 NAT-PT debugging is on
*Apr  2 02:47:25.367: IPv6 NAT: icmp src (2001:DB8:CAFE:FFFF::2) ->
(10.10.20.20), dst (2001:DB8:FEED::12) -> (10.10.10.10)
*Apr  2 02:47:25.367: IPv6 NAT: icmp src (10.10.10.10) ->
(2001:DB8:FEED::12), dst (10.10.20.20) -> (2001:DB8:CAFE:FFFF::2)
NAT-PT-Router#
```

Once again, verify the configuration by host A pinging host B, as shown in Example 11-6. Only hosts with the IPv6 source addresses of 2001:db8:cafe::/48 are permitted to be translated. The source IPv4 address will be allocated from the pool of IPv4 addresses, 10.10.20.10 through 10.10.20.30. The **debug ipv6 nat** command output confirms that the translation is using the pool of source IPv4 addresses listed in the **ipv6 nat v6v4 pool** command. In this case, the pool is using the first address in the list, 10.10.20.20.

Other Translation Techniques

Network Address Translation IPv6 to IPv4 (NAT64) and Network Address Translation – Protocol Translation (NAT-PT) are two of the more common IPv4-to-IPv6 translation methods but are not the only ones. IETF has defined additional translation techniques giving devices in IPv6-only networks the ability to communicate with devices in IPv4-only networks. The following gives a brief description of some of the other translation techniques available:

- **Transport Relay Translation (TRT):** TRT is similar to NAT-PT, using a TRT system to relay traffic between IPv4 and IPv6 domains. TRT enables IPv6-only hosts to exchange TCP and UDP traffic with IPv4-only hosts. TRT is defined in RFC 3142, An IPv6-to-IPv4 Transport Relay Translator.
- **IPv6 Rapid Deployment (6rd):** Like a 6to4 tunnel, 6rd utilizes stateless IPv6 in IPv4 encapsulation to transit an IPv4-only network infrastructure. Unlike 6to4 tunnels, a 6rd service provider uses one of its own IPv6 prefixes in place of a fixed 6to4 prefix. 6rd is defined in RFC 5569, IPv6 Rapid Deployment on IPv4 Infrastructures (6rd).
- **Dual-Stack Lite (DS-Lite):** DS-Lite is used by service providers to connect their customers using private IPv4 addresses to the IPv4 Internet, as shown in Figure 11-12. Between the IPv4 customer and the service provider is an IPv6 link. When a customer sends an IPv4 packet using a private (RFC 1918) source IPv4 address, the packet is encapsulated inside an IPv6 packet by the router and sent over the IPv6 network. At the other end of the tunnel, the IPv4 packet is decapsulated. The private IPv4 source address is then translated to a public IPv4 address using IPv4 NAT. DS-Lite and 6rd are tunneling mechanisms that typically work in conjunction with a translation mechanism.

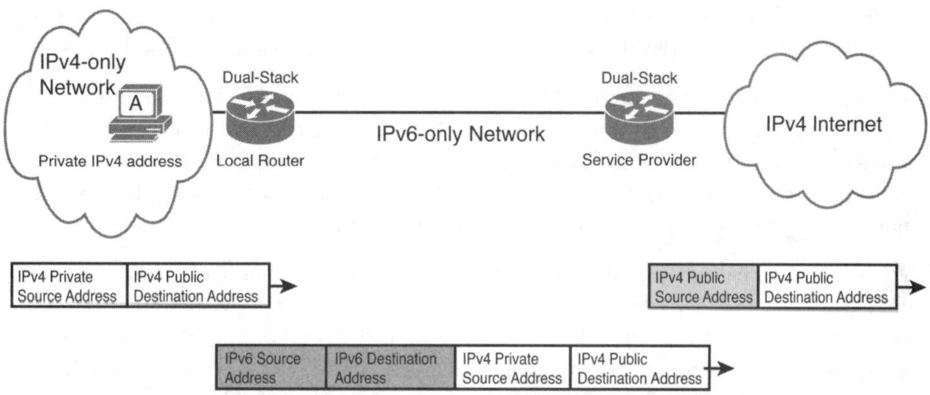

Figure 11-12 *Dual-Stack Lite*

Summary

Although several mechanisms have been established for the transition and coexistence of IPv4 and IPv6, native IPv6 infrastructures should be preferred and be the ultimate goal. In Chapter 10, "Dual-Stack and Tunneling," we explored dual-stack and tunneling techniques, and in this chapter, we looked into translation techniques like NAT64 and NAT-PT. Although dual-stack networks and tunneling have their limitations, they are far less restrictive than either form of NAT. NAT64 and NAT-PT should only be used when native IPv6 or other transitioning methods are not possible.

This chapter focused on two forms of NAT; NAT64, and NAT-PT. NAT64 is the recommended mechanism for IPv4-to-IPv6 transition and IPv4-IPv6 coexistence. Using DNS64, NAT64 allows IPv6-only clienst to initiate communications to IPv4-only servers, and IPv4-only clients to initiate communications with IPv6-only servers using static or manual bindings.

The DNS64 server functions as a normal DNS server for IPv6 AAAA records. If a quad-A (AAAA) record is not available the DNS64 servers will attempt to locate an IPv4 A record instead. If an A record is located, DNS64 converts the IPv4 A record into an IPv6 AAAA record using the NAT64 prefix. This gives the impression to the IPv6-only host that it can communicate with a server using IPv6. NAT64 does IP header translation between the two protocols.

NAT-PT allows devices in IPv6-only networks to be able to communicate with devices in IPv4-only networks. The NAT-PT router performs the translation between IPv6 and IPv4 addresses much like IPv4 NAT does between public and private IPv4 addresses. With NAT-PT, not only are the addresses translated between the two protocols but the other network layer fields are as well.

Both static and dynamic NAT-PT perform one-to-one mapping of IPv6 and IPv4 addresses. With static NAT-PT, each pair of IPv6-to-IPv4 addresses must be mapped individually. Dynamic NAT-PT provides the source address from a pool of source IPv4 addresses.

Although dual-stack, tunneling, and translation methods are not the ideal environment for networks to transition to IPv6, they are tools that can make this transition easier. IETF provides these and other methods to help make the transition to IPv6 a reality. A global Internet encompassing a vast variety of networks in every scenario imaginable makes it almost impossible for any one tool to work for every situation.

Wherever and whenever possible, native IPv6 is the way to go, but realistically, this cannot be the case in every environment. Now is the ideal time for network administrators to begin their familiarization with IPv6. Configuring devices (hosts, routers, and so on) as dual-stacked is a perfect way to begin familiarizing oneself with IPv6 while safely maintaining the existing IPv4 infrastructure.

Over the last few years in my research and implementation of IPv6, IPv6 has been a moving target. It is important to keep current on the RFCs, vendor implementations, and discussions involving IPv6 implementation. Many of the vendor features we have come to expect to secure our IPv4 devices are now becoming available for our IPv6 devices as well.

References

RFCs:

RFC 2766, *Network Address Translation - Protocol Translation (NAT-PT)*, G. Tsirtsis, Campio Communications, www.ietf.org/rfc/rfc2766, February 2000

RFC 3142, *An IPv6-to-IPv4 Transport Relay Translator*, J. Hagino, IIJ Research Laboratory, www.ietf.org/rfc/rfc3142, June 2001

RFC 4966, *Reasons to Move the Network Address Translator - Protocol Translator (NAT-PT) to Historic Status*, C. Aoun, Energize Urnet, www.ietf.org/rfc/rfc4966, July 2007

RFC 5569, *IPv6 Rapid Deployment on IPv4 Infrastructures (6rd)*, R. Despres, RD-IPtech, www.ietf.org/rfc/rfc5569, January 2010

RFC 6145, *IP/ICMP Translation Algorithm*, X. Li, CERNET Center/Tsinghua, www.ietf.org/rfc/rfc6145, April 2011

RFC 6146, *Stateful NAT64: Network Address and Protocol Translation*, M. Bagnulo, UC3M, www.ietf.org/rfc/rfc6146, April 2011

Websites:

Network Address Translator - Protocol Translator, www.cisco.com/en/US/prod/collateral/iosswrel/ps8802/ps6969/ps1835/prod_white_paper09186a008011ff51_ps6640_Products_White_Paper.html

Implementing NAT-PT for IPv6, www.cisco.com/en/US/docs/ios/ipv6/configuration/guide/ip6-nat_trnsln_ps6350_TSD_Products_Configuration_Guide_Chapter.html

Index

Numerics

A

B

C

D

E

F

G

H

I

J-K

L

M

N

O

P

Q-R

S

T

U

V

W-X-Y-Z

CISCO
Cisco Learning Network
Free Test Prep and Beyond.
Access review questions
Watch Quick Learning Modules (QLMS)
Search for jobs and network with others
Take self-assessments
Participate in study groups
Play online learning games
Register for a free membership
and get started now.
www.cisco.com/go/learningnetwork
Cisco Learning Network
A social learning site brought to you by Learning@Cisco

cisco.
IPv6 Fundamentals
A Straightforward Approach to Understanding IPv6
ciscopress.com
Rick Graziani